Books by Leonard Mosley

NONFICTION

BLOOD RELATIONS: *The Rise and Fall of the du Ponts of Delaware*   1980

DULLES: *A Biography of Eleanor, Allen, and John Foster Dulles and their Family Network*   1978

LINDBERGH: *A Biography*   1976

THE REICH MARSHAL: *A Biography of Hermann Goering*   1974

POWER PLAY: *Oil in the Middle East*   1973

BACKS TO THE WALL: *London in World War II*   1971

ON BORROWED TIME: *How World War II Began*   1969

HIROHITO: *Emperor of Japan*   1966

THE BATTLE OF BRITAIN   1965

HAILE SELASSIE: *The Conquering Lion*   1964

FACES FROM THE FIRE: *Biography of Sir Archibald McIndoe*   1962

THE GLORIOUS FAULT: *The Life of Lord Curzon*   1962

THE LAST DAYS OF THE BRITISH RAJ   1961

THE CAT AND THE MICE: *A German Spy in Cairo*   1960

DUEL FOR KILIMANJARO   1959

CASTLEROSSE: *The Life of a Bon Vivant*   1956

GIDEON GOES TO WAR: *A Biography of Orde Wingate*   1948

REPORT FROM GERMANY, 1945   1945

DOWNSTREAM, 1939   1939

SO FAR SO GOOD: *A Fragment of Autobiography*   1934

FICTION

THE SEDUCTIVE MIRROR   1952

EACH HAD A SONG   1951

WAR LORD   1950

NO MORE REMAINS   1938

SO I KILLED HER   1937

BLOOD
RELATIONS

BLOOD RELATIONS

*The Rise & Fall of
the du Ponts of Delaware*

LEONARD MOSLEY

HUTCHINSON

London Melbourne Sydney Auckland Johannesburg

Hutchinson & Co (Publishers) Ltd
An imprint of the Hutchinson Publishing Group
3 Fitzroy Square, London WIP 6JD

Hutchinson Group (Australia) Pty Ltd
30–32 Cremorne Street, Richmond South, Victoria 3121
P.O. Box 151, Broadway, New South Wales 2007

Hutchinson Group (NZ) Ltd
32–34 View Road, P.O. Box 40–086, Glenfield, Auckland 10

Hutchinson Group (SA) (Pty) Ltd
P.O. Box 337, Bergvlei 2012, South Africa

First published 1980

© Leonard Mosley 1980

Printed and bound in the United States of America

ISBN *0 09 142420 8*

ACKNOWLEDGMENTS

The du Ponts have always been a secretive clan. For generations they have deliberately eschewed the kind of publicity that has surrounded the rise of such other great national clans as the Rockefellers, the Mellons, the Roosevelts, the Guggenheims, and the Vanderbilts. But the du Ponts are, in fact, much more colorful than the public perceives them to be, and the history of the family, since its arrival in the United States nearly 180 years ago, is a saga full of every kind of human and social drama. But even those stories concerning the du Ponts, both laudable and venal, that have managed to break into the newspapers through walls of secrecy and phalanxes of tight-lipped public relations men have usually been only half-told, because of family determination that all shall not be revealed; and they have also very often been inaccurate, because of the difficulties journalists have encountered in getting at the facts.

Fortunately, in recent years the du Ponts have let down some of their defenses and have begun to allow historians and biographers a closer scrutiny of their professional and private lives. They have opened family documents for perusal by scholars at the Eleutherian Mills Historical Library at Greenville, Wilmington, Delaware. Here, on the grounds of the old Hagley powder mills overlooking the Brandywine River, the Historical Library, under the genial guidance of its general director, Walter J. Heacock, has assembled a treasure trove of family documents, company records, and other du Pont esoterica. In one of the most comfortable and pleasantly situated research libraries anywhere in the world, writers are now able to study the du Ponts' association with America from their earliest gunpowder days to their apotheosis as chemical pioneers.

It is true that the du Ponts have not wholly disarmed themselves against intruders. There are gaps in the correspondence and documentation in the library's collection, very often involving the most dramatic and sometimes the most scandalous moments in the family's history. Before turning over their letters and memoranda, certain members of the family did some careful winnowing in order to protect the reputations of their ancestors. At least three have declared that they would be damned if anyone, even scholars, would be allowed to discover what their fathers, their mothers, and their cousins had got up to on occasion, and at least one burned all the embarrassing letters his father had written, or had had written to him.

Furthermore, in the case of the two most prominent modern du Ponts, Pierre Samuel du Pont, who died in 1954, and Alfred Irénée du Pont, who died in 1935, whole sections of their correspondence have been sealed for fifty years. This could have been embarrassing for a study like this one, in which these two du Ponts play such prominent roles. Luckily, however, all the suppressed letters and other documents have been read by certain members of the family, as well as by some privileged scholars, some of whom are endowed with photographic memories and thus know some of the more dramatic sections by heart. I should like to thank them for sharing their knowledge with me, and I only wish they had allowed me to name them. It is one indication of how clannish the du Ponts still remain that they do not like "revelations" even about those members of the family now dead, and such would be their wrath that these amiable informants are unwilling to risk family censure by having themselves identified.

Aside from these, I have good reason to be grateful to the staff of the Historical Library for the help they so willingly gave me during the many months spent researching in their company. Dr. Heacock, who heads the

Eleutherian Mills–Hagley Foundation as well as the library and museum, gave me many pleasant and informative hours of his entertaining company. Dr. Richmond D. Williams, director of the library, was always available to discuss documentation with me, and Mrs. Betty B. Low, in charge of research and reference, was infallible in pointing me toward the obscure letter or document.

I am especially grateful to Mrs. Adeline Cook Strange, who runs Hagley Associates—the members of that group help preserve Brandywine buildings and traditions—for sharing with me her enthusiasm and interest in the du Ponts and Delaware. I wish I had been able to devote more space to her many stories, particularly those about the activities of her late father, the Reverend Philip Cook, who was bishop of Delaware in the twenties and thirties.

Not all my research was done at the library, of course. In Delaware I owe a debt of gratitude to Dr. E. A. Trabert, president of the University of Delaware, for giving a lunch in my honor at which he introduced all those members of the faculty who were experts on du Pont and the state and who might be of help to me. Dr. John Olson, dean of the Department of Chemical Engineering at the university, and his wife, Jean, were indefatigable in their efforts to broaden my knowledge and contacts in Delaware, and I am also most grateful to Russell Seibert, director of the Longwood Foundation, and his wife, Dennie, for introducing me to the floral wonders of P.S.'s old home by their kind invitation to a happy Thanksgiving dinner. I would like to thank Mr. Irving Shapiro, chairman of the board of E. I. du Pont de Nemours, for talking very frankly over a long period about his company and its family connections.

In Jacksonville, Florida, I had long talks, too, with that redoubtable nonagenarian, Mr. Edward Ball, who is chief trustee of the rich Alfred I. du Pont Foundation. He talked to me of his long association with his brother-in-law, and of his sister, the late Mrs. Jessie du Pont. I should also like to thank him for opening his files in the Florida National Bank Building in Jacksonville to enable me to retrace Alfred I. du Pont's remarkable exploits in Florida.

All the above, and many more—some of whom, as I pointed out, wish to remain anonymous—have contributed much of the information on which this book is based; but, of course, as always, the opinions expressed in it are mine and mine alone. The only one to whom that proviso does not apply is my fellow researcher, Deirdre Mosley, who sat in on all the interviews, read all the books, letters, and documents, and sometimes argued vigorously for her interpretations of them over my own. There are one or two occasions when she prevailed.

The Source Notes at the back of the book list documents and persons consulted.

CONTENTS

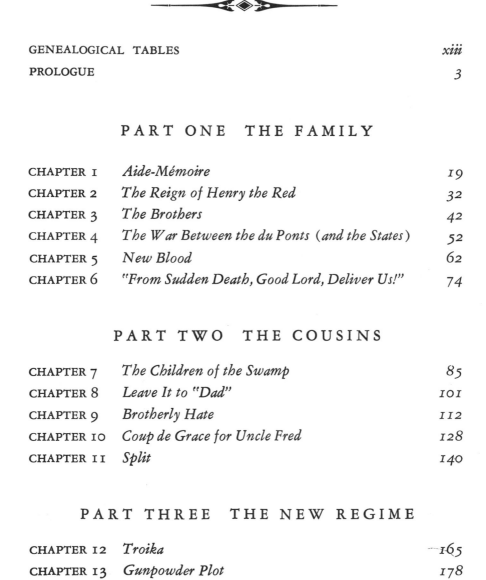

GENEALOGICAL TABLES   *xiii*

PROLOGUE   *3*

PART ONE   THE FAMILY

CHAPTER 1	*Aide-Mémoire*	*19*
CHAPTER 2	*The Reign of Henry the Red*	*32*
CHAPTER 3	*The Brothers*	*42*
CHAPTER 4	*The War Between the du Ponts (and the States)*	*52*
CHAPTER 5	*New Blood*	*62*
CHAPTER 6	*"From Sudden Death, Good Lord, Deliver Us!"*	*74*

PART TWO   THE COUSINS

CHAPTER 7	*The Children of the Swamp*	*85*
CHAPTER 8	*Leave It to "Dad"*	*101*
CHAPTER 9	*Brotherly Hate*	*112*
CHAPTER 10	*Coup de Grace for Uncle Fred*	*128*
CHAPTER 11	*Split*	*140*

PART THREE   THE NEW REGIME

CHAPTER 12	*Troika*	*165*
CHAPTER 13	*Gunpowder Plot*	*178*

CHAPTER 14   *Coleman's New Role*   *193*

CHAPTER 15   *Untrustworthy*   *208*

PART FOUR   COUP d'ETAT

CHAPTER 16   *Cousinly Coolness, Brotherly Love*   *223*

CHAPTER 17   *Patience Rewarded*   *238*

CHAPTER 18   *Feud*   *253*

CHAPTER 19   *Double-dyed Villains?*   *267*

CHAPTER 20   *Internal Combustion*   *281*

PART FIVE   ALL IN THE FAMILY

CHAPTER 21   *Spreading the Load*   *297*

CHAPTER 22   *Dirty Deals*   *309*

CHAPTER 23   *Filthy Rich*   *326*

CHAPTER 24   *Floridian*   *337*

CHAPTER 25   *Harvesting*   *347*

PART SIX   THE END OF AN EPOCH

CHAPTER 26   *Purity Hall*   *361*

CHAPTER 27   *Class Action*   *376*

CHAPTER 28   *Chain Reaction*   *390*

SOURCE NOTES   *401*

INDEX   *413*

ILLUSTRATIONS

(following page 140)

Pierre Samuel du Pont de Nemours, founder of the dynasty

Two of the powder mills on the banks of Brandywine Creek

Eleuthère Irénée du Pont I, founder of the firm

Alfred Victor du Pont I

Margaretta (Meta) LaMotte du Pont

Admiral Samuel Francis du Pont, "the father of Annapolis," and his wife, Sophie Marie

General Henry (the Red) du Pont, who made Du Pont the most powerful armaments firm in the country

Colonel Henry A. du Pont, who fought in the Civil War

The tragic couple Irénée du Pont II and his Southern wife, Charlotte Henderson

Swamp Hall

The dashing Lammot du Pont, a brilliant and inventive chemist

A family portrait, 1886: P. S. du Pont with his mother, brothers and sisters

The du Pont cousins and their friends, 1885

(following page 236)

P. S. du Pont at the age of twenty

Francis Gurney du Pont

The "Holy Brotherhood," Phillips Academy, 1880
    (COURTESY OF THE DU PONT FAMILY COLLECTIONS)

Alfred I. du Pont at M.I.T., 1883
    (COURTESY OF THE DU PONT FAMILY COLLECTIONS)

Bessie Gardner, Alfred I.'s first wife

Alfred I. in his personally designed motorcar, about 1890

Alfred's controversial second wife, Alicia Bradford
    (COURTESY OF THE DU PONT FAMILY COLLECTIONS)

Alicia Bradford du Pont with her daughter, Alicia
    (COURTESY OF THE DU PONT FAMILY COLLECTIONS)

Senator Colman du Pont, one of the three cousins who took over the company in 1902

P. S. du Pont and bandleader John Philip Sousa, 1930

The main conservatory at Longwood, P. S. du Pont's Pennsylvania estate

Irénée du Pont's estate, Granogue

Alice Belin, who married P.S. after a 23-year wait

P. S. du Pont and John J. Raskob, 1950

Nemours, Alfred I. du Pont's estate

Alfred with his third wife, Jessie Ball, in 1926
    (COURTESY OF THE DU PONT FAMILY COLLECTIONS)

UNLESS OTHERWISE NOTED, ILLUSTRATIONS ARE REPRINTED COURTESY OF THE ELEUTHERIAN MILLS HISTORICAL LIBRARY.

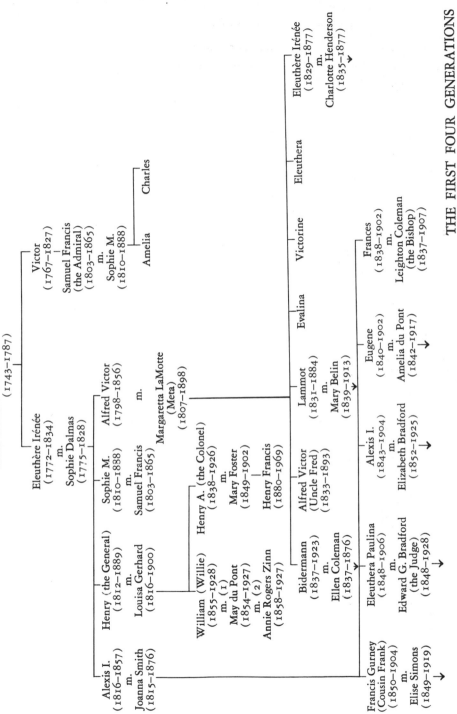

THE FIRST FOUR GENERATIONS

These charts are not intended to give a complete genealogical history of the du Pont family. They indicate the origins of those characters mentioned in this book but do not necessarily provide a comprehensive account of their extended families.

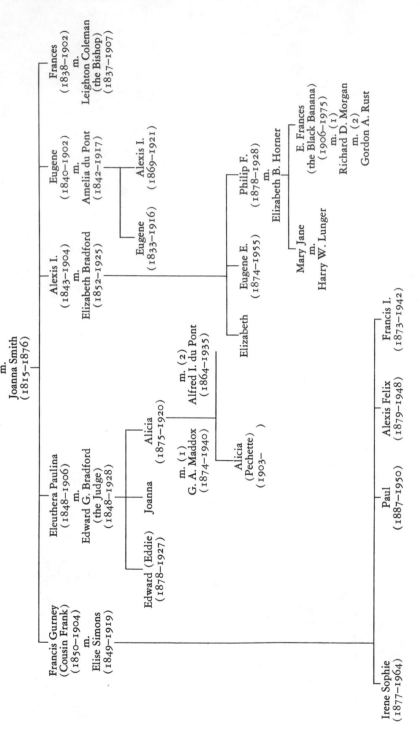

FAMILY OF ALEXIS I. DU PONT AND JOANNA SMITH

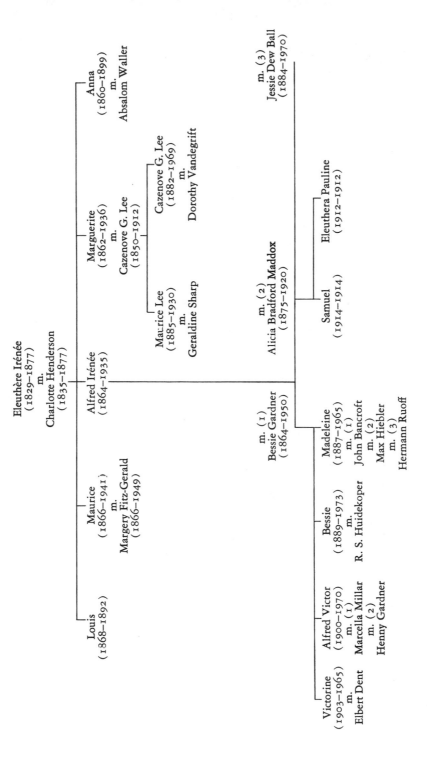

FAMILY OF ELEUTHÈRE IRÉNÉE DU PONT AND CHARLOTTE HENDERSON

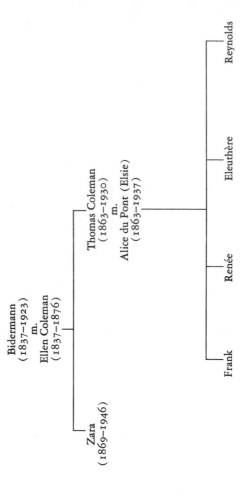

FAMILY OF BIDERMANN DU PONT AND ELLEN COLEMAN

Lammot
(1831–1884)
m.
Mary Belin
(1839–1913)

Louisa d'Andelot (Lou)
(1868–1926)
m.
Charles Copeland

Sophie M.
(1871–1894)
m.
Pierre Samuel
(1870–1954)
m.
Alice Belin

no issue

William K.
(1874–1907)
m.
Ethel Hallock
Henry Belin (Bese)
(1873–1902)
m.
Eleuthera Bradford (Eloo)

Henry Belin II
(1898–1970)

Irénée
(1876–1963)
m.
Irene Sophie du Pont
(1877–1961)

issue

Isabella d'Andelot
(1882–1946)
m.
Rodney Sharp

Lammot
(1880–1952)

m. (2)
Bertha Taylor
m. (3)
Caroline Hynson
(Stollenwerk)
m. (4)
Margaret Flett

m. (1)
Natalie Driver
Wilson

Pierre S. III
(1911–)
Jane Holcombe

Pierre S. IV
(the Governor)
m.
Elise R. Wood

Mary d'Andelot
(1878–1938)
m.
William Winder Laird

Margaretta
m.
Ruly Carpenter

Louisa d'Andelot

FAMILY OF LAMMOT DU PONT AND MARY BELIN

BLOOD RELATIONS

PROLOGUE

Death of a Loved Retainer

O N the morning of Friday, October 18, 1918, a special meeting of the executive committee of the E. I. du Pont de Nemours & Co. was called for 9:30 A.M. in the Du Pont Building in downtown Wilmington, Delaware. The moment had come for the biggest munitions company in the world to make vital decisions about its future.

For well over a hundred years Du Pont and the explosives it manufactured had played a major role in practically every war fought anywhere in the world, in Europe, in Canada and America, and from the deserts of North Africa to the river valleys of China and the jungles of South America. Its famous black powder had fired the rifles that annihilated both Indians and buffalos in the opening up of the American West. Its gunpowder had tipped the balance in favor of the North during the War Between the States. It had been Du Pont powder that ran the Anglo-French blockade of Sebastopol to reach Russian armies in the Crimea waiting desperately for ammunition, and it had been Du Pont powder with which French artillery subsequently mowed the Russians down. In Cuba and off Manila Colonel Theodore Roosevelt and Admiral Dewey blessed the volatility of Du Pont explosives during the hottest moments of the Spanish-American War.

But no armies in the history of warfare received so much gunpowder as Du Pont's arsenals furnished the British, French, and Americans during World War I. From 1914 onward the company's factories on the Brandywine River near Wilmington—and at half a dozen plants throughout the country—ground out powder for the Allied guns in France, and by 1917, when the United States came into the war, production rates were so high that Du Pont was making more in one day than it had manufactured during the whole of the Civil War.

Its output was so stupendous that by the autumn of 1918 more than one hundred thousand big guns of the Allied artillery along the western front in France were able to open up a continuous barrage against the German armies, with no fear of running out of ammunition. As a result, the Germans reeled back—those, that is, who survived the barrage—and were seeking an armistice.

When the members of the Du Pont executive committee assembled for their meeting on October 18, they did not know that the end of World War I was only twenty-three days away. But they were aware that the Germans were beaten and asking for negotiations. For the people of the warring nations, this news would have been reason to rejoice and be thankful that the terrible slaughter was all but over. For the men who ran the Du Pont organization, the prospect was rather more chastening. For them, it meant not just the end of the war but the end of a bonanza.

Soon the guns would be silent—and who would want, or be willing to pay for, Du Pont powder then? What would they do with all the new rolling mills that had been turning out explosives night and day for the past four years? How soon must they begin laying off the thousands of workmen—Poles, Irish, Czechs, Italians, and blacks from all parts of the United States—who had flocked into Wilmington to grab the good money Du Pont was paying for the dangerous work of mixing the explosives? What would they do with all the surplus powder lying around the mills now that the "war to end wars" was itself practically ended?

Most important of all, what would the Du Pont company do now in a postwar world where gunpowder would undoubtedly be a glut on the market?

For the answers to those and other questions, the members of the executive committee were relying upon the sage advice and guidance of the man who had called the meeting, their company president, Pierre Samuel du Pont. None of them doubted his ability to solve all their problems and plot their course through the stormy-looking postwar seas. It was he who had organized Du Pont's great wartime boom and, in helping the Allies win the war, had made these men rich beyond their wildest dreams. And now they were confident he would soon be telling them how Du Pont could become even more prosperous in peace than it had been in war.

The only trouble was, it was 9:31 A.M., and he had not turned up yet. P. S. du Pont had never been late for a meeting in his life. What could have happened to him? They stood around the boardroom and fretted, until one of them said:

"I hope to God he hasn't caught the flu."

All of them were suddenly silent—and apprehensive.

The influenza epidemic that was sweeping through Delaware and Pennsylvania in the fall of 1918 was more like a plague than an annual visitation of a virus. Brought back by American soldiers from Europe, where it had decimated the populations of Britain, France, and Italy, the flu germ had spread south and west from New York and claimed scores of thousands of victims. In Wilmington alone five hundred had already died from the disease, and thousands more were sick. Doctors were out of their wits trying to cope. The Du Pont company, which pretty well owned the city of Wilmington as well as the nearby powder mills, had already mobilized to take care of the mounting number of casualties. Passengers on the fast train from Washington to New York were chilled, when it halted at Wilmington depot, to see row after row of plain wooden coffins cluttering up the platform, and when one curious traveler asked a porter whether they were all full, he lugubriously replied:

"No, ma'am, but they soon will be."

The Du Pont company had had them shipped in after carefully calculating exactly how many Wilmington residents and Brandywine workmen were going to die in the great epidemic.

They had also done their best to prevent its spreading by discouraging visitors (and potential carriers) from coming into the city. To that end, they had reluctantly decided to turn guests away from their proudest showplace, the splendid new Hotel du Pont, which the company had built five years earlier to house well-to-do visitors or senior salesmen who came to do business with them. In a small town where the rest of the hotels had primitive plumbing, poor food and service, and, frequently, bugs, the Hotel du Pont was run on the lines of the best international establishments. Many an expert traveler judged it superior to more famous inns in New York, London, and Paris. Members of the du Pont family kept permanent suites there and used it for dances, banquets, and other celebrations too big for their own houses in the surrounding countryside.

But now, thanks to the menace of the dreaded flu virus, the hotel's great rooms, with their baroque ceilings and elaborately carved wooden walls, were empty, and the spacious dining room, famous for its cuisine, wine, and atmosphere, was closed down. Even the 1,251-seat theater,* which was an integral part of the hotel, had temporarily closed its doors to the opera and theater companies that made Wilmington a regular stop on their tours. It was a measure of the seriousness with which the Du Pont directors viewed the flu situation that the star chosen for the following week's show was the Chicago Opera's celebrated soprano, Mary Garden, and they had told her not to come.

But could the flu germ really have got to the great P. S. du Pont himself and laid him low?

The members of the executive committee, waiting in the boardroom as the minutes ticked away, found it hard to believe. Their president was forty-eight years old in 1918, and just as he had never missed a meeting or been late for one, neither had he ever had a day's illness in his life. Nevertheless, it was now 9:45 by the boardroom clock and there was still no sign of him, nor any message to say he was on his way.

Finally, it was P. S. du Pont's brother Irénée, nominal chairman of the executive committee, who decided to do something about it. Abruptly he slipped out of the boardroom and went along the corridor to his own office, where he picked up the telephone. When he returned, the other members looked at him expectantly, but his face was expressionless.

"My brother sends his apologies," he said. "A minor indisposition. He has asked me to go on with the meeting without him. Now, gentlemen . . ."

He must have been aware that his colleagues were astounded. How could they believe that "a minor indisposition" would keep their meticulous president away from such an important meeting? Was Irénée trying to conceal from them that P. S. du Pont had, in fact, caught the flu? Was he keeping silent about it because he knew what consequences a grave illness

---

* With, incidentally, the most comfortable seats of any auditorium in the nation, crafted especially for the long legs of du Pont males, and the broad beams so many of their spouses had been endowed with.

—or a death—could have on the company at such a vital moment in its history?

In fact, Irénée du Pont was saying so little about the real reason for his brother's absence because he was embarrassed. It was true that P. S. du Pont had not turned up for the meeting (had forgotten all about it, actually) because of the flu. But it was not that he had contracted the disease himself. It was simply that someone close to him was gravely ill with it, and that sick person, Irénée now realized, meant much more to his brother than anything else in the world, including the future of the Du Pont company.

Irénée's embarrassment stemmed from the fact that the person over whom his brother was agonizing, far from being his wife or one of his brothers, sisters, or cousins, was not even a member of his family. It was one of his brother's servants who had come down with the flu—his chauffeur, in fact. Yet, judging from the way P. S. du Pont was behaving, it was the greatest catastrophe of his life, and nothing was going to drag him away from the chauffeur's bedside.

Most observers of the industrial scene in October 1918 could have agreed that Pierre Samuel du Pont was one of the most resourceful and successful men of business in the United States. He was not yet as rich as a Ford, a Rockefeller, or a Mellon (though he would be), but it was because of his technical skill and organizing ability that the Du Pont company was, at that moment, the largest and most efficient gunpowder manufacturer in the world, supplying the armies of three great nations and half a dozen ancillary ones with all the explosives they could use. If it is true (and it probably is) that the Allied nations could not have won World War I without the aid of the Du Pont company, it is also true that the company could not have done it without the expertise and the constant supervision of P. S. du Pont. The war was making millions for him and the rest of his clan, tightening the company's grip on markets everywhere in the world, and he and his family would be investigated later on for the way in which they did it. He was already being accused of making far too much money, but no one could accuse him of not earning it. He had a reputation for never slacking on the job.

Until now, that is. Since his chauffeur had fallen ill a week ago, P.S., as everybody called him,* had hardly been near the office or the powder mills on the Brandywine River, five miles away. For the first time in his

* Except his brothers and sisters, and some of his cousins, who all called him Dad.

life, he was too preoccupied to make business decisions. It was as if the Du Pont company, to which he had dedicated his life, suddenly no longer meant anything to him.

Sixteen years earlier, in 1902, it had looked as if the stirring saga of the du Pont family enterprises would be coming to an end, after a hundred spectacular years. It was not that the family was in danger of dying out—it was, in fact, proliferating—but the future of the Du Pont company was in mortal peril. It had always been run by a system of dynastic selection and seniority, its successors always chosen from within the du Pont family itself. But the men who had taken charge around the turn of the century had proved to be weak and frightened members of the clan—stubborn, old-fashioned, and inefficient in their methods, lacking in courage and devotion to the company. They were so incompetent, in fact, that by 1902 they had practically run the fortunes of the Du Pont company into the ground and saw only one solution to their situation. They announced that they were going to sell out the famous powder yards to a rival firm.

That was the moment when P.S. and two of his du Pont cousins, Cousin Alfred I. and Cousin Coleman, came to the rescue of the family enterprise. Appalled at the prospect of the Du Pont powder yards being lost to the family, they managed to raise the wherewithal (if not exactly the money) to wrest control of the failing company from the palsied hands of their febrile relatives. Within a year the three cousins had more than restored the situation. Cousin Alfred I., loved and admired by the powder men—for he was a working powder man himself and had been burned in the same explosions—raised production and improved efficiency. Cousin P.S. took over the books and got order into the accounting and financing. Cousin Coleman, a customer's man if ever there was one, set about restoring Du Pont's markets, reputation, and prosperity. Du Pont quickly became big business again under the new regime, and the company's gunpowder was once more filling the bullets and shell cases of the arsenals of the world.

More than that. Du Pont was soon in a position, thanks to some sleight of hand on Cousin Coleman's part, to buy up most of their rivals or bring them into a competitive network, making the cousins arbiters of powder prices and markets from coast to coast. Within a decade of the transfer, the company was more powerful than ever before in its history, and the triumvirate could contemplate a future that promised ever-rising profits and the power and influence that went with them. Especially if, as seemed only too likely, a great war were to begin in Europe, making bullets and shells the currency of survival for the warring nations. Du Pont would be their mint.

The future did not work out quite as the cousins had planned. While Du Pont prospered the cousins quarreled. They shared the same bloodline; they were cut from the same cloth but in very different patterns. By the time the United States entered World War I in 1917, and the need for gunpowder made it a commodity as precious as gold, they had split up. The du Pont family was torn into factions with rancorous and sanguinary battles being fought among members of the clan who supported one cousin or the other. Du Ponts slammed doors in the faces of other du Ponts. Quarrels turned into long and bitter court cases, which would be fought all the way to the Supreme Court. It was a terrible time for the family.

But from it all, when the smoke had cleared away, it was P. S. du Pont who emerged the victor. He had bought out one cousin and ousted the other. By 1918 he was president of Du Pont and sole arbiter of its vast affairs. It was he who, from then on, would make all vital decisions, and he made it clear to all who worked for him that no important move would ever be made until he gave his approval.

Which was the reason why his continued absence from the office and powder yards in October 1918 was so painfully felt in Du Pont's boardroom. The war was ending, and important decisions about the future would have to be made. How could P.S. allow his chauffeur's illness to interfere with that? Speculation about their boss's state of mind was rife among the staff.

At about the same time that his brother was making his opening statement to the executive committee in the Du Pont boardroom in Wilmington, P. S. du Pont was conferring with his family doctor, U. Grant Gifford, a few miles away at Longwood House, in Pennsylvania.

P.S. and his wife gave as their official residence for tax purposes the Hotel du Pont in Wilmington, where they kept a permanent apartment (P.S. was president of the hotel board), and this would save them millions of dollars in the years to come. But in fact they spent much more time at their country residence just across the state line in Pennsylvania. The house and the 360-acre estate, called Longwood Gardens, near Kennett Square, is today open to visitors and famous for its conservatories and greenhouses, its fountains and *son et lumière* displays, but in those days it was still P.S.'s private fief, where he entertained his du Pont relatives and their friends at dances in his private ballroom, at masquerades in the gardens, and at recitals by famous artistes.

[9]

His wife, Alice, who was also his first cousin, had been visiting Long-wood ever since P.S. had purchased it in 1906, but it was only after they were married in 1915 that she came to know the great house room by room and to sit in with her husband as he discussed his plans for the estate. He was still building vast conservatories and houses to accommodate a staff of more than a hundred: gardeners, groundsmen, grooms, footmen, chauf-feurs, maidservants, and a butler.

Alice had been in love with P.S. as long as she could remember and from the age of twenty had been turning down suitors in the hope that one day P.S. would ask her to marry him. It had taken twenty-three years for him to make up his mind, and by the time they were married a year, Alice began to wonder why he had bothered. Their relationship stayed exactly the same as it had been before they pronounced their marriage vows. One of the qualities she had admired in P.S.—quite apart from her passionate love for him—was his kindly thoughtfulness toward his brothers, his sisters, his cousins, and his friends, and she had warmed to the way in which, ever since childhood, he had made it clear that he regarded her with brotherly affection. But after they were married, she expected, even impatiently and eagerly awaited, to judge by the feelings expressed in her diaries, something more than that. But those diaries, and her letters, reveal that she did not get it.

Both Alice and P.S. were intensely shy and introverted people and almost inarticulate so far as their personal feelings were concerned (though Alice did let herself go in those short agonized diary entries and in letters to her husband when she was away from him). P.S. never seemed to loosen up at all. It was true that once, when a favorite brother died of typhoid, he had broken down and cried, but that was the only time the family had seen him show emotion. He considered it unmanly to reveal any kind of distress, and even when he was in physical pain, he sternly eschewed painkilling drugs. Many years later, at the age of seventy-seven, when visiting Florida, he wrenched a ligament and was in great agony, but he wrote to a friend:

"Rod Sharp offered me an aspirin but I had the strength of character to refuse it. Hence my recovery!"

At least for the few first months of marriage it was possible to attribute the failure of the physical side of the relationship to the paralyzing shyness from which he suffered. But as he continued to rebuff Alice, gently but firmly, and life at Longwood resolved itself into a nightly regime of separate bedrooms, she began to anguish. What had marriage brought her? All she got from her adored husband was the same light, brotherly affection she had always known, unfailing kindness and concern for her everyday welfare, but an apparently total lack of awareness of the turmoil that was going on inside her.

What must have made it even harder for Alice was her growing realization that the easy intimacy with her husband that she desired almost as much as a sexual relationship—an intimacy she had so far failed to achieve —was reserved by P.S. for the young man who was his chauffeur, valet, and handyman, an employee of the Longwood estate named Lewes Mason.

Lewes and his married brother, Charlie, who had gone off to France a few months earlier as a doughboy in the United States Army, were among several young men employed at Longwood as gardeners, agricultural workers, repairmen, chef's assistants, and footmen. It was easy to see why Lewes Mason was her husband's favorite among them, for he was an exceptionally bright, cheerful, good-looking lad who obviously revered P.S. and spent all his time trying to please and amuse him. He succeeded to the extent that P.S. always seemed to have Lewes around—on trips, in the gardens, in his study in the big house, or in the ballroom listening, just the two of them, to music on the Victrola. Sometimes, when she interrupted them in the study, Alice must have had the feeling she was intruding, for they were often deeply immersed in conversation. Or they might be side by side behind the desk, poring over lists of figures, which turned out to be the portfolio of stocks and shares that P.S. was looking after for Lewes, and giving it all the care and attention he usually reserved for his own multimillion dollar investments.

It appears to be envy rather than jealousy that Alice Belin du Pont felt when she discovered the close and warm relationship between her husband and Lewes Mason; envy that this ruddy-faced boy seemed able to break through her husband's inhibiting shyness and penetrate the barrier he had built between his emotions and the outside world. How was it possible that a young man, and a servant at that, could succeed where she, his loving wife, had so abysmally failed? What sort of relationship did these two have that made them so snug, so free and easy, in each other's company? Did P.S. regard Lewes as a surrogate son, substitute for one for whom he secretly yearned? That was patently absurd; practically all his life he had had all the surrogate sons *and* daughters he needed in his brothers and sisters, whom he had looked after since his father had been killed when they were children. In any case, Alice had made it quite clear

to her husband that she was palpitatingly eager to give him a real son—
and one, moreover, who would be of the blood and able to carry on the
du Pont line.

There is no evidence to suggest that P. S. du Pont and Lewes Mason
ever had a physical homosexual relationship, and all the indications are that
P.S. would have been shocked at any suggestion that what he felt for his
chauffeur-valet might be the kind of deep sexual passion he was never to
know for his wife, or any other woman. As for Alice, if she had cherished any
"dark thoughts," as she called them, about the nature of her husband's relationship with Lewes, they were driven from her mind by the news she
received in the summer of 1918. P.S. went off one night in early June to
dine, he told Alice, at the Bellevue-Stratford Hotel, which the du Ponts
owned, in Philadelphia. She guessed, since Lewes was driving the car, that
the two would be having dinner together; she was not asked to go along.
What she did not know was that after leaving the big house, Lewes stopped
to pick up his niece, Anna, and that when the three of them reached the
Bellevue-Stratford, there was another young woman named Catherine Chalfont waiting to make a foursome.

That was the evening Lewes Mason introduced Catherine to P.S. as the
girl he "truly loved" and was going to marry before the end of the year.
Any doubts that Alice might have retained were dissipated by the manner
in which her husband appears to have taken this surprise announcement. It
seems that before this evening Lewes had not even informed him of Catherine Chalfont's existence. But, as P.S. told Alice later, he was "very happy"
and congratulated the couple, telling them that he would at once instruct
workmen at Longwood to build them a small house on the estate where
they could embark on married life. More than that: In the next few weeks
he wrote several times to Miss Chalfont, telling her what a wonderful husband she was getting, and sending her gifts of a tea set, a set of dishes, and
some solid silver teaspoons. Catherine wrote back to thank P.S.—"our
Daddy," as she called him—for his gifts and his praise. Lewes, she felt sure,
"is deserving of it all," and she added: "If in my making him happy I have
made others, it adds much to my own, for I can but say that I am the happiest girl in the world."

Alice must have been happy, too, for undoubtedly Lewes's marriage
would create a gap in P.S.'s life, and she was more than ready to fill it.

That autumn, germs of the virulent Spanish flu spread from New York
to Delaware and Pennsylvania. Alice, who traveled to Wilmington three or
four times a week to work with the Red Cross, was soon made aware that

scores and then hundreds were succumbing to the disease in the city. By the beginning of October the scourge was also finding victims in Philadelphia and then, its tentacles reaching southward, it found its way first to Media, then Kennett Square, and finally to Longwood itself. All over the farms and gardens, and inside the big house, staff were beginning to report sick. On October 10, 1918, when Alice returned from Red Cross work and a bond-raising drive in Wilmington, she found that one of the handymen, Gene, was down with the flu and that his wife, Edla, who worked at the house, had actually died of it.

Late that night P.S. came into Alice's dressing room to tell her that Lewes Mason had the flu. Could she come and help? She went down with her husband to Lewes's quarters and helped him put the young man to bed. He had a high fever. Next day P.S. said he was staying at Longwood, and Alice had her own chauffeur drive her into Wilmington for Red Cross work. When she got back late in the evening it was to be greeted by a cheerful P.S. who told her that Lewes was much better. He seemed so relieved that the following morning, a Saturday, he insisted on driving Alice into Wilmington, and they lunched together at the Hotel du Pont. But by the time they returned to Longwood, at about 2:30 in the afternoon, Lewes had had a relapse. P.S. went to the telephone and called Dr. Gifford.

Alice's diary entries for the week of October 13–20, 1918, show quite graphically how the drama (and the tragedy) in her life was building:

October 13th, Sunday. Had walk in a.m. & spent p.m. writing Loan letters. Upset over Lewnis [*sic*]. Lewis [*sic*] had had bad night.

October 14th, Monday. Fine. Spent morning visiting sick on place. Worried about Lewis. Sick again in p.m. P.S. up all night.

October 15th, Tuesday. Fine. Up very early because of worry. Went around farm to visit sick. Miss Love [a nurse] came and real sick regime started.

October 16th, Wednes. P.S. home all day. Irénée came for lunch and brought Mrs. Stofer. P.S. went to town in afternoon. Very anxious time . . .

October 17th, Thurs. Went around the sick and did the housekeeping. P.S. went to town. Very bad night. He out at midnight to Kennett.

Alice Belin was no gushing diarist. Her daily entries were rarely more than three or four lines in length, and the language was cryptic. She never wrote a sentence where a single word would do, and it was usually a monosyllable. But sometimes even single-line entries can hint at drama and deep emotion.

P.S. had spent the evening of October 17 spelling the nurse who was sitting with Lewes Mason, and at midnight they decided the young man's condition was worsening. P.S. usually telephoned the doctor when he needed him, but, possibly to give himself a break from the tension, he decided to go himself to bring him back to Longwood. But when he reached the clinic at Kennett Square, he discovered that Dr. Gifford was on his midnight rounds somewhere in the countryside; it was not until the following morning that he arrived at Longwood to see his patient. P.S., who had been up all night again, went with him into the sickroom, and afterward the two spent a long time in the gardens walking up and down in anxious consultation.

Alice had taken the precaution of calling in Lewes's fiancée, Catherine Chalfont, and summoning Mrs. Charlie Mason and her daughter, Anna, who lived on the estate, to come over to the big house. While they waited in turn to go into the sickroom to see Lewes, Alice went off to see her housekeeper, Mrs. Barre, into bed, for she too had contracted the flu. Then she came back to do what she could to comfort Catherine and the Masons. Alice asked them to stay the night; they would be called if there was a crisis.

But there was no possible way she could comfort her husband. He would not eat or talk and was either in or hovering outside the sickroom. Alice telephoned his brother-in-law, Rodney Sharp, who was also a colleague and good friend, to come over and persuade P.S. to rest, or to eat and drink. But he was immovable. He stayed where he was all Friday night and on through Saturday, passing the hot muggy hours in or near Lewes Mason's room. Meanwhile, Alice stayed in the background, watching and grieving, not over the dying boy but over her painfully suffering husband who was trying to face up to the implications of his impending loss. That night she wrote in her diary:

> October 19th, Saturday. Lewis not so well & gave up hope. Martha came. Rod stayed out. Lewis died at 7.30. P.S. all in. . . .

And that is practically all she wrote, except that, in the days to come, she mentioned Lewes's funeral ("very hard on P.S."), and a "long talk" she had had with her husband ("P.S. very sad and a very hard evening").

But there is one sentence in the diary that, by implication, is perhaps more poignant and revealing than all the rest because of the point at which it comes in the entries.

What did she do when Lewes Mason had been pronounced dead and her husband at last emerged from the sickroom? Did she approach him with words of sympathy and comfort? With the held-out hand of one who is still there and is offering, at this terrible moment, solace and a reaffirmation of her undying love? And what was P.S.'s reaction to her? Being Alice, she did not say. But what she did write seems to sum up the situation between her and her husband in that unhappy autumn of 1918 as no gush of words could have done:

. . . Hard realization of my place.

For one so hemmed-in as Alice Belin du Pont, it was a muffled moan of utter desolation.

As for P. S. du Pont himself, he confided in no diaries and did not talk about his feelings so that few people had any notion of the depth of his sorrow. In any case, the public would hardly have believed that a man so rich and powerful could have given his whole heart to a servant—or that he even had a heart to give. Like the rest of the du Ponts, P.S. was not supposed to be subject to the ills and sufferings of normal human beings. Was it not well known that when the du Ponts pricked themselves, other people bled? Was it not true that when tragedy threatened, they simply bought it off?

It was a legend P.S. was apt to encourage, and especially at this moment. For not only had he to guide the Du Pont company through the tricky challenges of the postwar world, he also had some bitter battles to fight and win with his du Pont cousins, still challenging his control of the company. It would be dangerous to let them know how badly he had been wounded by Lewes Mason's death. The more unscrupulous among them could easily make a great scandal out of it.

Part One

---◆---

THE FAMILY

CHAPTER 1

Aide-Mémoire

THE three du Pont cousins and their forebears and descendants with whom this narrative is chiefly concerned were feuding with each other in 1918 over which of them should have control of the great explosives and chemical company that bore their name, and it would be many years before the other two cousins finally accepted de jure what had already become de facto: that P. S. du Pont had made himself the man in charge.

In fact, all three cousins were lucky to be in a position to squabble among themselves over the destiny of E. I. du Pont de Nemours, for only a few years earlier they had been on the remote fringes of the operation. They had leaped into the breach left in the company's defenses by their uncles' neglect in the year 1902, when the uncles had decided to sell out, but they had not really expected to emerge in full control. The circumstances in which they achieved this domination are a choice chapter in the business history of the United States because of the finesse with which the three cousins carried it out, and because of the luck that rode with them during their maneuvers. To explain how it came about, it is necessary to go back a few generations to show how the Du Pont powder company became such a vital factor in United States affairs, and what nature of men they were who first made Du Pont and then all but destroyed it.

By this time the story of how the du Pont family left France toward the end of the eighteenth century and settled in the United States has become frayed in the retelling. I do not propose to spend more than a chapter on it, and those who would still prefer to reread it in detail will find a list of volumes dealing with that part of the du Pont story in the Source Notes. Here it will be sufficient to remember that it was another P.S., namely, Pierre Samuel du Pont de Nemours, who made the journey with his family.

Born in Paris on December 14, 1739, the son of a watchmaker, Pierre Samuel du Pont hated being apprenticed to his father's craft, preferring books and ledgers to hairsprings, and eventually broke away to educate and better himself. By 1774 he had been named inspector general of commerce under Louis XVI, was happily married with two small sons, Victor and Eleuthère Irénée, and had an estate in the country, Bois des Fosses. Ten years later Louis XVI granted him a patent of nobility, which enabled him to have a coat of arms and to tag "de Nemours" to his name; but in return he had, publicly at least, to renounce his Huguenot religion and espouse Roman Catholicism.

Then disaster struck Pierre Samuel. First his wife died young, and then came the French Revolution. Pierre Samuel was arrested and flung into jail while trying to defend Louis XVI from a Paris mob, and he narrowly escaped the guillotine, thanks mainly to the fall of Robespierre, who had been after his head.

He stayed clear of trouble for three years after his release from jail, but then, in 1797, he was arrested again, along with his son Eleuthère Irénée, and although they were released after only one night, Pierre Samuel, who had by then remarried, seems to have decided that emigration offered the only chance of security and freedom in the future for him and his family. He chose America because he was fired by the possibilities of that new and developing nation. He already knew much about it, thanks to a long-time correspondence with Thomas Jefferson and also to the stories told about it by his son Victor, who had been to the United States twice on diplomatic missions, once to witness the inauguration of George Washington and once to serve as consul general at Philadelphia.

Pierre Samuel's second wife went ahead to find a home for the family, but the rest of them—Pierre himself; Eleuthère Irénée, with his wife and first child; Victor and his wife; and some cousins—sailed for the United States aboard the *American Eagle* on October 2, 1799, from La Rochelle. The ship was leaky and the weather foul, and the du Ponts were soon suffering. Pierre Samuel, nearly sixty years old, was bent and in great pain from increasingly severe attacks of gout. Victor was cold and seasick, and the wives and children were nauseated by the boiled rats and weevily meal they were soon forced to eat. Only Eleuthère Irénée du Pont seemed to be impervious to the pains and trials of the voyage. But he was, in fact, suffering too, and the pain he was suppressing made the birthmark on his left cheek stand out lividly against the tense paleness of his face. His teeth, like those of many another Frenchman of his time, were rotting, and several had to come out during the voyage. Unlike his famous descendant, P. S. du Pont, who was proud of his false teeth "made by du Pont," which he considered "a great improvement on nature's manufacture," Irénée had no artificial ones to replace his own and endured in silence.

They were all thankful when they first sighted the American continent on the morning of New Year's Day, 1800, and ever since, the du Ponts have celebrated that day as the date of their arrival in the United States. In fact, the family did not actually go ashore until January 3, and not at New York, for which they had been aiming, but at Newport, Rhode Island, where their drifting ship finally dropped anchor. The oft-told story is that the hungry du Ponts knocked on the door of the first house they came to. Upon finding the house empty—the family away at church—they liberally helped themselves to the food heaped on the table, then left a gold coin and a note of thanks before going their way.

Pierre Samuel had no clear idea of what he and his family were going to do once they reached the shores of America. Before leaving France, he had formed a company called Du Pont de Nemours Père Fils et Cie and sold shares in it which raised him just under a quarter of a million francs plus the rents from fifty-six thousand acres in Kentucky that a French-Swiss banker, Jacques Bidermann, had given him in return for shares. But what was he to do once he got there? Go into land speculation? Thomas Jefferson had warned him of the heavy risks involved. Become a planter? He had had visions of starting a great agricultural enterprise to be called Pontiana, but once landed in America, he realized that his funds were inadequate. Start trading and build up a packet-boat system operating between the United States and France? That scheme never received from the French government the subsidy that Pierre Samuel had requested.

It so happened that before leaving France, Eleuthère Irénée du Pont had studied the manufacture of gunpowder under Lavoisier, a famous chemist, and had worked at the French government powder works at Essonne. He had even written a long thesis on different methods of manufacturing powder. Once established in the United States (the family had bought a house called Good Stay, at Bergen Point, New Jersey), Irénée went hunting one day with a French friend and, having flushed a covey of partridges in the marshes, opened fire—or, rather, misfired. He found that his gun, loaded with American-made powder, seemed to misfire about every other time he pulled the trigger. Speculating on whether he had simply bought dud powder or whether all American powder was like this, he went with his hunting companion to visit a factory in Pennsylvania and discovered that American methods of making gunpowder were years out of date and the quality of their product, abysmal. Irénée realized that with his knowledge he could easily produce a powder that would supersede the American product, and he went to his father to persuade him that one of the enterprises of Du Pont de Nemours Père Fils et Cie should be the establishment of a powder industry. Pierre Samuel was unreceptive; he thought gunpowder manufacture far below his lofty ideas, lower even than watchmaking, and it took all the arguments Irénée could produce to convince him otherwise. Finally he agreed to include powder making in the list of the company's concerns but insisted Irénée should become personally responsible not just for the establishment of a factory and its operation but also for one third of the money required to set it up.

Irénée accepted the challenge without hesitation and in April 1801 set sail for France, there to take a crash course in the latest powder-making know-how and also to raise more money for his new enterprise. His brother, Victor, went too, with fund-raising plans of his own.

Irénée was away for seven months, but his absence was more than worthwhile. His father's firm, Du Pont de Nemours Père Fils et Cie, had agreed to advance him twenty-four thousand dollars for his project. He decided that he would need at least another twelve thousand dollars to make his proposed powder mills a viable enterprise. In Paris he found a sympathetic ear given him by Jacques Bidermann, one of his father's original backers. Another of his father's friends, Mme de Staël, also received him and introduced him to her uncle, Louis Necker, whose brother was a government minister. Then there was a former colleague of Pierre Samuel's, one Louis Duquesnoy, who said he would come in. Between them they agreed to put up six thousand dollars.

On ' il 21, 1801, in Paris, Irénée incorporated a company for the "manufacture of military and sporting powder in the United States of America," assigning one share each (valued at two thousand dollars) to Bidermann, Necker, and Duquesnoy; eleven shares to Du Pont de Nemours Père Fils et Cie; and four shares to be made available to American investors.

But what turned Irénée's journey into a success far beyond his original hopes was a development from an entirely unexpected quarter: The French government came to his aid, too. In those days the British supplied most of America's gunpowder needs (except for the poor stuff that was manufactured locally), and the French were delighted to contemplate one of their nationals cutting into what was practically a British monopoly.

Immediately after the company's incorporation, the French government made it possible for Irénée to buy powder-making machinery at cost, allowed him to study and make notes of the latest powder-making processes at its experimental factory at Essonne, and helped him recruit experienced powder workers to take back with him to America. He returned to Bergen Point with his booty in July 1801 and brought with him other things besides machinery and powder men: clothes for his wife, Sophie, dolls and toys for his children, seeds and plants that he intended to plant and cultivate (for he was an enthusiastic botanist), and from Spain, seven merino sheep, famous for their silky long fleece, that he hoped to raise and breed in his new home, wherever it might be. In between powder making, of course.

Pierre Samuel had originally suggested that his son find a factory site close to Washington where he would have the ear of the elder du Pont's friend Thomas Jefferson, who was then president and therefore in a position to hand out contracts. But Irénée found nothing that was suitable in either Maryland or Virginia. He wrote his father that he found "the country, the people, the locale . . . all worthless" and proposed to go to Wilmington, Delaware, and take a look at the possibilities along the Brandywine River.

He found an ideal spot on the Brandywine Creek where the river, flowing in from Pennsylvania through the farmlands of northern Delaware, falls over one hundred and twenty feet in a course of less than four miles on its way to join first the Christina River at Wilmington and then the mighty Delaware River itself. Since Irénée would be driving his powder mills with power from waterwheels, he could hardly have hoped to find a more suitable location. But the man who owned it, a tight-fisted local Quaker named Jacob Broom, was a man who believed in driving a hard bargain. He had originally built a cotton mill on his property, only to have it destroyed by fire, and he had never bothered to rebuild it; and the land was so rocky that it was unsuitable for cultivation. But Broom demanded, and eventually got, $6,740 for his ninety-five acres along the creek, far more than the local going price. Since Delaware land could not be sold to foreigners (Irénée was still a French citizen), the new site was deeded to one William Hamon, a naturalized American of French extraction.

It turned out that Jacob Broom, in addition to his Quaker principles, had one other precept: The last drop of profit must be squeezed from a transaction. When he discovered that Eleuthère Irénée du Pont's plan was to utilize the Brandywine River for power, he saw one more possibility for profit. He owned a strip of land further upstream, and there he built a dam across the river to brake the force of the current to such an extent that it threatened to idle any waterwheels Irénée might install. The Frenchman was furious and spilled out his frustration in a letter to his father, enumerating the ways in which Americans, both officials and private persons, had sought to take advantage of him and make him feel "a foreigner":

> In spite of the equality, the rights of liberty, and the excellent government of this country, we foreigners are always in a position of inferiority to that of other citizens. We are not, as you say, among our equals; that is a truth that I have learned from daily contacts with Americans. This suggestion of inferiority—this prejudice of which one often feels the influence—offsets in my mind many of the advantages of America and makes me believe that if we could be free from debt we would all be happier in France.

He did not mean it. And hardheaded, determined character that he was, Irénée was certainly not going to allow a Quaker of English extraction (he shared with most Frenchmen of his day an antipathy to England and all things English) to outwit a Huguenot. Pacing the banks of the Brandywine, he suddenly came upon the solution. Broom owned only one side of the river upstream, and Irénée at once approached the owner of the land on the opposite bank and paid him one hundred dollars for the *water rights* along his stretch of the river. This gave him the right to destroy half of Broom's dam and set the Brandywine flowing swiftly again.

Delaware summers are as hot and humid as its winters are chill and damp, and it was in the midst of a more than usually muggy heat wave, on July 19, 1802, that Irénée brought his wife, Sophie, and their children to the small farm holding he had bought on the Brandywine. They arrived filthy, hot and caked with dust from a four-day journey by wagon over one hundred and thirty miles of deeply rutted cart tracks from Bergen Point, and the sight of the tiny, two-room stone cottage that was to be their future home must have shaken Sophie du Pont as much in spirit as the rigors of that journey had shaken her in body. Her brother, Charles, had brought in most of their furniture and other belongings by sea via New Castle, Delaware, and now beds and wardrobes spilled out onto the grass. The merinos were bleating in a pen close to the cottage, and the family dogs were joyfully leaping up at the children. But the sounds for which Irénée was listening, those of the mills going up along the creek, were missing, for work had been halted until he could arrive to explain the plans for his powder factory, over which the work force was sorely puzzled.

Another reason Irénée had chosen the Brandywine was its proximity to a colony of French immigrants in Wilmington, whom he hoped to recruit for his mills. Like Irénée himself, they spoke little English and were willing to work for far less than native American labor. But for building the mills he had been forced to recruit skilled construction workers from Pennsylvania, and they did not hesitate to make clear that they considered the building plans he had made crazily unsuitable. For one thing, there was going to be not one big factory but several small ones, with wide spaces of unused land in between them. Then, the buildings themselves were not even going to be of a piece. Three sides of each one of them were to be thickly walled with good solid stone, but the fourth side, the wall facing the Brandywine, was to be much less substantial. Most ridiculous of all, in a climate subject to heavy rains and snowfalls, the roof was to be of the thinnest kind of wood and to slope down steeply toward the creek. In America, his workmen-critics loudly told him, you did not build factories in separate little units, and what you did build you built solid.

Irénée's mastery of English was still poor, and it took him some time to explain that the eccentricities of his plans were carefully calculated to fit the character of his business. Powder making was a dangerous craft, and inevitably, there were going to be fires and explosions. Irénée was taking precautions so that when a mill blew up, only a small part of his operation would go sky-high. The full force of the blast, thanks to the thin wall and flimsy sloping roof, would explode toward the river, away from the vulnerable neighboring buildings and the men working inside them. It was a lesson he had learned from Lavoisier at the French powder works in Essonne, and it was meant to save lives and money.

Building resumed. But it was not until a year later that the first supplies of saltpeter were processed and refined, and not until the spring of 1804 that the waterwheels ground their first powder and the barrels began to be filled for shipment to its first customers from E. I. du Pont de Nemours and Company, Gunpowder Manufactory, Wilmington, Delaware.

During the next twelve months, E. I. du Pont de Nemours and Company made 44,907 pounds of black powder in the Brandywine mills, and had no trouble selling it. Good powder was in short supply, and Irénée made good powder. Secretary of War Henry Dearborn ordered a comparison test between the Brandywine product and the best English powder, and Irénée's proved "so superior" that the secretary ordered a hundred and twenty thousand pounds of army powder be sent to the Brandywine for "remaking." Irénée had expected to sell his powder for thirty-six dollars a hundredweight but discovered he could ask forty dollars and get it, with no complaints. Meanwhile, President Jefferson helped sales by telling Irénée confidentially that he had instructed the United States Army and Navy to buy Du Pont powders "whenever their wants may call for them." The navy called for twenty-two thousand pounds in 1805 and used it to pump cannonballs into the forts of Tripoli and Derna, on the Mediterranean, in its war against the pirates of the Barbary Coast.

Sales rose from ten thousand dollars in 1804 to forty-three thousand dollars in 1807, and there would have been quite a profit at the end of each year had the customers, particularly the government, paid their bills promptly. As it was, what profits there were got eaten up by the bank debts Irénée had incurred in getting Du Pont launched. With shareholders pressing for dividends and the bank dunning him for repayment, and with the responsibility for running the mills resting largely on his shoulders, Irénée complained bitterly of his problems and became subject to bouts of melancholia. As he wrote:

> The activity of my work helps me and is good for me in
> that it gives me less time to yield to the melancholy that never
> leaves me, and that, I am afraid, affects my health.

He found that the Delaware climate gave him chills, fevers, and
rheumatism and an almost permanent cough. After the first few months,
he had moved his family out of the tiny stone cottage into a new and
more commodious house, called Eleutherian Mills, on a slope overlooking
the Brandywine, where there was more air and sun; and there Sophie, his
wife, gave birth to four more children, two boys and two girls, although
her own physical condition was often as sickly as her husband's.

Irénée also worried about his brother, Victor, who was trying and failing to run a woolen mill from a stake he had advanced him, though he
could ill afford it.* Victor was cheerful and charming, and he easily weath-
ered the first big du Pont family scandal when his eldest daughter, Amelia,
married an Englishman who proved already to have a wife and family
back home. There was a child from the bigamous union, and Victor pulled
strings to have it legitimized while speeding the false husband back to England on the first available packet. But Amelia was heartbroken and said
she would never look at a man again. Nor did she. She was the ugly duck-
ling of Victor's family, and no one seemed to care when she disappeared
into seclusion. On the other hand, his three other children were more
comely and married more successfully. One of them, Samuel Francis, began
the custom of cousinly weddings among the du Ponts by marrying one of
Irénée's daughters, Sophie Madeleine. And though, from about this time,
Victor's children and descendants began to be squeezed out of the powder-
making (and therefore money-making) side of the du Pont activities, they
turned themselves into a sort of blood bank for Irénée's branch by providing his descendants with husbands and wives—a useful way of making
sure that control and succession stayed in the family.

Not that Irénée was against "outside" marriages for his children, so
long as there were practical as well as sentimental reasons behind the
union. In 1813, piqued by rumors that Irénée was not being frank with
his shareholders, the Franco-Swiss banker Jacques Bidermann dispatched
his son, Jacques Antoine, to Delaware to investigate the situation. Antoine
was impressed by the accomplishments achieved at the Brandywine mills
and reported back to his father that he had absolutely nothing to worry
about. Immediately attracted by Irénée's sincerity and seriousness, touched

* He also let him use his herd of merino sheep for wool.

by the sad expression on his pockmarked, lugubrious features, Antoine formed a rapport with the older man and stayed on to help him.

He was soon on visiting terms at Eleutherian Mills, the du Pont family home, and fell in love with Irénée's second daughter, Evalina, a bouncy, attractive girl of seventeen. Irénée gave his consent with no hesitation when Antoine asked for her hand in marriage, and happily welcomed him into the firm. It was one of the most successful marriages ever made by a du Pont.

Irénée had rather more doubts, however, when Ferdinand Bauduy emerged as a suitor for the hand of his eldest daughter, Victorine. Ferdinand was the son of Jean-Pierre Bauduy, an emigré from Haiti who had bought shares in the firm but expected participation beyond the extent of his holdings. Though the two young people were very much in love, Irénée hesitated, hating the thought of having a Bauduy in his family. He finally demanded a two-year separation to make sure that his daughter knew her own mind. She did. When Ferdinand Bauduy came back from a trip to France in 1813, Irénée finally gave his consent and they were married.

For a short time, at least, the bonds of marriage seemed to bring the fathers-in-law together. Then, a little over two months after the wedding ceremony, Ferdinand Bauduy came down with pneumonia and died. Like her cousin Amelia, Victorine, brokenhearted and inconsolable, swore a vow—and kept it—never to marry again. Ferdinand's death seemed to banish the resentment and envy Pierre Bauduy still cherished for Irénée, and he wrote to him:

> May this sorrow unite us; be my friend, for I have lost the best friend I had.

A few months later, however, he was snarling and backbiting as savagely as ever against Irénée's control of the company and busily stirring up intrigue among the shareholders in Paris against what he termed Irénée's extravagances. Business, in fact, was going splendidly. The trouble was that Irénée was trying to pay off many debts for which he had only moral responsibility—those incurred by his father, who had long ago returned to France, and by the bankruptcy of his father's original company, Du Pont de Nemours Père Fils et Cie.

The War of 1812 proved to be a bonanza for the Brandywine mills. The army sent in an immediate order for two hundred thousand pounds of the best powder. In that year Du Pont sold powder to the value of

$147,597, and the following year's receipts were $107,291. A panic set in when the British put Washington to the torch in 1814, and British naval guns began bombarding Lewes, in lower Delaware. Would the Du Pont mills be the next target? A militia (commanded by Victor) was hastily formed and stood guard along the Brandywine, but they never heard a British shot fired. And the Brandywine mills went on grinding black powder for American guns, the yards lit by swinging tallow lamps as the workers toiled around the clock to keep up with the orders.

The pressure was such that on the night of June 8, 1815, someone scuffed a pebble and sparked a grain of powder, and up went one of the mills. But only one. Irénée's foresight had paid off, and though nine men were killed and a whole building destroyed, the other buildings were saved. After the bits of the far-flung dead were scraped off the rocks and rescued from the Brandywine, the grinding went on. Antoine Bidermann, away at the time, wrote Irénée to suggest that the widows of the dead men be allowed to remain in their company homes, and put on pension; his father-in-law replied that he had already taken steps to see that this was done.*

It was a decade of fires and explosions. Just over a year later another fire broke out, reached a graining mill, and blew it up, this time fortunately with no casualties. But Irénée was forced to borrow thirty thousand dollars from a Philadelphia supply firm to get back in production. And then, in 1817, there was a third fire, an enormous one, and though it was eventually quenched with no explosion and no one killed, it did bring about the death of the founder of the du Pont family in America, old Pierre Samuel du Pont himself.

By 1817 Pierre Samuel should have been living out his old age back in his native France, for he had returned there with his wife in 1802 to help the new regime of Napoleon Bonaparte. He left America before Irénée got the powder mills working in Delaware, and made it clear that he did not intend to return.

When Thomas Jefferson heard that his friend was going home, he seized the opportunity to entrust him with letters and dispatches concerning the vexing problem of Louisiana, which, though nominally French, was increasingly being used by Americans as an outlet for goods and commu-

---

* Widows were encouraged by Irénée to take in unmarried powder men as lodgers, an arrangement that frequently led to their remarriage—and, of course, no further house was needed to set them up.

nications, and for their plantations. The local French were making difficulties. Pierre Samuel's cool handling of the affair helped quiet French
chauvinism, and the subsequent deal by which the Americans were able to
make the Louisiana Purchase, doubling at once the size of the United
States, owed much to his expertise as a go-between.

But it was his only success. Soon he was quarreling with Napoleon
and taking sides against him.

When Napoleon escaped from Elba in February 1815, gathered his
scattered armies together in the south of France, and began his march on
Paris, Pierre Samuel, who had experienced two previous imprisonments
for political activities and was convinced this time that he would end up
either on the guillotine or on Devil's Island, panicked and fled to Le Havre
to catch a boat to America, leaving behind his invalid wife, for whom
special transport arrangements would have had to be made.

Pierre Samuel's two sons welcomed him back to America with open
arms, and Pierre Samuel was allowed to resume his position as patriarch
of the du Ponts. Though bent and hobbled by gout and old age (he was
seventy-seven in 1815), he was able to lead an active life, receiving visiting statesmen, keeping up an avid correspondence with ex-President
Jefferson on their differing ideas of democracy,* and bustling crablike
around Brandywine Creek to keep an eye on the powder mills while his
son or young Antoine Bidermann was away.

It was during one of Irénée's absences, on July 16, 1817, that the
third fire occurred. A hogshead of charcoal, which its carrier thought was
burned out, rekindled and set the whole of a drying-house ablaze. The
alarm gong sounded to rouse the workers in their houses around the creek
and bring them down to fight the flames before they reached the powder
mills. Among those who responded to the call was old Pierre Samuel.

It was a particularly sticky conflagration, literally so, since scores of
full tar barrels were close to the fire and thus in danger of going up in
flames if they caught. They were too heavy to be carted away, and Antoine
Bidermann, who had taken charge, ordered them overturned so that their
contents would spill downhill toward the river, away from the flames.
Meanwhile, the fire pumps had gone dry, and the men, women, and chil-

* From one of their arguments emerged a letter that encapsulated Jefferson's
ideas of the American political ethic: "We both consider the people as our children,
and love them with parental affection. But you love them as infants whom you are afraid
to trust without nurses, and I as adults whom I freely leave to self-government." (Cited in
*Correspondence between Thomas Jefferson and Pierre Samuel du Pont de Nemours 1798–
1815,* ed. Dumas Malone, Boston: Houghton Mifflin, 1930.)

dren of the Brandywine had set up a bucket brigade in what turned out to be the direct path of the flowing tar. In minutes these fire fighters were up to their knees in the sticky mess, so thick they had trouble flinging themselves clear when a wall and a chimney of the drying-house collapsed.

Pierre Samuel passed the water buckets along with the rest of the workers until, hands bleeding, his stubbled chin and wisps of hair caked with tar and smoke, he collapsed, half-blinded and muscle-bound. He was carried up to his room in Eleutherian Mills and put to bed, and he was still there when Irénée got back.

Pierre Samuel never left his bed again. His two sons and their families gathered around his bedside, and while he was still lucid they kept thanking him for having been a good father and for the efforts he had made on their behalf. In truth, Thomas Jefferson had more reason to be grateful to him than did his younger son. Except, of course, that if it had not been for Pierre Samuel's decision in 1799, Eleuthère Irénée du Pont might never have come to the United States and never have pulled the trigger of a gun loaded with American powder—a misfire that was to have consequences not only for the du Ponts but for the world.

Pierre Samuel went into a coma on August 5, 1817, and died two days later. Messages of sympathy came from President Monroe, from Jefferson, and from many another American statesman. His mortal remains were buried under a white sandstone slab in a corner of Sand Hole Woods, within sight of Brandywine Creek. His was the first body consigned to what would henceforth become the du Pont family graveyard.

CHAPTER 2

The Reign of Henry the Red

Ａs Irénée du Pont came downstairs from his vigil beside his father's deathbed an onlooker thought (and later noted) that "he looked older and frailer than the corpse upstairs." But at forty-five years old, despite his sorry appearance, he was still a dynamo of energy, chasing government orders in Washington, putting in long hours at the powder yards, and traveling back and forth to the banks in Philadelphia, thirty-odd miles away, to discuss the company's loans. But melancholia consumed him. He rarely smiled, his shoulders bending, it seemed, under the weight of all the world's woes.

As the years passed, nothing that happened to him or to his enterprises was calculated to lighten his moods. In March, 1818, while Irénée was at the bank in Philadelphia, what appeared to be an act of sabotage by a disgruntled employee set off an explosion in a glazing mill, which blew up with a convulsive blast. This time all Irénée's precautions to limit the damage to the mills came to naught. Fragments of flaming wood landed on the drying sheds and ignited them, and then blazing embers caught the main magazine, causing an explosion that was heard in all the surrounding cities. Rows of powder men's cottages were completely demolished, and debris crashed through the walls and windows of Irénée's own home, smashing up the interior of the house.

While Antoine Bidermann once again directed the fire fighting, his wife, Evalina, and the rest of the du Pont women rounded up the workmen's wives to carry the wounded to a makeshift hospital, where burns and torn limbs were tended and screaming pain doused with liberal doses of whiskey. But thirty-six were already dead, and four more died from their wounds. Only eight bodies could be identified. The rest were blown to pieces, which had to be picked off the branches of blasted trees, from rocks, and from ruined buildings for days afterward.

Irénée, who had galloped his horse back from Philadelphia as soon as he heard the news, arrived to find that his wife, Sophie, had been hit in the side by a flying rock that had come through a window of Eleutherian Mills. She never really recovered from the shock and pain of the injury.

The explosion was a financial disaster of ruinous proportions. Practically the whole of the Brandywine yards, upper and lower, had been put out of action, and the upper yard was almost completely destroyed. The damage came to a hundred and twenty thousand dollars—more than the total fixed assets of the company. That meant Irénée would have to borrow even more money from the banks, to pay pensions to the widows, rebuild the upper yard, and restock the mills.

To add to his burdens, his old adversary, Bauduy, who had by now set up a rival explosives factory, chose this moment to sue him and incited a former shareholder in France to do likewise. At the same time, Talleyrand wrote to ask for the return of one hundred thousand francs that he had lent old Pierre Samuel (before his death) while he was still in Paris. All this meant more loans from the banks, and Irénée became physically and mentally hagridden just keeping up with the innumerable notes he was forced to sign. As he wrote:

> It is cruel to ride sixty miles every five or six days to meet one's notes, and so to waste one's time and one's life. God grant that some day I may get to the end of it.

But the burden grew no lighter and there were additional worries at home to darken his mind. In 1826 his fat and contented brother, Victor, serving then as a representative in the Delaware legislature—as "the people's friend"—went to a meeting in Philadelphia where he told his friends he had never felt better. Half an hour later he collapsed in the street outside his hotel and was pronounced dead soon afterward. Irénée grieved, for he had been deeply fond of his easygoing brother.

In 1828 his wife, Sophie, took to her bed and died. Irénée's widowed daughter, Victorine, still grieving over the untimely death of her young husband, made efforts to shake off her depression and take her mother's place in the household, but the sight of her sad and downcast features, as miserable as his own, only increased Irénée's sense of loss.

On October 31, 1834, he rode once more to Philadelphia for yet another session with his creditors, staying the night in the United States Hotel, which he and his brother had always used. Leaving the hotel the next morning, he was walking along the same stretch of sidewalk where Victor had collapsed eight years earlier, when suddenly he stumbled and dropped to the ground. Passersby carried him back to the hotel, where he died shortly afterward in his room, at the age of sixty-three.

Irénée was buried at Sand Hole Woods, to the left of his father's grave (Victor, as the older son, had been buried on the right). Immediately afterward his family met in the drawing room of Eleutherian Mills to discuss the situation created by Irénée's death. What was going to happen to Du Pont now? The company was leaderless, with a hundred and fifty thousand dollars in debt.

The female side of the du Pont family has never played a strong role in the boardroom or front-office affairs of the company. As a woman who is close to the family once remarked when asked what the eight daughters of a later member of the clan had done with their lives:

"They just got married."

A less kind observer called the du Pont women "the brood mares of the family stable."

But if that was their principal function, it did not prevent the strong-minded among them from influencing company policies and practices, some through their husbands in the bedroom, others through the sheer power of their personality to dominate the rest of the du Ponts. Evalina, wife of James Antoine Bidermann—he had now changed his first name from Jacques to James—was by no means the most potent personality in the long line of female du Ponts, but she had no doubt in her mind who should take over control of the company now that her father was dead, and it was certainly not one of her three brothers.

The eldest, Alfred Victor, was a first-class chemist whose experiments in powder making had already done much to improve the company's product, and he definitely had the appearance of a strong man. He was over six feet tall and broad shouldered, and his characteristically du Pont nose and cleft chin gave him an air of purposefulness and vigor. But appearances were deceptive; inside the big man was quite a small personality, and one, moreover, very much under the thumb of his pushy and often vindictive wife, Margaretta.

The second of Evalina's brothers, Henry, was cut from much tougher cloth (from storm-proof canvas, in fact), but he was only twenty-two years old and had just come out of the army. The youngest brother, Alexis I., was still in school and not, in Evalina's opinion, of leadership caliber.

So, once discussion of the succession began, she did not hesitate to persuade her three sisters to support her own proposal, which was that her husband, Antoine, should assume control of the company and handle its affairs until such time as their brothers, any or all of them, felt and were considered able to take over. Victorine, her elder sister, had no reason to disagree, for she had no husband to compete with Antoine. Eleuthera's new husband, Thomas Mackie Smith, was a practicing doctor in Wilmington and had no wish to change purgatives for explosives.* And Sophie Madeleine, wife and cousin of Lieutenant (later Admiral) Samuel Francis du Pont, knew her husband was firmly set on a career in the United States Navy.

James Antoine Bidermann held the temporary presidency of the Du Pont company for three years, during which time he turned its fortunes around. At the end of two years Antoine had earned enough for the company to enable him to sail to France and pay off all Pierre Samuel's old creditors as well as the shareholders (or their descendants) of the parent company, and when that was done, he wound up the affairs of the Du Pont de Nemours company in France. When he got back to the United States, he called the family together and proposed that a new company, an American one this time, be set up to take over all the assets of the enterprise on

---

* Although his chances of survival might have been better. A few years later Eleuthera, sent to her husband's surgery to get him a headache cure, brought him back a dose of aconite (wolfsbane) by mistake. He drank it down and, immediately realizing what had happened, calmly directed his wife and his brother-in-law's efforts to administer him emetics until the cramps began and he died.

the Brandywine. On April 1, 1837, a partnership with the title of E. I. du Pont de Nemours and Company was formed, with seven directors, Irénée's three sons and four daughters, all holding equal shares. Antoine was offered a directorship of his own, in addition to the one held by his wife, Evalina, but he refused it. He felt exhausted and told the family he was now retiring.

He had done well for the family, who received his resignation with a mixture of reluctance and apprehension. Who would replace him? Antoine pointed out that Alfred Victor, Irénée's oldest son, had been working at his side for the past three years and by then should have learned the ropes. So, on his recommendation, but mainly because Alfred Victor was the eldest son, the new partners elected him president of the new company in 1837.

It was a decision all of them (including Alfred himself) came to regret, for he simply was not made for the job. It should have been difficult even for the most incompetently run powder maker not to make money in the thirteen years after Alfred took over. In addition to the railroads pushing their way out west and the Indian wars, there were new farmlands to be cleared of trees, and there was even the great bonanza of the war with Mexico.

Yet by 1850 a downcast and exhausted Alfred had to confess to his brothers and sisters that E. I. du Pont de Nemours and Company, far from having run up a profit, was five hundred thousand dollars in debt. His wife, Margaretta, did not conceal her disgust for her husband's incompetency and mocked him in front of her six children. To their eldest son, Eleuthère Irénée II, she bitterly complained that his father's bungling was depriving him of his birthright, and that they would all be ruined if something were not soon done to restore the situation.

She was, therefore, fully in agreement with her du Pont in-laws when they held an emergency meeting to discuss what to do. One thing was certain: Alfred would have to go. He made that easy for them by telling them he had written out his resignation before coming to the meeting and was retiring from all future participation in the management of the company.

By the unanimous vote of the du Pont brothers and sisters, it was decided that Alfred's two younger brothers, Henry and Alexis, should take over the operation of the company. At which point Margaretta, declaring that her husband's failure was being unjustly visited on his sons, pleaded with her in-laws to add a third to the two new controllers of the company— her eldest son, young Eleuthère Irénée II. Knowing that they would never hear the last of it if they refused, for Margaretta was a virago when roused, the brothers and sisters agreed, even though Irénée was only twenty-one, in delicate health, and still learning the powder business.

So it seemed as if, from 1850 onward, E. I. du Pont de Nemours and Company would be controlled by a triumvirate of two brothers and their nephew. But one of the brothers had not the slightest doubt, right from the start, how it was going to work out. Henry du Pont already had the measure of his family and held them in affectionate contempt. As for his brother Alexis and his nephew Eleuthère Irénée II, he knew they would be afraid to object if he rode roughshod over them, and he was determined to swat them down if they dared to attempt it.

So far as Henry was concerned, he was now head of the Du Pont Company, and from then on it would be operated on his say-so and no one else's.

Henry du Pont was thirty-eight years old in 1850, and he had been itching to gain control of the company ever since the death of his father sixteen years earlier. Originally, he had set his heart on an army career and had taken part in some of the bloody encounters between the army and the Creek Indians then fighting bitterly to oppose the westward push of American civilization. He proved to be a splendid horseman and a fearless fighter and seemed to have a brilliant military career ahead of him. But shortly before his death, his father summoned him back to work in the Brandywine mills, and he had reluctantly resigned his commission, comforting himself with the thought that he would soon be head of Du Pont. But he had been passed over in the yards first by his brother-in-law, Antoine, and then by his ineffectual elder brother, Alfred. He swallowed with difficulty the subordinate position that professionally, socially, and economically a du Pont must expect if he was not boss of the company.

Short, burly, and strong as an ox, Henry had the familiar du Pont proboscis, of almost Cyrano-like proportions, but the equally familiar du Pont cleft chin was covered by a luxuriant beard. What made him stand out from the others was the brilliance of his blue eyes, as clear and hard as a mountain lake, and the flaming color of his beard and hair. Like most redheads, he was spiky and aggressive, took no insults lightly, and showed no mercy to weaklings. He despised his brother Alfred for having made a mess of his term as president, and there were strong rumors he had eased his frustration over Alfred's mismanagement by carrying on an affair with

Alfred's wife, Meta (as the family called Margaretta). It was even said that one day, while his father was away, young Irénée, his eldest son, had snooped on his mother and burst into her room at a moment when Uncle Henry had just climbed out of bed and was starting to dress. Irénée rushed at the interloper and lashed out, in a windmill of fists, at the squat, red, hairy, naked body, only to be held at arm's length by a cold, untroubled Henry, who then flung him onto the bed beside his mother, now cowering into the pillows. Irénée never forgave his mother his humiliation and her betrayal.

But Meta was far from being Henry's only conquest. In between fathering two sons and six daughters by his long-suffering wife, Louisa, he wenched methodically in town and countryside, and Philadelphia and Washington, too. His younger brother, Alexis, was a God-fearing man of such puritanical bent that he once had a Wilmington brothel, much patronized by some du Ponts, razed and a church built in its place. But Henry's taste was for gamier pursuits, at least until he took control of the company. Then he began wearing a top hat to increase his height and changed his life-style.

From the beginning he made it plain to other members of the family that there would henceforth be no passengers among them, and that each and every one of them would have to work for his or her living, either by qualifying for a job at the yards in the case of the males, or by mating and producing in the case of the females. Old Pierre Samuel had always counseled the du Ponts not to waste their time (or their sperm, for that matter) outside the family but to form a tightly knit group, taking no part in the life of the community beyond them, confining their working life to the mills and their social life to each others' homes.

"The marriages that I should prefer for our colony," he once wrote, "would be between the cousins. In that way we should be sure of honesty of soul and purity of blood."

He further counseled them to pool their resources and put them in the hands of the patriarch (or boss) of the family, who would dole out money to each of them according to need. It had particularly irked Henry, during his brother Alfred's reign, to have to go to him for every penny he wanted to spend and moreover to specify why he needed it. But now that he was boss himself, he quickly savored the pleasure of controlling the family money.

And it was Henry who would now decide where on the Brandywine each du Pont family unit would live. Families were shunted from one house to another, according to the size of their brood; if a couple wished to remain ensconced in one of the larger houses on the creek, it behooved them to keep breeding, for a more prolific member of the family might easily (at Henry's whim) unhouse them.

But where Henry differed from his father, from Antoine Bidermann, and from his brother Alfred was in his unwillingness to keep in house, food, and clothing any members of the colony who was not willing to earn his keep in the mills, or for whom there was no place. To cut costs and help wipe out the huge debts his brother had built up, he began an economy campaign, slicing the work force to 169 men—even when the orders came rolling in—stinting on bonus payments for night work and special jobs, and paring down running costs everywhere, even at the risk of impairing safety measures. In 1852 he experienced the first explosion under his new regime, and though only two men were killed, two of the mills were blown across the creek.* The explosion might well have been caused by the new pressures Henry was putting into application. But he chose to blame the carelessness of one of the workmen, William Cowan, whom he fired without severance pay and publicly excoriated, thus preventing him from getting another job. Cowan hanged himself some months later.

Henry's own son (there would be another later) was too young to go into the mills, but two of Alfred's four sons, Irénée and Lammot, were both of an age to work. Henry scarcely had any choice about Irénée, who had been made a member of the triumvirate (and Meta would have kicked up too much of a fuss, anyway). And he had no doubt at all that the younger brother, Lammot, would be a decided asset to the Du Pont company, for he was already showing signs of being a brilliant practical chemist. He would go far once he joined the Du Pont enterprise. But how far? Far enough to challenge Henry's own son's place in the company when his time came along?

Lammot du Pont returned from the University of Pennsylvania in 1852 with a degree in chemistry and almost immediately afterward joined the company to run the laboratory. It was the same one his father had used

---

* Du Pont powder workers never talked about getting killed in an explosion, rather they always called it "going across the creek," which phrase soon became a euphemism for death, both in the family and in the work force.

in his happier years before being kicked upstairs into the presidency, and Lammot was delighted to be able to juggle with the same phials, test tubes, powder mixes, and retorts that Alfred had so lovingly used. In addition, his work kept him well away from Henry du Pont, and that, he quickly learned, was something of an advantage.

He and his three brothers, Irénée, Fred, and Bidermann du Pont, still lived with their parents at Nemours, the family house overlooking the Brandywine Creek, and at supper almost every evening his elder brother would bitterly recount some new story of Henry's domineering ways in the yards. Irénée, despite his high-sounding title of partner and member of the Du Pont triumvirate, chose to work in the powder mills beside the workers, and each night he repeated their savage and often obscene comments on the stubborn and penny-pinching ways of their red-bearded boss.

Lammot noticed that his father seemed to turn his mind off as Irénée ranted on, except for a convulsive shudder of distaste, which occasionally seemed to shake his increasingly frail body. As for his mother, she would get up and leave the table, not daring to defend Henry du Pont against the vehement hatred of her eldest son.

There was only one time in the day when Lammot found it impossible to avoid contact with Henry, and that was at the end of the day shift on the Brandywine, when the boss followed an unfailing routine. He would call together his brother Alexis, who worked in the yards as general manager and superintendent, his nephews Irénée and Lammot, and Henry Belin, his accountant, and the five of them would walk around the mills on a tour of inspection. Henry was always in the lead, his top hat stuck on his flame of red hair, giving him equal height with the two rangy brothers and dwarfing the plump figure of the accountant. Belin would be in waistcoat and shirt-sleeves; the other three, in their caked and powdered working coveralls; but Henry wore cravat, white shirt, and dark suit, in addition to his polished top hat, though his pants were always carefully tucked into high black boots to prevent them gathering up the mud or dust of the yards.

Lammot noticed that the loud shouts and laughter that punctuated the working activity in the mills always ceased as Henry came by. He rapped out questions, listened to reports, inspected product, and made no comment. Then he led the quartet back to his office, where he went behind his beveled desk, pausing while he lit (if it was winter) three candles to illuminate the papers spread before him. Clearly, methodically, in a voice that brooked no interruption, he would pass judgment on what he had seen in the yards, instruct the other four about what should be done to improve matters, and tell them the decisions he had made about orders, policy, ways of working. After which, without waiting to ask their opinions, he would dismiss them.

Except that one evening in 1853 he looked across at Lammot and indicated he should stay behind. When the others had gone, Henry said:

"Get yourself cleaned up. You are coming up to the house for dinner tonight."

CHAPTER 3

The Brothers

Lammot du Pont was probably the most attractive figure the du Ponts ever produced. Not physically, perhaps, for though he had inherited his father's tall, bony frame and was broad shouldered and healthy looking, the pince-nez spectacles he had worn since boyhood and his shaven lip and under-the-chin beard gave him a professorial, even monastic, look, which aged him in appearance and made him seem, somehow, remote. He was, however, far from being so, and though there appear to be no photographs showing him smiling, his family's memories of him indicate that when he did so it transformed him, making him seem delightfully human.

Compared with those of his Uncle Henry, Lammot's eyes were a much grayer blue, without the cold, piercing quality of the older man's. He could be charming, but underlying the charm was a hard, driving self-confidence that made him impervious to all attempts to overawe him. He had no fear of anyone, least of all Henry, and he laughed at Irénée's concerned look when he reached home and told him of Henry's invitation.

In any case, he had a shrewd idea what was in the boss's mind. Ever since the Crimean War had begun, a few months earlier, the Du Pont yards had been doing a rousing business in black powder. Britain, France, and Turkey had gone to war with Russia. The men-o'-war of the first two nations had already passed through the Bosphorus into the Black Sea and were preparing to pump shells into czarist troops defending the Crimean shores of Russia before landing their own armies to annihilate them. Britain had its own supplies of powder, but French powder yards were running short, and in consequence the French government had sent an envoy from Washington to negotiate with Du Pont a contract for a large supply of black powder.

It so happened that the Frenchman's visit all but coincided with that of a representative of the czarist government, which was even more desperately in need of the powder it sought from Du Pont. The Russians had offered big money for a large consignment, and Henry had no compunction about selling to both sides (nor had any of the du Ponts, for that matter, so long as their own country was not involved). But there was one snag. The Frenchman had insisted that in return for the high price *he* was offering, Du Pont must pledge itself not to sell to France's enemies. Upon hearing about this from Henry, the Russian envoy had immediately added fifty percent to the price he was offering, and that, to Henry, was too good a bargain to miss.

The only trouble was, he pointed out to Lammot at dinner that night, the French would be furious if they learned about it, and would probably take drastic steps. How could Du Pont go on selling to France and still sell to the Russians, who were, he quietly added, insisting that Du Pont deliver the explosives to them in the Crimea, COD?

Lammot, who knew Wilmington Port and its captains well, replied that there were certainly ships in the harbor capable of taking a quarter of a million pounds of black powder (which is what the Russians had ordered) in their holds, and it would undoubtedly be possible to find a master bold and skilled enough to dodge any French or British blockade that might try to prevent his getting the cargo out of the Delaware Bay and across the ocean. Always provided, he added, that they paid him enough to take the risk.

Ah, but, interjected Henry, could such a master be trusted to accept the two million dollars the Russians were willing to pay for the gunpowder, and bring it back safely to the Brandywine?

It was then that Lammot realized why Henry had summoned him to dinner. He wanted him to go with the ship, personally see the explosives delivered to the Russians in the Crimea—and then bring back the money. It put an altogether different complexion on the affair. He had a new appreciation of the risks involved and would have preferred to talk it over with his father and brother. But Henry had sworn him to secrecy, pointing out that there were plenty of spies around willing to tip off the British or the French for the price of an ale, and any leak could jeopardize the deal.

Lammot had another glass of Henry's excellent burgundy and accepted the mission. Henry had chosen his man shrewdly enough. Lammot was twenty-three years old, heart-free, eager for adventure, and ripe for taking risks.

Lammot spent the next few days in the taverns near Wilmington Port, talking to American merchant captains. Meanwhile, Henry announced he was giving the young man a chance to do some business for the company and was therefore sending him off on a sales mission to New York and Canada, and on this pretext Lammot said good-bye to his parents and his brothers. But instead of taking the train north, he left for a rendezvous on the Delaware. In the meantime the powder mills had been working overtime getting a huge new consignment of powder ready for shipment, and day and night overladen mule wagons trundled through the streets of Wilmington with seven thousand five hundred barrels of Du Pont's best black powder on its way down to the Delaware.

Inevitably, the taverns were soon buzzing with speculation: Who had ordered such a vast amount of powder, and why was it being loaded onto only one ship?

In fact, Lammot had taken the precaution of chartering two merchantmen: The ship being watched by spies and gossips on the Wilmington dock front was actually taking fake powder barrels aboard and was bound for Charleston, South Carolina. When she set sail, British warships, apprised of its departure and tipped off that her destination was the Crimea, lay off Hampton Roads, outside the three-mile limit, and gave chase when she passed them.

Meanwhile, further downstream, another merchantman, with Lammot and the genuine cargo aboard, set sail in a different direction.

Later on, Lammot told the story of the voyage to a business colleague, Theodore Grasselli, who wrote some notes about it which his son found after his death.

They voyaged across the Atlantic without incident [Lammot told Grasselli]. At Gibraltar they lay to until a heavy fog permitted them to slip past. They eluded capture by one means or another in the Mediterranean and Black seas and as they neared Sebastopol, blockaded by three lines of war vessels, they encountered the real test.*

One of the last things Lammot du Pont had done before leaving Wilmington was to pay a large bribe to a French sailor for a list of the signals used by British and French ships when asked to identify themselves. He had not had need of them when crossing the Atlantic or passing through the Mediterranean and the Bosphorus Strait into the Black Sea, but as they approached the Crimean shore and Sebastopol, the moment came. Lammot pulled out his wallet and handed the list to the bosun. As they came abreast the first line of British men-o'-war, flags suddenly flew from the leading ship's yardarm demanding the signal that would take them through the blockade. The sailors jumped to, and up went the requisite flags. Lammot nervously watched as the British guns turned in the direction of the American vessel. One shot in the hold, or even the spark from a near miss, and a quarter of a million pounds of Du Pont black powder would blow them all to perdition. Would the signal get them through? Back came the message from the British signal flags: *Pass.*

There was a brisk onshore wind blowing; the master crammed on all canvas and all steam and turned the bows toward the faint smudge of land on the far horizon, and the sailors cheered as they raced for the shore. But Lammot was watching the British ships. New flags were flying, and they were not meant for the Americans but for the second line of blockade ships. Obviously the British were having second thoughts. Lammot grabbed the list back and consulted it to interpret the flags. *Stop and search,* they said. The second line of war vessels was turning now and making toward them.

They were being overhauled. Mr du Pont ordered all steam on and he took charge of the navigation. Shell came dangerously close—had one gone into the hold the venture would have ended in a flash and a roar. Shot whizzed through the rigging.**

But the American ship had the momentum and, weaving to evade the British gunners, at last managed to pull away. There was no longer any question of making Sebastopol Harbor, however. Lammot simply instructed

* Quoted by T. S. Grasselli, in a letter to Lammot du Pont II, July 28, 1928.
** Grasselli to du Pont, July 28, 1928.

the captain to keep the ship on a straight course, until, with a sudden lurch and a grind, they ran aground—fortunately on a sandy shore.

Within an hour Russian sailors and soldiers were coming aboard and pouring into the hold to begin the unloading of the precious powder with which they hoped to withstand the forthcoming siege of Sebastopol.

Lammot was carried ashore and acclaimed a hero. That night he heard himself and the American people toasted at the great banquet the Russian commander gave for him and the ship's captain.

Next day he went to see the czar's agent in Sebastopol and told him he was anxious to return to his own country. Could he have the two million dollars the Russian government owed E. I. du Pont de Nemours for the cargo of black powder?

"But, my dear sir," said the czar's agent, with some surprise, "it has already been paid. The money was handed over in Washington the moment your ship sailed out of Delaware Bay. Did not Mr. Henry du Pont tell you? That was the arrangement, and it was written into the contract."

By the time he returned to the United States, Lammot found there had been many changes back home at Nemours. His father was frail, ill, and afraid —so full of fears that each time there was a crash or a bang from the direction of the powder mills, he cringed and quavered. He was still only in his late fifties, but he looked like a pathetic old man and seemed obsessed with a black memory of the great explosions in the yard and "the blood, the blood, the blood. . . ." Lammot's mother, Meta, had turned into a virulent shrew who had less time than ever for her pathetic wreck of a husband and would obviously have been glad to see him go.

The house seemed empty and sad. His elder brother, Irénée, was frequently away from the Brandywine these days, drumming up contracts in Washington or visiting the powder warehouses in Richmond, Charleston, and New Orleans where Du Pont kept stocks for its southern customers.

As for his younger brothers, Fred and Bidermann, they had only been awaiting Lammot's return to tell him they were leaving home. Henry had made it plain that he had no place for them on the Brandywine and was not willing to keep them in idleness. Lammot, who was paid only a dollar a week more than the lower-salaried powder men, was unable to help them, and Alfred and Meta themselves were dependent on Henry's goodwill for the upkeep of their house, and general expenses. The boys had consulted their favorite member of the family, Aunt Sophie (the one who had married her cousin, Samuel du Pont of the United States Navy), and she had advised them to seek their fortunes elsewhere. She had secured them introductions to some distant relatives in Kentucky, and that was where they were going; they had simply waited for Lammot's return to say good-bye.

Alfred obliged Meta by not lingering too long. He died in his bed in 1856, still babbling about explosions, never having been sufficiently in possession of his faculties for Lammot to tell his father that, by using one of his old formulas, he had discovered a new method of using impure saltpeter in the making of black powder. The rougher quality would only do for second-grade powder, suitable for blasting in mines and excavations, and would not take the place of the saltpeter needed for gunpowder, but it would just about halve the cost of production for much of the day-to-day product.*

Alfred was interred to the left of the graves of his grandfather and father in the Sand Hole Woods cemetery. As the mourners left the graveyard, the tocsin sounded the alarm for a fire in the yards. Without waiting to take off their funeral clothes, all the du Ponts (including Fred and Bidermann, who had come up from Kentucky for the funeral) raced in to fight the flames. Their main job was to clamber to the sloping roofs of the press rooms and graining houses and wet them down against the danger of flying sparks.

An explosion was averted, but Lammot plunged through one of the frail roofs into a vat of mixing powder and scrambled out in the darkness, caked from head to foot with a coating of gunpowder, which would have turned him into a torch had a spark touched him. Alexis, working with the other fire fighters, emerged with his hands badly burned from helping to beat out the flames. As Aunt Sophie, who ran the dressing station, remarked later, if there *had* been an explosion, it "might very conceivably have wiped out the whole clan."

A year later, for the first time in the family's history, a du Pont died in an explosion. Alexis du Pont, younger brother of Boss Henry and second member of the ineffective triumvirate, worked as general manager and superintendent of the mills. The men liked him for the way he mucked in with them, and relished his macabre sense of humor.** Even behind his back

---

* Lammot du Pont was granted a patent for the new process in Washington in May 1857.

** In one mill accident a young apprentice swallowed a quantity of powder, and his irate mother arrived to ask Alexis what she should do. "Ma'am," he is said to have replied, "I suggest that you give him two rifle balls to swallow and make sure you don't point him at any other human being for a week."

they called him Mr. Alec, whereas Henry was known as The Ginger Bastard or names less complimentary.

On Saturday, August 22, 1857, Alexis came down to see how the repairs he had ordered for a graining mill in Hagley Yard (as the main yard was called) were proceeding. Looking into the mill, he noticed that a large mixing vat, heavily coated with old powder, had been left inside. If struck with a repairman's hammer or chisel, it could easily explode. He called seven men off the repair job and told them to help him get the vat out of the mill and into the open. It was too heavy a job for them, and as they strained, grunted, and staggered with it to the door of the mill one corner caught the stone wall and struck a spark, which ignited the cake of powder. They dropped the vat with a clang and struggled to beat out the flames; but on the way out they had left a trail of old powder behind them which suddenly ignited; the fire snaked its way across the floor and caught a tub of waste. There was a burst of flame, then a sudden explosion.

Three men were killed at once. A fourth, hurled across the yard, staggered to his feet and hurried blindly to his home across the creek, where he died at his wife's feet. Alexis was thrown thirty yards and got up to find that his clothes were ablaze. He raced across to the Brandywine and plunged into the stream, dousing the flames; but when he struggled upright in the racing water, he saw that a burning spar from the graining mill had been flung across the yard and landed on the roof of the press room. The press room was full of new powder.

He roared to the workmen to run for their lives, and then, scrambling out of the water, he rushed to the press room and climbed up to the roof. He was reaching for the flaming spar when the whole building exploded, but he did not die at once. The explosion report enumerated his injuries as "a compound fracture of the thigh, a wrenched back, a broken leg badly gashed about the calf, two broken ribs, both of which had punctured the lungs, and overall burns blackening the whole of his body." His eldest son, Eugene, home from college for the holidays, found his father in the wreckage of the yard, still conscious despite his appalling injuries; Alexis calmly instructed the lad to take off his suspenders and administer a tourniquet to his badly bleeding leg. Then the workmen arrived to carry him into the house.

For the next twenty-four hours he was conscious and in agony. But he managed to indicate that all the veterans of the powder mills, with whom he had worked side by side over the years, should be brought to the house so that he could see them for the last time. They filed in to say good-bye to him. Then he went into a coma and died two hours later.

Unlike his brothers, Alexis left instructions that there should be a religious ceremony before his interment, and a service was held in Christ's Church, which overlooked the Brandywine and the family graveyard. Then he was buried beside Alfred. He was forty-one years old.

Now only Henry and his nephew, Irénée, were left of the triumvirate. A year later Henry suggested that a third partner, Irénée's brother Lammot, should be added. But by the agreement that the three signed, Henry retained twenty shares, and Irénée and Lammot, three each.

In 1858 Irénée announced to his relatives on the Brandywine that he was going to marry Charlotte Henderson of Hanover, Virginia, and was piqued when no one seemed particularly pleased at his decision. Charlotte had not exactly made a good impression on the du Ponts when Irénée had first brought her to Delaware to visit his family, who thought she put on airs and was something of a minx. Used to the spacious life on a prosperous southern plantation and the busy social round in Washington, she seemed both surprised and disappointed at the meanness of the du Pont houses and their appointments, and depressed by their closeness to the noise, fumes, and dangers of the powder mills, not to mention the misty dampness of the Brandywine Valley. Nor did she approve of the clannishness of the du Ponts and the narrowness of their lives. There were exciting social events taking place in Philadelphia and even in Wilmington itself, some of whose social leaders she would often meet in the capital. Why were the du Ponts not a part of these enjoyable affairs? Could it be, she seemed to hint, that they were not good enough to be invited?

In any case, tall, slim Charlotte was far too pretty for the younger (and dumpier) du Pont women to have to look at; and she was much too pleased with her aristocratic southern background to satisfy their elders, some of whom she made to feel distinctly bourgeois. She had a feverish kind of flirtatious gaiety, which Lammot and Henry's son Henry Algernon, newly gazetted and down from West Point, found seductive, until they discovered that Charlotte could suddenly change her mood. First petulant, then accusing, and finally almost viperish, she would round on them, a burst of high color flooding her cheeks and a bright flashing in her dark eyes, and accuse them of "going too far" and "wanting to make a fool of dear Irénée."

She even managed to offend Irénée's beloved Aunt Sophie by talking lightly of a war between the states and remarking that if one came, those naval units loyal to the South would "blow the Yankee Navy out of the water." Since Sophie's husband was a Yankee navy captain, these were hardly well chosen words.

As for Meta du Pont, Irénée's mother made it plain from the start that she loathed the sight of her eldest son's southern belle, and told him crisply that if he insisted on marrying her and bringing her back to live at Nemours, he could certainly do so, but she would immediately move out. Irénée was not particularly cast down by Meta's reaction, but he was relieved when she finally consented to attend the wedding in Washington that October. Aunt Sophie, however, flatly refused to go. She sent the couple her best wishes and said she would do all she could for Charlotte once she came to live on the Brandywine, but go to the wedding she would not.

By the time Irénée brought his bride back to the Brandywine there was a slump in the powder business, and great discussions were going on about retrenchment. Irénée, his confidence buoyed up by his marriage, egged on to assert himself by his bride, decided to flex his muscles as one of the partners of Du Pont and recommended that the mills on the Brandywine be completely closed down, until conditions improved. It would have meant putting a work force of over two hundred out of their jobs, with no severance pay and no money while they found new employment, a prospect that Irénée did not seem to find of any concern. Nor did Henry, in fact. But he had two reasons for opposing Irénée's recommendation. In the first place, he was not going to accept any such drastic suggestion from his nephew, partner or not, for it would undermine his authority as boss of the enterprise. In the second place, he was anxious that the powder men on the Brandywine stay in place and not go wandering forth in search of new jobs because he was convinced that, in not too short a time, the mills would have need of them as never before. He believed that civil war was coming, and no matter which side Du Pont and Delaware found themselves on, there would be a booming market for gunpowder. Much as it hurt him to have to go on paying wages to his men when the orders were not there, he knew the investment would pay off once the war began. Other powder yards had already let their men go and would be desperate for powder men once the conflict started.

Unexpectedly, because she certainly did not like him, Henry found a vociferous ally in Aunt Sophie. She did extensive social work on Brandywine Creek and knew what unemployment would mean to the wives and children of the powder men. Therefore, quite aside from the possibility of civil war, she was very much for keeping on the work force and riding out the depression until the orders started coming in again. She rallied round to persuade her sisters to support her and sharply informed Irénée that when he did come back with his bride to the Brandywine, he would find the mills in operation as usual.

But where would the du Ponts and the Du Pont company stand if and when civil war came? Who were they for, North or South?

CHAPTER 4

---◆---

The War Between the du Ponts
(and the States)

T H E du Pont family was of two minds about the quarrel between the states, and so was Delaware. The downstate counties of Sussex and Kent, in what even then Wilmingtonians snidely referred to as Slower Delaware, were pretty solidly behind their southern neighbors on the Delmarva Peninsula, Maryland and Virginia, and were against emancipation. Even small tenant farmers seemed to be of a mind with the proprietors of the great plantations when it came to their attitude toward the Negroes. On the other hand, the people of northern Delaware, particularly in Wilmington and its industrial environs, felt close to *their* neighbor, Pennsylvania, which, for economic as well as moral reasons, was strongly against the policies of the South. So, though Delaware was a state below the Mason-Dixon line, that vaunted frontier separating two ways of life, not all Delawareans felt "Southern," and volunteers running the freedom trains of slaves escaping from Dixie, trying to get to the North and liberation, breathed a sigh of relief once they reached New Castle County, a way station in Delaware on the road to the Quaker receiving depot at Kennett Square, over the Pennsylvania line.

The du Ponts were likewise divided in their sentiments (and practical attitudes) and during the presidential election of 1860 there were often heated arguments between rival factions of the family. Irénée, of course, was strongly influenced by his southern wife, Charlotte, and he voted for the candidate of the Southern Democrats, John C. Breckenridge. Whereupon his mother, Meta du Pont, who would probably have been for the South if her daughter-in-law had not been southern, publicly espoused the cause of the abolitionists. Another du Pont who supported the Southern Democrat candidate was Cousin Charles, normally a liberal-minded and sympathetic man who had fought hard for the rights of the despised Irish immigrant Roman Catholics in Delaware; but he was now married and passionately fond of his new young wife, the daughter of a big Dover plantation owner with a large force of slaves. Besotted as he was, he found it impossible to resist her pro-Southern blandishments. This put him at odds with his brother, Captain Samuel Francis du Pont, and Samuel's wife, Sophie, both of whom were wholehearted backers of the new Republican party and its candidate, Abraham Lincoln. The brothers had been very close, but so great was the tension created by their opposing views that they did not speak for some time until Charles mollified his brother and sister-in-law by letting them know that although he was *for* the South he was *against* secession.

Sophie's sister, Evalina du Pont Bidermann (Antoine's wife), was also a strong supporter of Abraham Lincoln and was apt to give a tongue-lashing to those who were not. A meddlesome ally of Meta in her antagonism to Irénée's wife, Charlotte, she never missed a chance to make mischief between this beautiful newcomer and the rest of the family.

"It is Lina who makes me feel like an intruder," Charlotte said.

Lammot du Pont was torn. His two younger brothers, Fred and Bidermann, were in the South, and their letters made it obvious that they accepted without question the Southern point of view. Du Pont had warehouses stocked with gunpowder in many of the big southern cities, and the company could not afford to lose them. Moreover, just about this time Lammot had begun to lose his heart to the daughter of Du Pont's chief cashier and accountant, Henry Belin, for whom he had great admiration and respect. Henry Belin was strongly pro-South and prosecession, and just as ardently so was his daughter, Mary. Lammot's heart told him to vote for the South, but his head made him hesitate. It is probable that when the election came he did not vote at all.

But, of course, the key to the whole du Pont dilemma lay with the head of the family, Henry. Where did he stand?

To everyone's surprise, Henry was for compromise. After some hesitation, he told the family that he was voting neither for the lance bearer of the South, John Breckenridge, nor for the torchbearer of the North, Abraham Lincoln. Instead, he would support the candidate of the Constitutional Union party, John Bell, who favored reconciliation with the South, but not the breakup of the Union.*

It was a shrewd decision. He rightly surmised that Delaware as a whole would vote with the South for Breckenridge, but that the majority vote in the nation would be with the North for Lincoln. By publicly choosing the compromise candidate, he could be faulted neither by the state nor by the nation. He would show himself to be a man of reason and goodwill, voting for compromise to avert a catastrophe, and no one could accuse him of hoping to bring profit to Du Pont by supporting the counselors of war.

He advised the workers in the Brandywine to follow his example and vote for John Bell, but few of them followed that advice. The candidate of the Southern Democrats, John Breckenridge, won an easy majority in Delaware, thanks to the loaded votes of the big landowners in Sussex and Kent counties, but in Brandywine and the Christiana Hundred, where most of the Du Pont workers lived, Lincoln gained 617 votes against 664 for the other three candidates put together. And, of course, though he did not win the South, he won the presidency.

Henry was not displeased. War was now certain, he was sure, for stories were already circulating that South Carolina was gambling on secession—and the North would never stand for that. Once the die was cast, Du Pont could not help but win. And without having risked a stake.

For Charlotte du Pont the months that followed the election of Abraham Lincoln were miserable in the extreme, and nothing her adoring husband did for her could alleviate her depression. Irénée was a passionate, devoted, and attentive lover, and he ringingly declared that he would always stand as a barrier between her and the hostility of some members of the family.

* There was one other candidate, Stephen Douglas, representing the Northern Democrats.

He was furious when he heard that Lina had been gossiping about her. He urged his mother to show Charlotte some affection and warned that she risked losing a son by being so cold toward his wife; so, for a time, Meta made a show of being fond of her daughter-in-law.

Aunt Sophie, who was a semi-invalid, proved to be a friend in need. She spent much of her time entertaining Charlotte while Irénée was working in the yards, and even became fond of her, despite the sulky look that would cloud Charlotte's pretty face when she was bored, and her tendency to have tantrums when crossed in an argument. "She is a butterfly with a sting" is the way Sophie once described the girl. Of course, her sentiments about the South were quite impossible, and after a few sharp passages it was mutually agreed that the subject should not be brought up between them.

Most of the du Ponts had by this time accepted a war between the states as all but inevitable, and even Charles du Pont and his young wife now agreed that if it came, Du Pont and Delaware must side with the North. Irénée was aware that Charlotte would never be won over, but he pleaded with her to do her best to keep silent when the rest of the family spoke out against the South. Still she would stamp her tiny foot and, eyes flashing, tell him she would feel disloyal if she did so.

In the beginning the sheer passion of their relationship seems to have kept them going, and when, in 1860, she told Irénée she was pregnant, the bitterness left behind by their quarrels was sweetened by their mutual hope for a son, and for a few weeks there was calm. But the pregnancy proved false, and Charlotte's depression was so profound that Irénée thought she would be better away from the Brandywine. He was probably glad of the respite himself, for he was discovering that when Charlotte quarreled she could become violent; she would tear down curtains, fling vases, scratch and kick and bite, after which she would sink into a kind of stupor from which he could not rouse her.

The political situation seemed too tense for her to go to her parents' plantation in Hanover for more than a few days, so it was arranged that after her visit there she would stay with her sister and cousin in Alexandria, Virginia.

The visit seemed to revive her at first, and she sent back a flood of letters to all her du Pont aunts and in-laws describing her delight at being back in the southern social swim. But unfortunately, many of the people she was meeting were convinced as she was that secession was the only way out for the South, and in one of her letters to Evalina du Pont Bidermann she carelessly (or possibly deliberately) said so. Lina wasted no time in running with the letter to Meta, who, knowing it would hurt her, immediately raced across to tell Sophie.

Sophie was shocked. Secession would mean civil war, and war would mean that her husband, Samuel, would be involved and his life at risk. She could not resist writing to Charlotte at once to rebuke her. On March 6, 1861, at a moment when the situation between North and South was particularly tense, Charlotte wrote back from Alexandria:

> *Dear Aunt Sophie:*
>
> I am really very sorry to read how grieved the idea of me being a secessionist makes you, and am truly obliged to you for your kindness in telling me when you thought me in fault. I was not aware of having impressed my secessionist sentiments in my letter to Lina. The only thing I remember saying was, that we sang "Dixie" a great deal in Hanover and that there was some talk of making it our National Hymn of the Southern Confederacy. I was simply stating what the newspapers said.
>
> I am not a secessionist but neither am I a *submissionist.* I do not go for secession whether we have our rights or not but I do think that if we can have our rights, let us stay in the Union, but if we do not get them, then it is better to go out. I know it will be to our disadvantage to go out, but honorable war is better than dishonorable submission.
>
> If you hied South, you would think the same, for this is the prevailing sentiment with the exception of those who feel even more strongly about it. . . .

She was evidently going through one of her depressive states, for she added:

> Just now I have one of those little trials to bear. You know I have always disliked excessively to be alone, and now Fanny, and my cousin so soon going to leave me, I will be entirely alone . . . this is very hard for me to bear, as I am very dependent upon company. It is comforting however to know that it is good for me and sent for my good.

As the tensions increased in Washington and the South, Irénée wrote her to leave at once for New York, where he was going on a mission for the company. So it was to New York that Aunt Sophie, alarmed about Charlotte's state of mind, wrote to convey words of understanding and comfort. She enclosed a religious book for her to read, which would "help her to take heart." Charlotte wrote back that she was not going to read it:

> Do not think me ungrateful, it would be sheer hypocrisy for me to read the words of Jesus when I have not entered a church or opened a Bible for 10 months and never intend to again. A few years ago I little thought it should come to this. Why I was hardened it is not for me to know it is sufficient for me to know that it is so. I suppose I am justly cursed but then it is hard to have nothing to care for and nothing to look forward to however I am pretty well accustomed to it. Forgive me if I speak so plainly. . . . Your affectionate Niece.

On April 12, 1861 (three weeks after she wrote that letter), Fort Sumter was attacked and was forced to surrender five days later to the rebel forces. Even the doubters in the North and the waverers along the Mason-Dixon Line now lined up behind President Lincoln and urged him to retaliate. Fort Sumter gave him what he had been waiting for—the right to claim that the war was not of his choosing but had been forced upon him by the South.

A month after the Civil War began, Charlotte du Pont revealed to her husband that she was pregnant, and genuinely so this time. Irénée's expressions of happiness were cut short by the sight of Charlotte's tearful, unhappy face. By now Virginia, her home state, was in the war on the enemy side, and so was her family. How could she be joyful at the coming of a child whose father was manufacturing the means by which her own father and her brothers might soon be killed?

Even Henry Belin, who had never concealed his passionate support for the Southern cause, changed his mind after the attack on Fort Sumter. He declared himself outraged at the thought of South Carolina guns firing on the Stars and Stripes, and believed the rebels should be taught a lesson. In Kent and Sussex counties of lower Delaware sentiment was still overwhelmingly pro-South, but though scores of young men crossed the state line into Maryland and Virginia to join the Confederate forces, the votes were not there when some of the big slaveowners tried to get the representatives in Dover to put Delaware officially behind the Confederacy.

Henry du Pont, back on the Brandywine, lined up family and workers beneath the Stars and Stripes and led them in a ceremony of swearing allegiance to the flag and the Union cause. The only du Ponts not present were Aunt Sophie and Charlotte. No one worried about Sophie's absence. She was an invalid, and in any case there could be no doubt where her heart lay. But Charlotte was different, and Irénée turned scarlet with mortification when his mother scoffed at the excuse he gave for his wife's absence. "Women's troubles," he had said, and Meta had turned to her sister-in-law Lina and loudly remarked: "Rebel fever, more likely."

Henry went off to Washington to assure President Lincoln that Du Pont had willingly abandoned its explosives warehouses in Richmond, Charleston, and New Orleans and had informed the Confederacy that its mills would supply no more gunpowder to them for the duration of the conflict. But he pointed out that this could well put the Brandywine mills at risk from rebel attacks and attempts at sabotage by pro-Southern hotheads in Delaware. The president assured him that sufficient troops would be drafted at once to Wilmington to ensure his protection, and furthermore, the Union, grateful as it was for his self-sacrifice in spurning the South, would see that his mills were never short of orders for powder to fire the shells and bullets of Northern guns.

Lincoln kept his promise. In the next three years Du Pont yards worked twenty-four hours of the day and sold nearly four million dollars' worth of powder to the Union forces. Fifty-three of the company's powder men (the work force had been exempted from military service on the president's orders) lost their lives in explosions in the mills, but production never stopped—not for explosions or funerals or even when General Lee sent a Confederate force of three thousand men from Maryland with orders to take the Du Pont mills and blow them to bits. Lee's move was countered by the dispatch of twenty-five hundred Union troops from Pennsylvania, who camped near the Brandywine and, though they never had to fight the Confederate forces, did wreak some havoc among Brandywine wives and daughters. In fact, so many stories reached Henry of soldierly rape and molestation—as well as more amorous encounters—that he issued an order to the du Pont womenfolk forbidding them to walk abroad without a male escort until the hostilities ended.

The du Pont men emerged from the Civil War with their quota of heroes. Sophie's husband, now Admiral Samuel Francis du Pont, was the toast of the nation when, commanding the Union fleet blockading Charleston, he won a great battle with the rebels. Henry's son, Colonel Henry Algernon du Pont, won a brevet commission as lieutenant colonel for gallantry at the Battle of Cedar Creek, and Henry himself was created a major general by the governor of Delaware and given command of the state militia. Mightily proud of his title, he called himself General du Pont for the rest of his life, but, in truth, his most notable achievement was keeping the mills rolling through the stresses and strains of war.

It can hardly be said, however, that Henry got much help in his endeavors from his nephew and so-called partner Irénée, who was in no fit condition to face up to the crisis. Between worries over his wife's mental and physical condition and his feud with his termagant mother, Irénée was driving himself into illness and despair.

On the other hand, Lammot was the real hero of Du Pont's share of the victory, and he made his contribution on two widely different fronts: as a chemist and as an adventurer. In the months before war began, he had worked in Wilmingon, Philadelphia, and Washington with United States Army explosives expert Captain Thomas J. Rodman in the development of a new kind of gunpowder. Du Pont's famous black powder, even the most superior brand, was becoming outmoded. As cannons grew bigger and the cannonballs and other missiles they fired increased in size, it was discovered that black powder no longer had the propulsive power to hurl them great distances, or even, sometimes, to hurl them at all. Quite often the black powder's blasting effect simply blew the barrel to bits instead of thrusting the cannonball on its way to the target. Captain Rodman had come up with the idea of making gunpowder not as fine as dust or as rough as sand, but in much bigger grains, ranging in size from hailstones to tennis balls, which would burn at a slower rate of combustion and thus build up greater propulsive power.

It was Lammot who had taken Rodman's idea, made it a practical proposition, and then set out to persuade Henry to adapt a number of the Brandywine mills for its production. Henry was always opposed to new products and new ideas, stubbornly insisting on traditional routines and methods, and Lammot had a stormy time selling him on the new powder. Rodman called it Mammoth Powder, and it was with this new invention, manufactured exclusively by Du Pont, that the great ironclad of the Union Navy, the *Monitor,* had loaded her guns when she sailed out to meet the Confederate ironclad *Merrimack* in one of the decisive naval battles of the Civil War. Thanks to Mammoth Powder, the *Monitor* blew the *Merrimack* out of the water, and when news of the victory reached Henry du Pont, he summoned his workmen to a meeting in the Hagley Yard and told the cheering crowd of powder men that he would be paying them a bonus. Subsequently he took credit for having brought the miracle explosive to Du Pont. No doubt Lammot du Pont smiled cynically.

But it was not only in the laboratories that Lammot had distinguished himself during the Civil War.

In the summer of 1861, not long after the war had begun, Lammot received a summons to the White House and, on being shown in to the president, quickly discovered that the story of his exploit in running the British blockade to the Crimea had preceded him. Lincoln asked him if he would go on a similar mission on behalf of the Union government. He did not need to tell Lammot that if the war lasted a long time—and it was now beginning to appear that it would—the Union's supplies of refined saltpeter, without which good gunpowder could not be made, would soon be in short supply. The only source was Britain, which had a monopoly on the saltpeter mined in British India, and although it might have seemed simple just to put in a large order with the London merchants, there was a snag. The British were known to be sympathetic toward the Confederate cause, and there were rumors that they were willing to help the rebels in any way they could—for instance, by deliberately starving the Union of saltpeter, and so of gunpowder. Therefore, Lammot should sail at once for England, telling no one where he was going or the nature of his mission, and proceed to buy up every pound and every ounce of saltpeter he could cram into a ship, and bring it back at once.

Despite strenuous popular opposition in England, he brought back to America in March 1862 two thousand tons of the finest Indian saltpeter. He was rewarded by the personal thanks of the president, and a large new order from the government. The saltpeter he delivered lasted for nearly a year and enabled the Unionists to outgun the Confederacy on land and sea. It also moved Du Pont into the position of first powder maker to the nation, making the du Ponts rich in the process.

Lammot arrived back on the Brandywine just about the time his sister-in-law Charlotte du Pont was being delivered of her second child—and second daughter. Irénée had moved himself and his family into a new house, Swamp Hall, and allowed his mother to return to her old home, Nemours. But this was no gesture of reconciliation, and relations between Meta and her son had by no means improved. In fact, there had been a blazing row between them when Meta was revealed as the author of a Brandywine rumor that her daughter-in-law was working as a spy for the Confederacy and sheltering would-be saboteurs who had been seen skulking around the

Hagley Yard. Usually it was Evalina du Pont Bidermann who started this kind of gossip, but Evalina had died in 1863 after a short but painful illness, leaving the business of mischief-making in Meta's hands. When Irénée confronted his mother with this latest story and challenged her to deny that she had started it, she defiantly admitted the charge, and her son, his eyes blazing, raised a thin arm and would have struck her had not his cousin Charles swiftly intervened.

Charlotte herself was in no condition to refute any of the malicious gossip now circulating about her. Childbirth had weakened her in mind and body. And Irénée, too, was in failing health. In fact, he had tuberculosis, which would become a family scourge, and seemed to be constantly in a state of high feverish excitement. Charlotte could be even more frenetic on occasion. She gave way to fits of ungovernable rage and fury, in her unhappy frustration hitting out at everything in sight, slicing with her long nails at those near to her. Then she would sit in a dull stupor and dolefully hum a dirge for her beloved South, bemoaning the fate of her family and friends.

Charlotte and Irénée were two very sick people. But illness has never quenched the sexual appetite, and desperate unhappiness can often stimulate it. At Swamp Hall the nightly congress went on, and regularly, every two years, Charlotte gave birth to a new baby, with miscarriages in between. By 1868 she was the mother of five children, three of them boys. She was also very close to being certifiably insane.

CHAPTER 5

New Blood

EVERYONE on the Brandywine who survived the Civil War profited from it materially. The power men got a raise in wages of seventy-five percent, in addition, of course, to their exemption from the draft. Widows of the men killed on the job had their pensions increased by fifty percent. At the same time, General Henry upped the price of the gunpowder he sold to the government to thirty-three cents a pound (an increase of over one hundred percent), but some of his competitors were charging thirty-six cents, and in the beleaguered South the Confederate government was paying as much as three dollars a pound, when they could find the gunpowder to buy.

Between 1861 and 1865, when peace came at last, Du Pont made a profit of one million dollars. In 1864 General Henry reported his income for the year as one hundred and ten thousand dollars, more than twice as much as the next highest earner in Delaware. Irénée received twelve thousand five hundred dollars and Lammot ten thousand dollars, while Henry's two surviving sisters, Eleuthera and Sophie, got eight thousand dollars apiece, and his two surviving sisters-in-law, Meta and Joanna (widows of Alfred and Alexis), received seventy-five hundred dollars. There were three deaths in the family, and three more graves dug in the cemetery at Sand Hole Woods, in the four years the war lasted. Henry's oldest sister, Victorine, celibate and devoted to religion ever since the tragic end to her six-week honeymoon, died in her sleep in 1861. The death of Evalina du Pont Bidermann may have given Charlotte some respite from malicious gossip, but it had dealt a heavy blow to her husband, Antoine. With her passing he lost his zest for America and sailed back to France in 1863, a lonely old man of seventy-five. He died in Paris two years later.

Aunt Sophie's husband and cousin, Admiral Samuel Francis du Pont, also died, some said of a broken heart. He had heard himself acclaimed a hero after his great victory against the Confederate Navy off Charleston in the first phase of the war and seen himself attacked as a coward for his conduct in a subsequent sea battle. The shame never left him, and he died in 1865, still proclaiming his innocence and hoping against hope that his reputation would be restored. Sophie vowed to spend the rest of her life fighting to secure public restitution for her beloved husband's reputation. Eventually she succeeded (Du Pont Circle in Washington, D.C., was named after him as a gesture of mollification) but by that time no one but the du Ponts cared.

The end of the war left General Henry in an expansive mood, eager to branch out both personally and professionally. With a magniloquent stroke of his quill pen, he wrote "cancelled" across all the the contracts for powder that Du Pont had with the United States government and offered to buy back any surplus that was no longer required for war (at a discount, of course).*

He had grandiose ideas for the broadening of Du Pont's markets and the extension of its influence and power and was drawing up big plans for the next phase of the company's activities. But he would need the drive and ability of his nephew Lammot to help him, and for the moment the younger man's attention was absorbed in domestic matters. In any case, he had had an exhausting war and needed a period of relaxation. The General was willing to wait. In the interim he busied himself with the pleasurable task of demonstrating to the world that he had now become a noteworthy and successful man of substance, and that it was through him and his heir that the du Ponts would be remembered.

* Du Pont was still utilizing government surplus powder several years later.

He was inordinately proud of his elder son, Colonel Henry Algernon du Pont, and gave his reluctant agreement when the young colonel signified that, making the most of his distinguished war record, he would continue his military career. The General knew, however, that his son and heir would one day marry, leave the army, and come back to the Brandywine to take over his responsibilities at Du Pont. He would then need a house in keeping with his style and position, and Henry decided to provide him with one.

The General and his family were still living at Eleutherian Mills, which he had taken over on becoming president of the company. It was by no means grand enough for him, but the practical side of his character persuaded him that he should remain there because it was near enough to the powder yards for him to keep a close watch on activities there.* But that need not prevent him from adding to his acres (and stature) and becoming the biggest landlord in the district.

It so happened that there was a du Pont house available that would be eminently suited to his ambitious son and heir, and attached to it were great tracts of land that the General himself would be able to exploit. While his sister Evalina and her husband, Antoine Bidermann du Pont, were still alive they bought land along the Kennett Pike, near Wilmington and the Brandywine, and there built a house for themselves on the north slope of a valley. In Greek revival style, the brick and stucco building was a square structure with three stories, a flat roof, a porte-cochere in front, and a conservatory porch at the back. They called it Winterthur, after the Swiss town where Antoine's mother was born; and in later life, especially after Antoine's retirement from Du Pont's affairs, they devoted increasing amounts of attention to it, turning the rich lands of the estate into dairy farms and orchards, and the gardens surrounding the house into beds of flowering shrubs and exotic trees. The General bought it from Antoine and Evalina's only son, who had chosen to live in France.

General Henry now had 1,135 acres of land in northern Delaware, and he would soon purchase 800 acres more, making him the largest landowner in the state. He indulged his favorite hobby, experimental farming, all the while keeping a wary eye on the powder mills and waiting until Lammot was ready to go off on another mission, this time strictly for the good of Du Pont.

---

* If Henry was close enough to keep watch on the yards, the powder men were also close to him. He kept a pack of greyhounds, whippets, and lurchers in the kennels at Eleutherian Mills, and whenever they set up a chorus of excited baying, the men in the yards were warned that Henry would soon be coming down to inspect them, bringing the dogs with him—which gave them time to step up the rhythm of their activities.

By the time the Civil War ended, Lammot du Pont was thirty-four years old and still unmarried. At the funeral service for Admiral Samuel Francis du Pont he was reunited with his two brothers, Fred and Bidermann, who had spent the war on the other side, in Louisville, Kentucky, where things had gone well with them. Fred had brains and organizing ability, and he had built up thriving interests in paper mills and coal mines, with his brother Bidermann tagging along and sharing in his fortune. Bidermann had married a Kentucky girl named Ellen Coleman, and he brought her to the funeral with him, bossing her around and fussing about the way she handled their two-year-old son, Thomas Coleman du Pont, of whom he was bouncingly and jealously proud. The child seemed to prefer his uncle Fred, and Fred happily dangled the boy on his knee and made noises at him. But when Lammot asked him when he was going to have children of his own, Fred replied that he was planning to be a lifelong bachelor, adding, with a grin, that he preferred to spend modest amounts on "girls" rather than pay through the nose for a wife and family.

Lammot did not share Fred's fondness for other people's children, and by 1865 he had just about convinced himself that it was time he fathered some of his own, and furthermore, that he had found the young woman who could produce them for him. Over the years he had become increasingly fond of Mary Belin, the dark-eyed daughter of the Du Pont company's accountant. Increasingly drawn by her rather sultry beauty and the emotion that sometimes seemed to simmer behind her shy exterior, he realized by the time he returned from his mission to London in 1862 that he was in love with her. Although he must have guessed from her manner that she reciprocated his feelings, he had done nothing practical about it at the time for two reasons. First, he was aware that she was still recovering from a bout of tuberculosis. Having watched the ravages of that disease on his brother Irénée, and also dreading to have a sick or feeble wife like Charlotte, who should obviously never have had children, he preferred to wait and make sure that Mary's recovery was complete. Second, Mary Belin had Jewish blood. Her great-grandfather, Moses Homberg, had been a Philadelphia merchant. His eldest daughter (Mary's grandmother) had married a Frenchman and a practicing Christian, but to mollify her father she had retained her Jewish faith. Her daughter, however, though half-Jewish, had allowed herself to be married in a Protestant church when she plighted her troth to Henry Belin, then still a humble clerk in the Du Pont organization;

and Mary Belin never thought much about her Jewish antecedents. At least not until the du Ponts reminded her. To them she had one-quarter Jewish blood, and that made her a Jew. No du Pont had ever married a Jew, nor contemplated such a union.

Lammot du Pont was a cautious young man so far as his career at Du Pont was concerned, and he was not about to spoil it by creating a family crisis before it was necessary. So he bided his time until the moment arrived when Mary Belin showed evidence, from the robustness of her appearance and the sparkle in her eyes, that she had definitely thrown off her consumptiveness, and until he himself was in such a strong position at Du Pont that he need no longer care whether his relatives objected to Mary's background. In 1865 he asked Mary Belin for her hand and went to her father to secure his blessing.

Only then did he come home to Nemours and tell his mother of his decision. Predictably, Meta du Pont was outraged. After failing to move Lammot with dire warnings that he was ruining his chances by making a foolish marriage, she did what she had once done to Irénée in similar circumstances: She swore she would never stay in the same house as a woman of Mary Belin's antecedents; and this time, she added, she would *never* come back to Nemours. Lammot did not think his future wife would be the least bit unhappy with his mother's decision.

Meta du Pont did make one last attempt to prevent the marriage by pleading with her son to get General Henry's permission before taking the irrevocable step. But Lammot was unwilling to do that. Henry had recently been grumbling about the number of du Pont cousins who were marrying each other, for, unlike old Pierre Samuel, he believed the practice was dangerously thinning the family blood, and it was certainly producing its quota of miscarriages and freaks. But the General's opinion of Jews was well known in the family, and it was not enlightened. Later on, about Lammot's marriage, he remarked that it would have been "better to marry a cousin than marry a Jewess." Lammot was unwilling to risk a rebuff to himself and an insult to his wife-to-be by going cap in hand to the boss for his permission, though he did go across to Eleutherian Mills after the formal announcement had been made and ask for Henry's blessing, which was grudgingly given.

The rest of the family showed their distaste for the marriage and their contempt for Mary by ignoring her existence. In the normal course of du Pont life a new wife, soon after her installation on the Brandywine, would receive visits from the du Pont women one by one. In Mary's case, no one came to Nemours except her father, one or two friends from Philadelphia, and an occasional schoolfriend. There is no evidence, however, that Mary Belin du Pont was unduly cast down by the du Pont family's ostracism. In any case, she was totally wrapped up in her new husband and enraptured by the ever-new discoveries of a happy married life.

Lammot, on the other hand, was angered by the way in which his wife was being insulted, and soon made it plain that if it continued, he might well consider leaving the Brandywine and seeking his fortunes elsewhere, in a place where Mary's undoubted charms would be as much appreciated as his own talents. Word of his feelings reached General Henry, who must have been alarmed at the thought that his most valuable aide was threatening to leave, and decided to take appropriate action.

The du Ponts had a custom that began a year after they had landed in America. Their arrival had always been officially fixed by the family as New Year's Day, 1800, and ever since, on that day all the du Pont menfolk gathered together to visit, one by one, all the homes of the du Pont women on the Brandywine and in nearby Wilmington, handing over little gifts as tokens of their esteem and good wishes. On New Year's Day, 1866, Lammot du Pont faced the prospect that no one would be visiting Nemours, and though Mary, then pregnant with their first child, seemed—as she sat knitting in her rocking chair—to view their ostracism with equanimity, he was mortified, and his usually equable temperament seemed in danger of fraying.

His angry thoughts were interrupted by the sound of hooves, the crack of a whip, and the snort of a horse, and when Lammot looked through the window, there was General Henry drawing up in his buggy. A shiny Sunday top hat on his head, a carnation in his buttonhole, his red beard flecked with streaks of gray and flakes of snow, he came into the house with a bouquet in his hand, which he gravely presented to "the prettiest wife on the Brandywine." Mary blushed and rose to kiss the old man, mischief dancing in her brown eyes as she looked over his shoulder at her astonished husband.

Turning to Lammot, Henry told him to get his hat and coat. He would accompany the boss on his rounds of the du Pont houses for the rest of the day. Lammot protested. He was certainly not going to leave his wife alone. But Henry gestured out of the window and indicated, not without a foxy smile, that she was not likely to be alone very long. For another carriage had already drawn up at the gate, and Cousin Charles was descending, a box of candies in hand, to pay his respects to the newest du Pont wife.

Word had spread of General Henry's gesture, and the remaining male members of the clan—prodded by their alarmed and anxious wives and womenfolk—were making haste to follow suit. From now on, Mary would be accepted as one of the family.

The biggest competitor of the Du Pont powder company in the 1860s and 1870s was the eastern combine Laflin and Rand, and though Du Pont now regularly topped it in yearly sales, General Henry realized that it was too powerful a rival even for him to gobble up. But he had his eye on all the smaller companies, and in the next ten years he swallowed several of them in Pennsylvania and New York.

The rest of the du Pont family, even his nephew and partner Irénée, were now small fry in the Du Pont pool while the general kept a tight control on the shares and the profits for himself. But he still needed Lammot and therefore could not diminish the younger man's position in the company. Though Henry had no intention of allowing his nephew to take over when he departed—he had very different plans for his succession—he did allot him a good share in the profits and confide to him all the projects in which he was interested. He used Lammot as his front man to buy up competitors, and the young chemist now spent a good deal of time traveling the country looking for prospects, or making deals in the new Du Pont office at 70 Wall Street, in New York.

It was there, in 1872, that Henry called a meeting of Du Pont and nine of its nearest rivals. Four of them accepted, and two more sent letters saying they would endorse any agreement made by the majority. To their representatives he made a proposal that was to have important repercussions on the sale (and price) of gun and blasting powder in the United States. In the vigorous, thriving market for gunpowder now developing, why, he asked, should these companies waste so much time (and profits) on price wars? With so many new railroad, industrial, and mining projects burgeoning in all parts of the country, why not simply divide up sales and contracts among themselves?

These were the days before antitrust legislation, and the representatives were quick to agree with this proposal for the formation of what Lammot called the Gunpowder Trade Association. Price lists were drawn up, and minimum and maximum margins agreed upon. The country was divided into territories. Each company would have one territory where it had preference over the others in controlling sales; and in those common territories where it was agreed they should continue to compete, it was also agreed that the company that won a particular contract would compensate the others for having lost it.

Lammot was unanimously elected president of the new association (which the newspapers soon began to call the Powder Trust), and each participating company was apportioned votes, according to its size, for deciding future issues among them. Du Pont was given ten votes, as were Laflin and Rand, and Hazard. Oriental Powder Company got six votes, and the Austin, American, and Miami powder companies got four votes each. The three other big companies, which had failed to send a representative and had not replied to the invitation one way or the other, were, Lammot instructed his fellow members, to be subjected to concerted competitive pressure, which should soon indicate to them the nature of the new organization, and the fact that it had teeth.

In the next few months the Powder Trust demonstrated how hard it could bite. Masterminded by Lammot, measures were taken against the three large companies in New York and the Ohio Valley. The price of rifle powder was cut below cost, to $2.25, from $6.25, and blasting powder dropped to $0.80, from $2.75. The independents were soon crying for mercy. Two of them sold out, one to Du Pont and one to Laflin and Rand, and the third agreed to join the Powder Trust and accept its rules of conduct. The strategy of General Henry was now not only to buy up as many of the non-Trust rivals as he could but also to increase his influence in the Trust itself. One by one, the independents were crushed, and Du Pont moved in quickly to snap them up. First came the Sycamore Mills in Tennessee, then the Lake Superior Powder Company, the Hercules Torpedo and Powder Company, the Hecla Powder Company, and the Marcellus Powder Company. All were first driven to near bankruptcy by price-cutting (and sometimes by disastrous explosions, which, it was said, could well have been the result of sabotage) and then bought up.

At the same time, General Henry moved into the market and secretly bought up shares in the Hazard Company, giving him control of the company and also ten more votes in the Powder Trust. Hearing about this, Laflin and Rand went after Oriental and its six votes. Forewarned, Henry sent Lammot to propose an agreement to divide up Oriental and split its votes three apiece. Rather than face a costly stock-market fight, Laflin and Rand agreed. Now Du Pont had twenty-three votes; and Lammot soon added to this by traveling to Texas and buying up the Austin Powder Company, thus giving Du Pont another four votes, in all, twenty-seven of a total of forty-eight.

With the exception of California, where gold and silver miners had formed their own powder company during the Civil War and were doing big business in the West, the Powder Trust now controlled over ninety percent of the nation's business in gun and blasting powder. And Du Pont controlled the Powder Trust through its majority vote.

Henry seemed to be satisfied. At sixty-five he headed the biggest powder company in the United States, if not in the world. Millions of dollars in orders were coming into Du Pont mills, bringing with them huge profits. Customers had to buy at the Powder Trust's price, and Henry set that price for the Powder Trust, just as he took most of the profits for Du Pont.

But if Henry was sated, Lammot du Pont was not. He had escaped from the laboratories and tasted the stimulating challenges of power, and by now he had developed an appetite for it.

He also had a family to plan for. In 1866 Mary had given birth to her first child, a girl, and they christened her Isabella d'Andelot, after Mary's Jewish grandmother. Two years later Mary had given birth to a second child, also a girl, whom they called Louise d'Andelot. In 1870 Mary had borne Lammot his first son, and in great jubilation his father named him Pierre Samuel du Pont, after the founder of the clan. In the next thirteen years Mary Belin du Pont was to have eight more children, making eleven in all. But it was his first son, Pierre Samuel, upon whom Lammot rested his hopes and whose future prospects spurred his own ambitions.

But if Lammot and his family prospered, the situation of his older brother, Irénée, and his family grew steadily worse. Charlotte du Pont's condition had been deteriorating over the years, but she had continued to have babies until 1868. In that year she gave birth to her fifth and last child (and third son). Christened Louis Cazenove, he was so puny and frail that for a time the doctors feared he would not survive. Charlotte did not seem to care one way or the other. It was not so much that she neglected her children—she often had periods when she was passionately devoted to them—but sometimes she forgot their existence and would wander away on trips to New York or Virginia or Washington. During these periods Irénée would have to go down to the yards and ask a powder man to send up his daughter to act as nanny. He resented it when Charlotte would suddenly turn up again, unceremoniously throw out the nanny, and take over the nursery as if she had never been away. Invariably, the nanny would have hysterics, the children would cry, and Charlotte and Irénée would have a terrible quarrel.

Irénée tried his best to be sympathetic about his wife's mental condition, and du Pont family records indicate that he was a gentle and understanding man. But by the time his fifth child was born he was not exactly well balanced himself. The disease in his lungs was worsening, and he was coughing up blood. The acrid smell of the powder yards inevitably triggered a bout of coughing, and he stayed away more and more. He had long since ceased to communicate with his mother, whom he blamed for his wife's unhappy condition. Meta du Pont, for her part, had begun to regret her treatment of her daughter-in-law and had made several overtures for a reconciliation. In 1868 she timidly approached Charlotte with an offer to help with the children, but the result was disastrous. Charlotte drove her away from Swamp Hall, ordering her never to come near her again. The incident plunged Charlotte first into a paroxysm of rage and then into one of her fits of profound depression. She had once described how she felt on these occasions in a letter to Aunt Sophie:

> I suppose I was born in darkness so thick that no lights could penetrate—so I have groped and stumbled in a slough of despond from which there is no extrication. May others be more fortunate.

After her mother-in-law's abortive approach, Charlotte, languishing in her private misery, would not eat, wash, or move, and in despair, Irénée called in the doctors. It was decided that she be taken off to an asylum in Philadelphia until the heavy load on her mind lightened.

All this was bad enough for the unfortunate parents, but it must have been even worse for their children, who watched and shared in these miseries. By 1870, when things really began to deteriorate, the five children were ten, eight, six, four, and two years old, and the only bright moments in their unhappy lives seemed to occur either when their Uncle Lammot came to play with them, or when their Uncle Fred came up from Louisville, Kentucky, and stayed with them at Swamp Hall. Fred had quietly told the du Pont clan that if anything happened to Irénée and Charlotte, he would be responsible for the children. Uncle Fred was fun, and they adored him. He encouraged the two girls, Anna and Marguerite, to dress up and took special care to stimulate the interest of the eldest boy, Alfred Irénée, a morose and silent child.

Charlotte, released from the asylum, spent the summer of 1870 staying in hotels at Newport, Rhode Island, and Wellesley, Massachusetts, that specialized in the care of convalescents. But though mentally improved, she was restive and bored. "This is a lovely place," she wrote from Newport, "but there is no danger of anyone's suffering from undue excitement." She wanted to come home, but Irénée, increasingly upset by the devils Charlotte brought back with her to Swamp Hall, resisted it. By September she was complaining bitterly that though she had offered to return for the winter—her plan was to put the two girls in day school and teach the younger ones herself—her husband had ignored her offer. Now she heard through other members of the family that he had hired a governess for the children. "What think you of this treatment towards a wife and mother?" she wrote in a letter to Colonel Henry A. du Pont:

> I am raising children, laboured for them, and taught them until now, and here just before I am returning to them after my suffering illness is a governess engaged without any consultation with me. Had this been done whilst I was in the Asylum there might be some excuse for it, but here am I with a mind in full force, set aside in this manner. I am sure you can and will testify [Henry A. had been up to see her on behalf of the family] that I have been entirely myself this summer and come what may I know you will stand by me. . . . It is a thing I will not stand. Please excuse this scrawl. I am so agitated that I can scarcely command my pen. Here are my feelings again outraged in the most heartless manner, and should I again be made ill I take you to witness that I was entirely well before I received this unnecessary and unfeeling shock. . . .*

But two weeks later she was back at Swamp Hall and in a much more pliable mood. Introduced to the new governess, an Alsatian woman called Emma (there seems to be no record of her last name), Charlotte approved of her manner and qualifications and left shortly afterward on another long "convalescent" trip, this time to Baltimore and then across the Atlantic to England and France. She was away a year, during which time, with Irénée either too ill or unwilling to notice, Emma showed her true colors. She beat the three boys unmercifully, singling out Alfred I., the eldest, for particular punishment by lashing him across the bare back and buttocks until he bled. She starved the children, keeping the money given

* Charlotte du Pont to Colonel Henry A. du Pont, son of General Henry, Sept. 9, 1870.

her for household funds, and generally turned Swamp Hall into a place of dark misery for the five unhappy youngsters.

Then Charlotte came home, looking fit and relaxed, and the sunshine returned to Swamp Hall. Even Irénée got up to greet and embrace his wife. Charlotte heaped her children with presents—clothes and dolls for the girls, toy pistols for the boys—and laughter rang out as she recounted her adventures in Europe.

But later that same night Anna, the eldest girl, told her mother about the way the children had been treated by their Alsatian governess. At first Charlotte was incredulous. To prove that what she said was true, Anna took her mother into Alfred I.'s bedroom, pulled back the sheets, and showed her the weals and scabs on the boy's body. Without another word, Charlotte raced along the corridor to Emma's room, dragged the startled woman from her bed, and told her to leave the house at once.

While the governess packed, the boys and girls, joyful at the tyrant's departure, happy at their mother's return, built an effigy of Emma in the garden. They set it alight and sent up fireworks as the woman hurried down the drive into the darkness, the boys jeering at her as she went.

But Charlotte was not there to watch. She had already collapsed again, in Irénée's room, sobbing convulsively, then moaning and shrieking like the lost soul she was. Still shuddering and sobbing with rage, she was taken back to the asylum in Philadelphia. And this time—except for one short visit to her husband—she did not come back.

Irénée took to his bed. He wrote to his Aunt Sophie:

Dear Aunt:

I am too weak to write much. I see your kind note but you must not think that I ever have, or do, repine at God's will—he has given me much more of goods & blessings than I ever deserved— My troubles have all been brought on by myself & self reproach is the worst of all wretchedness. I am too weak to go on but hope you are well. Yrs always, Irénée. I am better today—

Charlotte du Pont died in the asylum on August 19, 1877. Her husband had a fatal haemorrhage when he heard the news. During her son's final hours, Meta du Pont arrived at Swamp Hill and asked for permission to say good-bye to him and beg his forgiveness. He summoned sufficient strength to say, "Never!" and then died, just six weeks after his wife.

Now what would happen to the children? A telegram was sent to Uncle Fred in Louisville, asking him to come at once.

CHAPTER 6

"From Sudden Death, Good Lord, Deliver Us!"

I N 1875 Lammot du Pont returned to Nemours from a long trip out west, in time for his son P.S.'s sixth birthday. He brought his son a multi-colored stick of hard toffee with the name San Francisco embedded in it, a small bag of gold from Sutter's Mill, and an elaborately decorated Mexican saddle for a pony he intended to buy him.* But he had in his pocket an even more valuable present for Du Pont and Uncle Henry. On his trip he had directed a campaign of undercutting and market stealing against the California Powder Company, and then, when the value of its profits dropped, he had bought up a large lump of the company's shares. Du Pont now owned forty-three percent of them, and the last big independent powder maker in the country had fallen under the company's control.

That purchase was to have a profound effect on the nature of the ex-

* Which, incidentally, P. S. du Pont rode only once. He was thrown, decided he hated horses, and thereafter avoided them.

plosives industry in the United States, and an even more devastating effect on Lammot du Pont and his family.

One of the reasons he had bought into California was that one million dollars of its capital was tied up in a new explosives process called dynamite, which, in Lammot's opinion, was soon going to blow all other blasting powders out of the competition. General Henry, stubbornly insisting that black powder would never be superseded, did not agree with him. In 1847, an Italian professor, Ascanio Sobrero of Turin, invented nitroglycerine, and Lammot had burst into Boss Henry's office to suggest that Du Pont take it up. "Too dangerous!" Henry had declared.

A series of disastrous explosions in Europe and the United States, caused by the careless use of nitroglycerine, confirmed Henry's opinion. The explosive was carried around in cans and containers as if it were lamp oil, and only too late was it realized that violent agitation released its terrible force, like an evil genie, to wreak havoc in streetcars and trains and crowded places. Soon there were laws to govern its public transportation, and Henry, who had suffered a similar ban for the far less dangerous practice of carting black powder, did not conceal his satisfaction.

Alfred Nobel, the Swedish chemist, was, however, enthusiastic about the potentials of nitroglycerine and had come up with special percussion caps and triggering devices for it. But this did not prevent his own factory in Sweden from blowing up when he started to make it in quantity. He went back to his laboratory to tame the monster and, after numerous experiments, came up with a mixture of powdered clay and nitroglycerine that turned into a putty. The putty could be molded into "sticks," which were easily and safely transportable and yet, when ignited by a fuse, exploded with a force that made black powder's blast seem like toy fireworks. Nobel called his development dynamite and made his fortune, and his name, from it. Soon orders for the new product were flowing in from all parts of the world, and large tracts of the United States were utilizing it—for the mines in the West, the sewer system in New York, and Rockefeller's new oil wells in Pennsylvania.

Only General Henry was opposed to it. He banned the storage of dynamite in Du Pont warehouses throughout the nation. He used his political muscle to try to extend the ban on railroad transportation of nitroglycerine to dynamite as well. He had always been a man of inflexible habits, and age had made them more rigid than ever. His daily routine never changed. He still used a quill pen and illuminated his desk with three candles. He still wore a top hat to work and trailed his pack of dogs after him when he walked around the powder mills. Black powder had made him the richest man in Delaware, and one of the most powerful men in the nation, and he was not going to abandon it for what he all but literally called a flash in the pan.

And so he was by no means pleased when he discovered that Lammot, in buying control of the California Powder Company, had in effect bought a million-dollar investment in dynamite. But it was too late to do anything about it, and he had to consent to the continuation of California's manufacture of dynamite. He would have been an idiot—and he was certainly not that—to have done otherwise, since the company was making a fortune selling its dynamite sticks to the booming silver, gold, copper, and zinc mines in the west. But General Henry was not happy, especially with Lammot.

Back in 1871 when the already sick Irénée was no longer able to stand the Brandywine's noxious fumes, General Henry had abruptly "accepted his resignation," as he told the family, adding that he would be replaced as partner by the son of Henry's brother Alexis, who had died in the explosion of 1857. This young man, Francis Gurney du Pont, was an able chemist, but he had an additional qualification that Henry considered much more valuable. Frank Gurney was intensely jealous and deeply loathed his cousin Lammot, and being a burly and aggressive character, he did not care who knew it.

A few years earlier Henry had given Frank's oldest brother, Eugene, a partnership on the grounds that he owed it to the dead Alexis, but principally he hoped Eugene would shoulder Lammot aside. It had not happened. Eugene and Lammot had got on with each other extremely well. But with Frank now a partner too, Henry hoped that when it came to a struggle for control, blood would tell, and Eugene would side with his brother in opposing Lammot.

The following year, in 1872, Henry made a move that finally persuaded Lammot that his dream of one day being the General's successor was futile. To an astonished gathering of the family, whom he had summoned to Winterthur—the house where his elder son, Colonel Henry Algernon du Pont, was now installed with his new wife, Pauline—he announced that both Henry Algernon and his brother, William, would henceforth be partners in the firm. All the du Ponts were flabbergasted at the news, for they knew neither of the boys had any qualifications for their new eminence. The only thing Henry Algernon knew about explosives was how to fire a gun—he had just retired from the army. William had even fewer qualifications. But no one could do anything to alter the decision, least of all Lammot.

General Henry had the votes, and in any case, the rest of the family was far too afraid of him to dare to oppose his wishes. The prospect of having to work with Colonel Henry Algernon du Pont, a pompous and bombastic prig with a giant-sized ego, was, however, too much for Lammot to contemplate. He quietly began taking the steps necessary to separate himself from the mainstream of Du Pont's operations.

By 1880 Lammot had made sufficient progress with his plans to bring them out into the open. He had had secret talks with Du Pont's biggest rival, Laflin and Rand, and they—being well aware of his talents—had agreed to help him finance a new undertaking. He had bought an isolated strip of land on the Repauno River, in New Jersey, and there he proposed to open his own dynamite factory. When General Henry was told about it, his initial reaction was to welcome the departure of his brilliant but disturbing and threatening nephew, but then it occurred to him that Lammot's defection might do Du Pont more harm than good. For all his dislike of it, Henry was already making money out of dynamite. Why not allow Lammot to make him some more? He reminded his nephew sharply that he was still a partner in Du Pont and therefore not legally in a position to set up on his own.

There was an acrid discussion, but in the end a compromise was reached. Instead of Laflin and Rand, Du Pont would be allowed to take a financial interest in the new company, but it would be run independently by Lammot, with neither Henry nor any of the other Du Pont partners having any say in its operations.*

Six months later the new factory was built. He brought in his work force from rival factories in Pennsylvania and New Jersey as well as from the Brandywine, and by 1881 the Repauno Mineral Company was producing (and selling) a ton of Atlas dynamite a day.

To avoid even the faintest chance that the General or the du Ponts might exercise any influence over him and his family, Lammot decided to

---

* In fact, Lammot did allow Henry's younger son, William, to join him in running the new company. William was neither Henry's favorite son nor Colonel Algernon's favorite brother, and both bitterly resented William's action.

move. He had found a house for them in Philadelphia, and that was where they would live—and where he would commute from, each day, to New Jersey—from now on.

From the first, the Repauno Mineral Company prospered. Lammot had, of course, teamed up with the Powder Trust and saw to it that he got a fair share of the market along with those other members who were now making dynamite. In the many open markets he went after sales by cutting prices to the bone and still showed a profit, mostly by improving efficiency in the works. He proved to be a good boss. He upped wages a dollar a week above Du Pont's rate, built the men a clubhouse, and used a newly installed telephone to beat his rivals to potential customers. His employees liked him because whenever there was a rush job, or when a new efficiency scheme was being organized, he came into the shops and rolled up his sleeves with the work force, sharing their labors—and their risks.

All efficiency schemes in the powder business are risky, but Lammot du Pont was always ready to experiment and cut corners in the hope that he could also cut prices. All through 1883 and the early weeks of 1884 he was working on an experiment that, he hoped, would streamline his production methods and increase Repauno's profits. The experiment involved treating nitroglycerine in such a way that the sulfuric acid used in its production could be saved, and used again. As an anonymous Du Pont associate explained it later:

> Up to 1883 practically all the sulphuric acid used in the manufacture of nitroglycerine was wasted. The entire charge consisting of nitroglycerine and sulphuric acid would be "drowned," as they called it, in large tanks of water, the diluted acid run off and the nitroglycerine remaining in the bottom of the tank washed to free it from traces of acid. In the belief that the sulphuric acid could be saved, Mr. du Pont called to his assistance at the Repauno works Walter N. Hill, who had been head of the Newport torpedo station, and together they undertook to solve this dangerous problem. The salvage of the acid might have been undertaken in comparative safety in any other industry than that of explosives, but there it became a great hazard. They succeeded, however, in settling the nitroglycerine and running off the sulphuric acid at its full strength (in the laboratories), and the outcome promised to reduce the cost of their nitroglycerine materially.

It was time, Lammot decided, to put the laboratory work to a practical trial in the glycerine house at Repauno. On March 29, 1884, he told his wife that this would be the day when they found out whether the experiment would really succeed. Mary had long since given up beseeching her husband to stop taking risks. He was fifty-three years old, rich enough to have servants in his home and a staff of chemists in his labs, and, she felt, he had reached an age when he should think first of his family. There were now ten children to consider, and she was pregnant with her eleventh. But she knew it was no use pleading. Lammot still lived for his experiments and could not imagine allowing anyone else to conduct one in his own works.

In any case, Lammot had not revealed to Mary how dangerous the experiment really was. What he had done the previous day was to prepare a vat of sulfuric acid and nitroglycerine and leave it overnight to develop what was known as a "strong" condition. Now he intended to try to regenerate the acid, knowing quite well what could happen to a mixture in such circumstances.

> Once L d P took some of the charge [a colleague wrote later] and let it stand overnight in a cup. In the morning he drew off a small quantity with a pipette and in carrying it into the laboratory a single drop fell on the ground and exploded like a percussion cap. This shows how sensitive it becomes when allowed to stand on the acids.

He was now going to deal with a whole vatful.

But on Saturday morning, when he arrived at Repauno, he was delayed in going to the mixing house, and by the time he began to walk across to it, things had started to happen. First a black laborer who helped move heavy materials came racing across the yard and, when asked where he was going, panted, "Things are getting too hot in there" (pointing at the mixing house), and continued on his way. Lammot hurried on and was met by his assistant, Walter Hill, who explained that the vat had begun to "fume" and they had better do something about it quickly. Lammot took one look and then shouted to all the other men in the house to run. At the same time, he and Hill grabbed a hose and started pumping water into the vat in the hope of drowning the fermentation.

But the water seemed only to enrage the bubbling mixture, which frothed in a violent fit of boiling and smoking. The genie had been unleashed and was roaring to go. Seeing that there was no hope of containing it, Lammot signaled to Hill, and they both ran for safety themselves. Lammot hoped the thick wall of a protection bank would save them, but he had failed to remember that three charges of nitroglycerine had been stored nearby the previous day. When the vat in the mixing house exploded, the nitroglycerine charges went up too, with a roar that could be heard across the water in Delaware.

No one came out of it alive.

News of the explosion was received on the Brandywine before it reached Philadelphia, and General Henry deputed Frank and Eugene du Pont to go across to New Jersey at once to find out what had happened. If Frank had any triumphant feelings over the death of his hated rival, he managed to conceal them in a show of pious sorrow. But he could not resist saying (in a letter to his younger brother, Alexis):

> Had they left one minute sooner they would be alive now. Lammot was anxious for the result of his experiment and did not wish to give up, and so stayed later than he would had the fuming taken place in the regular course of manufacture. . . .
>
> None of the bodies were [sic] badly mangled. Lammot was not disfigured in the face, but was crushed in body and ribs broken. I saw his body and was pleased to see that his face looked perfectly natural and peaceful, but death gave to the features a look of unutterable sadness that I do not remember to have seen on any other dead body. . . . I tell you this thing is heartrending, all our little differences with Lammot have vanished, I can bring myself to remember only the many, many pleasant hours I have spent with him, and the assistance he gave me from his experience when I first came [to the power mills]. I have scarcely had another thought but of him since the accident. He was universally loved. . . . I can only think of the fearful crash that ended his life without time for thought, and in the words so familiar to me from weekly use, "from sudden death, good Lord, deliver us," and pray that our family may be spared any more such afflictions.*

It was Frank who took the news of Lammot's death to Mary in Philadelphia. Since she shared her late husband's antipathy toward him, he could

* Francis Gurney du Pont to Alexis Irénée du Pont, April 1, 1884.

hardly have been a more unwelcome bearer of bad tidings. But perhaps the fact that it was an enemy rather than a sympathetic friend who broke the news to Mary gave her strength to absorb the shock without collapsing. To his surprise no doubt, Frank reported to his brother, "Mary is calm, and hopes no ill will come to her child, and thinks not."

He also wrote, "Lammot has left no will, and his capital is very much extended in various enterprises, and it is a big job for the executors."

The family gathered for the funeral at Sand Hole Woods, and with the possible exception of General Henry, his son Henry Algernon, and Cousin Frank, the sorrow was deeply felt, for Lammot had been a lovable man. Even Aunt Sophie, now seventy-four years old and very frail, insisted on attending despite the fact that this was the first time in many years that she had been outside her home, and her doctors warned her of the risk she was taking. She sat rigidly in her invalid chair beside Mary, who held firmly onto her steadying hand, for the widow was near her time. Ranged at Mary's side were her ten children, dressed in neat black suits and dresses, solemn, dry-eyed, and unfidgeting under the stern superintendence of their fourteen-year-old brother, Pierre Samuel du Pont, who already seemed to be taking the place of his dead father. All the uncles, aunts, and cousins were there too, and, of course, Fred and Bidermann, Lammot's two surviving brothers, who had come up from Kentucky. Uncle Fred was flanked by four of the five du Pont "orphans," the children of his other dead brother, Irénée; but the fifth of them, Alfred I., had moved across to stand with Bidermann's son, Thomas Coleman. They were the same age and had already formed a friendship that would soon mature into a more fruitful association.

It was certainly the biggest funeral ever held at Sand Hole Woods, for despite the unpleasant weather and the difficulties of travel, workmen and friends had come from many miles around to pay a last tribute to Lammot. That night Sophie wrote in her diary:

> Tuesday April 1st 1884. Louviers. A cloudy blustering day snowed somewhat in the morning occasional bursts of faint sunshine, very rare, raw and damp— Dear Lammot was burried [sic] at 1 o'clock, a very large funeral, and all the old neighbors and workmen that survived came all bearing testimony to his goodness and generosity of heart—calling him "poor man's friend"— Yes, he had that philanthropic spirit which characterized the preceding generation of du Ponts—which Biderman[n]

also inherits, alas becoming rapidly extinct in the rising generation I fear, a sad, sad day for me.

When the funeral was over, Uncle Fred went across to pay his respects to
his sister-in-law, Mary, and to her father, Henry Belin, and then he turned
to Mary's eldest son, P.S. It was the first time he had seen the boy in several years, and he was amazed at the changes in him. Though P.S. was only
fourteen, his height and solemn expression gave him quite a grown-up air,
and his manner and mode of speaking helped to strengthen that impression.

Bidermann was appointed executor of Lammot's estate (along with
Henry Belin), but Fred was made guardian of the children, just as seven
years earlier he had been made guardian of Irénée and Charlotte's children.
Fred had no doubt about Mary's ability to manage her family's affairs, but
he took his responsibilities seriously enough to want to assure young P.S.
that he would always be available to him for advice and help should it ever
be needed.

In later years P. S. du Pont remembered that moment at his father's
funeral because after he and his uncle had spoken, the two of them wandered over to Fred's other ward, Alfred I. du Pont, who was still standing
with Thomas Coleman. It was there, at Sand Hole Woods, that the three
cousins were together for the first time; the two older ones made stammer-
ing and inarticulate as they struggled to indicate their sympathy for the
younger one in his loss.

P.S. remembered that it was he who put them at their ease by thanking them gravely for their concern, and then the three young men together
joined the procession that General Henry and the more important members
of the du Pont family were leading back to Eleutherian Mills for the
funeral luncheon. The cousins were well aware of their minor place in the
hierarchy, and as he watched the automatic way in which some members
took precedence and others obediently fell back, P.S. realized that he, like
Alfred I. and, to a certain extent, Thomas Coleman, had now become one of
the "poor relations," and must learn to behave accordingly.

Part Two

THE COUSINS

CHAPTER 7

The Children of the Swamp

SWAMP HALL, where that sad couple Irénée and Charlotte du Pont had bred their five children, was one of the most spacious houses on the Brandywine, with ten bedrooms, lots of living space, stables, and outhouses. Like all the other houses on the estate, it was owned by the Du Pont company. From the days of the founder, it had been the practice for each du Pont who married to be given a house, a saddle horse, and a cow. The horse and cow were a gift, but the house was on loan.

Since General Henry was boss of Du Pont when Irénée and Charlotte died, it was to him that the rest of the du Ponts deferred when it came to deciding what should be done with Swamp Hall, and what arrangements should be made for the five orphans. Henry had no doubt about the house. Swamp Hall was one of the plum properties on the estate, and Irénée had done much to enlarge and improve it during the more active periods of his life. With its disposition in his hands, the head of the du Pont clan could

[85]

extract many a concession from his relatives, and he made it clear that Swamp Hall would now revert to the company.

The five children were a more complicated problem. It was true that Uncle Fred had promised to look after the orphans, and when the telegram arrived announcing Irénée's death, he had come up at once from Louisville. But, as he quickly explained to the relatives, he had not meant that he would personally and physically take care of the five children. How could he? Though he was an extremely rich man, with thriving paper mills and coal mines in Kentucky, he led a very simple life, occupying one room in the Galt Hotel in Louisville, eating in restaurants, and finding his entertainment in other people's houses (as it later turned out, in one house in particular). Uncle Fred had simply meant that he would always be around to superintend the affairs and welfare of his nephews and nieces. He willingly accepted the role of guardian, but where his wards would live was quite another question.

At the meeting where all this was discussed, under the leadership of General Henry, several du Pont families offered to take in one or another of the children. Some did it from kindness of heart, and others had more material motives. Irénée may have died an unhappy man, but he was not a poor one. He left an estate of $498,871.41, to be divided equally among his children and given to each one when he or she reached the age of twenty-one, and since shrewd Uncle Fred was going to invest the capital, they would each be quite rich when they reached their majority. Uncle Fred, knowing how his wards felt, pleaded that all five orphans be taken in by one family. The unhappy circumstances in which they had been raised had knitted them together into a unit bound by mutual suffering and adversity, and it would be tragic to separate them now. But no one was about to take in five children, and Henry had no compunction about splitting them up. So it was proposed by him, and thus automatically decided, that Swamp Hill revert to Du Pont, the five children be parceled out among four of the families, and Uncle Fred deputed to go across to Swamp Hall to tell them of the decision.

It so happened, however, that while the du Pont family council was in progress the five orphans were having their own meeting. Seventeen-year-old Anna presided, with her sister, Marguerite, fifteen, and her oldest brother, Alfred I., thirteen, taking leading parts. The remaining two boys, Maurice, eleven, and Louis, nine, were too young to be considered. In any case, they strongly agreed with what the other three were saying—and that was that under no circumstances would they allow their relatives either to evict them from Swamp Hall or to divide them up among the families on the Brandywine.

It was also agreed that if such an attempt were made, they would resist, physically. Alfred I., who had brought a shotgun to the meeting, firmly declared that they would have to carry his corpse out of the house, for he would not leave his home alive. Anna stoutly supported him, and so, more quaveringly, did Marguerite.

An hour or two later, when Uncle Fred arrived with his bad tidings, he found the orphans gathered on the front porch of Swamp Hall. Annie had a hatchet in her hand, Marguerite wielded a rolling pin from the kitchen, Alfred I. was loading his shotgun, Maurice held gingerly to an old flintlock pistol of his father's, and Louis was armed with his bow and a sheath of arrows. Uncle Fred, a warm, kindly, and understanding man, did not laugh at the spectacle but listened gravely as Annie explained that there was no reason to break up the family. There were servants in the house, and in any case, she was quite capable of running both home and family, since she had already done it more than once during her mother's illnesses. Why split them up when they could continue living together, as they had done for so long?

Fred went back to see General Henry and must have been at his most persuasive, for it was agreed that the orphans should be given a chance to prove themselves. They would be allowed to stay on at Swamp Hall under Annie's superintendence for a trial period, closely watched by the other du Pont women. Every day from then on, the coachman, Lytle, drove the two girls to school in Wilmington, and when they got back home in the afternoon, they set about making Swamp Hall cleaner and more shining than it had ever been in Charlotte's day. Alfred I. was at school in New Jersey, and the two younger boys were at another school in Philadelphia. The brothers could not wait to get home for their Christmas holidays. On arriving, they found a mature and confident Annie waiting to greet them.

She paraded them for inspection on the morning of Christmas Day to make sure they had changed out of their play clothes, scrubbed their hands and nails, washed their necks, and brushed their hair; then she and Marguerite marched them across the Brandywine to Christ's Church and into the Swamp Hall pew, under the approving eyes of the rest of the du Ponts. Rarely have small boys looked so clean or smelled so heavily of carbolic soap.

On New Year's Day, 1878, the du Pont men started their ritual round of visits to the women of the family. One by one, led by General Henry, they all made Swamp Hall their first call, piling their presents in the hall and kissing the grave but triumphant Annie, the lady of the house. She knew then that the probation period was over, and Swamp Hall would be the orphans' home for as long as they stayed together.

If Annie was the mother of Swamp Hall, there was no doubt that Alfred I. was its most interesting member. While his parents were alive he was a morose and moody child, driven into silence, and into himself, by the awful tension around the house. Their deaths released him. He had long since developed a passion for firearms and liked to go out, first with a twenty-two rifle and then with a shotgun, to pot rabbits and partridges around the Brandywine and bring back bagfuls of game. It seemed that the slaughter helped relieve him of some of the pressures at home. But after Irénée's death he became interested in more constructive hobbies: building steam engines, meddling with electricity and new electrical gadgets, practicing on the violin, trumpet, and other instruments, and singing in a Wilmington glee club. He was a strong and healthy young man who liked to show off his muscle. For a time he ran around Wilmington with a gang of young toughs who never challenged his leadership or mocked him for being one of the toffee-nosed du Ponts, because they knew he could beat any one of them in a fistfight anytime he was challenged.

From his grandfather, the founder of the company, he had inherited a fascination for powder making, and from the age of nine—while his father was still alive—he had been wandering around the yards, making friends with the men who had the dangerous job of mixing Du Pont's famous black powder. They noted how he sniffed the reek of explosives as if it were the scent of exotic flowers, and they accepted him as one of them, especially when he made it clear that he could not wait for the day when he would be working at the mixing vats beside them. One of his great adventures was to hitch a ride with one of the powder-wagon teams taking a load of exposives to the docks. He would hide in a ditch by the roadside so his family could not see him, and then emerge as the mule teams rattled by. If the driver was Bill Macklin, a friend of Alfred I.'s who managed the wagon teams, he would let the young boy climb aboard and then silently hand him the whip. Then Alfred I. knew that he was in charge of six ornery mules, responsible for keeping them to the smoothest parts of the road and away from the violent bump that would blow them all to perdition.

Alfred I. had one characteristic that was going to be troublesome to him: He was stubborn. When he made up his mind about something, he would refuse to budge. From the start he set himself against book learning on the grounds that through practical experiment he could learn all he wanted about the things that interested him. He hated academic tests and scholarly examinations. Once, when a master at school pointed out that he had only scored seventy-five points in an exam, the minimum to pass, he replied:

"Yes, and if the minimum had been 85, I would have scored that too."

To equip him for the position he would eventually hope to hold at Du Pont, Uncle Fred enrolled Alfred I. at the Massachusetts Institute of Technology in 1882. Du Pont was one of M.I.T.'s donors, so there was never very much difficulty about getting a place for one of the family, and it is doubtful that Alfred I. would have passed the written entrance exam otherwise. His spell at M.I.T. certainly did not do him much good so far as garnering scientific knowledge was concerned. His cousin, Thomas Coleman du Pont, had been there for a year when he arrived, and they became roommates. For Coleman, M.I.T. was a chance to get away from his domineering father and brighten his life (with the aid of the liberal allowance that his mother regularly sent him), and instead of attending courses, he was apt to prefer afternoons at the races, evenings at the local vaudeville houses, and late-night rendezvous with chorus girls from the shows. He took Alfred I. along with him, offering to pay for the shows, the champagne, and the girls, since Uncle Fred kept Alfred I. to a monthly allowance of only thirty dollars. To salve his pride and pay his own way, Alfred I. would sweep snow at a dollar an hour or do other odd jobs. One night, hoping to earn a thousand dollars, he climbed into the ring at a vaudeville show with the idea of knocking out John L. Sullivan, the bareknuckle heavyweight champion, who was top of the bill and issuing the challenge. The champion was even then on his way down hill, training on booze and doing most of his fighting with his chorus-girl wife, but he had no trouble taking care of young du Pont. Even so, he was impressed with Alfred I.'s pugnacity, courage, and capacity for punishment, and he eased the young man over sufficient rounds to earn him a fifty-dollar consolation prize. Afterward they met in the boxer's dressing room and, over a bottle of whiskey, drank to a friendship that was to last a lifetime. When Sullivan heard why Alfred I. had volunteered to be a chopping block, he offered to train him in pugilism. Soon Alfred I. was keeping up with Coleman by fighting (under an assumed name) in boxing rings around the Boston area, taking on all comers. His fights paid for the drink and the girls; as it turned out, he learned a lot more about physiology than he did about physics.

In fact, the abiding memory that Alfred I. carried away from his period at M.I.T. had nothing to do with the college at all. He had been fascinated with electricity, and especially with incandescent electric lighting, ever since he had been to an exhibition in Philadelphia as a boy. Now Thomas Alva Edison had come up with the invention of generators, switchboxes, and fuses, which made control of his incandescent lamp bulb possible. To demonstrate its possibilities, he lit Pearl Street Station in New York with his new system, and when Alfred I. passed through the station on his way to Boston, he marveled at the phenomenon of light.

Then, the following year, while he was still at M.I.T., he read an announcement that the Bijou Theater in Boston would become the first in the world to be lit by electric lights, using Edison's system. Alfred I. spent his savings to buy two tickets, and he never forgot the experience (though he did forget the girl he took with him). It was a night of double thrills, for the Bijou put on a performance of Gilbert and Sullivan's *Iolanthe,* one of his favorite operettas, and with the music lilting in his ears and the brilliant lights dazzling his eyes during the interval, he was ecstatic. When the end came, he dashed back to his rooms to recount to his cousin the wonders of his splendid evening.

"And what," asked Coleman, "did you do with Maisie?"

"Oh, my gosh," said Alfred I., "I completely forgot about her!"

From such a lack of academic application, it was hopeless, of course, to expect a degree, and in late 1884 Alfred I. du Pont dropped out. In any case, he had lost his partner in extrascholastic activities: Coleman had left school a few months before to go to work in one of his father's coal mines. On his way back to the Brandywine, Alfred I. stopped off in Philadelphia at yet another electrical exhibition, for it was his intention to convert Swamp Hall to electric lighting as soon as he reached home. By coincidence, Thomas Alva Edison himself was visiting the exhibition hall and was introduced to Alfred I. Impressed by the young man's knowledge of, and enthusiasm for, the new system, he invited him to the Edison Laboratory at Menlo Park, New Jersey. So in later life Alfred I. was able to say:

"I did not entirely waste my time during my student years. I made two distinguished friends. One made me see stars when he hit me, and the other made me see even brighter lights when he pressed a switch."

In 1885 he signed up at the Brandywine yards as an unskilled laborer at a wage of eighty-three dollars a month—twice as much as his fellow laborers were getting (after all, General Henry reasoned, he *was* a du Pont), but seven dollars less than the wages of the powder men whose skill he so much admired. It was a heavy job, and he needed all his muscle to handle it. He clocked in at 6:50 each morning and put in a twelve-hour day lugging kegs of powder, shifting saltpeter, soda, sulfur, and charcoal into the mixing sheds. It was also a dirty job; when he got home in the evening, Annie had covers down over the carpets to protect them from his caked boots and hurried him to the bathtub, complaining loudly that he "looked like a nigger minstrel." But it was not because of Annie that Alfred I. sent in a suggestion to the boss that shower baths should be installed in the yards; he was thinking of his fellow laborers who had no bathtubs to go home to.

Frank Gurney du Pont, by this time superintendent of the Hagley and Lower yards on the Brandywine, had been told by General Henry to keep a close watch on Alfred I.'s progress and to send him regular reports. Though Frank would never be a man to hand out praise, even when it was due, he had to grudgingly approve the young man's sense of application and willingness to sweat for his pay. At the end of three months Henry told him to put Alfred I. one step up the ladder, and the boy was informed that henceforward he would be working as an apprentice powder man, but with no increase in wages. He did not have to worry about that, however, because he was already a wealthy young man. Uncle Fred, who had handed his legacy over to him on his twenty-first birthday, had done well for his nephew: The amount that Irénée had left Alfred I. had more than doubled, to $104,000. But even if he had needed his wages, Alfred I. would probably not have complained, for he was too pleased at the prospect of actually being involved at last in the powder-making process.

To begin with, he was put to work in the Hagley Yard, where Du Pont made most of its money manufacturing what was known as soda powder, used mainly for blasting. Until Lammot du Pont had gone to work in the Du Pont laboratories, the raw materials for making explosives were sulfur, charcoal, and saltpeter—fine saltpeter for gunpowder, and rough or unrefined saltpeter for ordinary blasting powder. But saltpeter, as we have seen, was expensive and had to be imported. So Lammot had experimented until he found a much cheaper substitute, and one easily available: soda. He had perfected a soda powder that, though it would never be any use for guns, was perfectly adequate for industrial purposes. The process had been patented in his name and that of the Du Pont company, and prosperity had resulted. Du Pont was able to undersell every powder maker in the country, and by the time Alfred I. joined the company, it had the largest market for blasting powder in the nation. Alfred I. now began to learn in detail the method by which powder was produced. He helped to make saltpeter by boiling soda and potash, and he was shown how to pick the finest willow branches to make the special charcoal for gunpowder. "Next came the preparation of black dust at the composition house by grinding and mixing in fixed proportions of charcoal and sulphur," wrote Marquis James in a graphic account of life in the yards.

> Except during very high or low stages of the [Brandywine] creek, the composition house and all other mills with moving machinery were run by water power. Paralleling the Brandywine flowed a race, with sides of masonry, from which flumes carried the current to the water wheels. By means of shafting, set on piers about three feet above the ground, one water wheel might supply power to a number of mills. The grinding of the gears when this shafting changed direction was the loudest and most persistent sound in the yards. To avoid interruption of work during exceptionally high or low water, Francis G. du Pont had prevailed on his Uncle Henry to install a steam plant in Hagley Yard. It was built far up on the side of the hill and operated only at the rare times when water power failed.*

Alfred I. spent several weeks in the composition house making the black dust for the powder and was then transferred to a rolling mill for his first experience of the hazardous side of the process. It was here that he helped with the dangerous process of mixing black dust with saltpeter (or soda if they were making blasting powder) and then spreading it, for further pulverization, beneath two slowly revolving ten-ton iron wheels. The pulverization process took three hours for the best gunpowder, and if a wrench or a spade struck a spark during that period, if a bit of metal found its way into the mixture, or if the turning wheels grated on the bedplate, an explosion could well be ignited. James's account continues:

> Powdermen entered a rolling mill only to start or stop machinery at the beginning or the end of a run, or to add water

* Marquis James, *Alfred I. du Pont: The Family Rebel* (Indianapolis and New York: The Bobbs-Merrill Company, Inc., 1941).

to the composition about once an hour. Thus rolling mill work, though exacting, was not arduous. Crews spent their time while charges were being run in a rude clubhouse called the night shanty. There were bunks for those who wanted to sleep and benches for those content to gossip and chew tobacco. Though Alfred never chewed, he is said to have been the only du Pont to make a habit of sharing the bantering camaraderie of the night shanty.*

The next stage in the powder-making process, and in Alfred I.'s training, took place in the press room, where the pulverized dust from the rolling mills was shaped into slabs by a huge press and then broken up into brick-sized pieces for transfer to a graining mill. Here too the work was fraught with danger, especially since there was usually twenty to thirty times as much explosive material around in the press room as there was in the rolling mills. For that reason, the press room was tunneled into the side of a hill.

The last stages of the process occurred in the graining mill, where the presscakes, as they were called, were crushed to the proper size between corrugated rollers, and in the glazing mills, where graphite was added and the mixture poured into revolving hollow cylinders. This last stage was also one where a spark could start a murderous explosion, for the operation—in which the cylinders smoothed and polished the grains and filled their pores with graphite—took between eight and fourteen hours. It was only after this that the finished powder was kegged, branded, and taken to the magazines in the Upper Yard, ready to be shipped to new projects (or new wars) in all parts of the world.

It took Alfred I. du Pont just under two years to learn powder making from beginning to end, and to meet the exacting standards set by his cousin Frank. But by the end he was an expert powder man, and though none of them was ever likely to win such rapid promotion, his workmates did not grumble when Alfred I. was made assistant superintendent of the Hagley and Lower yards and had his wages raised to fifteen hundred dollars a year.

Alfred I. still signed in at 6:50 in the morning and still worked a twelve-hour day or, more often now, a twelve-hour night shift, but his reserves of

* James, *Alfred I. du Pont.*

energy were tremendous and he did not let his work interfere with his social activities. Now that he was in a white-collar job he often went straight from work to a performance at the Wilmington Opera House. On weekends he traveled to Philadelphia or New York for the symphony concerts, and passionately fond of music as he was, he continued to pursue his own music-making activities.

A distinguished former concertmaster from the Berlin Philharmonic, now teaching in Philadelphia, coached him in classical violin, and a well-known Brandywine square-dance fiddler taught him dance music. "Professor" Skimmerhorn, a black Wilmington musician, taught him the guitar. Alfred I. then organized an orchestra made up of Du Pont laborers, Wilmington shopkeepers, local doctors, and contractors—ten players in all, with himself doubling on the violin, piano, clarinet, and cornet. He called it the Tankopanicum Orchestra, Tankopanicum being the old Indian name for the Brandywine, but everybody in the neighborhood called it Al's Band. It played for powder men's dances and for socials at Christ's Church (the du Pont church) and Saint Joseph's (the Catholic church in Wilmington that most of the powder men and their families attended).

Nor did that end his extracurricular activities. Still fascinated by electricity, he had taken up Thomas Alva Edison's invitation to visit him at his laboratories at Menlo Park. He went there for the first time in the summer of 1884, before starting work in the Du Pont yards, and got such a warm welcome from the inventor that he became a regular visitor. Edison listened patiently to Alfred I.'s ideas and helped him produce his first successful electric gadget—a rattrap baited with cheese set on an electrified prong, which, when nuzzled by the rat, stunned or killed it at the same time as it activated the trapdoor.

It was Edison's work that had spurred Alfred I.'s ambition to bring the miracle of electric light to Swamp Hall, and shortly after his first visit to Menlo Park he hired two brothers named Mathewson to help him get the project going. Using models in Edison's laboratory, they built a generator and a motor to drive it, which they installed in the cellar of Swamp Hall. Then while Annie watched in skeptical amazement they hung wires around the house and fitted switches to the walls. Then presto! Swamp Hall suddenly blazed with light, the first house in the state of Delaware to have electricity. From all over Wilmington people came to marvel at the great house lighting up the countryside.

There was only one snag. The voltmeter on the generator had to be watched at all times, for if too many lights were turned on at once, their power would dim and the engine driving the generator would have to be speeded up; but then if half the lights were suddenly turned off, the current would be too strong and all the bulbs would burn out. Alfred I. had to pay one or other of the Mathewson brothers to stay permanently on duty, to watch the meter and rev up or cut the motor according to need— an outlay he could afford, but whose necessity irked him. Utilizing all the knowledge he had gleaned from Edison, he got down to the task of finding a solution to the problem. The result was a gadget that, when fitted to the generator, automatically controlled the supply of power. Its "inventor" was not a little irked when he took it to Menlo Park to show his mentor, only to discover that Edison had already come up with a rheostat of his own.

By the end of 1885 everybody in Wilmington as well as on the Brandywine knew Alfred I. du Pont, and he was a popular young man with all of them, workers and "gentry" alike. Whether cycling around the countryside on his old bike or playing an encore with Al's Band at a workmen's social, he always got a wave or a cheer.

As a powder man's wife has said:

> My father, Michael Gordon, was on the powder line, and he lived to be eighty-one. I knew Mr. Alfred when I was a girl growing up, and I want to say that he was a gentleman. He liked fun with the best of them and used to tease us about our fellows until we blushed like anything. But he did it like a gentleman and not like some of your rich young men, all too ready and willing to take advantage of a poor girl's ignorance or her love of a little finery.

Her husband added:

> Mr. Frank held himself aloft [sic] from those who worked for him. In six months Mr. Alfred knew the workmen better than Mr. Frank did after twenty-five years as our boss. . . . If Mr. Alfred knew you in Hagley he knew you on Market Street [Wilmington].*

And naturally enough, everyone, from Philadelphia to Wilmington and the Brandywine, began to wonder who would be the girl lucky enough to catch and marry him.

* Author's interview with Mr. and Mrs. Albert Buchanan cited in James, *Alfred I. du Pont.*

There had already been one marriage among the orphans. Marguerite did not even wait for her legacy before choosing a man she had met during a family celebration on the Brandywine. Cazenove G. Lee was, in fact, a cousin on Charlotte's side of the family. A Virginia-born lawyer in his late twenties, he was practicing in Washington. Marguerite was eighteen.

Alfred I. acted as best man at the wedding at Christ's Church and was happy for his little sister; but it did occur to him that one of these days Annie too was bound to meet and marry someone, and if so, what would happen to Swamp Hall? Would Annie and her husband automatically take it over, in effect persuading her three brothers that they had better look elsewhere for a home? Or would she depart, leaving behind a bachelor residence about which General Henry might well have reservations?

Alfred I.'s speculations began to take practical form in 1886, when he noticed that Annie was beginning to see a great deal of a young man named Absalom Waller, who, judging from his moony look and the sheep's eyes he continually cast in her direction, was, in Alfred I.'s opinion, absolutely besotted with his sister. He loved Swamp Hall and sincerely hoped it would be his home for a lifetime, but now he had to contemplate the prospect of a cuckoo coming into his comfortable nest.

It was in the spring of that year that another of his mother's relations, Annie Lee of Virginia, invited the orphans to her wedding in Hanover. Alfred I.'s second brother, Maurice, the happy-go-lucky member of the family, came down from M.I.T. and confided to him that he was bored with school, uninterested in Du Pont, and hated explosives because they were dangerous and so vulgarly noisy. From Yale came Alfred I.'s youngest brother, Louis, who was the dark horse among the orphans, broody, poetic, apt to have fits of passion over young ladies. He had actually brought one with him to Virginia for Annie Lee's wedding, and when Alfred I. ran his eye over the girl, he made up his mind about two things. First, she was far too worldly and sophisticated for his innocent younger brother, and second, she was just the sort of girl he was looking for for himself.

Her name was Bessie Gardner, and she too was a sort of cousin of the orphans, though a more remote one, again on their mother's side. Her father was an English professor at Yale, Dorsey Gardner, who was at that time working on a new edition of Webster's Dictionary. Bessie was well read and erudite, with an enormous fund of self-confidence, and she made no secret of the fact that she thought the orphan du Ponts not quite up to the standards set by herself and her family. She confided to her cousins that though Louis was a "dear boy," he was far too young and gauche for her taste, though she had tried, she assured them, to let the "poor thing" know that she was really flattered at having him fall in love with, as she put it, "an unworthy little creature like me." As for the older brother, Alfred I., why, she had been told he had not even been able to get a degree from M.I.T., and had they seen his awful hands, all black and pitted with dirt from those terrible powder mills?

Alfred I. was well aware from the start that Bessie, far from thinking herself unworthy of Louis, considered herself far superior to anyone in the world, with the possible exception of her father and the president of Yale. When the wedding was over, the four unmarried orphans, Annie, Alfred I., Maurice, and Louis, went to stay with Marguerite at her new home on New Hampshire Avenue in Washington, while Bessie took the train back to her family in New Haven. Once at his sister's house, Alfred I. went straight upstairs and wrote Bessie a letter that was to mark the beginning of a regular correspondence.

That autumn, soon after Louis went back to Yale, Alfred I. paid him a surprise visit. He also saw Bessie. A week or two later he was back again, and once more he spent some time with Bessie. She had apparently got used to the roughness of his hands and the smell of gunpowder in his clothes and had probably found out by this time that he not only had one hundred thousand dollars in the bank but was also doing well at Du Pont. Her father might be a distinguished professor but he had no money, and Bessie was intensely ambitious.

Bessie continued to see Louis, who continued to adore her, but neither she nor Alfred I. appears to have told him the way things were going. He was completely astonished when his brother arrived on yet another visit just before the Christmas vacation and, bouncing into Louis's room, flushed and beaming, demanded to be congratulated on his engagement.

"You don't mean you are going to marry Bessie?" said Louis.

Alfred I. was to say later that he had no idea at the time how much Bessie really meant to Louis, and was unaware that he and Bessie together were dealing Louis a blow from which he would never recover.

When a jubilant Alfred I. got back to Swamp Hall, he was greeted by an equally happy sister Annie. She too was engaged, at last, to Absalom Waller, and a date had been fixed for their wedding. Alfred hastily asked her whether she planned to live on at Swamp Hall, and was told that his sister and her husband-to-be would make their home in Wilmington. It was then that Alfred I. told Annie his news.

Anna Cazenove du Pont and Absalom Waller were married at Christ's Church, on the Brandywine, on December 22, 1886, and not only was Alfred I. best man once more to one of his sisters, but this time he also conducted his own Tankopanicum Orchestra at the reception at Swamp Hall.

Fifteen days later he and Bessie Gardner were married (on January 4, 1887) at Saint James's Church in Philadelphia. They left for a honeymoon in Bermuda, and while they were away the Mathewson brothers got busy unraveling the tangle of electric wires that still littered the floors of Swamp Hall, concealing them in panels in the walls. It was a surprise present for Bessie's homecoming, and Alfred I. had arranged it to impress her.

But when he turned on the switch as they came through the door, flooding the tidy reception lounge with light, Bessie's pretty face showed no sign of gratification. She was not only unimpressed but did not even seem to realize that a marvelous transformation had taken place.

"I shall really have to start doing something about this house," she said.

It was at that moment, Alfred I. said later, that he began to suspect his marriage might have been a mistake. His suspicions were not exactly allayed a little later when, as had been his custom, he invited the Tanko-panicum Orchestra to rehearse at Swamp Hall. Bessie retired to the back porch of the house. She was not, as it turned out, interested in music—at least not the kind of music the Tankopanicums played.

But if Alfred I. was having qualms about his new wife, General Henry was in no doubt whatsoever that she was quite the prettiest, wittiest, and cleverest female ever to come to the Brandywine. He approved of every-thing she did and said. He liked the way she altered the eating habits at Swamp Hall (and subsequently in all the other du Pont households) from main-meal-at-midday to dinner-in-the-evening, with the best napery, silver, glassware, and wine. When she told him she needed to make changes to the Swamp, he gallantly responded that Du Pont would pay her bills. It was quite an expensive promise, because Bessie installed four new bath-rooms, a billiards room, a new parlor and porch, and turned what had hitherto been a rather somber home into her ideal, a large chintzy heaven, rich in frills.

In the autumn of 1887 she gave Alfred I. his first child, a daughter, whom they christened Madeleine. General Henry offered to be godfather to Madie, as she was called, and told his grand-nephew he was raising his salary (to twenty-four hundred dollars a year). Alfred I. was glad of that. For the first time in his life, thanks to Bessie's many purchases, he had spent more than his salary and had been forced to dip into capital.

He comforted himself with the thought that if Bessie continued to win General Henry's warm regard and favor, her extravagances would be bearable. It could only mean that his own position in the du Pont hierarchy would be increasingly improved.

He received his first confirmation of this when he was called into Henry's office early in 1889 and told that he was being sent on an important mission for the company. Word of an alarming new development in the gunpowder business had reached Du Pont from its agents in Europe. Until now, thanks to Lammot du Pont's work in the company's labs, Du Pont had led the field in the improvement of powder processes, and one of his last achievements before his death had been to perfect a new powder called cocoa (because it was made from half-burned charcoal and looked brown), which had much greater propulsive power in larger caliber guns.

But now, it seemed, the French and the Belgians had moved a step ahead. They had produced what all explosives laboratories had been searching for and so far failed to perfect—smokeless powder. If it were true that the French and Belgians could now fire guns whose discharge could not be seen by the enemy, the whole pattern of armed combat would be altered, and every nation in the world would soon be in the market for the new product.

The General instructed Alfred I. that he was to go to Paris and buy, borrow, or steal the new process for smokeless powder, and also bring back the machinery by which it could be produced. He was to spare no expense. And to make his trip agreeable, the General added that his grand-nephew could take his charming wife and new baby along with him to keep him company in his off-duty hours.

It was not entirely favoritism, however, that secured the mission for Alfred I. He had worked on cocoa and already knew the general principles by which smokeless powder could be produced. Moreover, he was one of the last du Ponts to have French as a second language and would therefore be unlikely to find himself tongue-tied in Paris. On the other hand, within a few days of registering at the Hôtel des Deux Mondes in the French capital, Alfred realized that he was not going to get far with the French Ministry of War. He had been provided with all the necessary letters of introduction, including one from Secretary of State James G. Blaine, but when he presented himself to the Directorate of Powders and Saltpeters and made some casual inquiries about smokeless powder, he received polite but noncommittal answers. He could hear the doors slamming in his face. In no way, he decided, were the French going to help him. He decided instead to go to Brussels and approach the Belgian firm of Coopals, who had the process.

Alfred I. asked them whether they were ready to make a deal. They were, indeed, but there were other suitors for Coopals's hand. Was Mr. du Pont armed with sufficient authority to sign a contract? Alfred I. took a deep breath and said he was. The papers were drawn up. On behalf of the Du Pont company, he signed a deal not only for the rights to the smokeless powder but also for a shipment of machinery for making the Belgian version of cocoa gunpowder.

Confident that he had pulled off a coup for Du Pont, and that the General would reward him for it, Alfred I. sped back to Paris, where he had left Bessie and the baby, and then headed for Delaware. But by the time he returned to America, there was no question of General Henry's rewarding anybody. After seventy-seven years of perfect health, he had suddenly broken down.

He was mortally ill at the time of Alfred I.'s return, and he died on August 8, 1889.

He had already nominated his successors at Du Pont, and his grandnephew was not among them. The du Ponts chosen to succeed the General were frightened men, and they wanted no part of any deal Alfred I. had signed on behalf of the company. Smokeless powder? Who cared about smokeless powder when they already had so much unfinished business weighing on their minds?

CHAPTER 8

Leave It to "Dad"

T H E only du Pont who dared to be absent when General Henry was buried at Sand Hole Woods was Alfred I.'s brother Maurice, who had never liked the rude and dictatorial old man, anyway, and hated everything he stood for. Maurice had dropped out of, first, M.I.T., then Johns Hopkins, having reached the conclusion that he was not built for daily toil. Pocketing his family legacy (Uncle Fred had made more than one hundred thousand dollars for him, too), he had set off to see something of the world. When Alfred I. cabled him to come home for the funeral, Maurice cabled back from Ireland that he had "better things to do." He had indeed, one of the "better things" being a blonde Irish colleen named Margery Fitzgerald with whom he had become smitten in Cork.

Uncle Fred, Bidermann, and Coleman had, of course, made the journey from Kentucky. Fred was notorious for appearing around Louisville looking like a tramp, but he had the bloom on his cheek and the sparkle in his eyes of a man who was well served in every possible way, and the rumors going around the city bolstered this explanation for his air of self-satisfaction. It was whispered (he was too powerful for it to be said out loud) not only that he was a favored patron at the most expensive bordello in Louisville, but that its attractive madame, Maggie Payne, so doted on him that she had extended him the freedom of her personal favors as well. It was an arrangement that must have made a strong appeal to his famed frugality, as well as to his other passions.

Though Uncle Fred was now one of the richest men in Kentucky, having made a fortune from his paper mills, streetcars, and coal mines, he was everywhere well liked and respected. Despite his sexual dalliances and the sources of some of his income, no opprobrium attached to his name. Owners of Kentucky coal mines were not exactly loved at the time. The coalfields had been the scenes of bloody clashes between miners striking for better pay and conditions, and scabs and murderous thugs brought in by the owners to beat, terrorize, and starve them back into the pits. But Uncle Fred had made his brother the front man of the organization, and it was therefore Bidermann's ruthlessness that came under fire. Bidermann did not seem to mind. He was the hard member of the family, not averse to spilling a little blood if it would bring a few more dollars into the kitty. Nor, unlike Uncle Fred, had he any compunction about the obvious display of his wealth. He had built himself a large house and lived in conspicuous ostentation.

What did Coleman, Bidermann's son, think of his father's conduct? Since 1884 he had been working for the family-owned Central Coal and Iron Company at a soft-coal mine in Central City, Kentucky, and was learning what it was like to be a boss. He had, at first, made himself popular with the miners by mixing with them as his cousin Alfred I. had done with the powder men on the Brandywine. He joined them at football and baseball. He went to their dances and romanced their girls, who found no difficulty in falling for him, for he was tall, good-looking, charming and full of fun. His strongest romance was with one of the daughters of a mine foreman named Gish. He and the girl met at a miner's picnic, and he quickly separated her from her sister and took her for a boating trip on the lake. She was attracted by the enormous fund of exuberance bubbling inside his huge frame, and he was overwhelmed by her large, soulful eyes and calm, seraphic beauty. They were soon on first-name terms, and there were further meetings. But then both families intervened. Bidermann was furious at the

news that his son was "fouling his own nest," as he called it, by getting involved with a foreman's daughter. As for Gish, he probably realized that no
du Pont would ever be allowed to marry a girl from a miner's family, and
he packed his daughter off to stay with relatives in New York—and so Lillian Gish subsequently became a star of silent films instead of the mistress
(and maybe even the wife?) of Coleman du Pont.

It was after this incident (but certainly not because of it) that relations
between Coleman and the miners in Central City changed. One of his first
gestures as superintendent of the mine had been to arrange for all employees
in the pits to have a free bag of coal for Thanksgiving. But this did not
make up for the fact that the pitmen were paid a miserable $1.75 a day for
twelve hours down the shaft. Moreover, nearly all of them were kept in
debt by having to obtain much needed advances in the form of "flickers,"
which could only be exchanged at the company stores at eighty percent of
their face value.

In consequence, Coleman had to contend with a series of bitter strikes
which Bidermann ruthlessly put down. The final one, in 1888, practically
ended Coleman's interest in coal mining and consolidated his antipathy toward his father. Bidermann and his fellow mineowners were running into
hard times and insisted that the miners should "share" their sufferings. He
suggested a drop in their wages, which Coleman stoutly refused to accept.
But he did go along with Bidermann's alternative. The miners were paid according to the tonnage of coal they sent back to the pithead on the screened
and moving beltway. The mesh in the screen was one-and-a-half inches
across, and lumps of coal smaller than that size dropped through. Now
Bidermann ordered the mesh size to be increased to two inches, which meant
that the miners would have to dig more coal for their wages, since many
more lumps would drop through the mesh.

The miners walked out, and once more scab labor and strikebreakers
were brought in to starve them into surrender. This strike had ended only
just before General Henry's death and funeral, and the doleful look on
Coleman's usually cheerful face was therefore due not to Boss Henry's
passing but to his own sense of guilt and disenchantment. His du Pont
relatives, however, put his low spirits down to the fact that he had recently
got married to Alice du Pont—yet another cousin. Alice, a fresh-faced but
simpleminded girl called Elsie by everyone in the family, had been married
off to Coleman purely for dynastic reasons, and the relatives imagined that
she would put a crimp in his playboy style. They were quite wrong in that;

he had no intention of changing his happy-go-lucky ways. He was, however, worried about how he was going to get away from his father and out of the unhappy coalfields of Kentucky.

The chief mourners at the General's funeral were, of course, the partners who would succeed him as controllers of the company. Alfred I. had earnestly hoped to be numbered among them, but his apotheosis had come too late, and his benefit from the old man's death was not the block of shares big enough to enable him to demand a partnership, which he had expected, but a legacy of fifty thousand dollars. It was not to be sneezed at, of course, especially as Bessie was still running up bills, but it was far from the important position in Du Pont he had envisioned for himself.

Another who thought he might gain something from the General's will was Lammot's eldest son, P. S. du Pont, now a student at M.I.T. and, according to all reports, doing brilliantly. He wished for at least a mention in the testament and maybe even a promise that, in memory of his father's contribution to Du Pont's rise to fame and fortune, he would be taken into the company after graduation. But he was not mentioned.

With Henry's death there were now four partners left to run the company, two sons and two nephews. Colonel Henry Algernon and William du Pont, the two sons, had also inherited their father's considerable fortune, amounting to many millions. Henry Algernon still knew nothing about explosives, and William was living away from the Brandywine, having taken over the running of the Repauno Mineral Company in New Jersey after the death of Lammot. But both assumed that since Henry had been master of the company during his lifetime and they were his heirs, one or the other of them should now take over the presidency. The only question was which one? Upon this they could not agree, and there arose between them bitter squabbles over precedence, which were to drag on for some time.

Meanwhile it was agreed that the two nephews and active partners, the brothers Eugene and Francis Gurney du Pont, would be put in charge of the day-to-day running of the company. The idea that this couple would in future hold in their hands the destinies of both company and family filled Alfred I. with profound gloom. Eugene, a kindly man, was good for subordinate jobs but would never make a leader or an innovator. Frank Gurney was a good chemist and knowledgeable around the yards, but he had a surly temper, treated the men like cattle, and know nothing about the world of business where Du Pont sold its product.

General Henry had chosen a bad time to die, for there was something of a business recession in the United States and markets were shrinking. But this was the kind of situation in which Du Pont had always thrived, pushing its way into the market with new or cheaper products, shouldering its rivals aside, or, if they were in really deep trouble, buying them up and increasing the might of the Du Pont empire. Alfred I. quickly discovered that under Eugene and Frank (particularly Frank, for he was the dominant brother) a recession was no moment to expand but one in which to retrench. One of the last projects General Henry had ordered before he died was the building of a new refinery on the Brandywine; for this he had used a reserve of employees he kept on a permanent payroll so that they would always be available. Now that the refinery was finished, Frank gave them the sack at a moment's notice. Some of the men, aggrieved at the shabby treatment they had received after years of service, got their revenge by acts of sabotage. One burned down the barn of Eleutherian Mills. Another caused an explosion in the yards that killed two men. Alfred I. heartily approved when the saboteurs were found and jailed, but that did not stop him roundly criticizing Frank for his ham-handed handling of the labor force and his lack of backbone in facing up to Du Pont's future.

He had, understandably, done an enthusiastic job of selling to the new Du Pont bosses the contract he had signed in Belgium with Coopals and Company. With the machinery he had agreed to buy beginning to arrive on the Brandywine, and the bills for it coming due, he was flabbergasted when Frank not only refused to honor the contract but told Alfred I. to send the machinery back. That Alfred I. had not only signed the contract but given his word on Du Pont's behalf cut no ice with his bad-tempered uncle, nor did his contention that there was a glorious and profitable future ahead for Du Pont once it geared up to produce Coopals cocoa and Coopals smokeless powder.

Alfred I. angrily told Frank that the only quality he had inherited from General Henry was his stubborn unwillingness to move with the times. He accused his uncle of being both backward and frightened, and that touched a nerve.

With Henry's death there was room on the board for one more active director. But if Frank Gurney du Pont had had any intention of offering the post to Alfred I., this quarrel changed his mind. Instead he asked his youngest brother, Alexis, to accept a partnership, an unworthy act of nepotism that almost drove Alfred I. to resign from the company. He was only persuaded not to do so by his two other cousins, Coleman and P. S. du Pont, who urged him to stay on and fight.

Yes, he would stay, and yes, he would fight. But in the meantime what was he going to do about the contract with Coopals and Company, and who was going to pay for all that machinery?

It was then that the United States Army came to Alfred I.'s rescue. Having heard about the contract he had signed for smokeless powder, the army, unlike Frank Gurney du Pont, thought he had pulled off a considerable feat. An official wrote to Du Pont to congratulate the company on the astuteness and farsightedness of its young representative. When Du Pont let it be known that the company was not going to go ahead with the contract, and that the new senior partner had no faith in the future of smokeless powder, the army officials were appalled. Not only was government pressure applied to make Frank change his mind, but Du Pont was promised a subsidy if it began manufacturing the new product.

Frank, with ill grace, did an about-face, and Alfred jubilantly told Bessie that his honor had been saved. But with men like Eugene and Frank Gurney du Pont in charge, could the company also be saved—from every kind of disaster?

Among those who observed all these goings-on with not a little bitterness was Lammot du Pont's widow, Mary. As she marched her children away from General Henry's graveside, her eldest son, P.S., at her side, she grieved again over her husband's death and wondered how he would have restored the shabby situation in which Du Pont now found itself. She too had little faith in the ability of the new partners to keep Du Pont supreme in the tough, competitive world of powder making, but what worried her even more than supremacy was survival. Could Eugene and Frank even keep the company's head above water in the rough economic climate that seemed to be looming? Would not the fear that so obviously gripped them now turn to panic when the really serious decisions had to be made? Were they capable of keeping Du Pont floating long enough for rescue to arrive, rescue in the form of another du Pont with Lammot's qualities?

She had no doubt in her mind who that rescuer could be. It was not just maternal pride that persuaded her that he was, in fact, walking at her side at this moment. Perhaps her eldest son, P.S., could never become the brilliant chemist Lammot had been. Even though his scholastic record was first class in every way, she suspected he did not have her husband's zeal for experimentation, his ability to mix ingredients in a test tube and bring more out than he put in, his flair; but of his qualities for leadership and enterprise she was in no doubt, and though he was still only eighteen he was already making her job as the single parent of ten children easier to handle.

The shock of Lammot's death had been closely followed by the birth of her eleventh child—one had died at age five—a girl they had christened Margaretta and promptly called Peg, and Mary's recovery from grief and the accouchement had been slow. It was P.S., only fourteen at the time, who had looked after the household, kept the other children in line, and saw to it that they were clean, fed, and went regularly to school. It was no surprise that by the time Mary was fit enough to get around again, all of the children were calling P.S. Dad, and now that he was at M.I.T. she even called him Dad herself when she wrote to him. Sometimes she felt that, with the exception of the place beside her in bed, he had all but taken over from Lammot.

The only other area, actually, in which he had not yet matched Lammot was financial acumen. Lammot had made a great deal of money during his years on the Brandywine and at Repauno, and when his finances were finally worked out, it would be found that each of the children had inherited, as had Irénée's five children, fifty thousand dollars. But Lammot had died intestate, and that meant all the money was put in trust, and it was through the children's guardian, Uncle Fred, that the courts paid out their allowances. Fred's idea of what was enough was not that of either Mary or P.S.

At M.I.T., P.S. was always complaining that he was short of money. Alfred I. had supplemented his allowance from Uncle Fred by taking up public boxing, but his cousin P.S. was not capable of such resourcefulness nor had he the time. He was too busy studying. Every month he wrote to his mother informing her that Uncle Fred was "late again" and enclosing a carefully detailed list of his expenses and his debts. If the allowance did not come through soon, he added, "I am afraid that I shall have to live in the Poor House next year and beg cold scraps to eat." Uncle Fred always paid up in the end, of course, and it was not as if the family was short of money. Mary took P.S. and half of her children to London and Paris in the summer of 1890 (Alfred I. and Bessie du Pont went with them), and they had a house on Cape May, in New Jersey, for the summer months, when Philadelphia and Delaware got too sticky. But Mary du Pont had ambitions for her son, and she seethed at the thought that what she considered his heritage was being wasted because of the incompetence of Frank, Eugene, and Alexis.

Among the shrewder members of the du Pont family who observed the new generation for indications of who the leaders and shapers of the future might be, there was little doubt that P.S. would be an important one to watch. Alfred I., of course, was the most obviously promising and experienced, but he was too hot-headed and impetuous, too quick to make enemies, and, in any case, too involved in messy domestic situations. Already there were rumors that all was not going well in his marriage with Bessie.

On the other hand, P.S.'s credentials seemed impeccable. He had never made any secret of the fact that his ambition was to join Du Pont, and all his studies were directed toward that goal. He was quiet, efficient, and imperturbable and never seemed to lose his temper. When he came down from Philadelphia or Boston on a visit to his relatives on the Brandywine, all the du Pont mothers purred with approval. Tall, quite good-looking, for all his long du Pont nose, he could be especially charming and thoughtful toward women, they noted, instead of rough and cavalier as so many du Pont men were apt to be. The mothers began to go through the lists of eligibles, wondering which of his cousins he would marry, which one would help him most in his Du Pont career, which one would produce for him the healthiest children to carry on the dynasty. It did not occur to any of them (as it did not occur to Mary) that he might not be of the marrying kind. They did not think it strange that he never seemed to have a female friend at M.I.T., and they giggled but did not consider it unusual (nor was it) when Mary announced that P.S. had developed a "heavy crush" on his M.I.T. tutor, Dr. D. Drown. She read them a letter relating his efforts to win the esteem and approval of the doctor, whom, he said, "I will do anything to please."

"During the last month or so," he wrote on May 3, 1890, "Miss Bragg, Tilson and I have become quite celebrated in the labs."

> D.D. has a great mania for cleanliness and to please him Miss B. had quite a display of clean glassware one day. This raised my envy to hear D.D. praise it so I also began to clean up my glass to a most brilliant polish. Tilson also followed suit & Miss B. went on cleaning & I did a little better than her until it has

reached a point where one cannot have the least spot or tarnish on any article without being thrown out of the race. D.D. is greatly amused at some of our peaks of cleanliness & has named the aisle which our desks are on "Show Alley" & it has become known as such throughout the land.

It just showed, as far as his mother and his relatives were concerned, that he was fascinated with every aspect of his work.

The du Pont women continued to look speculatively over their daughters, wondering which one would win him. And Mary, making her own plans, wrote:

> Ethel Clark came up to visit B. on Saturday and was with us until Wednesday. I think she is one of the nicest girls I know [she was also extremely well connected] and I should be very glad if *you* will try to *cut Frank out.*

Frank was one of his cousins.

There had been some doubt to begin with, once Eugene and Frank Gurney du Pont took over, whether P.S. would be allowed to come into the Du Pont organization, even as a humble member of the work force. Despite Frank's honeyed words after Lammot's death, he had never really gotten over his dislike of Lammot, and Mary suspected that his antipathy now extended to Lammot's family, particularly toward any member who showed signs of inheriting her husband's talents. She was well aware that between themselves, Frank and his wife Lisa often referred to her still as "the Jewess," and she knew better than to propagate her son's cause by personal intervention with them. The sheer delight of repulsing and humiliating her would demolish any argument she might put forward in P.S.'s favor.

But she had gained *some* admirers during her stay on the Brandywine, and they included powerful members of the family. One of them was the old General's widow, Aunt Louisa, who liked Mary's children and was delighted when they wrote her letters headed "Dear Grans." Another was Eugene's wife, Amelia, who was not simply the wife of one of the senior partners but also a du Pont herself (theirs had been another cousinly marriage). It is true that she had great ambitions for her own son, Lex, so far as the control of Du Pont was concerned, but she certainly saw no reason why Mary's son should not rise in the company with him, to finish up as Lex's vice-president, perhaps? Mary took the time to confer with Aunt Louisa and Amelia at Henry's funeral, and she never failed to bring up P.S.'s future in the firm whenever she visited the Brandywine from then on. She knew that Amelia was well aware of her husband's weak nature, and that it would be difficult to persuade Eugene to push the cause of someone Frank did not like. But Amelia had her own ways of exercising pressure on her husband, and all through P.S.'s final year at M.I.T. she kept urging Eugene to back the young man's cause and wear down Frank's resistance. On February 2, 1890, she wrote in quiet triumph to P.S. to tell him she had got him a place at Du Pont.

P.S. was delighted and immediately wrote back to Amelia to say that he could not wait to start working on the Brandywine. But his great problem now was to decide where he would live.

Mary, when consulted, wrote to say she thought she had a solution. She would move the whole family back to the Brandywine and build a house there for them all. How would that be? But then, after several trips to Wilmington, she had second thoughts. On April 10, 1890, she wrote to her son again to tell him that her du Pont relatives, no doubt those with eligible daughters, had made great efforts to dissuade her:

> You will marry very early in life and therefore it is hardly worthwhile for us to change our residence on your account. This seems to be the opinion of Uncle Frank, Aunt Betty and Grandpa. . . .
>
> I want to know if you have shaved off your moustache. Charles Lenning declares that you have but I hope it's not true. He has shaved off his and is a perfect fright without it.

But the moustache was gone and would not reappear in her lifetime. Nor would she live to see a Mrs. P. S. du Pont (though she did not die for another twenty-three years).

The employment rolls of the Du Pont company record that one Pierre Samuel du Pont reported for work for the first time at the Upper Yard on the Brandywine on September 1, 1890. The old expression "put through the mill" was appropriate in P.S.'s case. He worked his way through the composition house, the rolling mills, the press rooms, the graining and glazing mills, and so far as the work was concerned it was a completely rewarding experience. But his relationship with his bosses was a different matter.

Frank Gurney du Pont made it plain from the start that he did not welcome the name of P. S. du Pont on the company's employment rolls, and he set out to put the young man through the mill in the less literal but altogether more unpleasant sense of that phrase.

CHAPTER 9

Brotherly Hate

THOUGH Eugene and Frank Gurney du Pont between them were now running the Du Pont company, they were never allowed to forget that the senior member of the whole enterprise was the elder son of the late General. And that son, Colonel Henry Algernon du Pont, was not an easy man to deal with. If, in fact, he had not been the richest of the du Ponts, those who had to work with him would have said that he was impossible.

The Colonel (as all du Pont relatives and Du Pont employees failed to call him at their peril) occupied the largest estate on the Brandywine, the great house his father had given him when he resigned from the army and entered the family business. It was here, to Winterthur, that he had brought his wife, Pauline, declaring that she would live like a princess, and this was no empty promise. Henceforward, anything she asked for she got, even her own railroad station on the line running through the estate, and her own post office, plus, of course, everything from caviar to diamond tiaras. She deserved it for putting up so patiently with her husband.

The Colonel was, of course, the family's Civil War hero, although it was not until thirty years after the event that Congress got around to awarding him the congressional Medal of Honor. And there were some who said he received it less for his military feats as a young man than his powerful position in the Republican party as an older one.

But there was no doubt that he had been a brave soldier. The only trouble was that he never let anyone forget it. He told endless stories about his skill, resourcefulness, and courage in battle, and because he was so rich —he was now worth at least eleven million dollars—no one ever dared to stop him, this being one of the crosses his du Pont relatives had to bear. The other was his snobbish passion for the family history. After the death of Aunt Sophie, who had been the family historian, the Colonel inherited her papers and from then on appointed himself recorder of du Pont triumphs. He omitted the more dismal of the family failures, censored the scandals, and wiped out of the family tree any member whose origin might suggest that the du Ponts, perhaps, had not been the most distinguished emigrants ever to leave France. He began, in short, the du Pont tradition of whitewashing the family chronicle.

If the Colonel could have had his way—and he certainly tried to have it—one of the names he would have expunged from the record was that of his only brother, William. William du Pont was seventeen years the Colonel's junior, and in most normal families that would have made the older a lifelong friend, defender, and protector of the younger. But the Colonel was, in fact, William's bitterest enemy. It was as if they did not share the same blood, so strong was their mutual antipathy. William was an equable and peaceable young man who only occasionally gave vent to outbursts of temper, and then usually under intolerable strain. He had been brought up by his father to respect and admire his brother as a great hero, but after years of watching him strut and posture, and of being pushed and bullied by him, he had come to the conclusion (reached by George S. Kaufman many years later) that "all heroes are horses' asses." He took to mocking the Colonel and calling him Stuffed Shirt or Tin Soldier, and this considerably increased his brother's vicious feelings toward him.

Their first big clash had come after their father's death, when the General could no longer keep the peace between them. Colonel Henry Algernon du Pont, as the General's elder son, had claimed his place as the rightful successor to the presidency of Du Pont and had been immediately challenged by William who pointed out that the General had left them equal shares in the company and that he himself was far better qualified for the presidency. Henry Algernon did not conceal his boredom with the processes by which du Pont made its money; whereas he, William, had worked on the mixing vats and had proved his mettle by taking over Repauno after Lammot's death, making a success of it. If it was a question of which one of the two should take over, his appointment would clearly be of most value to Du Pont.

Thereupon the ill feeling between the two brothers came to a head, and a blazing row ensued. The Brandywine was soon bubbling with gossip as the families speculated about how it would come out. P.S. tried to pump Lex, the son of Cousin Eugene, to find out what was going on.

"Do you know if the Cousin Willie affair is known by Lex?" he asked his sister Lou in a letter dated May 4, 1890.

> I tried to find out but only succeeded in learning that Willie and the Col. do not speak and that the latter always visits the office by special appointment with Cousin Eugene lest he might meet his beloved brother. I suppose Lex has, like me, been forbidden to mention the change in the firm.

By "the change in the firm" P.S. meant that William and the Colonel, after increasingly bitter and fruitless encounters, had at last agreed to a compromise, which was, in fact, a victory for the elder brother. The Colonel would take the nominal title of president but would leave the management of the company in the hands of Cousins Eugene and Francis Gurney. William would take no part in the running of Du Pont's operation on the Brandywine but would keep control of the Repauno Mineral Company, in New Jersey. To make all partners equal, both the Colonel and William also agreed to sell enough shares to Eugene, Francis Gurney, and their brother Alexis so that their holdings would be exactly equal—twenty shares each, for the five partners.

It was tacitly understood, at least by William, that the Colonel would, in future, stay away from the Brandywine and not interfere with Eugene and Francis Gurney's handling of business. But if the Colonel had made any such pact, he had no intention of keeping it.

Though it was quite true that he was far more interested in Winterthur, its farms and gardens, his family documents, his railroads, and his political ambitions, he could not refrain from meddling in Du Pont's affairs. He insisted on visiting the company's office each morning, always ready with an awkward question calculated to confound or confuse the three incompetent brothers. And then, satisfied that he had reminded them of who he was, he would depart for Winterthur, no doubt to work up some new plot against his brother, William.

For the Colonel was certainly not finished with William yet. Determined to squeeze him out of the company affiliate in New Jersey, then out of Du Pont entirely, and, finally, out of the family life, he was digging into his brother's private affairs for the scandalous material that would help ruin him.

When he came to think about Alfred I.'s position in the company, even a stubborn man like Frank Gurney du Pont had to realize that he could not sit on the young man forever. Keeping him down might even rebound against Frank himself, because Alfred I. had plenty of powerful du Ponts around the creek who were obligated to him and who owed him a favor in return. He had fitted up practically all their homes with electricity, even bringing a thousand-volt alternating system to the vast halls of Winterthur through a special dynamo he and the Mathewson brothers had designed. He brought electric lights to Eugene's home and then persuaded his uncle to let him illuminate the Brandywine yards and the new offices, replacing the old, dangerous oil lamps with brilliant incandescents. He electrified Christ's Church, the family place of worship, did the same for Saint Joseph's, the powder men's church, and then strung an extension to the vicarage, the school, and the nearby convent, thus increasing the esteem in which he was held by the workmen and winning the blessings of priest and nuns.

Even Frank, nagged by his wife, finally succumbed and asked Alfred I. to bring him light. After that, how could he refuse to admit Alfred I.'s value to the company? For, of course, he was well aware that Alfred I. was not merely clever with electricity but also knew more about how to run a powder-making firm than Frank did. Toward the end of 1889 he upped Alfred I.'s salary to six thousand dollars a year, and told him that though his title would remain assistant superintendent of the yards, he would, in fact, now be in complete charge. Frank, who held on to the title of chief superintendent, would concentrate on the mysteries of administration.

But Alfred I. was not satisfied. By this time he was well aware of how valuable he was to Du Pont. Without him, anything could happen, for no other member of the family had the confidence of the powder men, and the ability to organize their working programs.

There was only one other du Pont working in the Hagley yards at that time: a cousin from the other branch of the family, Charles du Pont, a good, solid chemist six years Alfred I.'s senior but very much under his thumb. He could be a useful ally in putting pressure on the brothers, and Alfred I. persuaded Charles to join him when he bearded the partners in their den and demanded recognition of their worth. Alfred I. and Charles wanted a partnership. Eugene, who had been expecting such a maneuver, promptly offered them each five-percent interest in the company. Charles was about to accept when Alfred I. burst in and indignantly rejected the offer. Didn't the brothers realize how much Du Pont now relied upon the two cousins? What would happen if they decided to leave? Who in the family was capable of taking their place? Instead of producing such insulting appeasements, Eugene and Frank should face the situation squarely and reward Charles and himself with what they really deserved—a partnership with at least a ten-percent interest for each.

While a pop-eyed and panicky Charles, and an outwardly self-confident Alfred I., waited the partners retired to the Colonel's room to consider. When they came back, it was evident that they had come to a very painful decision. The five partners (Eugene, Frank, the Colonel, William, and Alexis) would each sell four percent of their shares in Du Pont to the two younger men, giving them a total of ten percent each. The price would be $225,000 for each ten percent. Could they find the money? They could. Charles borrowed his share from William du Pont, who was all in favor of cutting into the Colonel's holding, even if it meant losing some of his own. Alfred I. used $25,000 of the legacy left him by the old General, $100,000 from his father's legacy, and borrowed $100,000 from Uncle Fred at seven percent.

He was twenty-five years old and now a partner in Du Pont. He would have been the happiest young man in the world had it not been for his life with Bessie, which was rapidly going to pieces.

In 1889, the same year that he became a partner, Bessie du Pont gave her husband a second daughter, christened the same name as her mother, though she was known to everybody as Bep. From then on, according to a remark Alfred I. once made to a close associate, he did not have any further sexual connection with his wife for a decade, and indeed no more children were born during that period. There appears to have been precious little emotional or domestic understanding between them either. They moved into separate bedrooms, and except for those occasions when Alfred I. squatted in front of the hearth with his two daughters, put on a Fourth of July fireworks display for the local children, hosted a dinner, or attended a du Pont function, husband and wife began to lead separate lives and grated on each other when they were forced to make social contact.

Was it Alfred I. or Bessie who decided on a ten-year hiatus in their sexual relations with each other? No one can now answer that question with certainty, although it might be relevant to remember that when the marriage did finally come to an end, it was Alfred I. who remarried twice more, and who was known to be having relationships with other women in between his subsequent marriages; whereas Bessie du Pont remained rigidly and determinedly single (and almost certainly celibate) for the rest of her life. But what was it that drove her husband from the family bed— and then just as suddenly back again? An unhappy experience with maternity (Bessie's first two babies were both difficult births) and a decision on her part not to risk it again? A frigidity that repelled or restrained her husband, who, it was well known, was a man whose enthusiasms were easily deflated?

Or was it the haunting presence of his youngest brother, Louis, who, from 1890 onward, often came to stay at Swamp Hall? Years had passed, but Louis had never got over Bessie's abandonment of him in favor of Alfred I. Ever since, he had let his life go to pieces and was now a wreck of the once-promising poet and literary young man. He had collected his legacy as soon as he reached twenty-one and had disappeared on a wild binge during which his brother lost all trace of him. He flunked out of Yale, then went on to Harvard for a year at the law school but failed there too because he spent most of his time drinking in saloons or carousing with the girls in New York brothels (where he was once picked up in a police raid). In between these periods he would suddenly turn up at Swamp Hall and moon around the house, looking soulfully at Bessie, who treated him like an importunate puppy.

Alfred I. had first become aware that Louis was still carrying the torch for Bessie when his middle brother, Maurice, came home from Europe at last and caused a family scandal. He had married the young girl he met in Ireland, and she was not in any way the kind of girl the du Ponts considered an appropriate wife for one of their kith and kin. By the 1890s the du Pont family thought of themselves as a sort of Franco-American aristocracy. It had begun to be tacitly understood among them that when the question of marriage arose, their eligible sons and daughters should choose their wives and husbands as carefully as the royal family of England, and much more carefully than the French and English aristocracy, who were beginning to pick up chorus girls and actresses and actually marry them. For practical purposes, and for dynastic reasons, the du Ponts preferred to continue their system of intermarriage, cousin to cousin, but if one of their eligibles *had* to go outside the blood to find a mate, that mate should be from either an aristocratic family (preferably European) or a really rich and successful line of WASP Americans. Sometimes an exception was made in favor of a non–du Pont male (usually one working for the Du Pont company), but only if he was obviously going to be so invaluable to the company—or to a rival—that marrying him off to one of the daughters was the only method of making sure he would not get away.

But a du Pont was expected to marry someone with *connections.* Any of them who failed to do so, who made a love match with someone not measuring up to du Pont criteria, caused shock and dismay inside the family —and also usually created a sensation in the American press, which shared the du Ponts' snobbish opinion of themselves.

So when Maurice du Pont, a charmer but otherwise largely untalented and unambitious, encountered the daughter of an Irish innkeeper and not only fell in love with her but married her, everyone on the Brandywine was appalled. The American press hastened to reveal the family's "shame" to the nation, and the New York *Herald* joyfully headlined its interview with Maurice: "HE MARRIED A BARMAID." The Wilmington *Evening Journal* (which was not owned by the family; the du Pont paper suppressed the story) called it "the sensation of two continents" and revealed that the bride was called "Tottie." (In fact, she was named Margery and sometimes called Meg.)

P. S. du Pont's sister Lou wrote to her brother at M.I.T.:

> Of course you have heard and seen all the accounts in the various papers of Maurice's marriage. Alas, for poor Maurice, the story is true. Miss FitzG. did stand behind the bar in the Green's Hotel, Queenstown. That morning when we stopped there did you see something of her? You can just imagine what a terrible hubbub this affair has created in the family. I never heard as much talking in all my life & I think the bride and groom may well be thankful that the Atlantic rolls between them and their enraged relatives. For my part, I think Maurice took a step he will repent always, but as far as in my power I will try to be kind & friendly to the girl, for his sake.

But Maurice decided not to allow the Atlantic to separate him and his new bride from the Brandywine, and he brought her back home. He was distinctly chagrined when the doors of all the houses of his most influential relatives were slammed in their faces. His aunt Amelia remarked:

"A London barmaid would have been bad enough. But an Irish barmaid!"

On the other hand, Alfred I., after the initial shock during which he referred to his brother as "that blooming idiot Maurice," welcomed him and his bride to Swamp Hall and informed them that they were to consider it their home as long as they remained in America. Margery, a pink-cheeked Celtic blonde with vivid blue eyes and a roguish smile, quickly won his heart. Within a few days he was both beguiled by her personality and as astonished as she was by the frigid refusal of the rest of the du Ponts to have her in their houses. He hoped she would help him cheer up his brother Louis, who was staying with them at the time. But Louis took one look at Maurice and Margery, fondly arm in arm, then burst into tears and tore out of the house. Alfred I. did not see him again for months.

In the meantime his relations with Bessie continued to grow more and more acerbic. Maurice and Margery eventually departed because they "could not bear to see the way Bessie [treated] Alfred." His two older sisters vowed they would never set foot in Swamp Hall again because they were appalled at the way Bessie "baited and taunted" him (about what they did not say).

To ease his frustration over the difficulties of his family life, Alfred I. had taken to hunting again. He purchased a small island in Chesapeake Bay, on the Little Choptank River, which could only be reached by ferryboat, and there he built a four-room shack, installed a couple of ex-slaves named Jim and Araminta Cook to look after it, and came across for weekends, banging away at bobtail quail and taking out his tension on these fortunately lightning-quick birds. Later on, when he felt a little less tense and misogamous, he began bringing friends across to join him and delighted in showing off the small electrically driven boat he had designed (with the help of Edison) for threading through the island's narrow waterways.*

He still had his orchestra, of course, though it no longer dared to rehearse at Swamp Hall, and the Tankopanicums by now had a new mem-

---

* Probably the first of its kind, the boat was driven by power from chlorine cells. Later Alfred I. replaced it with another boat powered by wet batteries of his own invention.

ber in the person of the latest recruit to the Brandywine, P. S. du Pont, who played the piano like one who had never had a lesson in his life. Nor had he. Furthermore, he could not read music—all right for popular airs but difficult when one of Alfred I.'s own compositions (for he wrote music, too) was being played. P.S. tried to concentrate while Alfred I. hummed the melody, but inevitably he made mistakes that even the rest of the orchestra could not cover up for him. A favorite family story tells of a well-attended concert in Wilmington. After one disastrous crescendo of wrong notes, Alfred I. could scarcely continue conducting, so angry was he at his cousin's maladroitness. On the way home Alfred I., still smouldering with annoyance, finally turned to his cousin and burst out:

"Pierre, when you made that terrible blunder tonight, I nearly came over to you, and I wished I had had a baseball bat in my hand instead of my baton."

"Alfred," replied P.S., soothingly, "if I'd had a baseball bat, I'd have handed it to you."

In November 1892 Louis appeared again out of nowhere and asked Alfred I. to put him up at Swamp Hall. He was only twenty-four years old but looked older than his brother; his hands shook, and alternately shamefaced and defiant, confessed that he had left Harvard and had no idea what he was going to do next. When Bessie came on the scene, she told him he needed cheering up, so that night she and Alfred I. were going to take him to the Wilmington Club Ball. She saw to it that he had a good time, too, saved several dances for him, and flirted, teased, and drank with him as she never did nowadays with Alfred I. But the next day, and the day after, he was again the puppy, always getting under Bessie's feet, and she had no time for him.

On December 2, Louis went back to the Wilmington Club where he retired to the library. It was midafternoon when a shot was heard. A club servant rushed to find out where it came from. In the library he discovered Louis du Pont sprawled across a chair, a pistol on the floor, and a bullet through his head.

The story reached the Wilmington *Evening Journal*, which was immune even to du Pont pressure, and while the family recoiled from the scandal down came the reporters from New York and Philadelphia to start a train of sensational speculation, broadly hinting that Bessie was the cause of the tragedy. At the coroner's inquiry no one mentioned Louis's unrequited passion, nor was Alfred I.'s routine testimony examined or questioned. Bessie did not put in an appearance.

The scandal took some time to die down, and while it kept making the headlines Alfred I., genuinely grieved at the loss of his brother, lapsed once again into one of those black periods he had not experienced since he was a boy, and avoided everyone on the Brandywine, particularly his friends among the powder men. If he blamed himself, or Bessie, for Louis's death, he said nothing about it to anyone. But at Swamp Hall the dark, unhappy atmosphere reeked even more of bitterness and strife. A young relative from the South, Ellen LaMotte, had come to be a companion for Bessie, and for a long time she took her mistress's part in the marital antagonisms. But after Louis's death she swung even more vehemently to Alfred I.'s side. Soon she was reporting in her letters home that the couple had begun quarreling violently, and that Bessie often spent the night following Alfred I. from room to room, quite often screaming at him. Ellen had become so unhappy that she asked permission to leave Swamp Hall and return home.

P. S. du Pont had all the pride and enthusiasm of his forebears when he started work with the company on the Brandywine, and he wrote to his mother back in Philadelphia that his chest swelled as he walked through the gates of the powder yards for the first time as a Du Pont employee.

"This is where my father, grandfather and great grandfather had entered the Company's employ," he reminded Mary, and added that he could not wait to get down to work. His cousin Charles gave him his first assignment, intended to utilize the chemical scholarship he had absorbed at M.I.T., plus, it was hoped, the inventive skill he had inherited from his father. But almost immediately upon entering the company's laboratories, he got a taste of how Du Pont was being allowed to run down. In Lammot's day the laboratories on the Brandywine had been the most modern in the nation, and chemists had come from all over the world to see and admire them. P.S. was appalled at their seediness now, and later, recalling his shock, wrote:

> The laboratory, so called, was in a deplorable condition. . . . The building was a one story addition to the Saltpetre Refinery, heavy stone walls and not too adequate windows. Equipment was almost nothing. A common kitchen range and one small spirit lamp were the only means of heating for chemical

work. No gas or electrical facilities, and a common kitchen sink and one ¾ inch tap the water supply. Distilled water came from a supply prepared for use in the refinery; the workmen called it "still-water" which referred more to its escape from ill-treatment more or less in its original condition than to any attained purity. Any unusual impurity was accounted for by the words "she must have boiled over." The laboratory contained no chemical reagents for making ordinary tests and the chemical balance did not deign to respond to the added weight of a few milligrams.

What the newspapers termed "the big gun of the Powder Trust," and certainly the largest maker of explosives in the nation, if not the world, did not even keep its labs in order. P.S. also was indignant at the lack of common business sense he saw all around him. Du Pont still relied on the Powder Trust for its share of the market, and the control of selling prices, despite the fact that the Trust had not bothered to modernize itself or change its image since its formation in 1872. After Lammot's death General Henry had purchased from the family two thirds of his share in the Repauno Mineral Company, giving Du Pont fifty-five percent of the stock in the company. Yet Cousin Eugene had never tried to integrate its dynamite and other high explosives operations into the parent organization, nor had he made any projection studies or efficiency plans or even separated company from personal spending by the partners. But for the moment there was little P.S. could do.

For eighteen months he quietly labored to learn all he could in the powder yards. He did not, as Alfred I. had done, make friends among the workers in the yards. That was not his nature; he was far too shy. But he wandered around and kept his eyes and ears open, he studied records, he followed the processes through, and he strove to improve conditions in the labs. At the end of this period he realized that the Brandywine had nothing more to teach him, and he was glad when Frank Gurney du Pont offered him a transfer. The United States Army had been joined by the navy in exerting pressure on the company to proceed with the production of smokeless powder, and the brothers had reluctantly given the go-ahead for the construction of a new factory at Carney's Point, New Jersey, just across the Delaware River from Wilmington. It had been decided that Frank would take over the running of the new factory, while Alfred I. would assume complete charge of day-to-day activities (though not administration) on the Brandywine Creek. Frank needed a scientist and chemist of his own caliber to get smokeless powder into production, and he asked P.S. to join him.

Mary du Pont had, by this time, come back to the du Pont colony on the Brandywine where she then built a house, called Saint Amour, for herself and her family, and it was arranged that from there P.S. should commute by ferry to Carney's Point each day. By now Mary really could not do without his help. She had begun to suffer from bouts of migraine headache that prostrated her or forced her to go away on trips, usually to stay with her brother, Henry Belin, and his family at his home in Scranton, Pennsylvania. It was the humid climate and general atmosphere of the Brandywine that seemed to bring on her migraines, and she really should never have returned there; but she was ambitious for her children, and among the du Pont colony there was a better chance of advancement for her sons and good marriages for her daughters. Her eldest daughter, Lou, who had grown up to be a highly intelligent and self-confident young woman, ran the household and controlled the servants at Saint Amour, but Mary still relied on P.S. to give advice to all her sons and daughters and keep them in line. He was the only one who could control them, and when they called him Dad, as they continued to do, it was as much a recognition of his place in their lives as a nickname.*

So henceforward, though he left at dawn and did not reach home again much before nine in the evening, he made the daily journey to Carney's Point through rain, snow, ice, and fog, ready, exhausted or not, to deal with the family's problems. Should his brother Bese (Henry Belin du Pont), two years his junior and just graduated from M.I.T., go to work for Du Pont, and if so, could P.S. persuade Alfred I. to give him a job? Should his twenty-two-year-old sister Sophie encourage the latest young man who had come calling upon her? She confessed she liked him a lot, but was she strong enough to think about marriage? Like Bese, she was weak about the chest, and childbirth might be the death of her. And what about his next brother, Irénée, who wanted to go into business with a friend? And his other brother, Lammot, who was complaining, as all of them had done before him, that Uncle Fred was periodically late in sending his allowance to M.I.T.?

In the midst of these domestic problems, he wrestled at Carney's Point with the processes of smokeless powder. Frank was beginning experiments to see whether the smokeless formulas Alfred I. had brought

---

* Even some of his nephews soon began to seek his help, and one of them regularly wrote him letters beginning "Dear Uncle Dad."

home from Belgium, combined with the United States Navy experiments with guncotton, could be adapted for use in large-caliber guns aboard ship. But the government contracts the company had received were for limited quantities of powder and might not be renewed. It was therefore desirable to develop a commercial use for smokeless powder. Should guncotton be adapted for shotguns and other sporting weapons? While Frank wrestled with the big guns, he assigned P.S. to work on shotgun powder and made it clear that he expected results. It was a challenge the young man was happy to accept. And luck was with him.

After a few experiments and a number of visits to the Navy Torpedo Station at Newport, Rhode Island, he realized that large-caliber guncotton would never be suitable for shotguns or rifles. But from one of those visits he brought back a quantity of wet guncotton pulp manufactured at the torpedo station, and when he started to break it down in the lab at Carney's Point, he recognized it as an old friend from his M.I.T. days.

> Without any very definite plan in mind [he wrote later], I transferred some of my guncotton to a pint or quart bottle about half-filled with water, shook it well and added some nitro-benzol while continuing the shaking. To my surprise the mixture separated into a mass of quite even spherical grains which remained apart—did not return to a single mass or adhere together. This was the discovery of Du Pont smokeless powder for shotguns.

He rushed around to Frank Gurney du Pont to demonstrate his discovery and was told by an initially skeptical and then none-too-pleased senior that his experiment was all very well, but it needed "improvements." These Frank said he would perfect himself. If any "improvements" were made they were of a minor nature, but they did enable Frank to have his name beside that of his nephew when the patent for the new process came to be granted.

P.S. bore his boss no grudge for forcing him to share the credit. As he wrote later:

> The inventive genius of Francis G. du Pont brought about the ultimate success of the chance discovery, therefore, it is proper to say that he was the real *inventor,* I the chance *discoverer.* The patent was issued in our joint names, which to me was quite sufficient recognition.

On the other hand, Frank now proceeded to do things to P.S. that he considered to be grossly unfair, and they gradually began to make his life at Carney's Point insupportable.

It was while P.S. was still breaking in at Du Pont that the bitter enmity between his two uncles, Colonel Henry Algernon and William du Pont, finally came to a head. It seemed that the Colonel, after some painstaking detective work, had finally got the goods on his detested brother. He called a meeting of the senior members of the family and in tones of mingled indignation and outrage revealed that William was betraying his wife, May (also a du Pont cousin). He had taken a mistress and had been seen making regular visits to the hussy's home in New Castle.

If the Colonel had expected this news to shock the rest of the family and infuriate them as much as it undoubtedly had him, he was disappointed. Du Pont men had been known to take mistresses before—look at Uncle Fred and Coleman, for instance. It was, in any case, well known to them all that the marriage between William and May du Pont had been a cousinly union that had gone wrong from the start, and neither had ever made any pretense about their loathing for each other. The family was not at all shaken by the news that William had looked elsewhere for female company and compensation, and they indicated they would not be surprised if May likewise looked for a suitable man. Anyway, what did the Colonel expect them to do about it? Drum William out of the family and the company because he was cheating on his wife? If that were to happen, they would soon be snowed under with resignations.

It was then that the Colonel dropped his bombshell: William's mistress, he revealed, was Mrs. Annie Rogers Zinn, and, of course, they all knew who she was. They did indeed. The beautiful young Mrs. Zinn was one of the belles of fashionable New Castle, the show town on the Delaware River, and until recently she had been a regular guest in du Pont houses. But in the past few months she had been involved in divorce proceedings against an exceedingly profligate as well as unfaithful husband; and that, even though there was a certain sympathy toward her, put her beyond the pale as far as the du Ponts were concerned. No-fault or not, divorcées were no longer the family's social equals, and even Mary du Pont, who had been a close friend, was being advised to cross Mrs. Zinn off her visiting list. The situation had created something of a family crisis in

November 1890, just after P.S. had joined Du Pont, when Mary decided to give a party. Should Mrs. Zinn be invited, and would the family be mortally offended if she were? P.S. had written to his sister Lou on November 11, 1890:

> On Sunday when we were enumerating the party guests Anne [Alfred I.'s sister] mentioned Mrs. Zinn and you intimated that she was to be asked. As you had told me before that she was not to be I intended asking you about it but forgot to do so.
>
> I hope that Mamma has decided not to cut her for I think that her position is entirely too uncertain to warrant doing so. You know the present stories blame Mr. Z entirely so I think it very hard to make the wife suffer for it.
>
> You know that a woman in such a position must have enough trouble without being forsaken by her former friends and that being cut by our family may mean a great deal in Wilmington. Hoping you may reconsider the case, I remain, Your loving brother.

Mary and Lou had decided to damn the relatives and invite her—a decision they came to regret, for the elegant and lovely Mrs. Zinn was snubbed by the du Pont women and, on their orders, ignored by the du Pont men. Alfred I. and P.S., who hated dancing, were forced to rush around to recruit their friends and bully them into filling up Mrs. Zinn's card.

Now here she was again—William's paramour! And not only that— the Colonel waited while they grew silent—William was now so taken with the woman that he intended to marry her and had already told May he was getting a divorce in order to do so.

That, of course, made it an entirely different situation, and the du Ponts audibly gasped at the news. There had *never* been a divorce in the family, and it was not to be borne. William must be made to see reason. Think of the scandal. Think of the reports in the press. William must be told that he could keep his mistress, but at all costs he must neither divorce May nor marry Mrs. Zinn. It was out of the question. The Colonel must talk to his brother.

The Colonel said he had done so and had been told to mind his own business. William was determined to go through with it. He had already left for South Dakota to establish residence and obtain a divorce.

In that case, the du Ponts agreed, steps must be taken.

"Leave it to me," said the Colonel, with satisfaction.

When William du Pont returned to Wilmington with his South Dakota divorce, he approached the authorities for a license to marry Mrs. Annie Rogers Zinn. He was asked for documentation, and so was Mrs. Zinn. Then weeks went by. The certificate was not forthcoming. Finally, exasperated by what were obviously deliberate delaying tactics, William and Annie sailed for London and were married there. But when their honeymoon was over, they did not return to the Brandywine, for the whole of the du Pont clan had made it plain that neither William nor his new bride would be welcome.

William was all for brazening it out, but Annie, already only too well aware of what a dose of du Pont ostracism was like, persuaded him otherwise. He resigned his presidency of the Repauno Mineral Company, he resigned his partnership in the Du Pont company (though he retained his shares), and he departed with his wife for Virginia, where he set up as a gentleman farmer at Montpelier, James Madison's old estate.

The Colonel did not care where his brother had gone, so long as he was out of the company, out of the Brandywine, and out of the family.

"I never wish to hear my brother's name mentioned again," he announced, and meant it.

CHAPTER 10

Coup de Grace for Uncle Fred

I~N the middle of the eighteenth century one of the du Pont connections,
Pierre de Montchanin,* spent some time in Switzerland, and there one day,
while riding in the Bernese Oberland, he took a bad fall when his mount
put its foot in a rabbit hole. The horse bolted in fright and Montchanin
would have had a long walk home if another rider had not happened by
and, seeing his plight, galloped across the fields and expertly reined in the
horse, bringing it back to him. When Montchanin looked up to thank the
horseman, he saw that his rescuer, though dressed in breeches and riding
astride, was a girl. She turned out to be the athletic, and extremely pretty,
daughter of a Geneva merchant, and within minutes they had fallen in
love. They arranged to meet secretly and rode together often after that,
and all was proper so long as they remained in their saddles. But when
they dismounted, the inevitable happened. Afterward, young Montchanin

* Anne de Montchanin, his sister, was to become the first wife of the du Pont
patriarch, Pierre Samuel.

fervently promised that as soon as he could let his parents know, they would announce their betrothal.

So far as the girl was concerned, it could not come a moment too soon, for she discovered that someone had seen her and threatened to tell her parents. But when she revealed this to young Montchanin, he took fright and the next day, without telling the girl or anyone else, mounted his horse and rode swiftly into France. Saddened but also infuriated at her lover's betrayal, the girl is said to have dressed in chevalier's clothing, glued a false moustache and beard to her pretty face, and galloped off in pursuit.

She came upon her fleeing swain on a lonely road near Annecy, and there, brushing and bumping his horse repeatedly, she forced him to dismount. Then, claiming to be her own brother, she leaped to the ground, pulled out her sword, and vowed to avenge the family dishonor. Being as good with a rapier as she was with a horse, she soon had Montchanin disarmed and at her mercy, awaiting the coup de grace.

It was then that she ripped off her whiskers and gave him a choice. Death—or marriage. He married her.

It seems almost certain that in Louisville, on the night of May 15, 1893, Uncle Fred was offered a similar alternative. Unfortunately, Uncle Fred, in contrast to Montchanin, hesitated. The result was a bullet in the heart and death a few minutes later.

In the circumstances, Uncle Fred's hesitation was understandable. Even though he was an unkempt, modest, and unassuming man, he was a du Pont, and the woman was far from being the young, beautiful daughter of a well-to-do merchant. She was, in fact, Maggie Payne, the madam whose brothel Uncle Fred had been patronizing so faithfully for many years and whose personal services he had long been given without charge. It had been a very pleasant arrangement until Maggie Payne made a highly unprofessional error and became pregnant. When she told Uncle Fred about it and said the baby was his, he replied that it could not possibly be so, since he was far too old to become a father (he was sixty at the time). A quarrel began when Maggie insisted, and Fred threatened to leave the bordello and never come back. In return, Maggie threatened to tell the world about the affair and create a scandal in all the newspapers.

Exactly what happened next no one has ever discovered. All that is known is that somehow a revolver appeared and a struggle ensued; then a single shot was fired and Uncle Fred fell dead with a bullet in the heart, spread-eagled across the bed of the best-known madam south of Baltimore. Maggie hastily dragged him over to a chair and, in case anyone wandered in, stuck a cigar between Uncle Fred's lifeless lips.

She did not call the police but conveyed a discreet message to Uncle Fred's brother, Bidermann du Pont, who immediately went to work. Within the hour a doctor and undertaker were in the house on West York Street. The doctor wrote out a certificate to the effect that an elderly citizen of Bowling Green, Kentucky, a certain James G. Johnson, had had a heart attack while disporting himself with one of the girls. The body (which had been carefully wiped clean of bloodstains) was put into a coffin, the undertaker announcing that he was taking it to the railroad depot for shipment to Johnson's home.

Instead, the hearse waited until evening and then discreetly made its way to the back entrance of Bidermann's mansion, Central Park, in Louisville. And it was from there, on the afternoon of May 16, 1893, that the announcement was made that Alfred Victor du Pont, director of the National Bank of Louisville, director of the Central Coal and Iron Company, director of the Johnson Steel Company, director of streetcar companies all the way from Indianapolis to Brooklyn, philanthropist, and beloved local eccentric, had died of "effusive apoplexy." The citizens mourned his passing, because he had been genuinely liked. The Louisville *Commercial,* in the course of a long obituary, referred to "the quiet and simple character of his life, unbroken in the scene of his death." And when a local memorial service was held, everybody turned up to pay a last tribute, even Maggie Payne and her girls, who stayed discreetly in the background. The police, who by now knew the truth about Unicle Fred's death, left her unmolested.

Nor did they do anything about it when a few days later, in response to a tip-off, the Cincinnati *Enquirer* came out with a front-page story about the true circumstances of the death. The paper was snapped up, and within hours every copy had been sold. But no one demanded an inquiry. The Louisville *Courier-Journal* even carried a front-page rebuke to those who paid credence to the "sensational and incorrect reports published in newspapers in other cities." It was the general wish that Uncle Fred be allowed to die as he had lived—discreetly.

Uncle Fred died intestate, leaving an estate amounting to more than two million dollars. Under the laws of Kentucky, half went to his mother, who was still living, and the rest was divided among his living brother, Bidermann, his living sister, Paulina, and the heirs of his two dead brothers,

Irénée du Pont (Alfred I.'s father) and Lammot du Pont (P.S.'s father). This meant that Alfred I., his two sisters, and one living brother got $62,500 each, and P.S. and his nine living brothers and sisters got $25,000 each. (Bidermann and Paulina du Pont, of course, got $250,000 each.)

This was a nice little nest egg, but hardly a huge fortune, for the two cousins Alfred I. and P.S. And of course, their third cousin, Coleman, as Bidermann's son, received nothing from the court-superintended division. But Uncle Fred had not forgotten them. It so happened that shortly before his death he went up to the Brandywine to stay with his mother. Now close to ninety and no longer the shrew who had once persecuted one daughter-in-law into the lunatic asylum and sneered at another's Jewish blood, Meta du Pont was an old woman filled with regrets and anxious to make amends. Uncle Fred told her that he wanted to leave something substantial to Coleman, Alfred I., and P.S.

Meta had plenty of money of her own, and under the division of Fred's estate she was now to get an additional one million dollars. Half of it was in the stock of Fred's favorite enterprise, the Johnson Company, which he and Tom Johnson had started to make rails, switches, and curved track and crossover points for streetcar systems. Meta now decided she would hand over this block of stock valued at half a million dollars, to be divided equally among Coleman, Alfred I., and P.S.

That gift could not have come at a better time for any of them. It gave immediate independence to Coleman, for whom life in the coalfields was now intolerable, and he and his wife and family took off almost immediately for Johnstown, Pennsylvania, where he became general manager of the steel company. Alfred I. found he now had more than enough to pay off the one hundred thousand dollars he had borrowed from Uncle Fred to buy his partnership in Du Pont. As for P. S. du Pont, in the first year of holding Johnson Company stock he received dividends of ten thousand dollars. He felt giddily rich. At twenty-three he had a personal fortune of one hundred seventy-five thousand dollars and practically his whole life before him.

But how was he going to deal with the runaround he was getting at Du Pont?

The death of Uncle Fred had put even heavier responsibilities on P.S.'s shoulders so far as his brothers and sisters were concerned, and that made him cautious in his business dealings with Frank Gurney du Pont. The court had made P.S. official guardian, in Fred's place, of the seven remaining children who were still under twenty-one, and he had control of the five hundred thousand dollars held in trust for them. He was appalled at the thought because, as he said, he "hardly knew the difference between a ledger book and legerdemain; at least they were both equally incomprehensible" to him.

He decided to go out to Johnstown to look over the plant in which he now had such a large interest and also to seek advice about investments. Uncle Fred's surviving partner, Tom Johnson, advised him to buy into streetcar stocks, which were booming at the time, and Coleman gaily told him to take a flyer in the stock market, where he himself was already beginning to make a considerable fortune. P.S. decided to be prudent, and although he did buy some streetcar stocks in his own behalf, he kept most of the children's money in safe and solid, if low-paying, mortgages. But he liked what he saw of the Johnson Company, and was happy when both Johnson and Coleman told him he would be welcome to join them there whenever he felt like it.

The trouble was, he did not want to leave Du Pont or the Brandywine. So far as the company was concerned, he felt he had a right to belong because of his blood and his line, and moreover, he was convinced he could do more than his uncles to improve its fortunes. He enjoyed working in the powder labs and experimenting to improve the product. He found Du Pont an exciting enterprise and feared that making rails for streetcar systems would be boring by comparison.

The only worry was Uncle Frank. P.S. had always been an even-tempered young man, and even when moved or disturbed, he seldom showed it to the outside world. But he had begun to confide to his sister Lou, as well as his brothers Belin, Irénée, and Lammot, that he was beginning to "dislike" Frank Gurney du Pont, and when P.S. used the word *dislike,* his family knew he meant hate. P.S. was well aware of the strength of his antipathy toward his boss, for it had turned life at Carney's Point into a chore instead of a joy. But when Lou advised him to be patient, he showed her a passage from a letter written by his ancestor and namesake, Pierre Samuel du Pont I, which, he said, helped to constrain him:

> There has always existed in our family a fault against which you should guard yourselves . . . it is a stubbornness, an inflexibility or tenacity of character which makes us very constant to our friends but very implacable to our enemies. I have seen

examples of this in my father who disapproved the same disposition in his elder brother. I myself am frequently conscious of being governed by it. Your aunt alone I have found without this grave fault, but I myself have nursed animosities too long. One should cultivate in himself the finer feelings and repress hateful passions.

P.S. tried to control his temper and be patient, but Frank made it difficult. He had now brought his son Francis I. to work at Carney's Point, and though Francis was inexperienced and three years P.S.'s junior, Frank gave him all the choice jobs and made it plain he should have preference.

In 1895 P.S.'s brother Belin du Pont graduated from M.I.T. and, thanks to Alfred I.'s help, was taken to work in the powder yards on the Brandywine. He served first in the saltpeter refinery and was appalled by the old-fashioned way in which it ran. "Even if the Refinery should burn down," he complained in a letter to P.S., "they would probably build it up just as it is now or if any changes were made I am sure I would not be consulted."

P.S. wrote back that if he thought conditions on the Brandywine were bad, he should see Carney's Point. They had had a sharp winter that year and Frank Gurney had been taken completely by surprise. "There is almost nothing for me to do," he told Belin,

the plant being practically shut down owing principally to F.G.'s methods of doing things. The gun-cotton dripping rooms are hardly heated at all and it is impossible for the men to do anything as they can not wrap up much and must wear rubber gloves. The ice is about one or two inches thick all over the floors as all the splash and drip of water freezes immediately. Our powder presses are also in a very bad way. We are using only one but we have to keep the others running [constantly] in order to prevent freezing. It is all the same old trouble of not looking ahead and making provision for things that are bound to occur sooner or later.

His head told him to leave the organization and go where his money was, but his heart urged him to stay.

Also, he relished life at Saint Amour with his mother and family, and he liked mixing with the rest of the du Ponts on the Brandywine. He felt at home with them and even had a warm spot for his pompous uncle,

Colonel Henry Algernon, who was always kind (if regal) to his family.
P.S. looked forward to the family parties, the charades, the parlor games,
and though he was surrounded by girls, and teased about them, they did not
seem to make him uncomfortable, as females from "outside" did. He knew
that his uncle Eugene and aunt Amelia hoped he would marry their daughter, whom his sister Lou always scornfully referred to as Your Bride, but
not even their overt matchmaking disturbed him. He was sorry whenever
he missed a party, and always asked Lou to fill him in with all the details
when he happened to be away.

So long as he was around, P.S. entered into the fun and games but at
the same time watched over his brothers and sisters like a fond parent; and
as Mary's migraines increased and she was less and less able to take charge
of family affairs, he and his sister Lou became father and mother of the
brood. Those were the days when not even money bought you immunity
from the diseases that today occur so infrequently as to make newspaper
headlines. Quite often whole communities succumbed to outbreaks of
typhoid, and dozens of deaths were accepted as normal.

Lou and her brother nursed the children through a whole catalogue
of illnesses—chickenpox, measles, scarlet fever, diphtheria—and thought
nothing of it. But now that they were grown up, it became apparent that
two of them—Sophie and Belin—were being threatened by a much more
serious scourge. Sophie, twenty-three in 1894, had long had a passion for
Charles Copeland, a lank, shy young man who came from a good Philadelphia family and had just signed on at Du Pont. In the family it was an
accepted fact that they would marry. But then Sophie, who had always
been a girl with a feverish gaiety, turned out to have a permanent temperature, too, and when she developed a cough and started spitting blood, the
doctors were called. The family was thunderstruck when it was revealed
that Sophie had a bad case of tuberculosis. True, there had been other con-
sumptives in the family, Uncle Irénée, Lammot's brother, had actually
died of the disease, but the du Ponts had always thought themselves a
strong and healthy clan subject only to the prevailing "epidemics."

As the months went by and Sophie's condition deteriorated, P.S. and
Lou consulted with their sister and advised her to give up any thought of
marrying Charles. In any case, the doctors wanted her away from the hu-
midity of Delaware, and it was decided Mary should take her to the Rocky
Mountains, where fresh air and sunshine might restore her health.

This was one of the unhappiest moments in P.S.'s early years. Not
only was he worried about Sophie, whom he adored, but his relations with

Frank at Carney's Point were worse than ever. Frank Gurney du Pont, with one of his sons, Francis I., already working at Carney's Point, now brought another, Felix, into the mill.* Felix was even more ignorant of explosives than Francis I., but once again Frank allowed him to shoulder P.S. aside and showed obvious favoritism toward him.

It was the moment, P.S. decided, to get out and do some hard thinking, so he announced he was taking a vacation to visit Sophie and his mother in Colorado Springs, Colorado, where they were staying at the Antlers Hotel.

There he received a telegram from Frank Gurney du Pont:

NO NEED TO COME HOME. YOUR SERVICES NOT MISSED HERE.

Then, perhaps having second thoughts about how this curt message might be received by his nephew, Cousin Frank followed it up on October 1, 1894, with a long letter, which was a fascinating mixture of insincerity and unction. *"My dear Pierre,"* it began,

> Your letter came to hand this morning, and I at once wired to you to the effect that there was no reason for you to feel that you ought to come home, and I wanted you to feel that in this I fully sympathized with you, and wished to convey quickly to you my wish that you should act as you thought best, and I hope that you so interpreted my telegram.

The letter contained a check for $333.33, which, Frank went on to say, was a raise in salary that he was awarding to P.S. *and* Lex (Felix) for the inconvenience, endured by both men, of having to travel to Carney's Point each day. He had had to go to the other partners for permission to make the raise:

> I found it to meet no opposition or criticism except that in one instance it was thought that you might not think it fair that Lex should receive as much as you, when his shorter time was considered, but I knew you so well that I scouted the idea as unworthy of your generous disposition. It is to be understood that these figures are to stand for some time, and I would impress upon you that all had been decided and acted upon before I had recieved [sic] your letter, so that what I have written has nothing

---

* Just to be confusing, Frank called Felix Lex for short. Lex was also what his brother Eugene called *his* son Alexis.

to do with what you may hereafter decide to do, and I would have you consider yourself as free to act just as you see proper and expedient for the present emergency.

Then came what P.S.'s sister Lou called "the guff":

Oh! my dear boy I wish I could convey to you all the sympathy I do so earnestly feel for you in you [sic] distress and trouble, what you have written confirms my worst fears, and had I not had so grievous an affliction myself, I could not feel as I do. Your time here is as nothing as compared to your sisters life, and you mus [sic] do just as seems best for her and your mother. You are not dependent upon your work for your sustenance, and can act as your conscience dictated, and this you must do without regard to the effect it will have upon us here. To intimate that you will not be missed [which is what he had said in his original telegram] would be to tell an untruth, Lex and I will indeed miss your ready work and the companionship we hold so dear.

It was the next passage that irritated P.S. most:

For myself I can say that it has not often fallen to my lot to feel towards a young man as I do to you, the intercourse with you has been to me much more than a business one, you know that my feelings towards your father were of the warmest affection, much more than even he ever knew. . . . As for the future, I wish to say that you need not think that you will be without a position. Should you wish to come back, you can always find a welcome here and should the exigencies of the work that you have so ably carried on require other arrangements, then I shall make it my business to see that other plans are made for you when you are able to resume business. My dear fellow, I have written you as I would to my own son.

He ended with a final note that made up P.S.'s mind about whether he should go back or not:

I can not close without a word about Lex, though I say it who perhaps should not. He has taken hold of the work where you left off and is doing all that could be desired, and the work has prospered, fortunately also, it has been rather free from

vexation too. . . . With kindest regards to your mother and
Sophie, I am Your affectionate cousin, Frank G. du Pont.

Alfred I. had been reporting to P.S. in Colorado that conditions at
Carney's Point were worse than ever. If Frank had allowed his dull and inexperienced son to take on P.S.'s work, the chaos was understandable.
Sophie's condition notwithstanding, the pull of Du Pont was too strong to
resist. P.S. told his mother he was going back at once. He said a fond good-
bye to his sister and, though genuinely sad to be leaving, comforted himself with the thought that there was really nothing that could be done for
the girl now.

He was quite right about that. Sophie du Pont died a few weeks later.

In the past the one thing that had constrained P.S. from resigning when
Frank became intolerable was that if he went, there would then be no
single member of his family working for Du Pont, and he knew that
neither his father nor his grandfather would have approved of that.

Now his brother Belin was employed in the Du Pont yards on the
Brandywine. If P.S. did decide to leave, his one consolation was that Belin
would be there to keep the family's flag flying—and worthily, for he was a
fine chemist and sure to do well in the company.

Belin was not only clever, he was also popular with the du Ponts. He
was the handsomest male member of the family. His chestnut-colored hair
was tossed back romantically from his broad forehead, his doelike brown
eyes sparkled with mischief, his sensitive, sensual lips nearly always curved
in a smile. The girls on the Brandywine doted on him, and though some of
them remarked that his eyebrows met in the middle, always a sign of a
black temper, he was never short of female admirers. Du Pont mothers regarded him fondly, and almost as favorably as they did P.S., as a suitable
catch for their daughters. And for a time it seemed that all would go well
with him.

It was true that Belin sometimes had a high flush and caught "bronchitis" easily, but Mary casually called it "the family cough," and despite
Sophie's tragic death plus the fact that one of her brothers had recently died
of TB in Scranton, she optimistically prophesied Belin would again be
healthy and normal once spring came back to Delaware. On the other
hand, P.S. and Lou were beginning to have premonitions, especially when

they caught their brother heaving distressfully in a dark corner, a handkerchief pressed to his lips.

Nevertheless, when Belin announced he was going to be married, everyone was happy for him, and overjoyed at his choice of a bride-to-be. She was Eleuthera Bradford, one of the two loveliest girls in Wilmington, the other being her younger sister, Alicia. Eleuthera was the daughter of United States Circuit Court Judge Edward Green Bradford, known far and wide for the delight he seemed to take in sending felons off to prison camps for long periods, no matter what the mitigating circumstances. He was a fire-eating punisher of sin in any form, and (though this was not generally known outside his family) a domestic tyrant who bullied his frail and charming wife and put the fear of God in his children. Even if Belin had not been quite such a catch, everyone said Eloo would be lucky to get away from her father, and surely her sister, Alicia, would not be long in following her.

For the family it was one of Eloo's added attractions that she was a cousin, for her mother had been born a du Pont. In the circumstances, geneticists probably would not have shared their enthusiasm. Eloo was a beautiful girl, but she was also known to have been extremely delicate in childhood.

Within a month of the wedding Eloo confided to her sister-in-law Lou that she was pregnant. In 1898 a son, Edward, was born. At his christening at Christ's Church, the relatives were uncomfortable as they watched the minuscule and apathetic baby being dipped in the font.

"He looks like a little white worm," one of them said.

But nothing, not even a sickly baby and Eloo's obvious lack of interest in it, seemed to mar the bliss of the newlyweds. While little Edward whimpered in his cot his mother dashed around buying up furniture and superintending heavy alterations to Louviers, the handsome house on the Brandywine assigned to them by Eugene du Pont, the senior active partner. Down at the yards Belin was not surprisingly proving himself an expert and highly capable addition to the staff of the yard boss, Cousin Charles, and no one paid much mind when he came down with another bad attack of "bronchitis" in January 1899. He was packed off for a holiday down South. Eloo went with him, of course, but the baby was left behind in the care of Lou, who adored babies. They came back again in April, and Lou wrote to P.S.:

Belin and Eloo were here last night for supper. . . . Belin looks better than when he went away, but none could accuse him of being stout. Has he written to you that their family will be encreased [sic] in the Fall. I am sorry it will be so soon, two babies are a good deal to look after, and Eloo don't seem very strong.

At about the same time that Eloo was giving birth to her second child (another son, named Henry Belin du Pont II) Belin suffered a really serious bout of "bronchitis" and soon left no one in any doubt that, like Sophie, he was suffering from TB. Once more his sister Lou took in the two babies and hired a wet nurse to feed the newborn. Belin and Eloo set out on what, over the next few years, would be a pathetic search for health. In the spring of 1900 Lou had planned a holiday in Europe, but she canceled it. She stayed on the Brandywine all summer, watching over the babies while the couple went from the Carolinas to Florida and eventually, as Sophie had done, to Colorado Springs, hoping that good dry air would bring about a miracle. Occasionally, and very reluctantly, Eloo would return to the Brandywine to see her children, but mostly because Lou called her back.

In July 1900 she made one of these unwilling visits and found the frail and puny first son, Edward, very ill indeed. In a panic, she wired Belin in Colorado, telling him to come home at once.

"He will make himself very sick," Lou wrote to P.S.,

taking that long journey in the hot weather and coming to the damp here after long acclimation [sic] to that dry climate. I can't understand Eloo, you know she won't stay with the baby, she says he looks so badly it makes her sick. To me they are an absolutely helpless pair to do anything with.

Little Edward died a few days later. Belin du Pont was at the funeral looking like a ghost.

CHAPTER 11

Split

EVEN in his youth P. S. du Pont was never rash or precipitate, and so he suffered under Frank Gurney du Pont's regime for nearly eight years before finally deciding to make the break, in 1898. In the previous year the smokeless powder factory at Carney's Point, alone among Du Pont's operations, had shown a loss—of seventy-five thousand dollars. Since smokeless powder was in short supply and the American armed forces were clamoring for it, the plant should have been the most profitable in the whole organization. P.S., who was incensed, put the blame squarely on Frank Gurney du Pont's shoulders, for he was in charge of production and had got the administration into such a muddle that the factory was quite unable to fulfill the orders that were flowing in.

Even though working with Frank had become intolerable, P.S. still hoped that if only he could get away from Carney's Point, he might still hang on to his Du Pont connection. He applied for a transfer back to the Brandywine yards where Alfred I., now the actual if not the titular boss of

Pierre Samuel du Pont de Nemours is usually regarded as the founder of the du Pont dynasty. It was he who brought his family from France to the New World in 1800, though he himself returned later to serve under Napoleon. A friend of Jefferson, with whom he kept up a lively correspondence, and such French luminaries as Madame de Staël and Talleyrand, he is generally credited with facilitating the transfer between France and the United States of that territory now known as the Louisiana Purchase.

Two of the Du Pont powder mills along the banks of Brandywine Creek, Wilmington, Delaware. Under working conditions a light wall covered the front of each mill, and this, together with the sloping roof, was so designed that, in the event of an explosion, they would blow out easily—and toward the creek—thus minimizing damage to adjacent mills.

Eleuthère Irénée du Pont I was the man who chose the site on the Brandywine and there founded the firm that was to grow into the most powerful armaments company in the world. But he had a hard time keeping Du Pont afloat. Dogged by mounting debts, tragic explosions and ill-health, he died in 1834, convinced that the Du Pont company would not long survive him.

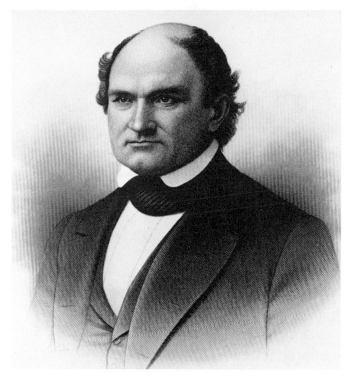

Alfred Victor du Pont I was the eldest son of E. I. du Pont, founder of the powder-making company, and he took over the firm sometime after his father's death. But his heart was not in the business, and his energy was sapped by his nagging, contemptuous wife, Meta. He eventually resigned in favor of his more relentless younger brother, Henry (the Red) du Pont.

Margaretta (Meta) LaMotte du Pont made life a misery for her husband, bullied her sons, and drove one of her daughters-in-law into the madhouse. She lived well into her nineties and left a sizeable fortune to her grandsons.

Admiral Samuel Francis du Pont married his cousin, Sophie Marie, daughter of the founder of the Du Pont explosives company and one of the best-loved members of the dynasty, but he preferred firing shells to manufacturing them and made a career in the navy. Generally regarded as the father of Annapolis naval academy, he achieved both fame and disgrace during the Civil War.

General Henry (the Red) du Pont was the ruthless master of the Brandywine who turned the Du Pont company into the most powerful armaments firm in the United States. He rode roughshod over his relatives and employees to get what he wanted and invented the Powder Trust to eliminate his rivals in business.

The dandy of the du Pont family was Colonel Henry A. du Pont, who fought in the Civil War and was later awarded a Congressional Medal of Honor. This photograph was taken in 1864.

Irénée du Pont II was one of the ill-starred members of the family. Son of a jealous and vitriolic mother, he chose a Southern bride, Charlotte Henderson, on the eve of the Civil War. She was baited and jeered at by her mother-in-law and other du Ponts, and weakened by difficult childbirths; Charlotte's mind gave way and she died in an asylum. Irénée blamed his mother for her death and refused to forgive her, even when he was dying.

After the tragic deaths of Charlotte and Irénée du Pont II, their five children were threatened with eviction from their home, Swamp Hall, which belonged to the Du Pont company. But led by the eldest son, Alfred I. du Pont, they locked themselves in and threatened with shotguns and clubs anyone who tried to put them out. They were allowed to stay and look after themselves. Swamp Hall was later the home of Alfred I., his first wife, Bessie, and their children, but he had the house razed after their marriage collapsed into divorce and acrimony.

Lammot du Pont was always considered to be the most charming and dashing member of the family. A brilliant and inventive chemist, he was also eager for adventure and went on two important missions during his career. Lammot was killed in an explosion in 1884, but his eldest son, P. S. du Pont, rose to become president of the modern Du Pont corporation.

A family portrait: P. S. du Pont with his mother, brothers and sisters, taken in 1886. Back row, left to right: Sophie, Mary, Louisa (Lou) and Lammot du Pont. Front row: Belin, Isabella, Margaretta, Mrs. Mary Belin du Pont, William K. and Irénée du Pont. P. S. is standing on the extreme right.

A portrait of the du Pont cousins and their friends taken in 1885. At the top, second from the left, is P. S. du Pont. In the second row, wearing a light dress and holding her hat, is his cousin, Alice Belin, whom he married thirty years later.

the Hagley mills, had told him his help would be welcome. Alfred I. was gearing up for the big orders he expected if and when the United States got itself involved in a war with Spain, and he offered P.S. a job as his assistant. He even hinted that there might be a more important job in the offing, since he himself was thinking of joining the United States Army when war came, and promised to recommend P.S. as his successor.

But when P.S. put in his application for transfer, the partners, on Frank's intervention, refused it.

Even in the face of this rebuff, P.S. did not rush things. He wrote to Tom Johnson and his cousin Coleman du Pont, who between them ran steel and streetcar companies in Kentucky, Texas, and Ohio, and mentioned that he was now definitely thinking of making a change. What could they offer him? Back came a joint reply offering him the presidency of the Johnson Company in Lorain, Ohio, at an annual salary of ten thousand dollars —four times what he was getting at Du Pont, and pretty good going for a young man of twenty-eight.

With the offer in his pocket, he wrote a formal letter to the Du Pont partners, telling them he would be leaving the company unless they could come up with a suitable proposition that could persuade him to stay. As he wrote to his brother Belin on January 27, 1899:

> They replied, also formally, that they would like to talk the whole matter over and would be glad to meet me at the office on the 26th. I went hardly hoping that they would have any definite offer. I was not disappointed for Cousin Eugene simply said that when things were reorganized there would be several good places to be filled and thought that I could fill any of them. No special place was mentioned and no salary offerred [sic] or any mention of giving or selling me an interest in the Company. I remarked that I had hoped for something more definite and Alfred, for the whole partnership was lined up against the wall, spoke up and said that he thought that as I had made a definite proposition that I was entitled to a definite answer. Nothing more was forthcoming so I got up with the remark that I thought that I understood the position and cleared out. I had not been home more than an hour before Charles and Alfred came over and started to tell me reasons why I should stay. They had all sorts of reforms that were going to be worked and I would probably have a chance to be head of the business end, etc. However I

told them that there had been reforms promised ever since last September and that I could not very well turn down a good offer for vague promises.

He added:

> Yesterday . . . I telegraphed Tom Johnson that I accepted his offer. Today at Carneys [sic] Point I told "F.G." of my decision. It is needless to say that he did not burst into tears or anything of the kind. I thought before that he was not anxious for me to stay and I am sure of it now.

P.S.'s brother Belin was delighted at the news, for he had strongly resented the way his elder brother had been pushed around. Belin wrote on January 30:

> I was very glad to receive your letter last night and to learn that you had decided to leave the Brandywine. I congratulate you on getting such a fine position as President of the Johnson Co. and getting away from such a disagreeable man as F.G. It is very evident that, from the way he acted, he never intended changing his ways at Carney's Pt. no matter how many reforms the company intended.
>
> Ma and the rest of us will miss you very much at Saint Amour, but I feel sure that all would rather have it so than to have F.G. have his way and have you underdog at Carney's Pt. . . . I am betting that after getting accustomed to your new work, you will get very lonely especially in the evening and the first thing you know a nice girl will turn up who will become Mrs Daddy. I will bet you a bottle of fizz that you will be engaged before you have been there a year.

P.S.'s last meeting with Frank appears to have been rather more acrimonious than he let it appear in his letters. Though there are no mentions of the meeting in the company records, there is a letter from Frank that throws some light on it. Some months later, much to P.S.'s embarrassment, his younger brother Irénée announced that he was going to marry Frank's daughter (and their cousin) Irene du Pont. Irénée asked P.S. if he would be best man at the wedding, but his brother, unwilling to meet the father of the bride face to face so soon after his resignation, refused. For Irénée's sake, and to prevent a family schism, he did, however, feel it necessary to write to Frank, assuring him that he was entrusting his daughter into safe hands and added that he hoped there was no ill feeling between them. Frank replied (on March 30, 1899):

> I feel quite safe in trusting the future of my daughter to Irénée. He's a manly fellow and I am sure is pure and free from faults, alas! now so common in young men. . . .
>
> In regard to the latter part of your letter, I would say that I have not the least personal feeling as to matters pertaining to your position with us. You will recall that I understood your meaning and in the presence of others assured myself that such was the case with them.
>
> Then I was careful to say as little as I could for fear that I might say something of a personal nature.
>
> Your proposition was to me thus made, in the shape of a mere business matter, and you simply stated that I must retire or you would. No allowance was made by you as to whether the change would be desirable for me or for the best results. Without any further question than asking advice of others, you accepted another position, and I do assure you that as for any dispute with you there was none on my part, and none has come up in my mind since. With best wishes for your wellfare [sic], I am yours sincerely, Francis Gurney du Pont.

By the time that letter was written, P.S. was far away in Ohio. But though he was working for the Johnson Company, he never had any doubt that one day he would come back to the Brandywine. He was simply in exile, awaiting the overthrow of the *ancien régime*.

Alfred I. was as chagrined as his cousin when Frank Gurney du Pont vetoed P.S.'s transfer from Carney's Point to the Brandywine, for his help would have been invaluable in the Hagley yards during the boom in production provoked by the Spanish-American War. When he first sensed that war was coming, Alfred I., an intensely patriotic young man, slipped away to Washington and offered his services to the army. He accepted a commission as a major in the Corps of Engineers, figuring that P.S. would be well able to take his place in the powder mills. But then in February 1898 the United States battleship *Maine* was blown up in Havana harbor, with the loss of 260 lives. The jingoists screamed for revenge. The secretary of war realized that by allowing Alfred I. to volunteer he had deprived the nation of its best powder man, and so he asked the young man to take off his uniform and get back to the Brandywine. At the same time Frank blocked P.S.'s transfer. So there was nothing else for Alfred I. to do but return to the job he knew best.

Even squalid wars (and the Spanish-American War was both squalid and unnecessary) produce their quotas of heroes, and this one was no exception. The avid prowar press made sure that they were remembered, and the world still hears a faint bell ringing when someone mentions Teddy Roosevelt's Rough Riders at San Juan Hill, Rowan's gallant "message to Garcia," Admiral Dewey at Manila Bay, and the destruction of the doomed fleet of Admiral Cervera.

But there was also a hero behind the lines, and he was unsung. Without Alfred I. du Pont the United States could easily have lost the Spanish-American War. Not for the last time, America had embarked on war lamentably unprepared on land and sea. The army was too small. The navy had not enough ships to protect the coastline had the Spaniards wished to make an attack or a landing. But more vital still, the big guns of the artillery and the battleships did not have enough powder, and even the infantry was short of bullets.

Just before war was declared, ordnance experts came to Carney's Point and sat down to a conference with Frank at which they asked him whether he could increase his production of smokeless powder to thirty thousand pounds a day and start shipping it within a week. Frank replied that it would take him months to get the plant ready for such an expansion, and that, in any case, it would be at least another half year after that before the powder could be dried and shipped. For months P.S. had been urging Frank to expand; and now, sitting in on the meeting, he was even more disgusted with his cousin's reply than were the ordnance officers. It gave him no comfort to realize that all Du Pont's so-called rivals, fellow members of the Powder Trust, were in a similar position. It was their lack of enterprise that had encouraged Frank's inertia to begin with.

The United States government had to face the fact that though the Spaniards were known to have smokeless powder, America would have to fight this war without it, and would be constantly giving away battle positions to an enemy capable of firing back without being seen. But would the United States forces even have enough ordinary powder to be able to fire at all?

The powder Alfred I. du Pont was producing in the yards on the

Brandywine was known as brown prismatic powder, and if the Spanish-American War had not come along, he had planned to call a halt and dismantle the machinery that made it, then retool for smokeless production. There was only one other small plant, in California, that still made brown powder, so everything depended upon whether Alfred I. could now give the army and navy enough. He pointed out that the capacity of the mills was three thousand pounds a day, and he could promise them that. The government, he was told, needed twenty thousand pounds a day—and within sixty days. Both Frank and Eugene threw up their hands. An impossible goal. But Alfred I., eager for a chance to show up his incompetent uncles, said he could do it. On one condition: that he be given a completely free hand. Eugene and Frank shrugged their shoulders. They had no alternative but to agree.

For the duration of the war Alfred I. moved into the powder mills and did not leave, either to eat or sleep. He had an intensely loyal and hard-working team of powder men under him, but he was well aware that without his constant presence production would never rise to the level that had been demanded of him. Now he set his workers an eighteen-hour day, and since there were no overtime rates in those days, they got the same eighteen cents an hour for the extra six hours that they were paid for the normal twelve-hour day. The only incentive was the sight of their boss, stripped to the waist, getting mucky beside them as they mixed and milled the powder, bedding down beside them when they snatched some sleep, and taking his meals with them. Like the other powder men's children, Alfred I.'s daughter Bep got up at dawn each day and brought her father's dinner pail to the mill gates; but she also prepared the meal, since Bessie was too estranged from her husband by this time to feel inclined to bother.

Before sixty days had passed, twenty thousand pounds of brown powder were being produced each day and loaded onto waiting trains.

It was quite a sight, the powder men told their wives: eight hundred square yards of zinc-lined boxes full of brown prismatic powder being shipped off to the war every day. Alfred I. and the Du Pont powder men were the only suppliers in the Spanish-American War who met their quotas. As one writer said later:

> The feat, to which public notice has not hitherto been directed, shines by contrast with the general conduct of a war begun on an Olympian note of mismanagement—no powder reserve—and continued in that vein to the end: cavalry without horses;

horses without saddles; infantry without shoes; vile rations; similar sanitation, thirteen men dying of disease for every one killed in action; regiments sent one place, tents and blankets another; troops poured into Cuba's steaming tropical summer clad in woolen uniforms. Had Alfred du Pont produced 5,000 pounds of prismatic powder a day instead of 20,000, it could be said, in mitigation, that his performance did not fall below the average of those charged with the administration of the war.*

On July 3, 1898, the Spanish admiral, Cervera, made his last attempt to relieve encircled Santiago, and his fleet was destroyed by American guns and Alfred I. du Pont's powder. Eleven days later Santiago surrendered, and on August 12 an armistice was signed.

For the first time in four months Alfred I. went home to Swamp Hall to clean himself up. Then he looked around for some relaxation. But not with Bessie.

In the ten years since the birth of their second daughter, Bessie and Alfred I. du Pont had not slept together, though there are indications that on several occasions Bessie did try to restore some sort of conjugal relations. In several of her letters to her brother, Lou du Pont mentions to P.S. that she found the "Alfred and Bessie misunderstanding" very sad to contemplate and wished Bessie would "try even harder" to "make it up" with her husband. "He looks very lonely," she added, and much in need of "cheerful company."

It was, in fact, a difficult time for Alfred I. After his heroic efforts in the yards during the summer, the peace that followed was an inevitable letdown, compounded by a worry that had been besetting him since the previous winter. He feared he was going deaf, and that would be a major tragedy for him, loving music as he did. He had had a bout of illness, probably viral pneumonia, a year earlier, and though he was up and about again after several weeks, he found that the sickness had left him with his hearing impaired. At first he had accepted the reassurances of the doctors who examined him, believing with them that it would all clear up when he was completely recovered. Only it had not. When he conducted the Tankopanicums now, his ears were no longer so sharply aware of discords;

* James, *Alfred I. du Pont.*

[146]

and when he went to a concert or to the opera in Philadelphia or New York, he heard the orchestra and the singers as if through a screen, still audible but muffled. It depressed him. He tried an ear trumpet for a time, but then decided it was too clumsy and eccentric.

Finally, he went to his friend Edison, who said he would find out whether anything could be done about an electrical hearing aid. But that would take time, and in the meantime Alfred I. suffered. Through all the years of his marital estrangement it was his music, even more than his gadgets, his hunting, and his work, that had helped to make life bearable. Now, angry at himself when he missed the subtleties of a concert, the whispered asides in an opera, the pianissimo passages in a recital, he petulantly abandoned music and flung himself into the new family passion. Automobiles were just becoming the talk of the nation, and naturally the du Ponts had been among the first to espouse them. To begin with, Alfred I. got himself a steam-driven carriage called a Locomobile but was quickly dissatisfied with its performance. He sold it to a buyer who was even more disappointed and wrote to Alfred I.:

"I just want to report on the Locomobile I bought of you. It is loco all right, but not so mobile."

Alfred I. sent him his money back. In the meantime his cousin P.S. had become so enthusiastic about internal combustion-driven cars that he had invested some of the family money in them. Alfred I. bought a different make and tinkered with its chain-driven system until he was so satisfied with it that he challenged all comers—including the French, who were among the automobile pioneers—to a race from Philadelphia to Wilmington. There were no takers, which is just as well, for his Haynes-Apperson frightened so many horses that it was banned from the roads.

Even Belin, despite his deteriorating health, could not help being fascinated with automobiles, and he wrote to his brother P.S. in the spring of 1889:

> Alfred has just ordered a Stanley* automobile which (according to him) is about perfect, can climb any hill, is noiseless and can be run by a baby. I suppose all stockholders in your Automobile Co. will be presented with automobiles. You can send mine by freight to Du Pont Siding, Monchanin Del.; have the tank filled as I would like to take her off the car and ride right home with it.

* Which had replaced the Haynes-Apperson.

But automobiles were made to be driven in the daytime, at least in those days, and Alfred I.'s other passion, hunting, was also a daylight pursuit. What was he to do with his nights?

He took to dropping in on some of the balls and germans, as small dancing evenings were called, which local society ladies gave in Wilmington, Scranton, Philadelphia, and even as far afield as Atlantic City in the summer. His brother Maurice and his wife, Margery, were staying in Atlantic City, preferring to keep away from their snobbish relatives on the Brandywine, and Alfred I. was with them one night in 1899 when he encountered the girl who was to change the course of his personal life.

Her name was Alicia Bradford, and she was the sister of Eleuthera Bradford, who had married Belin du Pont.

The two daughters of the tyrannous Judge Edward Green Bradford had responded in very different fashions to his harsh and dictatorial regime. Eleuthera's spirit had been broken early; frail, cowering, longing only for escape, she had grabbed Belin with both hands and thought him a wonderful refuge. Even a sick man was preferable to her father.

Alicia Bradford was made of different stuff. Like Eleuthera, she had suffered in childhood but thereafter had made up her mind to tolerate persecution no longer. She said later:

> As a child, I was terrified all the time—terrified of everything. Suddenly it came to me that my father was the cause of all this. He had wanted me to be a boy. I saw it all and made up my mind to get even.

As a result, she had grown up to be a young woman who shocked and scandalized her elders, infuriated and distressed other girls of her age in her social circle, and first disconcerted and then fascinated every man she met. She had worked hard at school, and she had a keen brain; she was shrewd, perceptive, knowledgeable, and never frivolous. She had a sharp and witty tongue that could shrivel any silly girl who got in her way, or any man she did not like. She despised the conventions of the times and went anywhere she wanted, without companions or chaperonage. She made it clear that she thought all the other girls in her circle were a bunch of sheep, terrified of offending against convention, and that she had no intention of obeying the stupid rules by which their activities were guided.

She also did not bother to conceal—and this was what particularly shocked her elders—that *she liked men,* more than her own sex. Since she was also quite potently attractive, and quite unscrupulous, no one's suitor, fiancé, or husband was safe from her.

Alicia Bradford and Alfred I. du Pont were, of course, no strangers to each other, Alicia's mother, Eleuthera Paulina du Pont Bradford, being Alfred I.'s aunt. They had been meeting at Brandywine christenings, weddings, and funerals since she was a child. But until their encounter in Atlantic City in 1899, Alicia had always seemed to treat Cousin Alfred as if he were a member of the older generation (he was, in fact, eleven years her senior), and, especially in the presence of his wife and children, had shown him a wary respect. But on the evening in question, at a soirée given by a reputedly flighty Wilmington matron in one of the Atlantic City hotels, she joined Alfred I., Maurice, and Margery and boldly asked her cousin if he would dance with her. He obliged. She then stayed with the trio for the remainder of the evening and, being in an unusually serene and happy mood, charmed and entertained them. She was especially nice and natural with Margery, who, having been bitten hard by du Pont frostiness in the past, was stimulated into hearty laughter by Alicia's takeoffs on some of her snobbier relatives. Alicia flirted gently but harmlessly with Maurice. And when she turned to Alfred I., it was to talk of music, cars, explosions at the yards, books she was reading, the developments of science, as if she instinctively knew exactly what his favorite interests were.

Alfred I. was delighted with her. He was staying overnight at the hotel, and after the party was over and the good-nights had been said, he decided to take a walk along the boardwalk to savor the evening. He had gone only a few hundred yards when he was joined by Alicia, who had breathlessly pursued him. They walked and talked for the next few hours, then returned to the hotel and went to their separate rooms. But both of them were aware that a relationship, though not yet physical, had begun between them.

When Alfred I. got back to Swamp Hall, it was immediately noticed in the household that he was relaxed, happy, amiable with everyone. He had brought back presents for the children, as usual, but he astonished Bessie by producing a trinket for her too; something, he said, he had picked up in Atlantic City and thought she might like. Bessie was so touched by the gesture, and by his continued good humor, that she decided to make one more attempt to patch up their differences and revive sexual relations.

She had chosen a propitious, not to say receptive, moment, and it worked. That was in mid-June 1899. A few weeks later she revealed to her husband that for the first time in ten years she was pregnant again. She was a trifle shattered that Alfred I., unlike everyone else on the Brandywine, all of whom seemed happy that the couple were reconciled, appeared crushed at the news. But there was no doubt whatsoever of his pleasure when on March 17, 1900, Bessie was delivered of a baby boy, their first son. He was christened Alfred Victor du Pont, and since his birth date was Saint Patrick's Day, every Irishman in the powder yards gathered on the grounds of Swamp Hall to drink the health of the boss and his heir.

Rumors about Alfred I. and Alicia Bradford were already circulating among the du Ponts, but curiously enough, Alicia did not seem to be troubled by the news of Bessie's triumph. She even attended the christening ceremony, congratulated the proud new mother, and did not appear at all upset.

In the circumstances (and Bessie did not know about them yet) there was no reason why she should be.

At the end of February 1899 P. S. du Pont arrived in Lorain, Ohio, to take control of the properties that the Johnson Company owned in that city, part of the conglomerate of steel, streetcar, and real estate companies that Uncle Fred and Tom Johnson had built up. Thanks to Uncle Fred and Grandmother Meta du Pont, P.S. now had stock in the companies worth one hundred thousand dollars, and in addition, he would be paid ten thousand dollars a year to streamline the Lorain operations and improve their profit-making capacity. He wrote home to his sister Lou on March 2, 1899, to say that he had already run into quite a few problems and that "upheavals" were in order. "However," he added,

> upheavals seem much easier of consummation here than at B'wine. So that I hope the affairs of this company may be sorted out before long.

He was not exactly enamored of the Ohio winter, he informed Lou. Describing the bad conditions in that town, he wrote:

> The milkman comes in a sleigh, though there is not a sign of snow anywhere. It is simply easier to slide on the mud than to drag wheels through it.

Almost simultaneously with P.S.'s appearance on the Johnson Company's payroll, his cousin Coleman du Pont decided to pull out. He and

Tom Johnson between them sold the steel company in Johnstown for a tidy sum, to what would eventually become the United States Steel Corporation, and Coleman then moved to Wilmington. He knew this would reunite his wife, Elsie, with her du Pont relatives on the Brandywine and would keep her entertained in the moments when she was not occupied with her four children (a fifth would be born in 1902). Meanwhile he was off to New York, Philadelphia, and points east to gamble on the stock exchange and wallow in the fleshpots. Coleman's appetite for gay parties and scantily clad chorus girls was never really appeased in his lifetime, and he said later that when he died, he hoped heaven would turn out to be the showgirls' dressing room of the Ziegfeld Follies. He once turned up for the Paris boat train to Cherbourg, after a business trip with P.S., with six of the prettiest *poules* from that famous Parisian bordello the Sphinx, and while he lavished champagne and caviare upon them they lavished him with attentions of a nature calculated to shock his more respectable cousin to the marrow. But when they reached Cherbourg, the *cocottes* stayed on the dock to wave good-bye while the cousins boarded the ship back to America.

"Thank heavens for that," said a relieved P.S. "I thought you were going to take them home as souvenirs."

For the moment, a threatened operation to Coleman's throat had put a crimp in his style of profligate living, but it did not prevent him from gambling in stocks or investing in real estate, and his bank balance was growing by millions every year. He was a shrewd operator despite his seemingly reckless investments, and he continually beseeched P.S. to follow his example and make some money for his "wards." P.S., however, was too prudent to do so.

For the next three years P.S. used Lorain as his base but traveled all over the United States in the Johnson Company's interest, buying up real estate and streetcar companies. With Coleman's departure he, though still under thirty, was the senior active partner in a million-dollar company. It was no mean responsibility, and it would have been a lonely job had he not had someone to share it with.

Back home on the Brandywine, they still hoped that this tall, gentle, thoughtful young man would marry one of his du Pont cousins. There were quite a few yet remaining to choose from, but his own family favored above all others his cousin Alice Belin, daughter of Harry, his mother's brother. Alice had been in love with P.S. since she was a little girl. In one of the first letters his mother, Mary, sent him after he arrived in Lorain, she wrote:

Alice Belin has been over, and says to tell you she certainly expected to find you here when she came as she understood you were not going to leave until the first of March. She is sorry. She misses you.

By the same post Lou wrote:

Alice [Belin] arrived at a late hour on Monday night, it was nearly half past eight, and was terribly disgusted not to find you here. She thought you would not go until the first of March and by coming Monday would have two days of your society. Alice I don't think is looking well. And ever since she has been here has had a pain in her stomach. She thinks she must have taken cold, as she has been living on tea, toast, whisky and paragoric [sic] without much beneficial result. She is not so pale today and thinks she feels somewhat better.

P.S. wrote back to his mother:

Tell Alice that I'm very sorry not to have seen her and that I hope that my wanderings may bring me to Scranton at times. Although we both may happen to visit B'wine together.

Alice herself, of course, wrote him nothing at all. She was not that sort of girl.

In the meantime P.S. had found for himself in Lorain a helpmeet who would give him all the support he needed at that stage in his life, and that support was of a kind that Alice Belin would never be able to provide. He had acquired a young male stenographer named John J. Raskob.

John Raskob was an earnest young man of nineteen when he first came to the attention of P. S. du Pont. As president of the Johnson Company's Lorain operation, P.S. had taken over from a man named Arthur J. Moxham.* Moxham had employed Raskob for a time in his office with such good results that he had offered to take him along when he moved north. But the young man was devoted to a widowed mother too delicate to travel, and he was determined to stay with her. As he wrote to P.S.:

As she is of a very nervous temperament and worries considerable about me, I have brought the matter before Mr. Moxham and he has kindly consented to release me and recommend me to anyone should I be able to secure a position.

---

* Whose son eventually married into the du Pont family.

[152]

He said Moxham had been paying him one hundred dollars a month, but he would be willing to accept eighty and should "earnestly endeavor to merit an increase in a short time." He got the job, and within months P.S. doubled his salary.

It was the beginning of one of the most famous associations in the history of American business, one that would make waves around the world, and soon the two were so close that those who came in contact with them began to make jokes about it. "P. S. du Pont is the one who breathes in and John Raskob the one who breathes out," said one. Another added: "Pierre and John can sit down in a room together for an hour without saying anything whatsoever to each other, and at the end of that hour, John will get to his feet and say: 'I agree.'" His disparagers described Raskob as P.S.'s valet, and the other du Ponts called him P.S.'s faithful squire.

So far as their personal relationship was concerned, they had much in common and established a rapport from the start. It was true that P.S. was pretty well an agnostic whereas John Raskob was a devout Roman Catholic. It was also true that there was a difference of eleven years in their ages. But their family backgrounds were uncannily similar. They had each lost their fathers at an early age and had thereafter been strongly influenced by their widowed mothers, for whom they had also provided much needed support. They were both the eldest son in a large family and had discovered early on that they were expected to look after and generally protect their younger brothers and sisters. In consequence, neither had passed a normal boyhood. Both had been forced to grow up and be responsible before their time, never knowing the careless rapture of irresponsible youth.

Within a year of their first meeting, P.S. trusted John J. Raskob so implicitly that he gave him power of attorney over all his affairs and, once Raskob was of age, made him joint guardian of his underage brothers and sisters. One of them would remain in Lorain, looking after the Johnson Company's affairs, while the other went forth to do a deal, and they never needed any unnecessary consultation to make a decision. When the deal was big enough (as, for instance, in the case of the Dallas Streetcar Company, which they bought up in 1901), they went together to conduct the discussions.

Soon both young men knew secrets about each other that they would never betray to a third person, yet John Raskob never presumed. It was years before he called his boss anything but Mr. du Pont, and decades later, when Raskob was a millionaire himself, he went on referring to him in that way when talking to business associates or members of the du Pont family.

But if P. S. du Pont had found himself a good companion in Lorain, Ohio, his heart was still on the Brandywine; what was happening to the family back there, as well as to the Du Pont company, was a matter of daily concern. P.S. returned to Delaware for brief stays at every opportunity, and he could not get enough news from home. He relied upon his sister Lou to send him a long weekly letter replete with all the gossip. Although he could not face being present at his brother Irénée's marriage to Frank Gurney's daughter, one wedding he did plan to return for was that of his brother William to a dark, slant-eyed beauty named Ethel Hallock. There was Armenian blood in her family, and Lou made the most of it:

> Ethel says she will not be married in the daytime. Evening is the only time for a wedding, and she wants everyone to wear full dress. She also said she preferred to wear a red wedding gown. Red was her favorite color, and she wanted to be married in it. I think her eastern blood must be creeping out. I have always heard red was the color worn by brides in the east.

Lou also kept him posted on her own affairs of the heart (she eventually married Charles Copeland, her dead sister Sophie's old beau), and the ups and downs of their brother Belin. One minute he was "breathless, distressed, spitting blood" and the next he was fighting fit. As Lou wrote:

> Mama was in to see Belin today, and found him much better. He has given up all Dr. Greenleaf's remedies and taken some of the medicine Dr. Battles gave him last winter in Asheville. Since he took it all traces of blood spitting have disappeared and he seems much better both in health and spirits.

P.S. continued to minister to his family's financial affairs and sent them regular accounts of his investments on their behalf. It must have taken him hours every week to compile the lists and keep up his correspondence with them all. And he was extremely generous with them. Lammot, his youngest brother, still at M.I.T., complained that he was now getting such a lavish allowance from P.S. that he had been forced to open a bank account.

At this time too, P.S. became passionately interested in promoting one other affair concerning the family, a celebration of the one hundredth anni-

versary of the du Ponts' arrival in the New World. He decided there must
be a commemoration worthy of the event, to which all living du Ponts in
the United States would be invited, on New Year's Day, 1900. In preparation for the event, he charged Lou to act as his go-between in making up
a photographic album depicting every single member of the du Pont family,
by blood or by marriage. The two of them, he said, would write to every
du Pont they could trace, asking for photographs of themselves and their
families. But he counseled her to go first to Winterthur to "consult" Cousin
Henry Algernon because the Colonel was "very touchy about anything to
do with the family" and if offended "he might get put out and not allow
anything he had to be copied." Since portraits of the original du Pont
ancestors and connections were all at Winterthur, a boycott by the Colonel
would effectively nullify their efforts.

For the rest of 1899 the correspondence between Lou and P.S. was
enlivened by her account of how her efforts were progressing. In July of
that year she went up to Winterthur with a Philadelphia photographer who
was to take pictures of the family portraits. She reported:

> The Col. was present and most agreeable, for him. We took
> Mr. and Mrs. Samuel, the portraits the Col. brought back from
> Paris, and we also took the Col's portrait. It is a very flattered
> [sic] portrait and much better looking than the Col. ever was.
>
> While I was up there the Col. called me into the parlor and
> asked if all the family were to be in the album and I not thinking
> said yes. Then, he said, that if Mr and Mrs Saulsbury and Mr and
> Mrs Wm du Pont were to be in, of course he would not take a
> copy.

Willard Saulsbury was the well-known family lawyer who had taken
May du Pont's case when her husband, William (the Colonel's brother),
had asked for a South Dakota divorce. William, of course, had gone on to
marry the pretty divorcée Annie Rogers Zinn and had been driven out of
Delaware by the Colonel. A little later, May du Pont had decided to marry
Willard Saulsbury, and the wedding had been celebrated in a Wilmington
church. The Colonel was so shocked that he had complained to the Reverend Leighton Coleman, bishop of Delaware; and the bishop (also married
to a du Pont) had thereupon dismissed from his church the unfortunate
rector who had dared to give a church wedding to the Colonel's divorced
sister-in-law, innocent party or not. She too had been expunged from Cousin
Henry's visiting list.

Now here was this disgraceful quartet trying to insinuate themselves back into the Brandywine by means of a photographic album. It was not to be tolerated.

Lou hastened to mend her fences with the Colonel.

> I said I have never heard you say who you would have in [she went on in her letter to P.S.], but that I was sure in his set of prints he would have anyone he wanted ommitted [sic]. He said he did not want this mentioned, except to you.
>
> I thought the less talk the better, but I suppose it was all right telling him he would have an expurgated edition.

It was not all right, of course, as P.S. pointed out to Lou in his next letter to her. The Colonel now had such a hatred of his brother, his brother's wife, and the Saulsburys that he did not wish merely to have them omitted from his own album, but rather he did not want any of their portraits to be used in the other albums, either. Lou had quietly been taking a poll of her relatives to find out how they stood on the question, and was convinced the majority of them were in favor of putting *every* du Pont's picture into the album. When she informed P.S. of this, he agreed that, in that case, the offending quartet should be asked to provide photographs of themselves. But he cautioned:

> For goodness' sake do not let anyone know of this as I fear that if the Col heard of it, he would refuse to appear in the album or at the dinner.

He also asked her to assure the Colonel that Brother Willie would not, of course, be asked to the dinner. But in the end he decided that the Colonel was too powerful to offend, since so much about the commemorative celebrations depended on him. Better to leave some gaps in the family portraiture—eliminating Willie, for one—than hazard ruining the dinner. A few weeks later Lou wrote:

> I send the [gold] leaf and unmounted photographs to the Col and yesterday had a call from him on the subject. He wants an album just like everybody else only he said he did not want May or Saulsbury or the Willies in it. I told him that the Willies were not in the book. He was evidently pleased as punch at that, and was most affable saying what a thoroughly good work it was you had gotten up, and generally flattering on all subjects. I was

almost sorry I did not strike him for something, for I am sure I would have gotten it.*

There was one controversial du Pont couple, however, who, P.S. and Lou resolved, were not going to be snubbed no matter how much the Colonel or anyone else objected: Alfred's happy-go-lucky brother, Maurice, and his Irish wife, Margery. So Lou was dispatched to Atlantic City to persuade them to postpone their imminent departure for Ireland and stay over for the centennial. Her report:

> It is very evident that Maurice wants to stay, but Margie is very sore about the B'wine still and says she don't feel as if she ever wanted to come back. My opinion is that Marguerite [sister of Maurice and Alfred, married to a Washington lawyer from an old Virginia family, and a great snob] has done a great deal toward keeping her off. Whether or not they can be kept here for eleven weeks longer . . . is a question.

Tiffany's of New York was commissioned to print the embossed invitations, with the du Pont coat of arms in color, inviting all the relatives to the centennial breakfast.** Then one of the du Pont girls fell seriously ill, and Lou reported she was praying every night for her recovery not, as she explained, because the sick one was not a "horrid person" but because of what would happen to Lou's cards if she were to die. She died, and Tiffany's had to print new cards with a black edge around them.

Then brother Irénée (called Buss by his family) informed her that his fiancée, Irene du Pont, was insisting on a January wedding.

"I do wish Buss had not taken January to be married," Lou complained. "What with Christmas, the Centennial and a wedding on top, we will all be bust."

But at long last the great day came. Satisfied that no alien or enemy eyes would be gazing at them, the Colonel brought along all the family portraits and all the family heirlooms for the other du Ponts to see. The guests had been enjoined to garb themselves in simple suits and dresses in keeping with what their forebears had been wearing when they landed on the American shore, but some of the best dressmakers in New York and Philadelphia had been commissioned to give most of them an elegance that

---

* The album and other preparations for the centenary had cost brother and sister a tidy sum, and they were hoping to recoup something from the relatives.

** Though held in the evening, it was called a breakfast because that was the first meal the du Pont ancestors had eaten on landing in the United States.

the early du Ponts perforce had lacked. Lou reported later that when one of the du Pont wives was rebuked for the splendor of her pearls, she had answered:

"But you see, they came from the sea too. I thought it was appropriate."

Of course, Willie and his wife, Annie, were not there, but he wrote to P.S. to say that he did not even remotely care. May Saulsbury was furious, on the other hand. To get her own back, she instructed Lou to be sure to let the Colonel and Bishop Leighton Coleman know that she and her husband, Willard, had given a large pension to the unfortunate rector who had married them and that he now had "a most fashionable and prosperous parish" in Switzerland.

Maurice and Margery du Pont had already gone back to Ireland after all. Margie had confided to Lou that she was pregnant and feared that the sight of all those terrible du Ponts gathered together might provoke her into a miscarriage. The last thing she wanted, Margie said, was for her baby to be born on the du Pont fiefdom of the Brandywine.

In spite of all the precautions, there was one scandal at the centennial breakfast, and that was caused by the beautiful and imperious Miss Alicia Bradford. Brought by her parents, Judge Edward and Eleuthera du Pont Bradford, she deserted them as soon as the feast was over and made her way across to where Alfred I. and Bessie du Pont were sitting. Coolly taking Cousin Alfred's hand, she drew him onto the dance floor and then spent most of the remainder of the evening in his company. The relatives were shocked. Of course it was true that Bessie du Pont was now seven months gone with child and in no condition to dance, but the watchful elders of the du Pont clan were scandalized not only by Alicia's effrontery in flaunting her power over Alfred I. so publicly but also by Alfred I.'s uncaring neglect of his pregnant wife. That pregnancy had seemed to proclaim an end to their estrangement . . . but observing the way Alfred I. and Alicia were holding each other, looking at each other, who could believe it?

What only a few of them knew was that Alfred I. and Bessie du Pont were, in fact, farther apart than ever, and he was now madly infatuated with Alicia. The evidence is scanty about what was taking place between them in the last five months of 1899, but it had certainly gone far beyond the fleeting intimacy of Atlantic City. What is hard to pin down is how far? Were they by this time having an affair?

Probably not. Alicia Bradford was still living at home, and even though she was a bold and uninhibited defier of convention, it would have been difficult for her to find a love nest where they could meet regularly. The trouble with being a du Pont was that everybody knew who you were, and every newspaper on the East Coast would have been after them had it become known that Judge Bradford's unconventional daughter and the famous Alfred I. du Pont were having a liaison.

Those moments they could manage had made Alfred I. more frustrated than ever, and more eager to find a way to separate Alicia from her bad-tempered and puritanical father and establish her in a place where they could meet discreetly. By the time the centennial dinner came around, he was able to tell her he had found a solution.

She must get married. Not to him—at least not for the moment. He could not possibly sue Bessie for divorce while she was pregnant and about to produce his child. No, Alicia must marry someone who could give her a home but who would not be around it too frequently himself, leaving the place clear instead for Alfred I. to visit: a surrogate husband with limited powers.

He even had the bridegroom picked out. His name was George Maddox, and he worked for Alfred I.

All the du Ponts were afterward to wonder how Alicia Bradford could possibly have entertained such an immoral proposal from her would-be lover. And it is true that at first Alicia seems to have had her own qualms.

Still, on February 9, 1900, when Lou du Pont went to Swamp Hall to visit Bessie and Alfred I., she had already heard rumors linking Alicia's name with George Maddox and had speculated about it with her intimates. Maddox was a minor engineer in the labs, and some grumbling had been heard among the chemists when Alfred I. suddenly promoted him to head of a department. He was a hulking, handsome, pleasant young man who made it plain he thought Mr. Alfred I. was the most wonderful person he had ever met, and all the chemists ruefully concluded that flattery of his boss was getting him everywhere. But then suddenly he was seen around with Alicia Bradford. Could it possibly be true that she—a du Pont girl, and a stuck-up one too, who could have had anyone she wanted—was serious about him? It was lucky, everybody said, that Judge Bradford had not heard about it yet. He would be outraged.

Lou wrote to P.S. in Lorain:

Today I lunched at Alfred's . . . while I was there Alicia came in. She asked me most particularly just what dates in June we were going abroad, and if we would be here until just before we sailed. She asked so many questions I really think she must be thinking of getting married.

A couple of weeks later (on February 25, 1900) she wrote:

Although Alicia said she was coming over for a special talk as soon as I got back from New York, she has not yet appeared. Perhaps I was wrong in thinking her wedding was in the wind.

What finally made up Alicia's mind was her father's reaction when the rumors finally reached him. Predictably, he exploded. What was this he had heard about his daughter compromising herself with a nonentity out of the powder yards? She must give up the association at once—he forbade it. At which Alicia calmly told her empurpled father that not only would she go on consorting with George Maddox but she was also going to marry him. She was of age. There was nothing he could do to stop her. Then, delighted to have so enraged her hated father, she hurried away to Alfred I. and told him to fix up the nuptials.

Alfred I. went to see George's parents, a humble couple who were grateful for the way the boss was looking after their son's future, and promised to pay all the expenses if they would make arrangements for the wedding. Between them, they began to draw up the guest list—which would not, of course, include Judge Bradford and his family. But Alfred I. promised the wedding would be at Christ's Church, the du Pont place of worship.

Then he began to have doubts. Was George Maddox possibly too young and too handsome for this proxy marriage to stay genuinely bogus? Would the bridegroom keep his part of the bargain? More important, would the bride?

"Alicia announces her nuptials for June," reported Lou to P.S. on April 29, 1900. But later in the same letter, she added:

We heard at Bess's that Alicia is not to be married in June after all, Mr and Mrs Maddox having met with some pecuniary loss. They say Alicia is broken hearted. It must be discouraging to be engaged in an indefinite manner.

She went on being engaged for another two years while Alfred I. wrestled with his doubts. Meanwhile he would often make a threesome with Alicia and George Maddox. But the scandalmongers on the Brandywine whispered that it was always George who parted from the other two, and not the other way round. There were also times when Alicia left the Brandywine to go to New York, supposedly to stay with relatives. At about the same time (May 11, 1901) Lou was writing to P.S.:

> Alfred is trying a new doctor in New York for his ears. This one cut a piece of bone out of his nose, as he said his nose mended wrong when he broke it [as a child], and all the passage from the back of his nose to his ears was stopped up. I do hope he will be benefitted. I have never seen anyone who really was. . . . Alfred goes to New York three days out of each week.

It was when news reached the du Ponts that he and Alicia had been seen with each other in New York, that Alfred I. decided he had better face up to the alternatives. Either he must emulate his uncle William du Pont and go to South Dakota for a divorce from Bessie, or permit the proxy marriage with George Maddox to go through.

It was no moment for a divorce. Cousin Eugene had died, and there were great goings-on in the Du Pont company. There were alarming rumors about what the senior partners were planning to do. It was no time to be away in South Dakota.*

On the other hand, he needed Alicia more than ever, and he needed her close by. What other solution was there—for the moment, anyway—than to marry her off to the complaisant George Maddox? He went back to George's parents and told them to make arrangements, for their son's wedding was on again.

Mary Alicia Heyward Bradford and George Maddox were married at Christ's Church, on the Brandywine, on April 30, 1902, and Alfred I. du Pont gave the bride away. Neither her father nor her mother was present, and two thirds of the du Ponts did not accept their invitations.

The wedding reception was held at Swamp Hall, and after it was over, after Alicia and George had departed for their honeymoon, after the last guests had gone, Alfred and Bessie du Pont were alone together. Since the birth of their son, Alfred Victor, two years before, relations between them had soured once more. But not tonight.

* Where a six-months residence was required.

Nine months later Bessie du Pont gave birth to her fourth and last child, a girl whom they christened Victorine.

A little earlier Alicia Bradford Maddox also gave birth to a daughter. She was given the same name as her mother, and christened Alicia Maddox. But Alfred I. always called her Pechette, which translates as "Little Sin."

Part Three

THE NEW REGIME

CHAPTER 12

Troika

O N January 27, 1902, Lou wrote to her brother P. S. du Pont that she had been to visit Cousin Eugene who was in bed with a heavy cold. The Du Pont company's senior partner looked so frail and feverish she thought he would not survive the night. He did that, but he died the following day, January 28, aged sixty-two.

His death created a crisis in the affairs of Du Pont. Eugene had served the company for forty-two years, and his hand, although shaky, had been the only one on the tiller since Boss Henry's death. Who would take his place as president?

Shortly after Eugene's burial at Sand Hole Woods, the five surviving partners were due to hold a meeting to discuss the nomination of a new president, and the future of the company. But Alfred I. did not bother to attend. His deafness had grown so serious that he could not always hear what was being said; and in any case, he was alienated from his fellow partners, who strongly disapproved of his affair with Alicia and his treatment of his wife. He knew they would outvote him on the presidency question and were not likely to listen to his advice. He had a fatalistic feeling that whether he was there or not, they would choose the wrong man.

By length of service, the logical successor to Eugene was his brother Francis Gurney du Pont, and though no one admired his capabilities or believed he had the qualifications for the job, the other four partners were resigned to the prospect of voting him in. But Frank surprised them by saying, the moment the partnership meeting was convened, that he "emphatically refused" to accept the presidency. His family knew what his partners did not: that he was a sick man.

The next logical contender was Colonel Henry Algernon du Pont, but he too demurred. He was now, at sixty-three doggedly trying to win himself a seat in the Senate or the Congress, and though he was having a frustrating time, he was not ready to give in yet. Moreover, as P. S. du Pont wrote later, he "was inclined to unload business cares and was quite unwilling to take on new responsibilities." And he had had no practical experience. His refusal of the presidency was received with relief.

But who else was there? The other two partners were Charles du Pont and the third brother of Eugene and Frank, Alexis I. du Pont. Charles was already a dying man and did not live out the year. Alexis, who had confined his career at Du Pont to representative and advisory duties, knew nothing about powder making, and he too was in poor health.*

That left the fifth partner, Alfred I. du Pont, as the only contender, and since he had not bothered to attend the meeting, they could discuss his qualifications (and his character) freely. He had already proved he knew more about powder making than the rest of them put together, but in the eyes of his fellow partners that did not outweigh the disadvantages of his character. Frank Gurney du Pont, as a report later put it, "had formed an exceedingly low estimate of Alfred Irénée's good judgment and business ability, which he did not hesitate to express." The Colonel then cleared his throat and declared that although he was "disposed to be more lenient," he did not think Alfred I. would inspire confidence among other members of the family, let alone in the business community beyond.

The others looked to Alexis, the third senior partner. Alexis would rather not have expressed an opinion but was well aware of what his domineering wife, Elizabeth, would say if he did not block Alfred I.'s progress. Elizabeth Bradford du Pont, a half sister of Judge Bradford, fully shared the judge's disgust over Alfred I.'s scandalous behavior with his outcast

---

* He died within a month of his brother Frank, in 1904.

daughter, Alicia. Alexis therefore made his opposition loud and clear. In the circumstances, Charles du Pont, Alfred I.'s only friend at the meeting, wisely kept his mouth shut.

But with the last remaining candidate eliminated, what were they to do? Wearily, after hours of fruitless discussion, the four partners reached what seemed to them the only possible solution. They would sell the Du Pont company. They would offer it lock, stock, and powder keg to their biggest and most respected rival, the Laflin and Rand Powder Company. For decades the two companies had dominated the explosives business through the Powder Trust. Laflin and Rand's president, J. Amory Haskell, was an old Du Pont hand who had until recently been head of the Repauno Mineral Company, which Lammot du Pont had started, and they all admired his ability. He would certainly do no harm to Du Pont's reputation or assets.

Then began discussions about who should run the company temporarily while the sale was being arranged. They eventually agreed on the choice of a young relative by marriage, Hamilton M. Barksdale (his wife was Charles du Pont's sister). He knew the powder business and had also once headed the Repauno Mineral Company. But when Barksdale was approached, he declined. He thought someone with the du Pont name should see the company through to its sale, and proposed to talk it over with Coleman du Pont, who was in Wilmington at the time. But by now Alfred I. had dragged himself away from his preoccupation with Alicia and his hearing troubles and had discovered what had been going on in his absence.

On Friday, February 14, 1902, a meeting of the stockholders of the company was called (as a subsequent company report put it) "for the purpose of taking action on the proposed disposal of their property. At this meeting a resolution was offered authorizing a sale to the Laflin & Rand Powder Company and appointing H. M. Barksdale as agent to negotiate."

Alfred I. made sure he did not miss that meeting. He came straight from the yards, still dressed in his coveralls, hands and face streaked with gunpowder. He took no part in the general discussion until the formal resolution was proposed. Then he rose and put forward an amendment specifying that the company should be sold to the highest bidder. When this was carried, and the meeting seemed to be over, Alfred I. spoke again.

"I will buy the business," he said.

The other partners looked at him in astonishment. The first to speak was Frank Gurney du Pont: It was, he said crisply, simply not possible.

"Why not?" Alfred I. asked.

Despite his outward calmness, he was considerably worked up by the cool way in which the other men around the table were proposing to sell out—just like that—a company that the du Ponts had spent a century to build up to its present eminence, spilling blood and sweat in the process. As he explained to his cousins later, it was an intolerable situation:

> I pointed out to [Frank] that the business was mine by all rights of heritage, that it was my birthright. I told him that I would pay as much as anybody else, and furthermore, I proposed to have it. I told him I would require a week to perfect the necessary arrangements looking towards the purchase of the business, and asked for that length of time.

The partners were struck dumb by this outburst, and no one spoke as Alfred I. shoved back his chair and prepared to leave. Then the Colonel rose.

"Gentlemen," he said, "I think I understand Alfred's sentiment in desiring to purchase the business, and I wish to say that it has my hearty approval, and I shall insist he be given the first opportunity to acquire the property."

With that voice in support of Alfred I., even Frank Gurney du Pont could not object. It was agreed that the junior partner be given a chance to produce.

Meanwhile the Colonel had followed Alfred I. out of the room and, grabbing him by the shoulder, said (and the stilted words are his version), "I assume, of course, although you said nothing about it, that Thomas Coleman and Pierre are, or will be, associated with you in the proposed purchase?"

Alfred I.'s reply, as the Colonel later remembered it, was "Yes, although as a matter of fact I have not heard from Pierre as yet, to whom I have written (or am about to write)."

The Colonel nodded. "With the understanding that Coleman and Pierre are associated with you in the proposition I assent to it most cordially and will do everything in my power to bring it about."

Pausing only to express his thanks, Alfred I. rushed out and leaped into his automobile. In a noxious cloud of blue smoke and backfires he sped downtown to Delaware Avenue, where Coleman and Elsie du Pont lived. He came right out with the proposition. Would Coleman now join him and help buy out the other partners?

It so happened that Coleman du Pont was going through a sticky financial period in the early part of 1902. He was rumored to have recently lost something like half a million dollars on the stock market, and he might very well have been about to lose more. But when strapped for money, Coleman usually was at his strongest and put his boldest front toward the world. He wore a self-confident mask for Alfred I. now. He too believed that his cousin, though a first-class powder man, was a bad organizer and an unstable character. It would never do to have him as president of Du Pont.

So Coleman made two conditions for his own participation. First, he must be given an absolutely free hand in organizing and managing the new company, and that meant he must be given the largest block of stock in the company. Second, their cousin P. S. du Pont must join them in the new venture, since P.S. had long since proved, as guardian of his brothers and sisters, and as director of the Johnson Company, that he knew his way around the business world—was, in fact, as good a manager as Coleman himself.

Alfred I. did not hesitate. He put out his hand, and they shook on it.

It was then that Coleman du Pont went to the telephone instrument in the hall and put through a long-distance call to P.S. in Lorain, Ohio. When the connection was made, he told P.S. he had agreed with Alfred I. "to accept the responsibility of the Presidency of the reorganization of E. I. du Pont de Nemours & Company," on the condition that P.S. agreed to oversee the financial part of the business. Would he do it?

P. S. du Pont wrote later:

> This was the most important and far-reaching decision of my life. No position, salary or interest in the business was offered but the three minute allowance of a telephone conversation was quite long enough for me to receive the account of the proposition placed before me, to make up my mind and give my reply in one word, *yes*.

He knew his two cousins were equally enthusiastic about the adventure now facing them:

> My commitment to join the enterprise, though made over the telephone only, bound me, by ties much stronger than a written contract, to stand by the old Company through thick and thin. Coleman had the same determination and, though only recently a citizen of Delaware and without close family ties, felt a commitment stronger than one to be broken by any unexpected development.

P.S. was convinced that Alfred I. "was equally enthusiastic," but, he added with a hint of the superiority that eventually goaded a cousinly quarrel, "as the question of administrative and financial leadership was paramount, perhaps [Alfred I.'s] responsibility seemed the least important of the three."

P.S. told John J. Raskob to begin closing up the files and preparing to leave for Delaware. Now all the three cousins had to do was find the money to make good Alfred I.'s offer. The old regime had put a selling price of twelve million dollars on the Du Pont assets, and the cousins had a week to find that sum. In available cash and credits they had less than one million among them.

It was, of course, the bargain of the century.

The three cousins may not have had the twelve million in ready cash, but there was no doubt, as they quickly discovered, that the Du Pont assets were worth at least double and possibly triple that amount. While P.S. was arranging for a successor in Lorain, Ohio,* and getting ready to come east, Alfred I. sneaked into the main office at the powder yards and started hauling out the ledgers in which Du Pont's holdings were listed. As a junior partner, he had never been allowed to peruse them; and from their condition, coated with dust, pages stuck together and yellow with powder, it appeared that none of the senior partners had examined them for some years, either. He was astounded at what he found.

Not only did Du Pont own the Brandywine yards and Carney's Point, but the company also had thriving mills in Pennsylvania, Iowa, and Tennessee. It still had the majority block of shares that Lammot du Pont had bought in the California Powder Company. It was the sole owner of the Hazard Powder Company. And it had considerable holdings in several other dynamite companies and explosives concerns. Alfred I., who had been drawing ten percent of the profits over the past few years, knew that the enterprise as a whole had never failed to do well, in spite of old-fashioned management and the failure of certain elements in the structure. He now realized that he and his cousins had the chance of buying up a gold mine. He computed the assets conservatively at twenty-four million dollars, and they were almost certainly worth very much more. The old partners simply had no idea of what rich resources they possessed, and of what fabulous potentialities they were divesting themselves.

* He put his brothers William and Irénée in charge for the time being.

But how to pay for it?

The cousins huddled in discussion. Where were they going to find the money? At which point Coleman du Pont said:

"We will not need money." And then, as they looked at him in astonishment: "Leave it to me."

Thomas Coleman du Pont was a born promoter, and a born seducer. Tall, with a du Pont nose of impressive proportions, a friendly smile on his face, and an air of enormous self-confidence, he had a charm that, as one less successful du Pont ruefully said, "could charm the birds off the trees, blood out of stone, gold bars out of bank vaults, and girls out of their dresses." He exuded capability and trustworthiness.

He went before a meeting of the old partners, and those tired and defeated men were like putty in his hands. He had to tell them, Coleman said, that he and his two cousins did not have the twelve million dollars they were asking for the assets of Du Pont. But did they really want twelve million in cash, anyway? Think of what an embarrassment it would be to them. Think of all the trouble they would have reinvesting it in something safe.

He had a much better idea. Instead of twelve million dollars in cash, he would give them a twenty-five-percent interest in the new company that the three cousins would be forming, and would pay them four-percent interest on twelve million dollars over the next thirty years—minus, of course, any interest they received from the profits of the new company.*

Alfred I. du Pont was astonished as he listened to Coleman talking. He was well aware that if he had made the proposition, the other partners would angrily have told him he was trying to acquire the company for nothing—which was true—and would undoubtedly have turned him down. But with a surprisingly scant expression of doubt, the proposition advanced by Coleman was accepted. The whole transaction, P.S. wrote later, "was one of mutual faith and intent to win success in the future."

But it was much more than that. It was high-powered salesmanship on the part of Coleman du Pont, and no one else could have got away with it. The three young men had taken over the biggest powder makers in the United States, and probably in the world. And it had not cost them a cent.**

P.S. wrote to his brother Irénée to tell him what had been happening,

---

* His proposal was not unlike a scheme by which the founder, Eleuthère Irénée du Pont, had financed the original company a century earlier, although he had paid six percent.

** Except for twenty-one hundred dollars in incorporation payments.

for until now he had kept even members of his family ignorant of these maneuvers:

> This [the purchase] will doubtless come as a great surprise to you. Nevertheless it seems to be a "go." I think there is going to be some tall hustling to get everything reorganized. We have not the slightest idea of what we are buying but in that we are probably not at a disadvantage as I think the [members of the] old Company have a very slim idea of the [value of the] property they possess.

The meeting at which Alfred I. had made his intervention took place on February 14, 1902. Exactly fifteen days later P. S. du Pont went down to the Brandywine with the idea of easing himself into the workings of the company while the Old Guard was still in situ. But he had a shock waiting for him. As he wrote later:

> Francis G. du Pont . . . came to the room which had been set aside for me and handed me a number of papers—the morning mail and other matters requiring immediate attention. He shook hands and with hearty good wishes departed, leaving the entire management of the Company to the prospective owners.

The cousins were on their own.

They had certainly taken possession of a viable enterprise. Upon examining the books further, they found they had $1 million in cash in the banks; $3 million in standard securities listed on the New York Stock Exchange; patents, goodwill, and other assets worth several million; plants conservatively valued at $10 million; and their interests in other companies.

They formally bought the assets of the old company for $2,100, or $700 each, and formed a new company called E. I. du Pont de Nemours and Company (1902), which, they declared, had a value of $24 million, of which $12 million would be issued in four-percent notes and 120,000 shares with a value of $100 each ($12 million in all). All the notes plus 33,600 shares of stock (worth $3.4 million) went to the old partners and stockholders and to the estate of the late Eugene du Pont. The remainder of the shares (86,400, worth $8.6 million) the three cousins split among themselves as "promoters' profits."

As the man who had pulled off the deal, and who would henceforth head the new company, Coleman reaped 43,200 shares and was named president. P.S. got 21,600 shares and was named treasurer. Alfred I. received 21,600 plus 3,000 shares (this last being his allotment of the purchase price as an old partner), making 24,600 shares in all.* He was named vice-president and general manager.

For Alfred I. the position was the fulfillment of a dream. All his life, ever since he had wandered around the Brandywine yards as a boy, he had hoped that one day he would be master of them. He loved the smell of powder. He enjoyed the comradeship he had with the men and the risks they shared in the mixing sheds and the rolling mills, where a sudden spark could blow them all to blazes.

He was well aware that the Brandywine mills were by now old-fashioned, their machinery obsolete, their quarters cramped and unnecessarily hazardous, the whole operation far too close to the living quarters where whole colonies of men, women, and children—du Ponts among them —were at risk. But he would not have it otherwise. He was a sentimental character who had a quite romantic idea of the working classes, at least so far as the Brandywine labor force was concerned, and it never occurred to him that they might not love the muck and sweat of the yards as much as he did. Had they not broken their backs together to save the nation during the Spanish-American War? He boasted that he considered the powder men part of his "family." Had anyone asked him why, then, he did not treat them as such, with the kinds of real rewards that "families" get for "belonging," like bonuses and profit-sharing, he would probably have replied that *his* powder men were not interested in money, so long as they got enough to live on. All they expected was praise from their boss and recognition of their best endeavors. They were in the yards, he would have added, not to grub for an extra nickel; rather, they were there because they had pride in their skills, a zest for challenging danger, and a respect for the Du Pont tradition. He loved his powder men as brothers, and he was certain they loved him back. As for the Brandywine yards, he could not imagine life without them, with his faithful labor force working there beside him.

His stupefaction was great, therefore, when Coleman du Pont, having made his first inspection tour of the mills, turned to Alfred I. and said:

"This place is out of date. Why don't we close it down and raze the whole thing?"

Aghast at the temerity of this outsider, Alfred I. did not stop to argue

* He also received $1.2 million in four-percent notes as his share of the purchase price.

but raced for the Brandywine offices where he confronted P.S. with Coleman's outrageous suggestion. He must be mad. Alfred I. had been a fool ever to allow him to become president. If that was how Coleman's mind was working, the new partnership would be a failure from the start.

P.S. was too keen an expert on cost factors not to know that Coleman was probably quite right. The yards were out of date. But this was no time to begin a quarrel. He went down to the yards to buttonhole Coleman and tell him to go slowly. So instead of closing the Brandywine, they agreed upon a modernization plan. New machinery was installed. New sheds were built. The water mills were heightened to bring in more power. Roads were regraded and straightened. An internal telephone system was installed. Meters were fitted in all the workers' houses—and those of the du Ponts, too—to encourage people to turn off the lights when not in use, thus reducing the cost of electricity. But at the same time, all the powder men's houses were fitted at last with baths and toilets.

As general manager, Alfred I. now had control of all the du Pont houses on the estate that were still owned by the company, and as it was with his great-grandfather, his grandfather, and his uncle before him, it was now in his power to decide who among the du Ponts should live where. Some of the family had, it is true, been allowed over the years to buy their houses. He himself, for instance, had been able to purchase Swamp Hall and some adjoining property, fifty-nine acres of it, for a consideration of "$5 and more."

But some of the best and biggest houses remained in the company's hands. Among them was the most palatial house on the estate, Louviers, which had once been the home of Admiral Samuel Francis and Sophie du Pont. But for the past few years the sitting tenant had been Belin du Pont, P.S.'s brother. Alfred I. was anxious to get him out. He wanted Louviers for a more active Du Pont employee, one George Maddox, who was just about to marry Alicia Bradford.

The three cousins took possession of the new Du Pont company on March 1, 1902, and Alfred I. became king of the Brandywine yards two days later. One of his first acts was to write to Belin du Pont to ask him to vacate Louviers as soon as possible, by mid-May at the latest.

He knew that Alicia and George Maddox would be returning from their honeymoon at the end of May, and he was determined to have Louviers ready for occupation by them when they returned. He had plans for

Alicia and George. He wanted Alicia close to him, in a house near enough to Swamp Hall for him to visit her by back lanes where he could avoid being seen; and he wanted George away when he made his visits. He had arranged that, too. He had told George he was being promoted yet again, this time to superintendent of the company's plants and customer depots in the Middle West. The job involved constant travel, and it could be rough country out there, he pointed out, hardly suitable for a gentle-born (and pregnant) wife.

The trouble was, Belin did not want to give up Louviers. He clung to the house as tenaciously as he did to life. Eloo had spent a large part of her dowry on making alterations to the house and decorating it in her style. The thought of some stranger soiling her treasures was more than either of them could bear. Belin, in particular, clung to his tenancy as a sort of talisman, as if sensing that in losing the house he would lose his fight to live. When he received Alfred I.'s letter asking him to quit he was at first in despair and then in a boiling fury. He was in Arizona by this time, on a ranch the family had bought him, for, they thought, the desert air would be good for his lungs. But though he was miles away from the Brandywine, he was still in touch with all the gossip (through his sister Lou, of course), and he had heard all the scandalous stories about Alicia Bradford's bogus marriage and her affair with Alfred I.

The thought that he was being asked to give up his precious Louviers, his last stake on the Brandywine, to accommodate a hussy and a cuckold was insupportable, and he scribbled a series of bitter (and libelous) letters to all and sundry.

He might have done better to appeal directly to his cousin, but even in his distress he could not bring himself to do so. In consequence, a formal letter from the Du Pont company arrived for Belin; his lease of Louviers, it announced, had been terminated, and Mr. and Mrs. George Maddox were now the official tenants. He handed the letter over to his mother. As she read it, Mary du Pont had a feeling that she was holding her son's death warrant.

On July 4, 1902, the three cousins arranged a celebration on the Brandywine to commemorate the centenary of the founding of the Du Pont company. Everybody was there (except Belin and Mary du Pont, of course), and for at least part of the day du Ponts and powder men and their families freely mixed. Alfred I. had arranged shooting matches, baseball games, tug-of-war competitions, dancing, band concerts, feasting and (soft) drinking, and, to end the day, a great fireworks display. Coleman wandered around the fields and yards, flirting with the wives and daughters, fascinating the powder men's children with displays of card and conjuring tricks at which he was adept. P.S. as usual stayed in the background but kept a benevolent eye on the proceedings and saw that there was no shortage of provisions.

At one point in the afternoon the three cousins gathered for a ceremony in the Brandywine office where that red-headed tyrant, General Henry du Pont, had once held sway. Gathered before the old boss's desk—lit for the occasion by three candles, his quill pens laid out in a row—was a small group of long-service workers from the yards. Behind Boss Henry's old desk were the survivors of the old regime, Frank Gurney, Alexis, Charles, and Colonel Henry Algernon du Pont. It was to the four older men that Pierre Gentieu, who had been with Du Pont since boyhood, now turned and said:

> Gentlemen of the old firm, you have been our leaders and friends for many years. We are sorry that you are leaving us, for we shall miss you.

Then, addressing the three young cousins, who stood in front of the desk, he said:

> What the new company will do, of course, we do not know. But let us hope that after one hundred years more as much good can be said of them as is said today of the du Ponts for the past century.

Probably only Alfred I. took seriously the sentimental ceremonial of bowing and scraping; he lingered with the veteran powder men, some of whom he had known since boyhood, while Coleman and P.S. hastened back to the celebrations outside. P.S. wrote to Belin later:

> The great Fourth of July picnic came off in great style, we had a perfect day though rather warm in the sun, and without the least danger of rain or thunder storm throughout so that everybody came and stayed to the very end. . . . As the fireworks lasted pretty late and as the day had been quite a long one for everybody we decided that we might as well shut down all of the mills on Saturday which I think is the first occasion of a holiday other than Fourth of July and Christmas being given

on the Brandywine. . . . Your affectionate brother, Pierre S. du Pont.

The letter was posted to Belin on July 7, 1902, for delivery to Santa Barbara, California, where he had gone on another desperate quest for a miracle-making climate. It was returned to P.S. a few days later, unopened. Belin du Pont had haemorrhaged and died while it was being written.

CHAPTER 13

Gunpowder Plot

T H E three cousins differed greatly not only in temperament, morals, and emotional makeup but also in their ambitions for the Du Pont company. Alfred I. du Pont would not have minded working with black powder on the Brandywine for the rest of his life, so long as the operation turned over a decent profit and left him time for his experiments, his music, his automobiles, his hunting trips, and his love affair. Coleman du Pont was interested in the Du Pont company solely as his means of making a fortune large enough to take him away from the Brandywine and provide him with a power base in New York. Du Pont might have made soap, or sausages, as far as he was concerned; all he knew about explosives was that they aggravated the condition of his chronically sore throat.

On the other hand, P. S. du Pont was enlivened, as much as a man of his nature could ever be, by the thought that Cousin Eugene's death had delivered the family business into his hands, and that he was responsible for its destiny. His pioneering forebears had created and fashioned the family business and turned it into a recognized name wherever shots were fired in sport or in anger. He could feel them tugging at him now as he wrestled with the ledgers in the office, whispering to him: We have made our family known and we have made it rich. It is now up to you to make it great.

How could that be achieved in any other way than by making Du Pont the biggest explosive company not just in the United States but in the world? It must be a company, moreover, that monopolized the explosives business so extensively that in the future no one would be able to make wars or blow up mountains without coming to Du Pont—and paying Du Pont prices. Once upon a time, thanks to the manipulations of old Boss Henry and P.S.'s father, Lammot du Pont, the company through membership in the Powder Trust, had been able to settle the policies of its rivals and split up the markets among the members of the Trust. But lately, owing to the laxness of the partners of the old regime, Du Pont's influence had waned, and the company had often had to be content with less than its fair share of the sales and the profits. P.S. hardly found this state of affairs satisfactory. As he told his cousins, what they should aim for now was not their fair share of the market but the lion's share—a monopoly of the orders at the prices Du Pont set.

Going through the company's books, P.S. noticed that Du Pont had some very valuable investments in the shares of rival powder companies, but in only one, the Hazard Powder Company, which Boss Henry had bought up secretly during his reign, did they have a controlling interest. In the eyes of the general public, and of most financial experts too, the three main and competing explosives companies in the United States in 1902 were Du Pont, Hazard, and Laflin and Rand. No one realized that Hazard was secretly under Du Pont control. And it was this that fired P.S.'s imagination and his ambitions. Du Pont already had a minority investment in Laflin and Rand. What if he could turn that into a majority investment—or even take over the whole firm? Then the Big Three would all be under Du Pont's control, and a monopoly of the explosives industry in America would be in the hands of the three cousins.

The prospect was so tantalizing that P.S. took time off to go to Scranton, Pennsylvania, to talk it over with his uncle Henry Belin. Uncle Harry, as P.S. called him, was his mother's brother and the father of Alice du Pont, who had pined over P.S. for years, and she was sorely disappointed when she discovered that it was the professional advice of her father that her young cousin was seeking and not her company. Uncle Harry (like his father before him) had become an expert accountant and was a sought-after adviser of banks and business enterprises, including Du Pont and Laflin and Rand. He had been through the ledgers of both companies and was quite familiar with their contents. He also knew that the three principal directors of Laflin and Rand, like the Old Guard at Du Pont, were "of fairly advanced age, knew the problems before the explosives industry and possibly were disturbed by the changes in the Du Pont management."

As P. S. du Pont described it later, the Laflin and Rand directors were "conservative and willing to drift," whereas they realized that Coleman du Pont had a reputation for being "progressive and aggressive," and they feared a knockdown war with him. If the cousins could come up with a good offer, they would be sorely tempted to sell.

It was at this point that Coleman du Pont was once more wheeled in for a concentrated exercise of his charm and salesmanship. By the time he arrived for the main discussion, the directors of Laflin and Rand had decided that what they wanted for their stockholders was $700 a share. This made P.S. and Alfred I. cringe. But Coleman was not fazed at all. Yes, he said, they would pay $700 a share (provided an examination of Laflin and Rand's books proved them to be satisfactory). Alfred I. protested that they could not afford such an amount, which came to no less than $6 million. How could a new company, needing all the money it could lay its hands on for raw material and development, dig up such a sum?

Coleman chuckled. "Don't worry," he said. "We are not going to pay them a nickel."

Once more he persuaded these tough, if tired, businessmen that the last thing they wanted was hard cash. He would pay them in bonds instead. For each seven-hundred-dollar share he would give the Laflin and Rand shareholders four hundred dollars in five-percent bonds of the Delaware Security Company and three hundred dollars in five-percent bonds of the Delaware Investment Company. The Delaware Security Company and the Delaware Investment Company were two holding companies that he had set up overnight, backed by collateral in the Du Pont company. To make his proposition seem even more tempting, he offered the Laflin and Rand shareholders a bonus of twenty percent of the par value of their bonds in the stock of the two companies.

The stockholders, P.S. later reported, "accepted this proposition as being too good to turn down."

As soon as they did so, Coleman sped back to P.S. and told him to get around to Laflin and Rand fast and verify the book value of the company while there was still time to back down. Of that visit, P.S. wrote:

> The *very private ledger* of the company was produced for my inspection. After a couple of hours I retired with a promise to return but instead I went immediately to Wilmington.

For he could hardly believe his eyes. Even more consistently than the Du Pont company, Laflin and Rand had undervalued its holdings and investments. Shares that Du Pont also possessed, and that the Old Guard had valued at $140, were in the Laflin and Rand books at $31, whereas they were worth at least $200 on the market. Other stocks were estimated according to their 1887 values instead of the much higher ones of 1902. Altogether, the book value of the company was millions of dollars more than the directors seemed to believe.

P.S. went straight to Coleman and urged him to clinch the deal at once:

> [I] advised Coleman to close the transaction at once, lest our inspection might lead the owners to resurvey their property and retire from their commitment. This advice was accepted and the purchase made as of July 1st, 1902, though all details of the transfer were not finished until October of that year.

The three cousins and their new Du Pont company were now masters of the United States gunpowder industry, the black blasting powder industry, and the dynamite industry east of the Mississippi valley. They were once more kings of the castle so far as the Powder Trust was concerned, for they owned nine of the seventeen companies outright and had large holdings in all but three of the eight remaining companies. Altogether, they now had fifty-four corporations under their control, and fifty-six percent of the national production. Coleman had brought off this financial coup at a cost of a cash outlay of eighty-five hundred dollars, divided among the three of them.

Coleman and P.S. then went to work to mold this unwieldy group of companies into one solid corporation. But this necessitated buying up the minority stockholders before their companies could be extinguished or incorporated, and in May 1903 Coleman set up the E. I. du Pont de Nemours Powder Company, with an authorized capital of $50 million, of which $30 million was issued in common and preferred stocks. Two thirds of this stock (and the controlling interest) was handed over to E. I. du Pont de Nemours and Company (1902), which the three cousins had formed after buying out the Old Guard. The other third was to be used, instead of cash, to buy out the minority holdings in the companies they now owned.

John Raskob was now working with Coleman du Pont, and these two shrewd operators knew that before the new corporation, the Du Pont de Nemours Powder Company, could begin operations, it must take out licenses to do business in various states of the union. Fees for licenses were calculated on the amount of the capitalization of the company, and the Powder Company's capitalization had been set at a high figure because the partners needed purchasing power. So yet another company was formed; called the E. I. du Pont Company, it was capitalized at only ten thousand dollars. All plants owned by the corporation were transferred to this company. Then the state licenses were applied for through the new company and granted at knockdown rates.

The operation was a brilliant success. The minority stockholders were bought out, and several other companies bought in, including the main California operators. As Marquis James has written:

> The success of the mopping-up process reduced the authority of the Gunpowder Trade Association [the Powder Trust] to that of a high school debating society. Authority rested with Du Pont. The Association was worse than a hollow shell. It was a source of potential embarrassment, some of its restrictive provisions being clearly in contravention of the Sherman Anti-Trust Law. In 1904 Du Pont pulled out of the Association, abrogating the agreements on prices and trade territories under its aegis. In one instance Du Pont paid $100,000 and in another $140,000 to get rid of such agreements. The Association collapsed.

Du Pont now really controlled the market, and the three cousins set to work driving out every vulnerable competitor. By 1905 they had such a stranglehold on the industry that they manufactured 64.6 percent of all soda blasting powder sold in the United States, 80 percent of all saltpeter blasting powder, 72.5 percent of all dynamite, and 75 percent of all black sporting powder. They also produced 100 percent of the smokeless powder manufactured by private firms for military use.*

Having broken the Powder Trust, Coleman now began to wonder

---

* The United States government had an ordnance factory making a small amount of smokeless powder.

whether he could challenge and beat the international powder manufacturers too. For many years the Du Pont company had paid dues to an international association that controlled world explosives markets as the Powder Trust had once controlled those of the United States. It not only divided the globe up among its members but exchanged patents and information. The Du Pont interests had exclusive rights to these patents (as well as markets) in the United States, Mexico, and Central America, and British and German interests controlled the markets in the rest of the world, with the exception of South America, which was, as P.S. described it, a "happy hunting ground for all parties."

> All secret processes were included with the patents [he wrote later]. An annual payment by Du Pont to the Europeans was provided. Undoubtedly, both sides benefitted by the acquisition of the patents and secret processes and equally undoubtedly the loss of the use of these assets deterred the Du Pont company from branching out into foreign business, which it had no intention of doing at any rate as it was very fully occupied at home. The Europeans were quite willing to surrender their rights for the United States though it seemed evident that they would have frustrated a Du Pont invasion into any valuable part of their territory.

Should they now go all out for a global market and drive out the British and Germans as they had their home rivals? Coleman was all for it. But P.S., on the urging of John Raskob, was more prudent. He advised his cousin to curb his appetite until Du Pont had digested what it had already swallowed.

So, instead, Coleman concentrated on the final stroke of his domestic campaign. He disbanded the ten-thousand-dollar makeshift company, which had served its purpose now that state licenses had been secured, and transferred all its invaluable assets to the Du Pont de Nemours Powder Company, which received as well the assets of all the companies that their other purchases had brought in. When the cousins had first taken over Du Pont, the company controlled thirty-six percent of the nation's powder markets. By 1905 Du Pont did seventy-five percent of the business. That was an impressive enough figure. But some of the statistics that the financial experts now began to unearth were even more astonishing.

The cousins had taken over Du Pont and Hazard, and then bought out Laflin and Rand, for a cash outlay of $8,500. That was in 1902. By

1905 the value of Du Pont's combined assets was $59,955,000. Commenting on that figure, P.S. noted:

> Of course, since we were du Ponts we were always more likely to under- rather than overvalue our assets, so that sum must be considered a conservative estimate.

When Alfred I. du Pont installed Alicia Bradford Maddox in Louviers, on the Brandywine estate, he had planned to visit her two or three times a week while her husband, George Maddox, was away, and no one would be any the wiser about their clandestine affair. But Alicia was never one to sit around and wait like a kept woman; and when Alfred I.'s visits dwindled from two or three times a week to sometimes none at all, she let him know in angry tone and terms just what she thought of the way he was neglecting her. It was useless for him to explain that he was now a partner in a new and developing Du Pont company, which was undergoing convulsive changes, and that his part in the revolution was taking up most of his time. That she was to accept second place to an explosives company made Alicia shrill, and she showed Alfred I. a side of her nature he had not realized existed. It appears to have somewhat deflated his ardor, and that did not please Alicia at all; she became scornful as well as resentful.

Had it not been for the challenges accompanying his new role with Du Pont, Alfred I. would have been an unhappy man. His deafness had grown much worse, so much so that he had been reluctantly obliged to give up the conductorship of the Tankopanicum Orchestra and pass the baton to his assistant, Jimmy Dashiell. He got little comfort from the fact that his friend and mentor, Thomas Alva Edison, was also deaf; the affliction did not seem to trouble the great man to anything like the same degree. Edison was still fond of his exuberant protégé and always delighted to see him at Menlo Park. He spent hours listening to Alfred I. pour out his ideas and helping him perfect his plans for an electric motorboat, his latest project. But when the subject of deafness came up and Alfred I. bitterly lamented his inability to hear what people were saying, Edison shrugged his shoulders and replied:

"But think of all the foolishness you no longer have to listen to."

Had it been simply conversation with his fellow men that Alfred I. was now missing, he would have agreed that deafness was no disadvantage. But unlike the inventor, he loved music passionately, and without its soothing sounds to solace him in his darker moments he felt himself withering.

In fact, Edison was much more sympathetic toward Alfred I.'s physical problem than he outwardly indicated, and it seems likely that he spent some time pondering how best he could help. In the end he introduced the young man to one of his fellow inventors, Dr. Miller Reese Hutchison, who Edison suggested might have a solution to the problem.

The moment he met Hutchison, Alfred I. realized he was in the presence of a kindred spirit. The scientist was bubbling over with new ideas, several of which he had turned into viable projects. He had installed an air-conditioning unit of his own invention in his New York office at One Madison Avenue and was in the process of developing it for use in hotels, trains, and offices; he had fitted in his automobile the first self-starter ever to replace the crank handle on a car; and his automobile's wheels were equipped with detachable rims of a new design that made wheel-changing simple. He had plans all over his office for new telephone systems, improvements to cinecameras and phonographs, and the development of wireless telegraphy. Alfred I. was so impressed that he almost forgot his deafness and thought only of encouraging Hutchison to press ahead with his inventions, even offering to go into partnership with him.

But Hutchison explained that Edison had just come up with an invitation to join him in his experimentations at Menlo Park, and at this news Alfred I. at once withdrew his suggestion and urged him to accept that offer.

"Serve the great master," he said. "There will still be time in other years for us to do the things I really want to do."

Hutchison had a solution for Alfred I.'s hearing problem but, after examining his ears, warned him that it would only be temporary. Some years earlier he had invented the akouphone, an instrument that amplified consonants (which deaf people mostly miss) rather than vowel sounds. He had presented one to Queen Alexandra, the wife of King Edward VII of England, and it had worked so well that the king had presented Hutchison with a gold medal.

Armed with an akouphone, Alfred I. took Hutchison with him to a symphony concert in New York. For the first time in a year the music sounded in his ears with bell-like clarity and he was so delighted that afterward he embraced the inventor and burst into tears. Happy though he was at having provided his new friend with an effective hearing aid, Hutchison still felt constrained to remind him that his deafness was of a type that would worsen from year to year. His condition was incurable, and one day he would be stone deaf. He must regard the akouphone only as a temporary relief. Alfred I. replied that he would face that grim prospect when the time came. In the meanwhile he could hear again—and that was enough.

Unfortunately, however not only could he hear music with the aid of his new apparatus but he could also hear every syllable of Alicia's petulant complaints. One of Alfred I.'s troubles with women was that he went through life idealizing them, looking up to them as goddesses without faults, and therefore being repeatedly cast down when they proved to be less than perfect, fell into moods, caught colds, became bad tempered, menstruated, developed wrinkles, and often proved to have if not feet of clay, then bunions. He expected the passions and ecstasies of the honeymoon to endure forever and was shattered when they did not. In all probability this is what had put the first blight on his relationship with his wife, Bessie, and it now showed signs of doing the same with his mistress.

His profound sense of disappointment and disillusion with Alicia was hardly alleviated by an encounter he had around this time with another woman, this one perfect beyond his wildest imaginings. In earlier times he had done most of his weekend shooting at Cherry Island, on Chesapeake Bay, but lately he had found an even more congenial place for his hunting parties. This was Ball's Island, Virginia, the home of two families, the Hardings and the Balls. The Balls traced their ancestry back to the early English settlers in Virginia and were proud that one of them had married George Washington's sister; but all of them had seen better times and now scraped a modest living out of the island soil. The arrival of Mr. Alfred I. and his party was a great event for all, because he always insisted the weekend should conclude with a feast and general celebration, for which he footed the bill. A country fiddler and a banjoist played for dancing, and Mr. Alfred I. often strummed on the piano. Moreover, when he returned to Wilmington, Alfred I. carried with him information from Mrs. Fanny Harding, a widow, that members of both families were in need of a little ready cash for new shotguns, clothes, books, or travel expenses, and he posted off a check to her, with instructions to spread the money around anonymously.

The Hardings and the Balls between them had four sons and six daughters, and there was no doubt which two of them stood out. Little Ed Ball, a boy who swam through the island swamps and woods like a tadpole, and who could smell a covey of bobtails a mile off, was as sharp as a needle and as mischievous as a puppy. He was a never-failing source of amusement as he performed his tricks for the distinguished guests.

But it was to little Ed's sister, Jessie Ball, that Alfred I.'s eyes were constantly drawn. She was sixteen years old, already a teacher at the local village school, and everybody's darling. Tall, dark-haired, dark-eyed, with a long graceful neck and narrow waist, she was a warming delight to Alfred I.'s gaze, whether she was wading barefoot in the island mud, clad only in a muslin dress, or decked out for the evening in long skirt and wasp-waisted, high-necked blouse, with her hair done up in a chignon. By day she was a tomboy. By night she was the most roguishly charming creature he had ever met, teasing and flirting with him outrageously, mocking him for his clumsy, clodhopping way of dancing, but indicating with every long look of her sparkling brown eyes that she thought him a most wonderful person. Alfred I. had to keep reminding himself that she was only sixteen. And her mother had to keep reminding Jessie (as she recalled later) that this visitor from the mainland was twenty years her senior, far above her station in life, and, moreover, married.

Yet he wrote to her when he was back home in Wilmington. One night, toward the end of a party, and a weekend, Mrs. Ball had insisted that the hour was late and Jessie and her sister must go off to bed. Jessie had gone reluctantly and not before making Alfred I. promise to write. Even then, she confessed later, she was in love with this tall, burly, clumsy, *boyishly shy* man, but though he gave her an avuncular peck and said he would not forget, she had never imagined he would take her seriously. But, to her delight, a few days later the letter came. "Dear Jessie," Alfred I. wrote,

> You see I can keep my promise about writing to you although I am quite sure you have forgotten all about it (the promise) and its author. It matters little, however, as I write so badly as to make my letters, to all but experts on chirography, absolutely unintelligible. My little visit was most delightful, and I was very blue at having to leave. I had hoped that you and your sister would be in at the finish, or in other words stay with us until the boat left, and as it was nearly an hour late we could all have seen just that much more of you. Did we not have a fine time the night of the dance? I'll never forgive you for preferring the orchestra to me. I always knew I danced poorly, but never had it rubbed in like that. However, my revenge will come some day.

After Jessie's youthful charms, invigorating him like a fresh spring breeze, the heavy summer sultriness of Alicia was even harder to bear, especially when it presaged a devastating storm of raging temper and tears. Moreover, tired of waiting around for his increasingly infrequent visits, Alicia had started to go over to Swamp Hall to beard Alfred I. in his den. Ignoring his wife and the listening children, she would proceed to berate her reluctant lover and then, in a fit of remorse, fling herself sobbing into his arms. After it had happened for about the fifth or sixth time, Bessie du Pont found the situation so intolerable that she decided to leave, taking the children with her.

It was agreed she would go off on an extended trip to Europe, and in the summer of 1904 Bessie and her four children sailed for France. They settled in Brussels, in an apartment. The two oldest daughters, Madie and Bep, entered a local school, and Bessie looked after four-year-old Alfred Victor and one-year-old Victorine.

From then on, Alicia spent as much time at Swamp Hall as she did at Louviers, and some of the acrimony, though none of the passion, went out of her stormy relationship with Alfred I. The du Ponts on the Brandywine were shocked to their marrows, and Judge Bradford was heard around Wilmington declaring that Alfred I. ought to be horsewhipped, and Alicia, stoned as a harlot and a slut. Among the cousins, P.S., though strongly disapproving not so much of Alicia but of the way Bessie was being treated, nevertheless kept a stiff upper lip. Coleman, however, was loud in his denunciations of Alfred I.'s behavior.

"I may give Elsie a rough time," he said, "but I would never treat her the way Alfred treats Bessie. He ought to be ashamed, fouling his own nest like that."

The closer liaison with Alicia did not, however, prevent Alfred I. from making his trips to Ball's Island, Virginia. If anything, these grew more frequent, and the joy of each visit was the chance of meeting young and lovely Jessie Ball, whose pleasure in his company was increasingly noticed on the island. Alfred I.'s behavior was always as circumspect as that of an uncle with his niece, but his face was a mirror of his feelings, and those he was unable to conceal. Jessie Ball also made it clear to any of the young men on the island who might have had ideas about her that they were not in the running, especially when the Big Man from the mainland was there.

In November 1904, some three-and-a-half months after Bessie du Pont left for Europe, Alfred I. telegraphed Ball's Island that he was bringing down a small party of hunters from Wilmington. He arrived with William Scott, divisional superintendent of the Du Pont mills at Wapwallopen, Pennsylvania, Frank Mathewson, his aid in electrical experiments, and Joe Weldy, a volunteer fireman from Wilmington. Jessie Ball was on the dockside to meet them. She told them that breakfast was waiting but she had to hurry off to school. Alfred I. proposed that they all go off immediately into the woods for a bit of shooting before they ate.

The four men were spread out across the fields, concealed from one another by trees and hedges, when Scott heard a sound: It must be a bird rising, he thought. He wheeled and fired in the direction of a copse, where Mathewson and Alfred I. were hiding. Mathewson flung himself to the ground, but Alfred I. was slower. Mathewson saw his boss's cap flying in the air; then Alfred I. reeled, dropped his gun, and fell to his knees. "By the time I got to him," Mathewson reported, "I could see nothing but blood all over his face. He keeled over and lay so still I thought he was dead."

But a few seconds later Alfred I. was struggling to get to his feet. He was groggy, but Weldy and Mathewson supported him as they started to walk him back toward the Harding house. A groaning and sobbing Scott followed; he was so stricken at what he had done, and in such audible distress, that Alfred I. finally turned to him and said, "Buck up, Scott, you couldn't help it." Mathewson knew his boss well enough to realize Alfred I. was in great pain but was not going to show it.

When the men reached the house and started bathing Alfred I.'s face, they discovered that one of the shots had torn into his eye. One of the Harding boys was sent to town for a doctor, and Jessie Ball was alerted at the schoolhouse. She ended her class as quickly as she could, then rushed to the Harding house. But she arrived too late. Alfred I. was already on his way back to the mainland (and expert medical help), and she could just see his boat vanishing around a bend in the bay. In tears, she turned and went back home to wait for news of her first, last, and only love.

It was not until the following day that Alfred I. du Pont was finally wheeled into an operating room at the University of Pennsylvania Hospital in Philadelphia, where an eye specialist, Dr. G. E. de Schweinitz, was waiting to examine him. By that time everybody on the Brandywine knew what had happened, and the story of the accident was a major news item in the Wilmington and Philadelphia papers. Alicia Bradford Maddox rushed to the hospital at once, and there was an awkward moment in the waiting room: Alfred I.'s sister Marguerite Lee was there, and she and Alicia were not on speaking terms. Luckily, Father W. J. Scott of Saint Joseph's Roman Catholic Church, Wilmington, had also arrived. Sent there by the powder men to keep them informed of the boss's progress, the priest, a jovial type, was so full of praise for Alfred I.'s good works, and so determinedly and cheerfully optimistic, that the hostility between the two women was never allowed to erupt. Also present in the waiting room was one of Alfred I.'s old friends, Wallis Huidekoper, on a visit to Philadelphia from his ranch in South Dakota, and he helped Father Scott to keep the peace.

The long vigil ended when Dr. Schweinitz finally appeared. But there was no cause for rejoicing. The specialist gave his patient only a fifty-fifty chance of retaining the sight of his wounded eye, and complicated surgery would be required to repair the damage. After that, only total rest, immobilization, and complete freedom from any irritation or upset could ensure the success of the operation and the well-being of the patient. Obviously, Alfred I. had told the doctor to keep the women out of the way, because Schweinitz added that in the circumstances he thought it would be best if neither Mrs. Lee nor Mrs. Maddox excited the patient by her presence. On the other hand, he had asked to talk to Mr. Huidekoper about a personal matter.

Alicia and Marguerite made their separate departures while Huidekoper was shown into Alfred I.'s room, where he found the patient calm and reasonably cheerful. The first thing Alfred I. did was ask his friend to write at once to his wife, Bessie, in Brussels to tell her of the accident; Huidekoper was to assure her that though he was not likely to see well from the damaged eye again, he would be out of the hospital in a week or two. Alfred I. stressed that Huidekoper should write rather than cable, for fear of upsetting his children.

A week later Bessie du Pont cabled to Dr. Schweinitz:

WIRE ME ALFRED DU PONT'S CONDITION. SAILING ON NEXT BOAT.

Ten days later she and her eldest daughter, Madie, were in New York. They took the first train down to Philadelphia. The news that they were on their way had the exact effect on Alfred I. that the doctor had hoped to avoid: It "frightfully distressed him both mentally and physically."

Madie, who had always preferred her father to her mother (not unnaturally, for she was his favorite daughter and he spoiled her), did not enhance her father's physical condition when she flung herself into his arms. On the other hand, Bessie du Pont, who had been warned by the doctor, remained aloof and distant. This too did more harm than good. Madie resented her mother's attitude and afterward said: "She never once showed any pity, never once said: 'Alfred, I am sorry this has happened to you.' Not a kiss; nothing."

The sight of his wife stirred all the resentment and guilt that were marinating in Alfred I. and created such an obvious mental turmoil that Madie called the doctor, who ordered both women from the room. When Bessie came back alone the following day, she was told that her husband did not wish to see her and advised her to return to Brussels.

A few days later she and Madie sailed back to Europe to rejoin the other three children.

But the damage had been done, though whether by Madie's boisterous show of affection, or Bessie's lack of it, no one will ever know. Shortly after his wife's departure, Alfred I. checked himself out of the hospital. He spent Christmas at Swamp Hall, where he gave a party for the powder men's children, with Alicia acting as his hostess. The effort was too much for him, and he collapsed. Forty-eight hours later Dr. Schweinitz operated and removed the wounded eye. Afterward, when he was strong enough to travel, Alfred I. left for convalescence in Florida, wearing an eye patch until such time as an artificial eye could be fitted.

He went alone. He would not allow Alicia to accompany him but left her festering with her own emotional wounds at Louviers. It was reported that her husband, George Maddox, had turned up from the Middle West, but Alicia had locked him out of the house.

In the spring of 1905 P. S. du Pont went on a business trip to Europe to talk to the Nobel Explosives Company in England and the Société Nobel in France. Bessie du Pont had by now moved to Paris, and his sister Lou, now Mrs. Charles Copeland and pregnant with her first child, had asked him to visit with her while he was there and see how she was getting on.

"I am quite anxious to know if you succeeded in seeing [Bessie]," she wrote to P.S. on March 20, 1905.

> I hope you did. Her letter was mainly about her returning to this country and asking my advice on the matter. She inclosed [sic] a letter from [her brother] Coz who had just come from seeing A who was very cutting about her not returning to Alfred when he was hurt, and ignoring entirely the fact she had come home and been sent back. I have not seen Alfred except on the

street since his return. At any rate I think it is very hard to settle other peoples [sic] difficulties, they say they tell you all, but there are often little things, that change the entire look of things. I have just written to her and advised her to stay where she was. I said she knew best how they parted, and if she could I advised her to send Coz's letter to Alfred, to tell him it hurt her very much, and if he wished it she was ready to return to him at once. Her judgment being to leave the two girls to finish their music but she would do whatever he wished. I told her Alicia had been here all the time he was away, and that I had heard no one mention their names together since his return. That I would overlook her existence and most likely the entire affair was about over. I think Alicia glories in her unconventionalities and parades to the public eye, the worst side of the whole affair. I do hope the Alfreds will get together again and peace be restored.

But Bessie had made up her mind that if there was the faintest suspicion that Alfred I. wanted her back, she would leap at it. Lou wrote to P.S. again on March 30:

> . . . A letter from Bessie saying she and the children would all land here tomorrow. She said Alfred had written her a very angry letter saying he wished she would send the three eldest children home to him, & she and the baby stay on the other side always. So she said she was packing right up, & they would all return at once.
>
> Of course this about what Alfred wrote is between ourselves. I can't say I envy Bessie her position. It seems to me what fault there is is on his side, & he is trying to put the blame on her. I think he has more or less [made up his mind] & there is very little one can say to a person like that but it don't make Bessie have any easier position. He insisted on the family all going abroad, would not let Bessie stay when she came home to him, and now is mad because she is away. I am afraid there will be a public sho[wdown] yet.

CHAPTER 14

Coleman's New Role

COLEMAN du Pont was bored. For four years he had relished the power and heady excitement provided by his presidency of the new company, and wallowed in the praise lavished on him for his genius as a salesman and promoter. He had bought up the opposition. He had built the grand new Du Pont Building in downtown Wilmington and opened a flashy office in New York. But lately he sensed he was becoming more of a figurehead than a vital cog in the machine, especially as the company got down to the serious business of selling more explosives than anyone else.

For a time Coleman had dreamed of making a pact with Nobel in England and France, and I. G. Farben and Krupps in Germany, to form one great global explosives combine that would control the whole of the world market. No country would then be able to make war without the combine's permission, and Coleman saw himself as not just the fixer of dynamite prices but also an international power broker, the friend and adviser of kings and presidents, the arbiter of global conflicts, the man who could start the guns firing or order them stopped. For, of course, he saw himself as the man in charge of the combine.

Quietly and gently, P. S. du Pont put these dreams to rest. Although the three cousins, as senior partners, remained in control of the company, they had formed two committees to decide general and financial policy, and over both of these P.S. had begun to exercise effective control. Two members of his immediate family sat on the committees: his brother Irénée and his brother-in-law, Charles Copeland. In addition, Arthur Moxham, who had worked with P.S. in the Johnson Company, was a senior director, and Eugene's son Alexis I., formerly a classmate of P.S.'s at M.I.T., was also a member. Finally, P.S. had brought in another protégé, Victor, brother of the former Old Guard partner Charles du Pont.

Among them, they voted in favor of domestic rather than global expansion, and P.S. then took off for Europe on a less ambitious, but not less effective, mission. He came back with an agreement, signed by his European rivals, to renew patents and consultation agreements that would keep the powerful British and German interests out of Du Pont's North and Central American markets.

P.S. was beginning to show himself as a deft and smart negotiator in those situations that did not require Coleman's salesmanship and flair. He could drive bargains. Foreign company chiefs (particularly the head of the powerful British Nobel group, Sir Harry McGowan, with whom he formed a close friendship) came to admire his integrity. They also knew he could be tough. A wily Austrian named Dr. Siegfried Singer, head of the Nobel industrial combine in France, once tried to pull a fast one on him by bribing the Mexican government to bar all other companies and nations from their market, in return for a large dynamite factory, which he would build for them. The Mexican market was one of Du Pont's most profitable outlets, and until Singer came along with his bribes, it had been the company's exclusive territory.

Coleman, panic-stricken at the thought of losing everything to the interloper, was all in favor of making a deal with Singer, either going into partnership with him or buying him out. P.S. and the executive committee, however, advised a strategy of watching and waiting. Several months later, after Du Pont had been shut out of the market and Société Nobel's Mexican dynamite factory had begun operations, there was a mysterious explosion. It was fortunately not serious and only closed down the factory for a week or two. But as soon as the yards had been rebuilt, there was a bigger and much more devastating explosion. It would take months to repair the damage. The Mexican government came, sombrero in hand, to beg Du Pont to start resupplying them. P.S. agreed to do so—at a price.

So Coleman now began to feel unwanted, unnecessary. He spent more and more time in New York, working out real estate deals. His new interest was hotels. As he gave so many of his famous parties in hotels, he thought it might be cheaper to do so if he owned one and got the rooms, the help, and the champagne (if not the showgirls) at cut-rate prices. Nowadays, when he came down to Wilmington, it was just as likely to be for a consultation on politics with his uncle Colonel Henry Algernon du Pont as for a meeting of the financial committee.

The Colonel had been trying for years to get himself a seat in the United States Senate as a representative from Delaware, and considering the influence of the du Ponts in this small state, it should have been easy. The family controlled the newspapers and were the biggest employers in the state. They had all the money they needed to spread around in the right places. Yet each time, the Colonel had been frustrated. It was neither his pomposity nor his high-handed manner that had blocked him; rather it was a gaudy political operator named John Edward O'Sullivan Addicks, who wanted the Senate seat for himself. He was prepared to bribe anyone to secure it, and there were plenty of takers in downstate Delaware.

Addicks, a ward heeler from Philadelphia, had made millions from building and operating gas plants in Boston, Brooklyn, and Chicago. He too had failed to win a Senate seat from Delaware for himself, but by shrewd use of political maneuvers and money, he had blocked all other contenders—including the Colonel. Not all the Colonel's righteous indignation against this upstart, this vulgarian, this *manipulator,* could alter the situation. But Coleman could.

Coleman du Pont made his appearance on the political scene as campaign manager for the Colonel in the 1906 elections. It was going to be a rough fight, and the last person he wanted to have around while it was being fought was the Colonel, whose very proper principles could well be outraged by some of the low blows that were about to be traded. He was persuaded to take himself and his wife across the ocean on a European vacation while Coleman loaded his big guns—with du Pont money.

Coleman's efforts took him nearly a year, and siphoned off a considerable amount of the Colonel's considerable fortune, but when he got back to Delaware, his jubilant nephew met him with the news that "we have the rat on the run." On June 13, 1906, the Delaware Republican caucus elected the Colonel senator by a vote of 20 to 10. That same day Addicks took the train for New York and never returned to Delaware again.

Coleman found the no-holds-barred fisticuffs of Delaware politics much to his liking, and he was eager for more. Then a visit to the Colonel in his Senate office gave him a taste of what national politics was like, and he vowed that he too would become a senator one day.

Meantime he allowed the day-to-day activities of the Du Pont company to pass more and more into the hands of his amiable and able cousin P.S. He preferred to spend his time in New York, attending to more interesting and more entertaining matters.

Just about the time the Colonel was realizing his ambition to become the family's first senator, P. S. du Pont received news that was by no means so pleasant. Over the years, his relationship with his chief aide, John J. Raskob, had grown closer than ever. It was rare nowadays for P.S. to make a decision without first discussing it with J.J.R. He consulted him about everything: his business, his automobiles, his clothes, his home. They went everywhere together—to the opera in Philadelphia, to theaters and restaurants in New York (where they shared a joint apartment), on voyages to Europe, the West Indies, California, and South America. Over the years, P.S., still as single and celibate as ever, had continued to live at home with his now-aging mother, Mary du Pont, who still hoped to see him married to her dear niece, Alice Belin. Finally, to escape from her unquenchable instincts for matchmaking P.S. began to look for a place of his own, and with John Raskob's help he found it. In 1906 he bought an old Pennsylvania mansion with considerable grounds and gardens, just over the state line from Wilmington. The house, called Peirce's Park, had rooms to accommodate plenty of guests, should he wish to invite them. He showed it off proudly to his relatives and discussed with Raskob his grandiose plans for turning it into one of the showplaces of the region.

But if P. S. du Pont had every intention of remaining a lifelong bachelor, John Raskob had other ideas. How he managed to find the time for it was one of those mysteries, but Raskob sandwiched a busy life with the opposite sex in between his sessions with his boss. In the spring of 1906 he did what other close male friends of P.S.'s were destined to do in years to come, and produced a girl for his inspection and approval. Her name was Helena Springer Green, whom he had met, he said, while she was visiting her aunt in Wilmington. She was a good Roman Catholic, and he planned to marry her.

If P.S. was shaken by his confidant's sudden plunge into matrimony, he did not show it. What must have made him happy, and possibly mollified him, was Raskob's fervent declaration that his marriage would make no difference whatsoever in his devotion to his boss, to whom he would always be loyal and faithful.

As if to emphasize this, Raskob kept up a steady stream of letters to P.S. all through his honeymoon. Married at Wilmington Cathedral on June 18, 1906, he penned his first message from Albany forty-eight hours later, "almost," as Coleman later remarked, "before he and his bride can have got their breaths back."

"*Dear Dady,*"* Raskob wrote,

> You surely will be much interested to hear from me, so I am going to scribble a few lines while waiting for our train.
>
> After leaving Monday, Helena and I went to Philadelphia and then on to New York where we spent Monday and Tuesday. This morning we took the Day Line from New York to Albany and the trip is exceedingly interesting and pretty. To add to one's pleasure they have good music on board all day— an orchestra in the afternoon and a band in the morning. Several selections from the prettiest operas were played. The meals are very very good and the general comfort of the passengers is well taken care of. . . .
>
> I wish, Dady, that there was another girl somewhere in the world, as good and dear as Helena, for you. Its [sic] thoroughly impossible for anyone not happily married to appreciate my happiness since Monday. Words cannot describe the feel that comes over a man when he fully realizes that a good girl places her whole future in his care and keeping. God Grant that nothing will ever tempt me to betray that confidence for life would never be worth living thereafter. No one could ever be more dear, thoughtful, upright, honest and loving than Helena and I only hope that her husband will prove worthy of her. My love for Helena seems to have grown as much during the last few days as it did in the weeks and weeks before. Please don't think me foolish for writing to you in this way, Dady: I know you wont [sic] for

* Raskob usually used the du Pont family nickname Daddy or Dad in his letters to P.S., but this was an exception.

we have known each other too long and too well for either to misunderstand or think the other foolish. I know my happiness concerns you as much if not more than all else so this letter (though
foolish to anyone but you) will be mailed.

Helena wishes to be remembered most kindly to you and
would send some of her love were I not so selfish.

Hoping that you are happy and not worrying too much, believe me as ever, Yours most sincerely, John.

Leaving for Buffalo tonight.

P.S. wrote back from Saint Amour, his mother's home, two days
later (June 22, 1906). *"Dear John,"* he began,

I hope that I have not delayed writing too long to catch you
in Buffalo though it does seem a little doubtful.

Your letter from Albany was received and I can assure you
was heartily enjoyed by me. You know well enough that your
happiness is too much to me to make me think foolish anything
you may say about yourself. I have been thinking of you a great
deal since you left and am glad to learn that my best wishes for
you have been realized. . . . I hope that you will let me send
my love to Helena as well as to you. Tell her that I can not make
it Mrs Raskob so if she objects to Helena from me I shall have to
address her as "say" for the rest of my life. . . . Again with best
wishes, I remain very sincerely your, Pierre S. du Pont.

In one line of his letter to Raskob P.S. had reported, "we are all well and
nothing very new," but in fact there were many problems on the Brandywine at that moment and they concerned both "family" and company. The
family worries were, of course, over the gossip and scandal of which Alfred I. and Alicia Maddox were now the center. Like the newspapers in
Philadelphia and New York, every du Pont was anxiously awaiting the next
sensational development in their affair.

P.S. and his cousin Alfred I. had enjoyed a warm and comradely relationship since boyhood. If Alfred I. was sometimes affectionately contemptuous toward his more respectable cousin, gently mocking his antipathy
to sport and hunting, his clumsiness with his hands (especially when playing
the piano), his preference for working with words and figures rather than
"honest" gunpowder, P.S. was much more indulgent in return. He had

always overlooked Alfred I.'s stubbornness, temper, sudden flashes of irrational dislikes and prejudices, because he knew that Alfred was fundamentally kind, brave, and sensitive. It was sometimes hard to understand what queer motives drove him, what peculiar bees were buzzing in his big head, why he suddenly acted as he did. But though he often did unforgivable things, P.S. always forgave him.

Their relationship had, if anything, warmed even more since the hunting accident in which Alfred I. lost his eye. When P.S.'s father, Lammot du Pont, was killed, it was Alfred I. who had put his arm around the boy's shoulder and comforted him, knowing instinctively that though he showed no sign of it, P.S. was the one in Lammot's family (aside from Mary) who felt most pain. When the tables were turned, it was P.S. who had come to comfort Alfred I., understanding that behind his cheery exterior and shoulder-shrugging, he was grievously hurt by what had happened to him. The result was that as late as April 1905 Alfred I. was writing to his cousin in terms that he would never have used to any other man, confessing a sense of weakness he always concealed from others:

> My eye has gotten fairly strong, although for some reason or other I do not seem to be able to do much more than my regular work; reading seems to be out of the question. However, that may fix itself in time. My general health is pretty good, but I lack the old snap which was mine before the accident; I doubt, however, that it will come back.

He signed it "with my best love, affectionately."

But the next year changed the relationship between them and strained P.S.'s indulgence toward his big, burly, unruly cousin to its limit. P.S. had done his best (though it was against his principles) to accept that the marriage between his cousin and Bessie was irretrievably destroyed, and he was by no means as scandalized as some of the other du Ponts professed to be over Alfred I.'s affair with Alicia. He was even glad when Alfred I. at last made up his mind first to separate from Bessie and then to divorce her, and was much less censorious than his other cousin, Coleman, when Alfred I. took six months off to establish residence in South Dakota in order to get his decree.

What did offend P.S. was the manner in which his cousin repeatedly embarrassed and humiliated his wife by conducting his affair with Alicia in public. At the beginning of 1906 it was obvious that Alicia was pregnant again. Anybody capable of simple arithmetic must have wondered how her husband, George Maddox, could possibly be the father of the child; his absences from Wilmington were more frequent than ever, and everybody knew that Alicia had slammed the door of Louviers in his face. No one, on the other hand, seemed happier about the forthcoming event than Alfred I., and there were rumors, circulated in shocked whispers, that he had even brought his mistress over to Swamp Hall to parade her swollen belly before an increasingly tearful Bessie.

This, P.S. considered unforgivable, especially since he agreed with his sister Lou that the ruined marriage was "all Alfred's fault." He rather liked Bessie, anyway, admiring her stiff upper lip and well-bred, intelligent conversation. How could Alfred I. prefer a shameless hussy like Alicia?

In April 1906 the shameless hussy was plunged into her share of misery by the death of her infant son shortly after birth. Alicia, who had dearly yearned to produce a boy (for Alfred I.?), was grief-stricken, her disappointment so profound that an unhappy Alfred I., who had been hesitating for some months, immediately left to procure the divorce for which Alicia had been pleading. While he was doing his six months in South Dakota, his mistress left for a convalescent trip to Europe, only to be further cast down by news from Wilmington that her mother—her only surreptitious connection with her estranged family—had died, and that her husband, George Maddox, revolting at last against his role as cuckold, had entered a suit in a Wilmington court charging Alfred I. with alienation of his wife's affection.

Alicia handled this crisis as quickly and effectively as she had handled all her dealings with her husband. She squelched the divorce proceedings by buying George off with a sizable check and then wired Alfred I. in South Dakota that she had entered her own suit for divorce from Maddox in Wilmington. Alfred I. was alarmed. The exact telegram has been destroyed, but he apparently telegraphed back:

NOT WILMINGTON. WITHDRAW AT ONCE. LEAVE IT TO ME.

He came back to the Brandywine free of his marriage to Bessie and, having moved out of Swamp Hall, established himself on an estate called Rock Farms, near Wilmington. Alicia was not there to greet him. She seemed to have disappeared, and it was announced that she had made a brief return to America but had left again, almost immediately, for Europe.

A financial settlement had already been drawn up between Alfred I. and Bessie du Pont, and P. S. du Pont had been involved in it. His view of his cousin did not improve when he read the terms that Bessie had been forced to accept. As treasurer of Du Pont, he was well aware that Alfred I. was a very rich man. His stocks in the company alone amounted to nearly four million dollars, and he had other investments, as well as income and dividends amounting to nearly two hundred thousand dollars a year—a vast fortune in 1906.

Yet the trust fund he had set up for his wife and children, it seemed to P.S., erred on the side of meanness. It consisted of four-percent Du Pont bonds valued at six hundred thousand dollars, yielding twenty-four thousand dollars a year. The income was guaranteed to Bessie so long as she remained unmarried, and from it she was to support herself and her four children, feed and clothe them, and pay the cost of their education. In the event of her death or remarriage, the income reverted to Alfred I. Should Alfred I. die, the income was to be shared among the children equally until the youngest reached the age of twenty-five, when the six hundred thousand dollars was to be divided equally among them. The agreement also stipulated that if the income from the bonds ever exceeded twenty-five thousand dollars, the difference would go to Alfred I. and not to his wife and family.

It was not exactly generous, especially since Bessie, in accepting it, agreed to forego her dower rights and pledged herself not to contest any will that Alfred I. made subsequently.

Two trustees were appointed, one to represent Alfred I., and the other, Bessie. Alfred I. chose a Philadelphia attorney George Quintard Horwitz, and Bessie asked P. S. du Pont to be her trustee. P.S. accepted reluctantly, and only because he felt sorry for Bessie. But he anticipated trouble.

In the autumn of 1907 it was revealed that Alicia Bradford Maddox, far from being away in Europe, had been hiding in a house in Carlisle, Pennsylvania, establishing her own residence for divorce. A complaisant judge considered her case in secrecy and granted her a decree, though not without some gentle persuasion on Alfred I.'s part. So now the way was clear for both of them. On Tuesday, October 15, 1907, Alfred I. wrote to P.S.:

My dear Pierre:

As Alicia has done me the great honor and for me the great happiness of becoming my wife, I shall be absent from the office this week and possibly longer. Mr. Connable will look after matters as usual during my absence and on my return I will make an effort to see you soon. . . . I am sorry not to have had a chance to see your new country place before my marriage to my dearest

Alicia, but trust my visit to Peirce's Park has merely been post-
poned. With my kindest regards . . . Alfred I. du Pont.

It was as near as he could come to hinting that P.S. should not allow
the marriage, and the circumstances surrounding it, to come between them
and spoil their friendship. But Alfred I. was asking too much, even of his
mild and understanding cousin. He was never invited to Peirce's Park—or
Longwood Gardens, as it later became.

Nor did P.S. or Cousin Coleman pay a formal visit to Rock Farms,
where Alfred I. and Alicia established themselves after their marriage,
though P.S.'s sister Lou was one of their first visitors and reported to her
brother, "They already look like an old married couple—even bicker at
each other like marrieds do."

Fifteen years had passed since the Colonel's brother, Willie du Pont,
had scandalized the family by getting a divorce and marrying Annie Zinn,
but though legally terminated marriages were by now commonplace occur-
rences, they were still anathema to the du Ponts. A few members of the
family were willing to accept the facts and admit Alicia to their social
circle, but not the more powerful ones. Particularly outraged was Colonel
Henry Algernon, who sent a message to Coleman from the United States
Senate decreeing the same banishment for Alfred I. as had been ordered for
Willie, and the same ostracism for Alicia as had been ordained for William's
ex-wife, May, who had dared to marry again.

Coleman called Alfred I. into his office and told him:

"Al, now you've done it. The family will never stand for this. Don't
you think you'd better sell out to me and get out of here?"

"I'll see them in hell first," said Alfred I.

When the Colonel, then in Washington, heard that his outrageous
nephew refused to go, he turned to his old ally, the bishop of Delaware.
The Reverend Leighton Coleman's spade beard shook with indignation and
disgust as he confronted the problem presented by the stubbornness of his
immoral cousin.* He in turn consulted with the relatives of Alfred I.'s
shameless consort, Alicia: her father, Judge Bradford, and her puritanical
aunt, Emily Bradford du Pont. How could they wipe clean the family
escutcheon? If Alfred I. refused to go, they obviously could not drive him
out of the Brandywine or carry him out on a rail. But, they decided, perhaps
they could salvage what was left of the family honor by making life uncomfortable for those who continued to associate with the two sinners. The

---

* For the bishop was a du Pont too.

Philadelphia newspapers had announced that Alfred I. and his bride had been married in New York "with only immediate members of the family present." Judge Bradford was outraged at the implied suggestion that he had been there, and he proposed to make a public announcement denying that *any* of his family had been present. But then the rumor spread that there had been two witnesses, Alfred I.'s brother Maurice and Alicia's brother, Edward Bradford, Jr. Could this be true? Had young Bradford dared to defy his father? Bishop Coleman sent off a telegram:

> ESSENTIAL TO KNOW IF YOU ATTENDED SO CALLED WED-
> DING ALICIA AND ALFRED DUPONT. ANSWER AT ONCE.
> LEIGHTON COLEMAN.

Eddie Bradford was a twenty-nine-year-old lawyer just getting established in Wilmington, where he relied a great deal on his family connections and, of course, on his father's judicial eminence. He was well aware that his practice would be damaged if both the bishop and the judge turned against him. But he loved his sister Alicia, and he finally wrote back to Bishop Coleman to say that he had done what he had thought right, and stood by his sister.

Meanwhile Alicia and Alfred I. made their life together at Rock Farms as if nothing had happened, except that their union was legal at last. There were fashionable dinner parties, trips to Florida aboard Alfred I.'s new yacht, which he had christened *Alicia,* and get-togethers with Alicia's New York and Philadelphia friends and the few members of the du Pont family with whom the couple were still on visiting terms.

After Coleman's outburst ("Al, now you've done it") an effort was made on all sides to patch things up between the cousins, for, after all, they were still partners in the Du Pont company and had to work together. But though a semblance of friendliness was established, it was only superficial, and there was no longer any genuine social contact between them. They met on stag occasions but did not visit between houses. Coleman told his family to stay away from Alicia. As for P.S., he found himself in an increasingly invidious position, thanks to Alfred I.'s behavior toward his divorced wife and the children.

One of the clauses in the divorce agreement had stipulated that though Bessie was to look after the children, Alfred I. was to have visiting rights, and for a time the children continued to see him regularly. On these occasions Alfred I. could not resist asking them how they were getting on with their mother, and one or another of them—all but Alfred Victor—inevitably told tales. A quiet, subdued boy with little to say for himself, Alfred Victor had effectively terminated his relationship with his father by making plain his dislike of Alicia. When asked if he would like to go to live with his father and his "new mother," he had violently shaken his head, and it says much for Alfred I.'s state of mind that he was not to forgive his son for the implied insult.

On the other hand, his eldest daughter, Madie, a petulant and willful girl, complained bitterly about the way Bessie was "neglecting" her. Now twenty years old, pretty, vain, and restive, she was, one suspects, ready to do anything to get away from her mother's control.

In response to her tales against Bessie Alfred I. wrote angry letters to his trustee, G. Q. Horwitz, and Horwitz in turn wrote to P.S. enumerating instructions for, and grievances against, Bessie. He declared that his client was angry at the "very painful and most regretable [sic] situation with regard to his daughter and felt that there was no other course to pursue but to 'make proper provision for the support of Miss Madeleine du Pont in the manner to which her position in society would entitle her.' " Horwitz made it clear that by this last remark his client did not mean that he was allocating more allowance to Bessie for her daughter, but that he expected his ex-wife to give Madie more money from the allowance she was already receiving. Bessie then protested to P.S. that she could not possibly give Madie more from the small amount Alfred allowed her.

On December 9, 1907, a little over a month after Alfred I. and Alicia were married, Madie went herself to Philadelphia to see Horwitz and complain of her mother's parsimony and general unpleasantness toward her. When P.S. was informed of this visit, he suggested that Madie come over for a talk. She refused but demanded that her mother increase her allowance to three thousand dollars a year. Bessie, meanwhile, came to cry on P.S.'s shoulder, claiming that she already provided Madie with food and lodging, and Madie was not entitled to physical support outside the home. Horwitz replied that his client "totally rejected" this argument, and added:

> It is not only incumbent upon Miss Madeleine's mother to give her an offer of a home to live and eat in, but she must so act toward her daughter that she can live there. . . . If Mrs du Pont makes the house in which she lives so uncomfortable that her daughter cannot dwell there, then of course, it cannot be said that she is offering to her daughter a home, and she would have to provide her with a home elsewhere.

It was an obvious hint that Madie was planning to leave the maternal nest, and unlike P.S., who was worried about Bessie's reaction, Alfred I. and Alicia were delighted. They were convinced that Madie wanted to come and live with them, which for both of them, constituted a triumph over the ex-wife who seemed to be getting altogether too much attention and sympathy from the rest of the du Ponts. Madie meanwhile wrote directly to P.S. to plead with Bessie to give her the three-thousand-dollar-a-year allowance that would enable her to get by. Commenting on that sum, she noted:

"I should have to economize in order to make $3,000 meet expenses. . . . In the event of my going abroad with a chaperone, I could not possibly get along with less than $4,500."

She had no intention of going abroad with a chaperone, however. She stayed a few days with her doting father and a triumphant Alicia, then suddenly disappeared. Madie, the family was to learn, had eloped with a young Princeton graduate named John Bancroft, and the couple had taken off for France. Alfred I.'s reaction was to instruct Horwitz to write to P.S. "My legal opinion," that letter was to state, "is that the marriage of Miss du Pont does not in any way change the responsibility of her mother to support her."

Meanwhile Madie and John Bancroft had reached Germany, where the new wife promptly left her husband for a German student, Max Hiebler, with whom she spent the rest of her honeymoon in Berlin. By the end of it she was pregnant, but by whom?

In the midst of all this, P.S. was also embroiled in a family drama of his own. Throughout 1907, in addition to running the company and acting as arbiter of his cousin's domestic problems, he had been involved in the defense of a court case that the United States government had brought against Du Pont and that would continue to occupy his time for the next three years. The company was being sued on charges of contravening the Sherman Antitrust Act, and things were not going well for Du Pont. To begin with, since Alfred I. was completely preoccupied with his own affairs, and Coleman was in the hospital, undergoing a throat operation, P.S. was the only senior partner concerned with the company's rebuttal of the government's case and had spent many hours closeted with the lawyers.

In the circumstances, he was glad when the court adjourned the antitrust case over Christmas, 1907, enabling him to return to the Brandywine to relax for the holidays. There was a family party at Saint Amour, with his mother presiding over a happy gathering of her surviving sons and daughters: Irénée (with his wife Irene), Bill (with his wife Ethel), the youngest son, Lammot (with the first of his many wives, Nathalie), Lou (with husband Charles Copeland), Mary d'Andelot (married to William Winder Laird), Bella (with husband Rodney Sharp), and Margaretta (with husband Ruly Carpenter); plus their brood of children and, of course, P.S.

All the grown-ups had something in common, either blood or profession, for, with the exception of William Winder Laird, who was a banker, all the husbands of the du Pont women worked for the company, as did all their sons. Copeland, Sharp, and Carpenter would all one day preside over the Du Pont company. Irénée sat on the executive committee, and Lammot (not the brightest man in the world but a fine chemist) was nurturing his own plans for the company's future.

The remaining son, Bill, was the brother P.S. loved best. He was an easygoing, unambitious soul who never believed in too much hard work but had such a sunny disposition that no one minded very much. Even P.S., who did not approve of slackers, indulged his brother and used him as a sort of superior "go-fer" in connection with his own affairs as well as those of the company. He had never seen Bill happier than this particular Christmas, immensely proud of his darkly beautiful wife, Ethel (dressed in her favorite color, red), and of his three small children, brown-eyed imps of mischief.

At one point in the festivities Bill and his wife went off to have dinner with Rodney and Bella Sharp at their Wilmington home. Sharp had just received a supply of oysters from the Chesapeake and knew Bill (though not his wife) thought nothing more delicious. Exactly how it happened will always remain a mystery, but when Bill came home, having consumed several dozen of the bivalves, he complained of feeling ill. Next day he was running a high temperature, and when the doctor was summoned, he diagnosed typhoid fever. P.S. was called in and heard the doctor counsel Ethel that she must try her best to prevent her husband from having paroxysms: One of the dangers of typhoid was that the agony might become so intense that the bowels could burst with the violence of the reaction, and this was usually fatal.

P.S. elected to sit with Bill, and never left his bedside. Each time Bill was racked with convulsions, P.S. would fling himself on the bed and hold his brother tight, to prevent a fatal rupture. But the fever did not abate, and the violent paroxysms did not cease. After forty-eight hours Bill commenced writhing again, and once more P.S. pressed him down with the whole weight of his body. But not even all his strength could restrain the monster that had taken hold of his brother. With one gigantic, convulsive shudder, Bill died—"in my arms," as P.S. simply put it, later.

He came out to the waiting relatives in a daze, and when one of them asked for news about Bill, he did something that astonished them all. Tears came to his eyes, and he collapsed into a chair, sobbing as if his heart was broken. It was the first time any of them had ever seen P.S. cry.

CHAPTER 15

---◆---

Untrustworthy

Nᴏᴛ even the death of his favorite brother could delay P. S. du Pont's return to Washington, where the antitrust suit was to resume after the holiday break. He stayed in Delaware only long enough to see William's body lowered into his grave at Sand Hole Woods, then went back to the capital to return to court, where the case against Du Pont had begun to take on worrying elements.

The trouble was that when the government suit first came along, none of the cousins had taken it seriously. What had given them a sense of security, a positive conviction that the suit would be thrown out, was in large part the questionable motivation of its originator, a certain Robert J. Waddell. A former employee of the Du Pont company, Waddell had worked out of Cincinnati as a go-getting salesman, then, after a quarrel with his bosses, had branched out on his own as president of the Buckeye Powder Company and proceeded to run up against Du Pont's competitive tactics. His company had trouble surviving, and Waddell—probably rightly—attributed his lack of success to the cut-price and often cut-throat competition the Du Pont organization turned against any firm that stood in its way.

Waddell thirsted for revenge against the ruthless Du Pont machine, which was, he believed, deliberately driving him out of business, and he went to Washington and managed to arrange an appearance before the Senate Appropriations Committee. His testimony created something of a sensation. When he left Du Pont, he had taken with him a bundle of letters, memoranda, price agreements, and contracts, which he now proceeded to wave before the senators.

A fluent and convincing witness, he had some tantalizing revelations to make about the Du Pont method. For instance, he described how Coleman du Pont employed a chief mechanic at the Brandywine works who always seemed to live better, in a bigger house, and with more money than could reasonably be expected of someone in his position. Waddell would tell the senators why. The role of the chief mechanic, one George Seitz, was to travel to places were rival firms were operating, and there he would apply for a job as a mechanic under an assumed name. Once hired, he would keep his eyes and ears open, discover the company's strengths and weaknesses, who its customers were, what methods and machines it used. Then he would report back to Coleman with material that enabled him to assess the value of the rival, undercut its costs, and steal its customers, before making an offer to buy it up at a bargain rate. Seitz kept his job as a Du Pont snoop secret, Waddell maintained, but "you should see the size of his tax return!"

He went on to accuse Coleman of "engineering" Colonel Henry Algernon du Pont's election to the Senate for the sole purpose of having a member of the family there to wheel and deal on the company's behalf. He charged that the Du Pont Powder Trust and its family directors were "an absolute and exclusive monopoly for the manufacture" of all government military gunpowder, that they were "daily, continually and openly defy[ing] and break[ing] the laws of the states and the United States," and then demanded of the senators:

"How much faith can be placed in the [du Ponts'] loyalty and patriotism in time of emergency and distress?"

He urged the government to end Du Pont's stranglehold on the supply of gunpowder to the United States Army and Navy. And he demanded that they be sued under the Sherman Act.

Because Waddell was a disgruntled ex-employee and competitor, and because he mixed a lot of lies and half-truths with his charges, P.S. had scoffed at the suggestion that he could be a danger. Nor had he or Coleman been worried when the Chicago *Tribune* and other newspapers took up Waddell's cry. But the nation was in the mood for hitting out at big business, and President Theodore Roosevelt's "big stick" had already begun flaying such giant (and restrictive) corporations as Standard Oil and the American Tobacco Company. The Justice Department announced that Du Pont would be prosecuted.

Waddell heaped anti-Du Pont evidence on the desks of the Justice Department lawyers. He gave them all his correspondence and other documentation on the Powder Trust and handed over even more incriminating evidence about Du Pont's close collaboration with British, French, and German interests to keep tight control over the world market. What he had to say was so cumulatively damning that although the trust-busting regime of Theodore Roosevelt gave way in 1910 to the more conservative sentiments of the Republican president Taft, the court still brought in a guilty verdict against Du Pont: that they had maintained an illegal association to dominate the explosives industry and regulate prices "not according to any law of supply and demand, but according to the will of the parties to the said contract."

Coleman had been ill, off and on, during the course of the case, so much so that the executive committee of Du Pont had voted to make P.S. acting president in his place. But Coleman had insisted that since the antitrust case was so obviously "political," he, who knew politics, should take charge of it. He was astonished and then furious when the verdict was announced, and blamed not his own strategy but the tactics the lawyers had adopted. And he grew even more bitter against them when they sent Du Pont a bill for three hundred thousand dollars. P.S., on the other hand, was convinced it was politics that had done them in. If the Colonel had not entangled himself in so many controversial battles during his fight to get elected to the Senate, and if the du Pont name had not been plastered in headlines all over the country during his campaign, the company would never have attracted the attention of the Senate and started the furor that led up to the suit. P.S., in short, blamed Coleman. Without his cousin's help, the Colonel would never have become a senator and started all the fuss.

Coleman did not seem to be aware of how seriously endangered the family business was, and went out of his way to insult the government lawyers. He could not believe the court order that the Du Pont trust be busted, as Standard Oil and American Tobacco had been. He was given a deadline: If by a certain date he could not produce a plan to break up the company, then the government would do it for him.

It was at this critical moment that P.S. intervened. With only weeks to go before the lawyers from Washington moved in, he came up with a plan. Although Du Pont had long since taken the companies it had bought up under its corporate wing, many of them still operated under their separate names. Now he wiped them out of existence with a simple stroke of the pen. E. I. du Pont de Nemours, Hazard Powder Company, Eastern Dynamite Company, Laflin and Rand Powder Company, California Investment Company, Delaware Security Company, and Delaware Investment Company were all consigned to oblivion. All that remained was the E. I. du Pont de Nemours Powder Company. P.S. then lopped off branches of its operations and used them to create two new companies: the Hercules Powder Company, which was given one of Du Pont's patented formulae, and the Atlas Powder Company, likewise given a Du Pont patented process. The new companies, P.S. declared, would be completely independent of the Du Pont organization.*

Under Teddy Roosevelt's administration, it is doubtful that the plan would have been accepted, since it left Du Pont pretty well intact. Though it was a costly exercise in corporate dismemberment and (on paper, at least) left the company millions of dollars poorer, it was far from being the complete breakup that the court's verdict had predicated.

The court accepted it, and P.S. was satisfied. But not with his cousins and fellow partners, Coleman and Alfred I. du Pont.

Everybody was beginning to be dissatisfied with Alfred I. Despite the breakup ordained by the court, Du Pont was doing bigger business than ever. Profits were running at over $6 million dollars a year, dividends of twelve percent were being paid, and nearly $1.5 million was being carried forward each year to swell Du Pont's capital. But there was one activity that was not bringing in anything like its proportionate amount of profit when compared with Du Pont's other products. This was black powder, which Alfred I. and his teams continued to make in the aging mills along the Brandywine. The market for the powder was shrinking as newer and

---

* He did not stress that each company would be headed by a former Du Pont executive.

more powerful products took its place, and if Coleman had had his way, the whole line would have been closed down for good.

But Alfred I. simply would not have it. He was wedded to black powder and passionately fond of the processes, as well as the men who mixed and milled and glazed it. P.S. and other veterans of the Brandywine yards understood his obsession. Making black powder was a man's job, and among their fellow employees at Du Pont, the powder men of the Brandywine mills were a special elite. Compared with them, other explosives workers were by now as safe as clerks in an office. Nearly all the teams of men who worked with Alfred I. had lost brothers, fathers, mates, in the explosions that had ripped through the creek over the years; their hands, faces, and bodies bore the marks of the fires and other calamities they had endured.

P.S., who had lost a father in a mill disaster, who had been through explosions himself while working in the yards, understood the ties of spilt blood that bound his cousin to the Brandywine, and realized that Alfred I., unstable as he was about this time, clung to the mills like a castaway to a rock in a storm. Once more he counseled Coleman to be patient and let Alfred I. keep his black powder, for the time being, anyway. But he too was growing tired of his cousin's increasing unreliability in matters beyond the business in the yards. Alfred I. was no longer pulling his weight as a senior partner in the company. His personal life was causing disturbances among the du Pont clan whose members were, after all, important shareholders. Not only was his deafness making it difficult for him to hear, it was also making him bad tempered, and sometimes furiously angry, when he misinterpreted what was being said.

P.S. quietly dropped him from the financial and executive committees of the Du Pont company, ostensibly because of his deafness. But the real reason was that, shy as he was and terrified of displays of naked emotion, P.S. found Alfred I.'s passionate outbursts to be extremely embarrassing. For his own peace of mind, he decided, it was better to keep Alfred I. out of the office and decision-making meetings.

He would probably have been more sympathetic if his cousin had not continued to be so beastly to his ex-wife and children. P.S., as trustee for Bessie, was still in the middle of the family quarrel, and hating every moment of it. Madie had already embarked on her stormy marriage to John Bancroft—which would soon end in scandal and divorce—but Alfred I. continued to harass Bessie about giving her an adequate allowance. P.S. wrote to him (through his trustee, G. Q. Horwitz):

> I might record that Mrs du Pont has had no message from
> Mrs Bancroft since the latter's marriage and is absolutely with-
> out means of communication with her. It would, therefore, seem
> that the daughter should make some communication in regard
> to provision that may be needed for her maintenance.

But if Bessie did not know where Madie was, Alfred I. did. He sent
his new wife, Alicia, off to Paris where Madie was having a baby. He had
instructed Alicia to bring his daughter and her child back to America. But
as soon as the baby was born, Bancroft sued for divorce, naming the young
German, Max Hiebler, with whom Madie had interrupted her honeymoon
for an amorous adventure in Berlin, *and* the baby in his suit. So instead of
coming back to Wilmington, Madie left for Berlin to show off her son to
her lover. Only after another idyll did she return to Delaware. In the
meantime Alfred I. and his attorney had been at work: Young Bancroft
had been persuaded to withdraw his suit, and there was a sort of reconciliation. But though they began living with each other again, Madie was still
far from satisfied with her husband, and gossip about her scandalous goings-
on in Wilmington, New York, and Philadelphia was soon the talk of the
family. Coleman sent Alfred I. a bunch of slanderous letters about Madie's
infidelities. And angry at the thought that his cousin had been made privy
to Madie's affairs, Alfred I. wrote him back a cold letter, which did nothing
to improve relations between the two partners.

Then Madie was pregnant again. By whom, no one ever found out
this time, except that Bancroft insisted the child was not his. This time
nothing could dissuade him from filing suit for divorce. Madie moved in
with her father and stepmother, but that did not last long, either. Alicia
Bradford du Pont was trying hard to have a baby of her own—a son, she
hoped, for Alfred I.—and as her time approached, she became increasingly
irritable with her stepdaughter, particularly after Madie gave birth to a baby
boy, so easily. Alicia's own pregnancy ended painfully, and ignominiously,
in the birth of a baby girl who only lived a few hours. Once again she had
failed to give the man she loved a legal child, and she was not only miserable but ready to lash out because of her failure. She turned her self-hatred
on her stepdaughter and venomously attacked her until Madie packed her
bags and moved out.

Madie then did something for which Alfred I. never really forgave
her. She went to see Elsie du Pont, Coleman's wife, and poured out everything about her quarrels with her stepmother. Elsie did not fail to carry

the tale all over the Brandywine. At the same time, she agreed with Madie that it might be best if she got away from Delaware and her father. She lent her money for her fare to Germany, and there Madie was reunited with her old lover, Max Hiebler. They were married some months later.

Compared with what had happened to the Colonel's brother, Willie, Alfred I. had come out of his scandals unscathed. Willie had been banished. Alfred I. was still on the Brandywine, as large and as defiant as ever. And though an increasingly antagonistic Coleman continually badgered P.S. to help him get rid of the cousin whom he now regarded as "a burden on the company and a bounder into the bargain," P.S. counseled caution. He believed that Alfred I. was now so unbalanced and unrealistic that he would sign his own death warrant with the company, and it would not be necessary for his cousins to write it for him.

In any case, P.S. considered it unwise for them to expel Alfred I. simply because he was acting foolishly and unpleasantly in his private life. Let him go on offending the family as much as he liked. His behavior would simply create an atmosphere in which, once he made a mistake in the affairs of the company, he could be eliminated without protest. In other words, give him all the rope he demanded—in his personal as well as his business life—and wait for him to hang himself.

It was a shrewd decision, but it did not please everybody in the du Pont clan, and it certainly did not make P.S.'s life as trustee for Bessie easier. Alfred I., if sympathetic for a time toward Madie and her problems, had become extremely hostile toward his three other children, particularly his only son, Alfred Victor, and that produced new worries for P.S. Until his marriage to Alicia, Alfred I. had welcomed the visits of his son and two other daughters and kept up a cheery and affectionate correspondence with them. He addressed Alfred Victor as "My dear little Man" and ended letters to him with the words "kiss yourself in the glass for me and see how it tastes." But now he slammed the doors on all of them.

Not that this banishment of his children stopped his interfering with the way Bessie looked after them. To the contrary, P.S. soon found himself involved in an acrimonious correspondence over the question of Alfred Victor's education. The boy, now going on ten years old, was a withdrawn, nervous, and emotionally unstable lad who clung to his mother (in both his features and his nervous gestures he was uncannily like his father). P.S. agreed with Bessie that he needed careful handling and would be the better for an education close to home where his mother could keep an eye on him.

Alfred I. was furious when he heard about this. He wrote to both trustees:

> It is best for the future of my son, Alfred Victor du Pont, that he be placed at school where he will have the advantage accruing from associating with boys of his own age and the benefit resulting from the guidance and supervision of men. I deem this necessary in order that such qualities as he may possess will have every chance of full development, and he has now reached an age when this development should begin. I will ask you to inform Mrs. B. G. du Pont of my decision so that the boy may be prepared to leave when my arrangements have been perfected, due notice of which will be given you.

So an unwilling Alfred Victor was sent off to boarding school, not quite sure whether he was being removed from his mother's protection for his own good or for the simple reason that he had become a convenient pawn in a squalid postmarital game.

A psychiatrist could have told P.S. and the rest of the du Ponts that the way to placate Alfred I. was to stop making such a fuss over his harassed ex-wife. While Bessie was getting all the family's sympathetic attention Alicia was being ignored, and Alfred I. found that intolerable. But since several of the du Ponts derived a positive pleasure from hitting back at Alfred I. through Bessie, a showdown was inevitable.

Ironically enough, in view of the fact that Alfred I. could no longer listen to it, music was what brought things to a head. While he was still married to Bessie, and keeping up appearances so far as their relations were concerned, Alfred I. would take her to concerts and operas in Philadelphia, New York, and Wilmington, and Bessie relished these occasions, particularly the Wilmington concerts where she met members of fashionable local society with whom the du Ponts did not normally mix. Soon she was introducing other du Ponts at these occasions, and so marked the beginning of the end of du Pont seclusion from Wilmington's *haut monde*. In particular, one of her introductions brought about a rapprochement between the family and the pretty but formidable leader of local society, Mrs. Henry B. Thompson, wife of the chairman of the board of trustees of Princeton University.

Mrs. Thompson was a friend of Presidents McKinley and Taft and a patron of Woodrow Wilson, then a professor at Princeton, and strong men quailed when her blue eyes turned frigid. She decided who was acceptable, and who was not, in Wilmington society, and once the du Ponts came into her purview, she deftly picked those who might help her consolidate her power and influence, and ruthlessly discarded the lesser fry. One whom she chose as a most useful ally was the widow of the late Dr. Alexis du Pont, one of the Old Guard partners. This formidable lady, Mrs. Elizabeth Bradford du Pont, was also the sister of Judge Bradford and the aunt of Alicia Bradford du Pont. Despite Alicia's marriage to Alfred I., Aunt Elizabeth still regarded her as a slut.

Someone in Wilmington had the bright idea to give the city a symphony orchestra of its very own, and when the local rich were approached for contributions to make this possible, no one gave more generously than Alfred I. His gift was so munificent, in fact, that no one grumbled or objected when he suggested that his friend Jimmy Dashiell, who had become conductor of the Tankopanicum Orchestra after Alfred I.'s retirement, should become concertmaster. Another friend of his, August Rodemann of the Philadelphia Orchestra, was named conductor. Alfred I. looked forward to the first concert, which he proposed to follow, since he would not be able to hear a note, by reading a score of the music, as well as observing the expressions on Alicia's face as she listened to the actual sounds.

Mrs. Thompson was named head of the women's committee responsible for arranging the first performance of the new orchestra, and it was left to her to choose the time and the venue. Through her connections in Washington, she contrived a small triumph. The new United States battleship *Delaware,* the navy's latest and most powerful ship, was scheduled to visit Wilmington October 5–9, 1910, and Mrs. Thompson planned a concert in aid of a fund to buy silver for the ship's mess. Alfred I. immediately sent a hundred-dollar contribution to the Silver Fund and waited for his friend Jimmy Dashiell to send him a copy of the program.

Dashiell by this time had a proof copy, and knowing how Alfred I. felt, he was embarrassed. For there on the front page, prominent among the list of patronesses, were the names of Bessie Gardner du Pont and Elizabeth Bradford du Pont, but not Alicia du Pont's.

Dashiell went to see Mrs. Thompson and protested that Alicia, as wife of the orchestra's principal financial supporter, should surely be up there on the roster of patronesses. Mrs. Thompson replied sharply that she would never consider insulting her friends Bessie and Elizabeth (or herself, for that matter) by putting the name of *that woman* alongside theirs. Dashiell then went to see the mayor of Wilmington, to whom he prophesied all sorts of disasters if something was not done. The mayor thereupon decreed that new programs and notepaper be printed, with Alicia's name included. But it was brought to Alfred I.'s notice that letters petitioning various likely subscribers for support of the forthcoming concert were sent out on the old notepaper—without Alicia's name. Dashiell, furthermore, glumly informed him that Mrs. Thompson and "other ladies" had gathered in the furnace room of the Century Club, in downtown Wilmington, where they ceremonially burned four thousand sheets of the new notepaper with Alicia's name on it.

Alfred I. then formally withdrew his financial support of both con-cert and orchestra, which shortly afterward was forced to disband. And that would have been the shoddy end of the affair had not a kind friend come to tell Alfred I. that some of the ladies at the burning ceremony had made scandalous remarks about Alicia's morals, about her previous marriage, and about the paternity of her little daughter, Alicia.

He immediately filed a suit for slander against the supposed authors of these malicious stories. One of them was the widow of a Wilmington manufacturer, Mrs. Mary Bush, whose adopted son had married Joanna du Pont Bradford. Joanna was Alicia's sister, and no love was lost between them. The other defendant was Alicia's aunt, Elizabeth Bradford du Pont.

For a time not a word leaked out about the rash step Alfred I. had taken to protect his wife's honor. The Wilmington newspapers were all tightly controlled by the du Pont family, and their editors were forbidden to publish anything about the case. But frustrated reporters, sitting on the biggest local story in years, could not keep silent for long. They leaked the news to New York and Philadelphia papers, and suddenly, on the front pages of all of them, the du Ponts' dirty linen was once more on view. "THE WOMEN'S WAR THAT CONVULSES DELAWARE" was the headline in the Philadelphia *North American,* and the New York *World* spoke of the slanderous allegations as being "of such a nature that they cannot be published."

Of course, the case never came to court. Even Alfred I. realized after a time that he had been more recklessly foolish than usual in taking his grievances against his wife's enemies to the law. Whether he won or not, Alicia would be damaged. But it took Alicia herself, who had never been consulted by her husband, to tell him he was acting like a stupid idiot. It was she who forced him to withdraw.

But now the enmity between Alfred I. and his in-laws was out in the open, and he placed the blame squarely on Bessie du Pont. Unable to secure redress in court, he hit out in the way he calculated would be most hurtful to his detested ex-wife. He had just completed the building of a new home for himself and Alicia on the outskirts of the Brandywine. A huge, splendid house, part French château, part pillared southern plantation mansion, it was three stories high, with limestone façades looking out on the rolling green wooded hills of Delaware and Pennsylvania. It had seventy-seven rooms and was surrounded by a high wall. He named it Nemours.

Just before he moved in with Alicia, he picked up James Smyth, the man who had built it for him, and drove with him to a spot overlooking Swamp Hall, the place where he and his brothers and sisters had been born, where his father and mother had fought, and bred and died, and where Bessie du Pont and three of his own children were now living.

"Smyth," said Alfred I., "I want you to pull down that house."

The builder looked at him in astonishment.

"I mean it," Alfred I. said. "I want it razed to the ground—brick by brick. And I want you to start tomorrow."

Coleman was appalled at Alfred I.'s cruelty. All he wanted now was to be rid of his malevolent cousin. To his surprise, P.S. agreed that Alfred I. should go—not because of his treatment of Bessie du Pont and his children, nor because of all the scandalous gossip and the resentment against him in the family, but because of his poor head for business.

P.S. pointed out that despite the fact that black powder was now selling worse than ever, his cousin had refused to heed P.S.'s advice to slow down production. Instead, he had insisted on opening a new half-million-dollar plant at Welpen, Minnesota. The operation had been a dismal failure. The plant would have to be sold at a considerable loss. P.S. indicated that the executive committee, of which he was chairman, was not likely to be pleased about this wretched performance on Alfred I.'s part.

They were not. Meeting in January 1911, they unanimously voted to relieve Alfred I. du Pont of his position as general manager of the Brandywine yards. Coleman's brother-in-law, H. M. Barksdale, was voted in as general manager in his place, and P.S.'s youngest brother, Lammot, was put in charge of the black-powder operation.

Word quickly spread through the yards that Mr. Alfred was out, and a meeting of the veteran powder men was organized. A delegation went down to his office, where he was clearing out his papers, to read him an emotional farewell and hand him a silver cup.

Alfred I. listened in silence, showing no sign of emotion. Then he began to thank them, his voice, as the powder men noted, "so husky you could hear it scraping."

They all wiped the grimy tears from their eyes, and Alfred I. went back to Nemours to inform Alicia of what had been done to him. He told her to start packing; they would be taking off for Europe, where he would think about what to do next.

But before they sailed, he made one other trip, to Ball's Island, Virginia, which he had not visited since his marriage to Alicia. Nor had he seen anything of his dream of perfect girlhood, the brown-haired Jessie Ball. Her brother, Ed, watched them walk off together along the island shore but had no idea what was said during the hour they were away. All he does remember is that when Alfred I. left the next day to go back to the mainland, he said:

"Take care of your sister, Edward. I'll be back one day. But now I have to go away and fight."

Ed Ball bought the big city newspapers over the next few weeks and kept looking for news of a war. It took some time before he realized that what Mr. Alfred was talking about was not a new conflict in which American troops would be engaged but a war between the Big Man and his cousins.

Part Four

COUP D'ETAT

CHAPTER 16

Cousinly Coolness, Brotherly Love

I T had been some time since Bessie du Pont and her aunt Elizabeth Bradford du Pont had started taking the richer and more cultivated members of the still basically provincial du Pont family downtown to concerts, plays, and charity balls. The menfolk of the family, of course, had been going into the city regularly ever since the Du Pont Building opened its doors in downtown Wilmington, and were now members of the exclusive clubs for leading lights of the community.

But what really changed the attitude of the du Ponts to Wilmington and its social life was the opening in 1913 of the splendid new Hotel du Pont, which had been built to mop up some of the surplus cash now flowing into the company's coffers. The du Ponts almost without exception were tremendously proud of the new hotel, pronouncing it "absolutely spiffy," and were equally excited about the 1,251-seat Playhouse Theatre it housed. Minor members of the family who had rarely eaten outside a du Pont home in their lives came downtown now for lunch or dinner and stayed on to see a play or a musical on tour from New York. And naturally, balls, hitherto confined to a poky municipal hall or held in private houses, now blossomed into brilliant fetes in the great hotel dining room, with its minstrel gallery for the orchestra.* No expense had been spared to make the hotel as modern, comfortable, and luxurious as any in New York or Europe, and reaping a profit from it was the last thing the Du Pont directors had envisioned. It would be a showcase for the prestige of the company.

Only Alfred I. was sniffy about it, and that was probably because Alicia was ill, and he did not attend the opening night, fearing snubs from her relations. In a letter to a friend, Mrs. Louise B. Angell, Alfred I. wrote:

> The Hotel is rapidly turning into a first class saloon. No guests are allowed to remain more than a certain time unless they become drunk. In order to make the Hotel pay it is necessary that the bars distribute sufficient liquor on a basis of 100% profit. I do not know whether you received an accurate account of the opening evening at the Hotel. The tables had been engaged several months in advance, consequently nothing but the crème de la crème could gain admission. If the City's Tatler, Bill Scott, is to be accredited, the scene in the Rathskeller placed Le Rat Mort at a serious advantage. After each incumbent had surrounded a quart of champagne, tables were pushed against the walls and the various participants in this Saturnalia started to turkey trot in a way which caused Mr. Scott to rush across the room to poor Aunt Mary: "Mrs. du Pont, are we in Berlin or Paris? This surely is not Wilmington."

Money was now flowing so copiously to Du Pont that Coleman was making $600,000 a year and P.S. $350,000. Alfred I.'s share was $400,000, despite the fact that he was no longer actively engaged in the day-to-day affairs of the company—and it had to be spent on something. Alfred I. lavished Alicia with presents, including a ruby from Tiffany's said to be worth $150,000. His great new house, Nemours, was rumored to have cost over $2 million at a time when the dollar was worth at least ten times what it is today.

But he was not happy there. When his builder, James Smyth, had finished the great wall that surrounded the Nemours estate, Alfred I. had told him to put spikes and embedded glass on top, for, as he said, "That wall's to keep out intruders, mainly of the name of du Pont."

* Until 1918, when the magnificent Gold Ballroom was added to the hotel.

Expensive pictures and antiques were shipped in from Europe and the Orient, and the grounds around the house were turned into ornate ornamental gardens. But there were few guests and fewer parties to show off the gaudy, tasteless, impersonal splendors. Alicia had been ill ever since the death of her baby and did not want visitors to see her. In the aftermath of childbirth she had become partly crippled, which prevented her from pursuing her favorite sport, riding, and something had happened to her eyes, so that her sight was poor, even with glasses. She was miserable, bitter, shrewish, and hard to live with, but Alfred I. was surprisingly gentle and patient with her, as he never had been when she was her normal, full-blooded, arrogant self.

Everybody said Alfred I. had only built Nemours because he was jealous of his cousin's new home and was determined to outdo it. In extravagances he had certainly succeeded, but P.S.'s house, Longwood Gardens (formerly Peirce's Park), would always be superior in the elegance of its design and the passion that had gone into its furnishings and its opulent greenhouses and gardens. P.S. had already installed a small ballroom. Now gardeners were at work reshaping the two hundred acres of grounds that rolled across the Pennsylvania countryside, and workmen were making the pools and installing the heating for six acres of greenhouses and conservatories in which he planned to grow flowers and exotic plants from all over the world, at all times of the year.

P.S. spent every leisure moment from Du Pont overseeing the work and operation of Longwood. He already had a large staff of employees, and each newcomer was handed a 160-page handbook containing precise instructions for the running of the house and grounds and describing the duties of those who worked there. He ran the house like a well-oiled business operation: breakfast 7:15–7:30 A.M., except Sunday when it was 9 A.M.; light lunch promptly at 1 P.M.; and dinner at 7 P.M., always of six courses, starting with caviare followed by soup, roast or poultry, a relish, salad, dessert, and coffee.

"Pierre was fastidious," wrote the authors of the official Du Pont story.

He looked after the wine cellar himself and he left detailed instructions for the care of his house. The silver, for example, was in charge of the caretaker. The tableware and nearly all other pieces were all plated, and therefore of little real value; but the knives, forks and spoons were sterling silver. Pierre directed that they be "guarded and counted frequently, so as to insure against loss." All tableware was to be polished at least once a week or more frequently if necessary. Pierre even concerned himself with the use of candles. "The metal candlesticks throughout the house," he instructed, "are to be placed in their various positions about the dwelling each morning and, at the same time, are to be replenished with fresh candles, excepting the single bedroom candlesticks, where the partially burned candles may be allowed to remain." Pierre's directions for the care of every phase of his house and garden were equally detailed.

P.S.'s mother, Mary du Pont, used to tease her eldest son about his finicky ways, chiding him that the running of a household was women's work and that he needed a wife experienced in such matters to assume the burden. She did not add that she knew just the woman for the job, because she had practically given up hope that P.S. would ever get around to marrying Alice Belin. From 1910 onwards P.S. began giving an annual summer garden party at Longwood, and Alice Belin was always among those present. As Mary watched her walking through the gardens with P.S., hanging on his every word, she wondered whether she would live to see her twenty years of scheming bear fruit. But it was not to be. In 1913, shortly after attending the opening of the Hotel du Pont, Mary du Pont died. She was buried at Sand Hole Woods. Alice Belin was, of course, at the funeral, ready to comfort P.S. for a loss he felt deeply. It was a moment, she was later to confess, when she thought the love of her life was ready to turn to her at last, especially when he took her arm after the burial service and asked her to accompany him in his chauffeur-driven car back to Longwood.

At the huge house, with Mary's strong presence still hovering in the great rooms as if to remind P.S. of her deathbed wish, it seemed as if this strangely shy and introverted man might finally be ready to pop the question to which Alice had had the answer ready since well before the turn of the century. But then his brothers, Irénée and Lammot, arrived, and they were interrupted. There were business matters to discuss, which even their mother's funeral could not postpone.

Coleman du Pont had known he was sick for many years, but except for those moments when the pain was too much, or an operation too urgent to be dodged, he ignored his illness and went on with life as if he were a healthy man. There is a favorite story about him that tells how once, lifting the settee cushion of a hotel suite he had just entered, he found a pair of silk cami-knickers. Handing them to the porter, he remarked:

"Take these out and have them filled."

In fact, the owner of the lingerie in question was probably waiting for him in the bathroom, because it was a rare occasion when any hotel suite Coleman occupied, sick or not, did not come equipped with hot-and-cold-running chorus girls as well as the usual plumbing. Though his plump and fatalistic wife, Elsie, now four times the size of the wraith he had married, affected to ignore his marital infidelities, she was, in fact, deeply hurt by them and regularly poured out her woes into the ears of her daughters or her eldest son. But the rest of the du Ponts, to whom Coleman was always helpful in the case of the men and gallant in the case of the women, never seemed to condemn him for his adventures as they did in the case of Alfred I. He was always so cheerful about them, as he was about everything— even his illnesses.

Between 1911 and 1914 Coleman was in and out of the hospital about five times, for various operations. Alfred I. du Pont was later to suggest, in sepulchral tones, that Coleman was suffering from "a social disease caused by his excesses." But in fact it was almost certainly pancreatitis that was creeping up on him. In the circumstances, one wonders how he found the time, the energy, the drive, and the sexual potency, not to mention the fund of good humor, to carry on as he did.

In 1909, in furtherance of his own political ambitions in Delaware and of the Colonel's interests as the state's representative in the United States Senate, Coleman bought the Wilmington *Evening Star* for one hundred thousand dollars, to use for his own and the family's propaganda. At the same time he made a remarkably expensive public gesture calculated both to fulfill a dire Delaware need and to keep his name before the voters: He offered to build a superhighway spanning one hundred and three miles separating Wilmington from the state capital, Dover, and on beyond to the Maryland state border. It was to have an all-weather pavement for high-speed motor traffic, slower lanes for trucks and horse-drawn vehicles, and a trolleyway. He guaranteed the cost of the road up to forty-four thousand dollars a mile, which, excluding the cost of the bridge necessary to span the Delaware Canal (he expected the state to pay for this), would amount to over four million dollars.

Though road connections between Wilmington and Dover were at that time impassable every winter, the legislators did not welcome Coleman's offer with open arms. They suspected he had some ulterior motive (which, with the exception of resultant political kudos, he did not), and began arguing about it. So did the farmers of lower Delaware, who immediately raised the price of land through those parts of their farms where they estimated the road would go.

While they were arguing, Coleman threw other irons in the fire, particularly in New York, where his heart (as well as the majority of his heartthrobs) lay. In 1912 the Equitable Life Assurance Society's New York headquarters burned down, and Coleman paid $13.5 million for the plot. He agreed to build a new thirty-six-story building at an estimated cost of $14.6 million, though eventually the amount came to $28.5 million. He also built the McAlpin Hotel in New York in partnership with President Taft's brother and took a large slice of the ownership of the Waldorf-Astoria Hotel. His idea was to start a chain of fashionable and expensive New York hotels—and he no doubt envisioned an endless vista of hotel parties whose bills he would be able to charge to expenses.

All this frenetic activity, combined with his occasional disappearance into hospitals, made him an infrequent attendant at the meetings of the executive and financial committees in Wilmington, and though P.S. was automatically voted into the chair in his place, Coleman's absence caused irritation. It was felt that Coleman, like Alfred I., was not pulling his weight, which also made the younger du Ponts restive. The company was not exactly losing money, but there was a national recession: Du Pont's gross receipts in 1913 had dropped to $26,675,000 from $36,524,000 the previous year, and profits had fallen to $5,347,000 from $6,871,000. It was the first setback since the cousins had taken over, and P.S. did not like it at all.

He sensed that the cousinly combination was beginning to lose its snap, and that it was time to make some changes. Both Coleman and Alfred I. were now fifty years old, and they were increasingly preoccupied with matters that had nothing to do with Du Pont. P.S. was still only forty-four, and though he yearned to spend more time in his greenhouses and gardens at Longwood, his sense of responsibility toward his now orphaned brothers and sisters had reasserted itself with new vehemence. More than ever he was Dad to them, and they looked to him for guidance and put their fortunes and their futures in his hands. Since those fortunes and futures rested squarely on the continuing prosperity of Du Pont, he could not possibly loosen his grip on its control. Nor could he afford to carry dead weights, such as Coleman and Alfred I. were gradually becoming.

Therefore, why not divest the company of its tricousinly control and substitute a fraternal regime with more youth, expertise, and dynamism? His younger brother Irénée was already on the executive committee and proving himself a first-class administrator and organizer of Du Pont affairs. And Lammot, his youngest brother, was in the labs and showing himself to be a brilliant chemist—and new developments in chemistry, P.S. believed, were going to revolutionize Du Pont's methods and products in the future as they had done in his father's day. With himself as their guide and adviser, the three brothers could revitalize Du Pont just at a time when an injection of adrenaline was needed.

It would be untrue to say that the idea of a triumvirate of brothers, in place of a triumvirate of cousins, had already come to flower in his mind in 1913 and 1914, but it was certainly germinating even then. By this time it was clear to him that his cousins would have to go. But how could he get rid of Alfred I.? And would Coleman be willing to sell out?

By 1913 P. S. du Pont no longer had any compunction about shaking off Alfred I. because, in his opinion, his cousin had finally put himself beyond the pale by his treatment of his ex-wife and children.

The private letters Alfred I. began writing in this period to his cousins and others, are locked up at the Eleutherian Mills Historical Library and will not be released until the end of the century, but those who have read them say they are not only scurrilous in the extreme but display the same signs of mental disarray that his mother, poor mad Charlotte, revealed in her correspondence. He was abysmally unhappy and had begun blaming everybody but himself for his miseries.

Everything had by now gone wrong in his personal life. Though not yet stone-deaf, he could no longer hear even a two-way conversation without a hearing aid and was hopelessly confused at meetings. His new glass eye seemed like a perfect twin of his good eye, but, in fact, it gave him constant pain, which forced him to retire at frequent intervals to take it out. Alicia was sick and miserable and found her only entertainment in taunting and baiting her husband, whom she had begun to suspect of infidelities. Alfred I.'s English valet, Thomas Horncastle, had caught her going through his master's desk, and knew she must have discovered the letters Jessie Ball was now writing him regularly, but it was over his occasional flings with girls from the powder men's families (about which friends did not fail to inform her) that Alicia jeered at him. As Lou reported to her brother P.S.:

> Alicia says Alfred has found a new aphrodisiac. She remarked that it seems the smell of powder on the Brandywine girls really ignites him!!!

In his misery Alfred I. was prepared to lash out at anybody in the hope that hurting them might ease his own agony and sense of defeat. On February 13, 1913, he struck out at his own son. On that day the Democratic representative from Delaware City rose in the House of Representatives at Dover and introduced a bill entitled "An Act to change the name of Alfred Victor du Pont to Dorsey Cazenove du Pont." He had already informed his fellow party members in the lobbies that the divorced du Pont parents, Alfred I. and Bessie, had mutually agreed to the name change, so the bill was passed and sent to the Senate.

But then both Bessie and the New York newspapers got wind of the story (which did not, of course, appear in the Wilmington press), and while the New York *Times* and the *Sun* speculated about the reasons behind this remarkable bill Bessie rushed to P.S. for advice. He summoned his lawyers, and next day an attorney representing Bessie appeared in Dover to make it clear to the representatives that Alfred Victor's mother had not only not consented to the name change but vigorously opposed it. This announcement caused a sensation in the House.

Alfred I. then issued a public statement:

> I wish to say that this bill was introduced by me and not by the boy's mother, Mrs. B. G. du Pont, as certain papers have erroneously stated. This change [of name] was requested by me for reasons to me sufficient and at the moment not of public concern.

What reasons? The representatives in Dover, particularly the anti–du Pont Democrats, were dying to know. Was Alfred I. suggesting that Alfred Victor was not his son? That Bessie, perhaps, had been unfaithful to him with, say, Cazenove Lee, who was Bessie's cousin but also married to Alfred I.'s hated sister Marguerite? The only way they could find out was to call Alfred I. du Pont before them and hear his evidence from his own lips. But the only evidence he produced when he appeared before a private meeting of the House committee was a copy of the trust agreement he and Bessie du Pont had signed. He said he had not seen his son, Alfred Victor, for four years, and when pressed by the chairman about why he wished to change the boy's name, he reluctantly replied that he felt he would one day "bring disgrace" on his father. That was all he was prepared to say, except that he had chosen the names *Dorsey Cazenove* as a "courtesy" to his ex-wife, for they came from her family.

P.S., meanwhile, had been doing some rapid defensive checking, and at the same meeting he had Bessie's lawyer read a report from the headmaster of Hallock School, which Alfred Victor was attending, giving him excellent marks for character and intelligence. But P.S. relied (and rightly) on a letter, written by the boy to his mother, to make its mark on the committee:

> Please can you tell me why Father is trying to change my name? I do not understand it, and my schoolmates keep asking me questions.

That did it. The Democrats had a majority and were by this time ranged behind Alfred I., who had sent down a professional lobbyist with scads of money to spend; but when it came to the final vote, the bill was defeated by 17 votes to 15, thanks to five Democrat abstentions. Alfred Victor du Pont kept his name. But P.S. never forgave Alfred I. for having humiliated his own son.

At first it looked as if the problem of eliminating Coleman was going to be much more of an ordeal than getting rid of Alfred I. For Cousin Coleman, suddenly announcing he "had never felt in better health," reappeared on the Brandywine and gave every sign of snatching back the reins of the presidency from P.S. He was soon criticizing many of the decisions his cousin and the executive committee had made, and ranged himself on the side of executives who disagreed with P.S. This produced strained relations between the cousins, and Coleman threatened to quit. But P.S. could not possibly allow him to leave in anger. If he went, it had to be amicably. Alfred I.'s behavior had already caused too much dissension in the family, and nothing could be allowed to further alienate the du Ponts from one another.

The situation grew worse during the summer of 1914, and on August 24 Coleman wrote a letter to P.S., which he marked "Confidential and for you only."

It was a long and moiling document, full of past grievances and reproaches, but its main point was contained in one of its final paragraphs:

"I have always said that when a President cannot control his board of directors and have the support of his board it was time for him to quit and for the board to get a new President. I am now as close to the line that were it not for my belief that it would make your task harder, my resignation would go in to take effect Sept. 1st."

He suggested the appointment of two outside arbitrators to settle the differences between them. Coleman and P.S. would agree beforehand to be bound by their finding and suggested solution even if it meant that one cousin take full control and buy the other out.

For the moment P.S. was in no position to buy his cousin out. He did not have enough family support behind him. And he was certainly not willing to let strangers come in and arbitrate between them. So he wrote Coleman an appeasing letter and decided to bide his time. But there was no longer room in the company for both of them. Moreover, until he could be certain of his family's continued involvement, he had no intention of going himself.

As a result of the court's decision in the antitrust suit, Du Pont had taken certain (if hardly stringent) measures to break its stranglehold on the domestic explosives business. But it had taken no steps to end its global arrangements with the explosives trusts in England, France, and Germany. In the spring of 1914, in fact, P. S. du Pont consulted with his brother Irénée, now a vice-president, and decided to strengthen rather than weaken Du Pont's agreements with the international cartel.

On May 19, 1914, Irénée showed his brother a new agreement that he proposed to take to England where he would persuade the Europeans to sign it. It would consolidate and, if possible, reinforce Du Pont's monopoly in the Western Hemisphere. The proposed agreement put it this way:

> First, divide the world into Eastern countries and Western countries. Eastern countries [which Britain and Europe would control] to include European, Asiatic and African countries. Western [under Du Pont control] to include United States, Mexico and such South American countries as the Europeans will acquiesce in.
>
> When we become possessed of an invention, we shall decide whether it shall be patented or maintained as a secret process. Should we decide that we will patent it, upon filing application

we will disclose to them the nature of the invention and ask which Eastern countries they desire that patent be taken out, and will cause to be filed application in such at their expense. Prior to their making use of such patent, or in any case within two years thereafter, we will come to an agreement for a proper compensation basis. . . .

Should we elect to maintain the process as a secret, we will disclose to them the nature of the process and prior to their use of same, and in no case in less than two years thereafter, we will determine with them a proper basis of compensation, by which we will grant an exclusive license [to them] to utilize such secret process in all Eastern countries. Should they become possessed of an invention a like procedure will be followed.

By the time Irénée reached London, in June 1914, the prospect of war in Europe loomed large, but the British, French, and German explosives trusts were still meeting, as if unaware of the possibility of conflict between them. Du Pont was extremely anxious to get out of paying a high price for the royalties they owed on an Anglo-German patent for Ballistite, which they had been using since 1910 in the manufacturing of shells. The other members of the cartel were demanding $137,000 in royalties per year, but Irénée, realizing that one or another of the Europeans was going to be heavily dependent on Du Pont for supplies in the near future, drove a hard bargain. He settled for retroactive payment of $75,000, and the same amount for future use, and persuaded them to throw in another of their patents as well.

By the time the agreement came before the executive committee in Wilmington, World War I had begun, and the Nobel-Dynamite Trust Company of Britain was out of touch with its former partner in Germany. On August 26, 1914, one of the British directors wrote to Irénée du Pont about what he termed "the unfortunate international complications on this side." Would it be possible, he asked, "for the Europeans to execute the Agreements now under consideration by your Executive"? He added:

You will appreciate that it is quite impossible at the moment for us to communicate with our German associates and it has occurred to us to suggest that, if it is agreeable to you, the Nobel-Dynamite Trust Company can execute the Agreements, or give you a letter indicating their willingness to do so. . . . While we are at present prevented by force majeure from calling upon our German interests to carry out the arrangement, we shall of course seek the earliest opportunity of doing so.

Irénée was all for Du Pont signing the agreement at once and waiting until the end of the war—which he did not think would be of long duration—for the Germans to countersign. But P.S. was more cautious. He suspected the war might go on a long time, and he was not sure which side would win. In the circumstances, he wanted that German countersignature. He conferred with the company's legal adviser, Judge John P. Laffley, and from their discussions and maneuvers a go-between emerged in the person of Edward Kraftmeier, a Swiss subject working for the British Nobel Company, whose passport enabled him to travel freely through the war areas. On February 4, 1914, Judge Laffley wrote to Irénée:

> . . . Re Nobel agreement, I will prepare a resolution for the next meeting of the Board of Directors, authorizing Mr. Mathesius to sign the contracts. . . . Mr Kraftmeier advised me that . . . the contracts be signed in London by the Du Pont Co. and the Nobel's, and that then all four contracts should be returned to us, and that we should then send them to Mr Aughslager [Dr. G. Aufschlager of German Nobel's] at Hamburg with the request that he have all four copies executed by the German party to the agreement. I told Mr Kraftmeier I saw no objection if they desired to proceed in that way and that we should do so [but] I am wondering what would happen to the contracts if the German Censor examined sufficiently to enable him to know what they are. . . . It might be very embarrassing to our German friends if these contracts should fall into the hands of the German Censors.

But even as that letter was being written, P.S. was clambering down from the fence so far as the European war was concerned. He had been conferring with an old friend of the Du Pont company, Dwight Morrow. A director of the Morgan banking interests, Morrow was a fervent supporter of the Allies and had won his bank over to his point of view to such an extent that the Morgan interests were ready to bankroll British purchases in the United States for the duration of the war. He told P.S. he had advised the British to purchase their explosives from Du Pont.

So P.S. no longer cared whether the Germans signed the agreement or not. Like Boss Henry at the start of the Civil War, he had chosen sides.

In his view, it was now clear that the British were going to win the war, and it was the British he was backing. He wrote to Coleman (who was convalescing from an operation at the Mayo Clinic, in Rochester, Minnesota) on January 25, 1915:

> Since my last letter, the Nobel Company has closed for 6,500,000 more pounds of powder and gun cotton on account of the British Government. . . . Col. Buckner has taken up the question of supplying the powder for the British Government with J. P. Morgan and Company who have been appointed financial agents for the purchase of supplies. . . . It is difficult to judge the effect of earnings by this extraordinary business. In the neighborhood of 100% seems a fair guess.

But would Du Pont be able to cope with the rush of orders they were now getting?

> You probably do not realize how much this extraordinary military business has diverted attention from the routine of the company's business. . . . The Engineering Department has expanded beyond our wildest dreams. Those in the Smokeless Operating Department have seized men from the other departments to quickly meet demands.

Du Pont's orders to date, he added, amounted to 55,999,575 pounds of cannon, rifle, guncotton, and triton powder, more than at any time in its history; and the company had offers of purchase of another 14,027,500 pounds.

He believed, but did not say to Coleman, that the tremendous effort in which Du Pont was now involved could only be turned into a success if he (P.S.) and he alone had command of the company and its operational policies. Was Coleman, with only half his stomach left after his recent operation, now ready to withdraw? And would he sell out to his cousin, or was he going to go after what the market would bear for his share of Du Pont?

A rumor had suddenly come to the surface, and P.S. made haste to let his cousin know that he had heard it.

"My New York visit," he wrote in the same letter to Coleman,

> was to meet Mr. Kraftmeier, who, with his wife and daughter, arrived on the LUSITANIA Saturday. He had cabled he wished to

meet Irénée and me immediately on his arrival. I supposed that
his mission was to place additional orders so we took Col. Buckner [now Du Pont's selling agent] along and were much surprised to find Mr. K. made no mention of orders. Finally, after
he succeeded in drawing me aside, he told me that they had a
report that Kuhn, Loeb and Company of New York (who are a
pro-German firm) had gained control of our company through
the embarrassment of one of our large stockholders and that
they on that account had fears concerning the [British] orders
placed with us. I, of course, assured him that nothing of the kind
had happened or would happen; that all orders would be filled
according to contract without any shadow of a doubt. He seemed
somewhat relieved to hear this and said this was one of the important things that brought him over.

There was only one stockholder in Du Pont with a large enough holding to give the pro-German bankers, Kuhn, Loeb and Company, control
of the company if he sold out to them, and both Coleman and P.S. knew
who it was—Coleman himself. Could he really be planning to sell out to
the "other side"?

To probe further, P.S. wrote him on January 28. "For a period of
time covering this extraordinary war situation," he suggested in that letter,
the four largest stockholders in Du Pont should place their stock together,
"with an agreement that the certificates would not be sold or used as collateral unless by common consent."*

P.S. added:

Personally, I think it is a good idea, as our ability to state
positively that control of the stock was absolutely safe would put
our foreign orders in much better position. Our business with the
side of the Allies is so large now it may mean to them the turning point of the war. It is, therefore, of the utmost importance
that they know our situation. If you approve the plan . . . it
would be a very good thing to tell Mr. Kraftmeier that we have
determined to do this in order to assure our customers of the
true situation.

* The four largest stockholders in Du Pont at this time were, in order of the importance of their holdings, Coleman du Pont, Alfred I. du Pont, P. S. du Pont, and
William du Pont. Although banished from the company, William still held on to his
stock. His brother, Colonel Henry Algernon du Pont, had divested himself of his holdings when he became a United States senator.

P. S. du Pont at the age of twenty.

P. S. du Pont's biggest enemy in the family was his uncle, Francis Gurney du Pont, who, with his brother, Eugene, took over the company towards the end of the last century. As a result of their quarrels P. S. resigned but came back later to buy out his uncles and turn Du Pont into an internationally known corporation.

Alfred I. du Pont (STANDING LEFT) *with his brothers, Louis* (SEATED LEFT) *and Maurice* (SEATED RIGHT) *and two other members of the "Holy Brotherhood" at Phillips Academy, Andover, Massachusetts, in 1880.*

Alfred I. du Pont as a student at MIT in 1883. He paid his way by boxing in local matches around Boston, and became a close friend of John L. Sullivan, then heavyweight boxing champion of the world.

Bessie Gardner was a distant relative of the du Ponts who met and married the temperamental Alfred I., one of the Three Cousins who founded the modern Du Pont company. Although she bore him three daughters and a son, it was far from a successful union. Alfred I.'s messy affairs with other du Pont women and his subsequent divorce caused a great scandal in the family and his banishment from the firm.

All the du Ponts were mad about motorcars—they finally bought up General Motors. Among the first in Delaware to own a car was Alfred I. du Pont, seen here (around 1890) in his personally designed "special."

Alfred I. du Pont's first wife was a cousin, and so was his second. Alicia Bradford's relationship with Alfred caused some stormy family encounters and much scandal before they were finally married in 1907.

Alicia Bradford du Pont with her daughter, Alicia, who was born while she was married to Alfred I. du Pont's assistant, George Maddox, and whom Alfred always called Pechette —"Little Sin."

Senator Coleman du Pont was the most gregarious of the three cousins who took over Du Pont in 1902. Despite a lifelong struggle with serious illness, he contrived to enjoy, as he once put it, "good food, good wine and bad women." He was also a genius at promoting a deal, and it was thanks to his powers of persuasion that the du Pont uncles turned over a company then valued at $19,000,000 for a cash outlay of only $2,100.

The famous composer and bandleader John Philip Sousa was a friend of P. S. du Pont and often came to play at Longwood Gardens. This picture was taken on August 26, 1930.

The most successful of the du Pont family houses is Longwood, in Pennsylvania, which P. S. du Pont created from a small farm originally known as Peirce's Park. Set in 400 acres of rolling farmland, it was turned into a park with ornamental gardens and fountains and an open-air arena for plays and concerts. The house is surrounded by six acres of conservatories and greenhouses where P.S. raised orchids, rare flowers and shrubs. This is a view of the main conservatory, leading to the house. Inside the house is a ballroom equipped with a 10,010-pipe organ, the second largest in the United States.

In the beginning, the Du Pont company owned all the houses on the Brandywine, where the mills were established, and the head of the firm assigned living quarters as and when they were needed. But as the cousins grew richer, they began building estates of their own. Granogue, one of the biggest, was built by Irénée du Pont. Set in 250 acres of ground, the great house includes a ballroom and concert organ.

Alice Belin married P. S. du Pont in 1915, after waiting 23 years. The marriage was full of dashed hopes and disappointments for Alice. She never conceived the son she had hoped for, nor any other children. Alice was deaf from an early age—note the hearing aid in this picture.

There is a file in the du Pont archives at the Eleutherian Mills Historical Library marked "Letters between P. S. du Pont and John J. Raskob—Confidential." It is empty. But Raskob and P.S. had no secrets from each other. This picture was taken at Longwood Gardens in 1950, during the 150th birthday celebration of the du Pont family's arrival in America.

Alfred I. du Pont was always jealous of the great house and gardens his cousin P.S. had created at Longwood, Pennsylvania. After his stormy second marriage, he decided to build a great house of his own. Called Nemours, the estate is modeled on Versailles and surrounded by a nine-foot wall. It is now a hospital for crippled children.

Feuds with his du Pont cousins drove Alfred I. du Pont out of Delaware. He moved with his third wife, Jessie Ball, to Florida, where this picture was taken in 1926.

Coleman chose deliberately to misunderstand this letter and wrote back protesting that the Allies were trying to dictate to Du Pont. He was damned if he was going to allow them to get away with that. The company could sell to whom it liked—to the Germans, too, if they sent in the orders. P.S. hastened to agree. As he wrote on February 5, 1915:

> If they [the Germans] come forward with orders in quantity, similar to the orders of the Allied nations we would be willing to sell; but we would not be willing to place small orders, say, five or ten million pounds, with the Germans giving them access to our factories, through which means they might cause great damage and loss of profits far in excess of the above mentioned orders.

Coleman never did tell P.S. whether he had, in fact, been dickering with Kuhn, Loeb and Company. But he confided to his cousin something that was much more important. He announced that he felt it was about time the younger men and junior executives in Du Pont had a bigger stake in the fortunes of the company, and proposed to do something about it. He was willing to sell 20,700 shares of Du Pont common stock for the benefit of senior employees, the purchase price to be financed from the company treasury.

He wanted $160 a share, or just over $3 million for the whole block of stock. It was a high price, for Du Pont shares at the time he made his offer were being quoted at around $137. But P.S. was not concerned about that. All he cared about was that once Coleman sold 20,700 of his shares, he would no longer be the majority holder and no longer in control of the company.

No matter what anybody said, he was determined to take Coleman up on his offer.

CHAPTER 17

Patience Rewarded

As far back as the early 1890s Alice Belin, then a twenty-year-old student at Bryn Mawr, was in love with her cousin P. S. du Pont and convinced that one day she would marry him. In those days, with her blue eyes, contrasting brown hair and sun-bronzed face, she was one of the most attractive girls on campus, and one of the merriest. Princeton students and Scranton beaux came chasing her, and she was always one of the popular belles at Scranton Country Club dances.

She had her share of romances, and to judge by the sentimental relics later found among her effects, some of them had been serious. There is an envelope containing a reddish-brown tress marked "Jack's hair," which belonged to one John Daw, who wrote to her:

> Dear Alice Belin
> > Hast thou no feelin'
> > > To see me kneelin'
> > > > Day after day?

And in the same handwriting:

A dog may look at a Queen—no harm to the Queen, I hope.

Underneath is scribbled

<u>Dear, dear</u> Jack.

But all her suitors had been spurned in the end, for reasons her family well understood. Alice was waiting for P.S. to ask her to marry him. Both her father, Henry (Harry) Belin, and P.S.'s mother, Mary Belin du Pont, were strongly in favor of it. Harry Belin was a successful accountant who already looked after many of Du Pont's interests, and one of his sons ran an explosives works in Scranton that, if not owned by Du Pont, had close connections with it. Clearly a marriage between the two cousins would knit up quite a few mutual interests, and so it would have Mary and Harry's approval whether or not Alice was in love with P.S. Her adoration, and the fact that she thought him the handsomest, the cleverest, the most charming, and the nicest man she had ever met, simply added passion to practical considerations. As for P.S.'s feelings toward Alice, they all knew he had been her friend since childhood and was quite obviously fond of her. What more could one ask than that?

Still the years went by, and P.S. did not pop the expected question. The fact that he had not proposed to another girl, or even shown a particular interest in anyone else, gave the family hope. He was too hardworking, too anxious to get started, they had thought at first. He could hardly marry while he was off in mid-America making his fortune, they had said when he left for Lorain, Ohio. His new responsibilities were taking up too much of his time, they had decided, when he took over the company with his cousins in 1902.

Alice Belin herself had become convinced that it would happen at last when P.S.'s mother died. But if P.S. had had any intention of filling with Alice the gap left in his life by his mother's death, he failed to ask the necessary question.

In 1915 Alice Belin was forty-three years old and P. S. du Pont forty-five. Everyone had pretty well resigned themselves to the thought that in P.S. they had a perennial family bachelor; and that was a pity for dear Alice, since, at her age, she could hardly expect to marry anyone else. It seemed sad, after having waited so long—twenty-three years.

But then, that spring, Alice Belin's heart began to sing. Suddenly P.S. was seeking her out. It was no longer she who made pretexts to come to

Wilmington from Scranton and engineered excuses for seeing him in the Brandywine houses. He actually began to write to ask her when she was coming over.

It is unlikely that she wasted time wondering why he was now so interested in her despite his deep involvement with developments at Du Pont. Her father told her that some sort of a revolution was taking place in the company, and that P.S. was likely to emerge the master of everything. But she was far too happy at seeing so much of him to be bothered with all this, and if her father speculated about how P.S. could possibly find the time, Alice did not.

All through May and June 1915 she was seeing him practically every day. She toured the conservatories of Longwood with him and listened while he explained his ambitions for the orchid houses or discoursed on the nature and flowering habits of obscure but exotic shrubs. With his chauffeur-handyman, Charlie Mason, newly arrived on the estate with his wife, family, and younger brother, Lewes, she drove through the Pennsylvania hills or to the country club, where they played golf together or strolled around the course. At the end of these Longwood visits P.S.'s youngest house servant, Lewes Mason, would come forward, ruddy-cheeked, shyly grinning, and hand her a box of orchids, a bouquet of lovely roses, or a basket of the special fruits (melons, peaches, or nectarines) P.S. was now cultivating.

Until 1915 Alice's diary had been not only perfunctory but gloomy as well, and mostly concerned with the rain or heat or cold or headaches. But now, though the entries were still short, they became, for her, quite ecstatic. On June 11 P.S. gave a small dinner party and dance at Longwood in her honor. It seems likely this was the night he got around to asking the all-important question, for Alice wrote the next day:

> Wonderful day . . . lovely party . . . supper & watched dancing with P.S.

She stayed on the Brandywine, seeing P.S. every day and walking around (her cousin Lou remarked) "as if someone [had] told her where the fairy gold [was] buried." On Sunday, June 20, she went back to Scranton, where she wrote in her diary:

> Unpacked & finally told Mother and Father.

There, it was done. The fading Juliet had captured her aging Romeo at last.

That same day P.S. wrote to Henry Belin, Jr., from Longwood:

Dear Uncle:

Alice said that she would tell you that she has consented to share my lot in life but I do want her consent to have your approval. No man can claim to merit the sacrifice that a woman must make in marrying but he can promise to do all in his power to compensate for what she gives. The promise I give, may I be capable of carrying it into effect!

Our long years of association together leave you pretty well informed as to my character and position, at forty-five a man has little hope of change for his imperfections but if your observations can suggest a line of endeavor that will make me more worthy of Alice I shall take the greatest pleasure in applying myself toward that end.

If you and Aunt Greta will consider that you are not giving up a daughter but are taking on another son I shall be very happy and shall try to merit a place in your family circle.

The engagement was officially announced by Alice's parents on June 25, 1915, and the marriage fixed for October.

From Alfred I.'s point of view, Coleman du Pont's offer to sell a large part of his Du Pont holdings could not have come at a worse time, because Alfred was sick with worry over personal problems. In the spring of 1914 Alicia had told him that she was pregnant again, and despite the frailness of her health, he hoped yet again that she was going to give him a son. Together they walked down to the little grave on the grounds of Nemours where their baby girl had been buried, and they prayed for a son, in the hope that the child would give Alicia back her pride and restore their failing marriage.

That summer, afraid the humid heat of Delaware would be bad for her, Alfred I. persuaded his wife to take a European vacation and sent with her (all expenses paid, of course) her brother, Edward Bradford, Jr. Eddie was now a state representative in Dover and generally accepted as Alfred I.'s spokesman both in the House and in the Delaware Republican party. The trip was a great success and both Alicia and her brother wrote back glowing accounts of their travels through Burgundy. Alfred I. planned to sail to France in August and meet them in Paris before bringing his wife home again.

But on August 4, 1914, the war began, and the German military machine rolled across the farmlands of France, threatening the French capital itself. Alfred I. was frantic. He did not for a moment worry about his daughter, Madie, in Germany, whose husband had already been called up into the kaiser's army, but the thought that Alicia, pregnant with his child, might be trapped in France was almost too much to bear. He could not get a passage to France himself, and he could not make contact with his wife.

Eventually, Alicia got back to America. But the worry had done her no good, and for months Alfred I. hovered over the doctors' shoulders, making sure that his wife did nothing to provoke a miscarriage. On October 21, 1914, her time came. It was a difficult labor, but after many hours Alicia gave birth—to a son. Still the doctors were concerned. Both mother and child were in poor condition.

Alfred I. already had a clergyman standing by, and within hours of the birth a christening ceremony was held beside Alicia's bed. Alfred I. could not name his son after himself because his other son, Alfred Victor, had already preempted the name, so he was christened Samuel du Pont. The father wept tears of joy as Samuel's puny little body was dipped in the makeshift font, but he was dry-eyed later in the evening when the doctors came in to tell him that the child had died.

The baby was buried on October 22 beside his little sister, and Alfred I. plunged into a profound depression from which he found it difficult to emerge, especially for considerations of business.

In consequence, when his cousin P.S. summoned him to a meeting of three of the four principal shareholders (Coleman being absent) where he was told that Coleman was prepared to sell a block of shares, he paid little attention. Once the details had been made clear to Alfred I.—for he had difficulty hearing—he snorted and said Coleman's price was far too high. P.S. seemed to think that the war would last a long time and profits would increase, but Alfred I. was not sure about that. It would certainly be too risky to pay $160 a share; he believed $125 a share would be a much fairer offer. William du Pont, who had personal reasons for being on Alfred I.'s side, agreed with him, and they so voted. On the other hand, P.S. voted to accept the $160 offer.

And this is where the misunderstanding, deliberate or not, arose to split the du Pont family down the middle. Alfred I. was later to contend that he had meant only to indicate his readiness to negotiate, although he thought Coleman was asking too much. P.S., on the other hand, maintained that his cousins had turned the offer down flat, and that he had been outvoted, two to one. The minutes of the meeting in the Du Pont archives do not answer the question either way. They simply say:

PURCHASE OF STOCK OWNED BY T. C. DU PONT

P. S. du Pont presented letters of T. C. du Pont offering to sell 20,700 shares of common stock of this Company at $160 per share. Moved and carried (P. S. du Pont voting in the negative) "that Mr. P. S. du Pont be instructed to advise Mr. L. L. Dunham, attorney for Mr. T. C. du Pont that we do not feel justified in paying more than $125 per share for this stock.

This resolution was offered by Alfred orally.*

Was P.S. trying to trick Alfred I.? It looks suspiciously as if that was the way his mind began to work in the weeks that followed the so-called turndown by Alfred I. and William du Pont. When he reported to his board of directors, a week after the original meeting to discuss Coleman's offer, he wrote:

The committee [that is, P.S., Alfred I., and William] expressed the feeling that we were not justified in paying more than $125 a share and asked Mr. P. S. du Pont *to take the matter up with Mr. T. C. du Pont further* [italics mine].

On the other hand, on February 10, 1915, when the three men met again at a regular finance-committee meeting, Alfred I. asked his cousin how the "negotiations" with Coleman were going.

"Why, they are all off," said P.S. "They were called off shortly after you and Willie turned down the offer in December."

Alfred I. immediately protested that the offer had not been turned down.

"There was merely a difference of opinion as to price," he said, "and it was my understanding that you were to convey to T.C. through Mr. Dunham that we believe the price of $160 a share excessive, and we suggested $125 as a proper price at that time."

"That was not my understanding," said P.S. "My understanding was that you turned down T.C.'s offer definitely."

Alfred I. consulted with his cousin Willie and then turned back to P.S.

"There seems to have been some misunderstanding as to the position taken by Willie and myself," he said, "and I desire to have this matter

* Vol. I, p. 172, Du Pont Co. records.

cleared up. You have unintentionally misinformed T.C. and I suggest Willie and I write to T.C. setting forth our views."

But either his mind was not up to the talk or he was relying on his cousinly ties to persuade Coleman to reopen the negotiations, for the letter he wrote was extremely tactless and it still quoted the figure of $125 a share, with no suggestion that he and Willie were ready to agree on a compromise figure. Nor does Alfred I. seem to have noticed that word of Du Pont's bulging order book had gone around the markets, and that the company's shares were now being quoted at $203. Even at the original figure of $160 Coleman would now be losing $890,000 on the deal at current market value. At $125 a share he would stand to lose $1,614,000. He wrote back:

Dear Alfred:

I am in receipt of your letter of February 16 [1915] and have read it several times. I cannot, however, make out why you wrote it.

The truth of the matter was that the time was past for haggling over price, and that he had already wired P.S. to tell him that he had withdrawn the offer. And, he added slyly, how many of his *own shares* was Alfred I. prepared to sell to Du Pont junior executives at $125 a share? "Probably I can join you with an offer," he wrote.

What Coleman did not reveal to Alfred I. or to Cousin Willie was that some nifty negotiations of a different kind were now going on behind their backs. Nor did P.S. mention a word to either of them, though he was deeply involved in the proceedings. Coleman had received some bad news from his surgeons at the Mayo Clinic and knew he would shortly have to undergo another operation. He was not sure that he would survive the ordeal this time. The moment had come to sell out completely. He summoned his right-hand man, Lew Dunham, who then took the train to Wilmington where he conferred with P.S. and *his* right-hand man, John J. Raskob.* Dunham confided that Coleman was prepared to sell out twenty thousand, forty thousand, or even sixty thousand (his total holdings) shares of common stock and a large block of preferred stock. But he was no longer willing to sell at $160. He wanted the market price of $200, and if he could not get it from his cousins, he would go to the stock exchange for it.

P.S. called a meeting to discuss this grave situation. Significantly, he did not invite Alfred I. or Willie to be present. Instead, only his brothers,

* Who had now risen to be treasurer of Du Pont.

Irénée and Lammot, his brother-in-law Ruly Carpenter, and John J. Raskob were there. P.S. pointed out that the family firm was facing a crisis. If Coleman sold on the open market, the family would lose control of Du Pont after 113 years. Such control could well pass, as Dr. Kraftmeier had direly predicted, through Kuhn, Loeb into pro-German hands, and Du Pont's booming business with the Allies would be ruined. But on the other hand, what was the alternative? Looking around the table at his relations—whose financial success he readily acknowledged—he pointed out:

"We do not have enough cash between us to meet the amount we need to buy Coleman out."

Now this is where the question of P.S.'s motives arises. He must have known by then that Alfred I., despite his incompetent letter to Coleman, was still ready to make a deal. He must also have known that with Cousin Alfred I. and Cousin Willie once more in the game, there would be quite enough money to meet Coleman's price, even if it had risen to two hundred dollars a share. All he had to do was call in his cousins, present them with the facts of the emergency, and enlist their help. Alfred I. was as anxious as he was to keep Du Pont in the family.

Then why did he not ask his cousins to the meeting? Why did he tell only his brothers, his brother-in-law, and his treasurer that they were the last hopes for saving the company?

P.S.'s own explanation of his actions, made many years later, is lame and unpersuasive:

Alfred's conduct had been vague and inconsistent, and there was no time to be lost.

Was time really so pressing that Alfred I. could not be summoned from Nemours, six miles away, and a telegram sent to Willie? Yet the only alternative P.S. presented to his assembled relations was either (*a*) to find the money to buy out Coleman themselves or (*b*) to let Du Pont pass into the hands of strangers. And, he said, they just did not have the cash for the first alternative.

It was at this moment that John J. Raskob rose to his feet and thereupon proceeded to repay every favor he had ever received from his boss. A tiny man, teetering on tiptoe in his size seven shoes to achieve some height amid these hulking du Ponts, he was a very different character from the young man P.S. had once employed as a reluctant stenographer in Lorain, Ohio. Pince-nez added a glint to his button-bright eyes, he smelled of expensive facial lotion, and his dapper silk suit had been cut for him in Savile Row. He exuded self-confidence and addressed the meeting as one among his equals, except when he turned to his boss and all the old deference came back into his voice.

He had been thinking, he told the men around the table, about a conversation he had had a few days before with his good friend Dwight Morrow of J. P. Morgan and Company. Morrow had reminded him that J. P. Morgan was a banking enterprise and therefore interested in the money-lending business. The firm had lent money to the British government to pay Du Pont for the powder the nation was buying for the war. Why should it not lend money to Du Pont's senior partner to enable him to secure the company and go on producing that powder for the British? As P.S. put it later:

> John Raskob, with his usual financial acumen, believed that the purchase of Coleman's entire holdings could be arranged with the assistance of the New York banks. . . . Raskob proceeded along to the office of J. P. Morgan and Company on the next day, February 19. Mr. William H. Porter, one of the Morgan partners, whom Raskob had known for quite ten years, became interested in trying to place the loan. He thought it could be done.

If P.S. and his group were to buy out all Coleman's stock, they would need, Raskob calculated, around $14 million. As P.S. later wrote:

> Mr. Porter went out to make inquiries and reported on his return that he felt satisfied that $10,000,000 could be placed and was hopeful of placing the whole $14,000,000 that was needed. Raskob returned as far as Philadelphia that evening and met Pierre there. On the morning of the 20th Mr. Porter telephoned that the proposition was to be taken up by the Morgan partners and soon after informed Raskob that the plan was satisfactory.

By this time one other du Pont had been invited to join what P.S. was now calling the syndicate. He was the son of the late Eugene du Pont and therefore holder of a considerable block of company shares. In the names of himself, Irénée and Lammot du Pont, Ruly Carpenter, Cousin Alexis, and John J. Raskob, he then telegraphed a definite offer to Coleman. There was a forty-eight-hour delay while some details and prices were ironed out, and then Coleman wired back:

PROPOSITION ACCEPTED FOR ENTIRE HOLDINGS. . . .

He surrendered 63,214 shares of common stock at $200 and 13,898 shares of preferred stock at $85, for a total purchase price of $13,831,865. But not all this money would have to be borrowed from J. P. Morgan. Coleman agreed to accept $8,000,000 in cash, and a note from the purchasers for the remaining $5,831,865 at six-percent interest over seven years. So the syndicate needed only $8,500,000 from Morgan (the $500,-000 being for "expenses") to cover the payment to Coleman, and they agreed to borrow this over eighteen months at six percent. The six members of the syndicate thereupon formed themselves into a corporation called Du Pont Securities Company to carry through the deal.*

Still no word of the negotiations had reached other members of the family, let alone the press. When Alfred I. and P.S. met in the corridors of the Du Pont Building, they stopped to chat about Coleman's "obstinacy," and P.S. uttered not a word about what had happened. Yet he had two letters in his pocket from Coleman that would have told Alfred I. everything. One of them said:

Dear Pierre:

No one will ever know the sacrifice I made in giving up being the largest stockholder and President of the Powder Company. The position I would rather hold than any in the world.

1st. I feel certain that in doing this I am doing what is best for the Powder Co.

2nd. That I am doing what would have pleased Uncle Lammot, Aunt Mary and Bill and what is best for their children who are dearer to me than any people in God's green earth except my own family.

3rd. That any possible differences between you and me is removed.

4th. That I am losing money—to hell with the last.

The other letter, written on the same day, was in reply to one from P.S. asking Coleman to remain silent. "I realize," Coleman wrote,

that to keep the sale of stock quiet until <u>you are ready</u> is so important that I have not thought it wise to even dictate confirmation of telegrams and conversations & really wanted to whisper when talking on the phone.

* Its name was later changed to Christiana Securities.

It was not until the weekend of February 22, 1915, that word at last leaked out. P.S. decided that he was not going to be greedy about the coup he had brought off, and he took $1 million out of his stake in the new acquisition and gave 1,250 shares, valued at $125,000, in Du Pont securities to each of his two brothers, Irénée and Lammot, and the same amount to John J. Raskob. He then called in four members of the Du Pont executive staff—Harry F. Brown (in charge of smokeless powder), Henry G. Haskell (in charge of high explosives), William Coyne (in charge of nonmilitary sales), and F. G. Tallman (in charge of sales)—and handed them 1,250 shares each.

Still P.S. did not call Alfred I. or Cousin Willie, nor did he consider making any allotments to them. Instead, he sent an order to the Du Pont–controlled newspaper telling it what story to run on Sunday, February 23. And the two other senior stockholders learned what had been done behind their backs from the front-page headline in the *Sunday Star:*

COLEMAN DU PONT SELLS OUT HIS ENTIRE POWDER HOLDINGS

His Stock Bought by Pierre S. du Pont and Others Active in Company

The first of the major stockholders to react was Willie du Pont, who telegraphed his cousin P.S.:

PAPERS STATE YOU HAVE PURCHASED COLEMAN'S STOCK. I PRESUME FOR THE COMPANY. ANY OTHER ACTION I SHOULD CONSIDER A BREACH OF FAITH.

On Monday Alfred I. went to the Du Pont Building in Wilmington and waited, in his office down the hall, for his cousin to come and see him. But P.S. did not appear. Finally Alfred I. picked up the telephone and asked his cousin to walk the necessary fifty paces. As P.S. came through the door Alfred I., flushed and grim-faced, said:

"Pierre, don't do this thing! . . . It is wrong! . . . The stock which you have acquired does not belong to you but to the company which you represent. I therefore ask you to turn this stock over to the company."

P.S. denied that he had "used the company's credit in any way" in finding the money to buy out Coleman, and said that therefore he could not do as his cousin wished.

"Pierre," said Alfred I., "your father and my father were brothers. Neither of those men would have approved, I am confident, of what you have done. For their sake, as well as for your own, put that stock in the company's treasury. You can't afford to . . . injure your business reputation. Pierre, I ask you."

P.S. said that what had been done could not be undone.

"Then you refuse to make this concession I ask?"

"I do," P.S. said, and walked out of the room.

Each side now began to look around for supporters in the war of du Pont versus du Pont that was destined to rip the family apart.

The Belins were a Pennsylvania family, and in normal circumstances their daughter Alice and P. S. du Pont would have been married from her home in Scranton. But then somebody pointed out that a law had been passed in the state forbidding the marriage of first cousins. P.S. had not yet discovered the tax advantages of a home address in Delaware, and he was a registered Pennsylvanian too. Coleman's wife, Elsie, wrote to suggest he give her address as his home and celebrate the marriage at Christ's Church, on the Brandywine, but since the family was now split over the share-purchase business, that might have created painful gaps in the guest list. Instead, it was decided to have a quiet wedding in New York, where no one worried about the consanguinity of the bride and groom. Alice's brother, Ferdinand Lammot Belin, who was head of the Aetna Explosives Company of Scranton, Pennsylvania, had an apartment at Four Hundred Park Avenue, in New York City, and it was there that they were married on October 6, 1915. Considering the monosyllabic nature of her usual entries, Alice positively gushed over the event in her diary that night:

> October 6th 1915. Cloudy then cleared. Best day of life. Shopped went to apartment. Saw Bertha and Mary. Jolly lunch. Back to apartment. Rehearsal. Dressed. Wedding at 5.30. 8 to New York [railroad station?]. Coat of furs. Ritz in Phila.

The honeymoon was spent motoring from Philadelphia to Washington, where they spent two days ("sightseeing"), then through the Shenandoah Valley to Augusta, Georgia, and on to Sulphur Springs and Warm Springs. The wartime boom showed no sign of slackening, and P.S. could not be away from Du Pont for long, so they drove back to Longwood via Gettysburg by October 20.

How did the honeymoon go, this fulfillment of a twenty-three-year-old dream? In her diaries Alice does not say, nor do her letters written during this period give a hint of what life with the man she loved felt like and what propinquity had done to the nature of their relationship. But there are clues here and there to indicate that perhaps it was not quite so idyllic as she had so long dreamed it would be.

Scattered through the short entries in Alice's diaries at regular intervals is a symbol, which she inserts and sometimes rings: "O.L." Consultations with those familiar with her diaries have produced no definite explanation of its meaning; these readers have pointed out, however, that, with an occasional exception, the "O.L." comes at monthly intervals and could be the reminder of a regular natural physiological occurrence. (One female expert on the du Pont papers speculated that it might stand for *"Oh Lordy! that old thing again!"*)

Whatever its meaning, the symbol "O.L." is marked down in Alice's diary right at the beginning of her honeymoon with P.S., and if the experts are right, her relations with her new husband cannot have been launched smoothly. Nor do the entries in the days succeeding their return give any indication of marital bliss:

October 22 1915. Fine. Very busy morning unpacking selves. Father came at 1.30. Lunch. Talk. Went in for P.S.

Talk with her father about what? Had P.S. gone to the office so as to leave them alone?

Oct. 23 Saturday. Fine. P.S. stayed out. Father went home & Motsy [Lammot] came worked all day & got pantry settled. Weary evening.

Married only fifteen days, and already talking of a "weary evening"? And then, on December 3:

Very weary and gave P.S. a treat of tears.

Is this an indication that married life is not all that Alice hoped it would be? One asks the questions, but neither the diaries nor letters give the answers.

It is only gradually in their relationship that the truth begins to emerge, as Alice slowly realizes that although she might love her gentle and thoughtful husband more and more each day, marriage to P. S. du Pont is not by any means as fulfilling as she thought it was going to be. For the moment she blames nobody but herself and copies out a prayer:

> God! what a world the world would be if under Thy hand it were governed as man governs the world which he himself creates. As I have governed mine! Tolerance for none but self, pity for none but self, all written, judged, measured, watched in terms of self. Rid me of that! Help me to see self. Help me to see w. others eyes not with my own.

In any case, what time could P.S. have had to spare for his wife when he was deep in the process of gaining control of the biggest explosives company in the world?

Du Pont was now doing so well out of the war that the value of its shares was going through the roof, and so were the profits. The returns for 1914 showed a modest profit of $5,796,000 "due to more of the military business getting into the earnings than . . . estimates had shown." But P.S. was well aware that this was only the beginning.

"The decrees of Fate in this regard could not have been better planned for our interests," he wrote early in 1915,

> that is it was highly desirable to show some increased earnings but very undesirable to bring into the year 1914 any extraordinary amount due to military business. We all think it highly inadvisable to publish extraordinary earnings until the annual report of 1915, say, about March of 1916. Meantime we propose to abandon quarterly statements.

In fact, Du Pont sales to the Allies were now so high that the February 1915 orders alone amounted to $58,932,000, more than the whole of the company's gross receipts for 1913. Profits for the year rocketed up to nearly $60,000,000, ten times those of 1914. This worried neutralists and pro-Germans in Washington who were against gearing up the American industrial machine to help the Allies win the war, and there was a strong movement to curb trading activities that favored one side in the conflict against the other. Some congressmen turned their attention specifically against Du Pont and proposed a law to ban the company from trading directly with the "belligerents," in this case, Britain, France, and Russia.

P.S. was not worried, for Du Pont had already taken precautions against any such prohibitions and had insisted on signing contracts only within the territorial United States, leaving it up to the buyers as to how they would ship the gunpowder over to Europe. As he wrote in 1915:

> We have given a great deal of consideration to the proposed law prohibiting shipments of powder, which law seems unlikely of passage; as its terms would seem to seriously infringe upon International Law. Moreover, from our point of view we are not concerned; as all of our contracts are for deliveries in the United States and have no relation to the question of shipment of material. In the last contract entered into by us with Nobel (for accounts of Vickers, London) 4,300,000, they took the precaution to make the contract for delivery to their [neutral] Spanish house, which deals with belligerent nations only. I suppose that a similar change could be made in other contracts if it was found necessary.

He added that the company had also begun taking precautions about sabotage, since German agents had already been active in the New Jersey dock areas, destroying shipments on their way to the Allies. The navy had assigned some patrol ships to the Chesapeake and the Delaware River, and militiamen were now stationed around the various plants.

On November 30, 1915, the saboteurs penetrated the yards and four mills blew. Eight men died. Thereafter, the guards around the mills were tripled, and every visitor was searched and had to sign in before entry; and employees signed a document pledging themselves not to talk about company business or the nature of the work they were doing.

By this time Du Pont had taken, through Morgan and Company, $100 million in bonds from the British and French governments in payment for powder and other arms that the company had supplied to the Allies. As Ruly Carpenter remarked:

"Our company has been very careful not to choose sides in the war going on in Europe. On the other hand, I don't think we can afford to let the British lose the war."

P.S. was not worried about that. He was concerned about who was going to win the lawsuit that Alfred I. had instituted against him and other members of the syndicate.

CHAPTER 18

Feud

THE wartime boom in Du Pont stocks was such that within seven weeks of buying Coleman's shares at $200, P.S. and his syndicate found that they were worth $300 on the open market. Preferred stock too had gone up from $85 to $90. The rise was so swift and spectacular that on April 17, 1915, P.S. was able to announce that Du Pont Securities Company (which he and the syndicate had formed to exploit Coleman's shares) had made enough money to pay off the more than $13 million it owed to Coleman and J. P. Morgan and Company, and still have plenty of money left in the kitty. In fact, shares in Du Pont Securities were now worth $198.20 each, with no debts outstanding.

P.S. looked around for a method of winning friends and influence in the du Pont family through this happy state of affairs. Alfred I. was running around like a wounded bull, looking for a cousin to gore, but so far P.S. had deftly eluded him. At each meeting of the executive committee since their confrontation after the share sale, P.S. and his syndicate members had out-maneuvered him. Repeatedly, Alfred I. and his supporters had been out-voted in their attempts to change the Coleman transaction from a syndicate operation to a Du Pont company deal. Finally, thwarted and out of temper, unable to follow what his quiet-spoken cousin was saying, Alfred I. had stalked out. P.S. had been formally voted in as president of Du Pont in Coleman's place and had got down to the day-to-day task of running the business. But he knew that Alfred I. had gone away only to lick his wounds and plan his counterattack. He would be back, and more dangerous once he recovered his balance.

What the new president of Du Pont now needed, he decided, was allies in the family to back him up once the real battle began. The success of Du Pont Securities gave him a chance to buy their support. Money, he reasoned, was thicker than blood. He sent for a list of the principal family shareholders in the Du Pont company and then wrote to each one of them:

> Now that this whole transaction is definitely closed, I offer
> you an opportunity to become a shareholder in the Du Pont Secur-
> ties Company.

If they would surrender their ordinary Du Pont shares, he went on, he would give them in exchange Du Pont Securities shares worth fifty per-cent more. For instance, each of the sons of the late (and so far as P.S. was concerned, unlamented) Francis Gurney du Pont had inherited 222.75 shares of Du Pont common stock worth $66,825. If they would hand them over, he would issue in exchange 500 Du Pont Securities shares worth $99,100. He made similar offers to the sons of the former Old Guard mem-bers Eugene du Pont and Dr. Alexis du Pont. And with his brothers, Irénée and Lammot, already in his camp, he thought it advisable to bring in his brothers-in-law, Charles Copeland, William Winder Laird, and Rodney Sharp, by making them the same offer.

It was a clever ploy and partially successful. Two of Frank Gurney du Pont's sons accepted the offer, and two turned it down. Eugene du Pont's son Alexis was already in the syndicate, and Eugene junior said he too would come in. Of Dr. Alexis du Pont's sons, two accepted the offer, and the third, Philip, curtly refused it. It soon became apparent that so far as this wrangle was concerned, the camps could be divided into the Saints and the Sinners.

P.S. undoubtedly had the powerful and respectable members of the family on his side. (He also had eleven members of the Du Pont board of fifteen.) Alfred I., on the other hand, found that his sympathizers and supporters included Cousin Willie, who had shocked the family by becoming the first du Pont to get a divorce; Cousin May du Pont Saulsbury, who was also divorced; Francis I. du Pont, a brilliant but temperamental chemist; Coleman's sister, Zara du Pont, a hell-bent socialist and a family rebel; and Philip du Pont, a playboy and the family poet. Philip's reputation in the du Pont family was that of being weak-willed and apt to say yes to any proposition that was made to him, so P.S. might have won him over had Philip not been ill with typhoid when the offer came. By the time he recovered, however, it was Alfred I. who got to him first.

That was the reason why, on December 30, 1915, it was in Philip du Pont's name that a suit was brought against P. S. du Pont and his associates in Du Pont Securities, charging them with defrauding the company, and P.S. with acting for himself in purchasing Coleman's stock "in violation of his trust as an officer, director and confidential representative of the E. I. du Pont de Nemours Powder Company."

The suit did not simply set cousin against cousin. It split apart brothers and sisters, and came between mothers and sons. The mother of Philip du Pont was Elizabeth Bradford du Pont, archenemy of Alfred I. and Alicia, and naturally she was wholeheartedly on P.S.'s side. She too had had an offer to exchange her Du Pont shares for stock in Du Pont Securities and had unhesitatingly done so. She was shocked when Philip revealed that he had thrown in his lot with Alfred I.

"I am much distressed," she wrote P.S.

that Philip, who has always expressed the greatest admiration for you—and still does—should have brought this suit. He never told me, and I knew nothing of it until the day the papers came out with it. Had I known of it, I could have tried to persuade him not to bring it. I realize how you have borne the burden of this business for 7 years while Coleman was ill and other big stock holders absence [sic] and what we all owe to you and can only say again how sorry I am that my son should have any thing to do with such a suit.

The Colonel thundered down from his Senate office in Washington to announce that Philip was a fool and Alfred I. his evil genius, and told P.S. that the columns of his newspaper, the Wilmington *Evening Journal,* were open to him to reply to the scurrilous articles that were now appearing in Alfred I.'s Wilmington *News.* His old ally, Aunt Amy, hastened to add her support:

My dear Pierre,

I am so worried about the suit Philip has brought against the company and indignant at the injustice to you in the articles in the papers. I know all you did about Coleman's stock was to prevent Alfred getting into power, and the best for everyone interested in the Company.

I shall always put great confidence in your management of our interests.

Although the suit was filed in Philip du Pont's name ("on behalf of the interests of the small shareholders"), P.S. did not need to be told that Alfred I. was masterminding and bankrolling it, and he now made a move that, he hoped, would finally frighten off his cousin by confronting him with P.S.'s power and influence in the company.

Du Pont's annual meeting was due to be held in March, and P.S. went out to scramble for proxies, intending to use them, combined with his own shares and those of his supporters, to vote Alfred I. off the company board. On his side, Alfred I. pleaded with stockholders to hold back their shares until the courts had decided the case. But the tide ran strongly in his cousin's favor, and when the vote came, P.S. had 411,053 shares out of a total of 593,224, while the Sinners could only muster 3,621 out of the 181,191 they controlled.

"With the smoothness of a well-oiled machine," as the Philadelphia *Public Ledger* put it, the annual meeting voted to dismiss Alfred I. du Pont from the board of directors of the company. He then came out into the open, since he no longer had anything to lose, and joined his own name and those of other Sinners to that of Philip du Pont as plaintiffs in the forthcoming suit. All over the nation stories about the du Pont family began to appear in the press, some of them maliciously anti-Alfred I., many of them devoted to Coleman's peccadilloes, and most of them virulently anti-big business. The family cowered in the face of all the publicity, though quite a large amount of it was, in fact, initiated by employees of one side or the other seeking to discredit their opponents.

P.S. made one last attempt to persuade his cousin to call off the suit, pleading with him to agree to a talk "cousin to cousin," but if he was hoping for a reconciliation, he could have had no conception of the sense of outrage Alfred I. was feeling over what he considered to be his cousin's underhandedness. Alfred sent back a curt refusal by way of a servant.

From then on, their only communication was in the form of frigid complaints, delivered usually through a third party. Alfred I.'s wife, Alicia, now owned Louviers, the house on the Brandywine estate that he had taken away from P.S.'s brother Belin in order to install her there when she was still his mistress. But the neighboring house and the lawns surrounding it still belonged to the Du Pont company, and word reached P.S. that Alfred I. was having soil removed and carted up to Louviers, to which P.S. responded with a frigid letter saying,

> I have ordered the work stopped and request that you see that none of your people trespass on the company's property in any way to do damage in the future.

But in snooping on Alfred I., Du Pont employees had been doing some of their own trespassing on *his* property, and this maddened him. On July 11, 1916, he had a secretary, Ruth Brereton, write:

> I wish to inform you that the act of trespass on Mrs. Alfred I. du Pont's property "Louviers" was not the first of its kind, as after each of the many explosions which have occurred in Hagley Yard under your management persons representing themselves as being sent by your Department have visited this property, for the stated purpose of inspecting the damage done.
>
> Mr du Pont is informed by the caretaker that after one of those explosions some time ago, you personally made a thorough inspection of the house. Mr du Pont is naturally astonished that you should interest yourself in private property in which the Du Pont Company cannot possibly have any concern.
>
> The property is amply posted with signs and there is no excuse for acts of this nature, and in future such interferences will be dealt with under trespass laws of Delaware.

Since the du Ponts by this time pretty well controlled the state—they owned the newspapers, they collected the tolls along the turnpikes, they operated what schools existed, they manipulated state and local government, they had a member of the family in the Senate and made sure Delaware's Congressmen voted in accordance with family wishes—no one really doubted that they were also in a position to control the courts. The suit taken out by Alfred I., Philip du Pont, and other Sinners had been filed in Delaware, and so it caused absolutely no surprise at all when it was announced that Judge Bradford, Alfred I.'s father-in-law, would be in charge of the case. When none of Alfred I.'s lawyers protested, apparently unaware that the judge positively loathed his son-in-law, P.S. must have been tempted to let things run their course. In matters concerning Alfred I. and Alicia, Judge Bradford could be relied upon to let his prejudices overcome any tendency to judicial impartiality. However, P.S.'s own sense of fair play asserted itself (his enemies said it was his knowledge that any obvious judicial bias would be appealed), and he prevailed upon the judge to step down in favor of a colleague from Philadelphia.

P.S. had a deep conviction that every move he made in the matter of the shares had been fair, honest, aboveboard. He believed he had acted in the best interests of the family and of the company, and he expected the courts to confirm that his motives had been impeccable and his probity beyond reproach. He was shattered when the court decided otherwise.

Judge J. Whitaker Thompson delivered his judgment on April 12, 1917, and used some hard words to describe P.S.'s actions in the share deal, which were, the judge said, "colored by trickery and concealment." He concluded:

> It is asserted by counsel for the defendants that when Coleman withdrew his offer, the duty on Pierre's part of acting for the Company was at an end and he was free to act for his individual interests. It must be assumed that Coleman's conclusion to withdraw the offer, qualified as it was . . . was effected by Pierre's breach of fidelity he owed to the company in misinforming and misleading Coleman as to the real action of the Finance Committee. . . . The evidence irresistibly forces the conclusion that there was a deliberate intention on Pierre's part to conceal from Alfred . . . correspondence which would have . . . disproved Pierre's statement that the offer had been "turned down" on December 23rd.

Judge Thompson therefore decided he could not uphold the action P.S. had taken, since to do so "would be contrary to conscience and good morals," and he declared it invalid.

P.S. was stunned. It was the first time in his career that his honesty of purpose and the purity of his motives had been found wanting, and it was to nag him for the rest of his life. He went to his death still feeling that the court had done him an injustice. For the moment, he took absolutely no comfort at all from his lawyers when, all smiles, they told him that the verdict wasn't so bad, after all.

They were quite right, even if P.S. did not see it that way. For if Alfred I. and his supporters had won the court battle, it soon became obvious that they were going to lose the war for control of Du Pont.

The judge reasoned in his verdict that there had been no proper expression by the company's shareholders as to whether Coleman's stock should be acquired. He described the board of directors as unfit to pass on the matter, as they were personally biased. He therefore ordered that it must be for the shareholders to decide the question, and that the old Coleman shares should be held back from the voting. He ordered that a referendum take place, with a court-appointed official to supervise it.

The result was a foregone conclusion. As Alfred I. wrote to his attorney:

> By ordering this matter to be referred to the stockholders . . . Judge Thompson has badly muddled what otherwise would have been a perfect opinion. . . . The Court, itself, has determined that the interests of the Company have been violated. This is not a point left for the stockholders to vote upon. We have the unheard of situation where a matter is presented to stockholders to vote on wherein one portion of the stockholders will vote for it, because it is to their personal interests and the interests of the Corporation to do so, and the other portion will vote against it because it would be inimical to their interests.

He mobilized his newspapers and his publicity men to flood the public and the family with arguments supporting his point of view, but he had no chance against the Du Pont company machine, which brought to bear all its big guns. Stockholders were made aware that the shares P.S. had bought only a little more than a year previously for $13 million were now worth $43 million. A former associate of the United States Supreme Court, Charles Evans Hughes, was brought in (at a fee of $50,000) to examine the court's verdict. He pronounced it faulty in blaming P.S.

When the voting results were announced, the defeat Alfred I. had anticipated was even greater than he feared. Not unnaturally, every officer and director of the company voted in P.S.'s favor. So did 60 out of 65 members of the du Pont family (not counting Alfred I. and his supporters). The final result was 312,587 in favor of P.S. and his associates keeping Coleman's shares, and 140,842 against.

But still neither was satisfied. Alfred I. wanted the voting figure thrown out. P.S. wanted his reputation as an honest broker restored. He was not entirely displeased when he learned his cousin had decided to enter an appeal, hoping to get the original condemnation of P.S. upheld but the voting clause abrogated. P.S. saw it as a new opportunity to reverse the verdict entirely, and he told his lawyers to spare no effort and no expense to upset the findings of Judge Thompson's court.

To Alfred I.'s chagrin, that was just what happened. In the court of appeal Judge Joseph Buffington overturned the lower court's verdict completely and described P.S. as "most earnest in his efforts and sincere in his purpose" and one who had "done his whole duty as an officer of the Company." He made it so clear that he did not think Alfred I. had a case at all that an application by him to take it to the Supreme Court was denied.

From P.S.'s point of view it was complete vindication of his motives, and well worth all the trouble and expense. To those who expressed amazement that Judge Buffington's opinions could be so much at variance with those of Judge Thompson, he pointed out that the higher court had more time to ponder on "purity of intentions." Alfred I. had darker ideas about why it had happened.

P.S. was just beginning to get the bills from his lawyers for the cases involving his quarrels with Alfred I., and they amounted to $1,130,000. That seemed to be a large sum to pay even for the restoration of his honor, but it had been worth it. On the other hand, one suspects that his conscience was not entirely clear. As he wrote to his cousin:

> I still wonder, Coleman, why you did it and why I did it also.

Coleman, who was still very ill, sent back a rambling letter that could not have given P.S. much comfort:

> Remember, you were on the ground and knew all. I was still far from well and knew nothing except that you were in the saddle and running things against some opposition.

Well, at least the opposition had now gone away.

Everybody was doing well out of the war in Europe, but none so well as the du Ponts and the Du Pont company. In 1915 Alfred I. made $3,050,089 in payments and dividends, although no longer particularly active in the company. During the first half of 1916, after he had been voted off the board, he received $3,848,617.90, which he took part in cash ($963,219.10) and part ($2,885,398.80) in Anglo-French bonds.

By 1917 P.S. was making even more. When the United States declared war on Germany, he was $55 million richer than he had been in 1913, and Du Pont's profits were topping $100 million a year.

P.S. did not conceal from the rest of the family that he was utterly and completely on the side of the Allies, but he did his best to keep the company distanced from those who were publicly working to push the United States into the war. Disingenuously, he wrote to Mrs. Lindon Bates, chairman of the women's section of the Movement for National Preparedness:

> Our company has found it necessary to take the position of neutrality in the effort for preparedness. We are large manufacturers of powder for military purposes, and, therefore think it unwise to take part in a movement which should be settled without bias by the country at large.

He took issue with the leaders of the Senate antiwar movement, Robert M. La Follette and William J. Stone, who charged Du Pont was behind the "preparedness" propaganda that was flooding the country. As he pointed out:

> At the beginning of the agitation I, as President of the Du Pont Company, issued a circular requesting that officers and employees of the company refrain from contributions to and active interest in such organizations.

But in fact, he knew most of the huge payments for powder that were coming to the company from the Allies via J. P. Morgan and Company were largely in French and British bonds, which would be useless if those two countries lost the war, and would jump in value if the United States joined in and brought the conflict to a close all the more quickly.

What was clear to him was that if and when America did come in, even the major expansion of Du Pont's capacity that he had effected would be incapable of keeping up with demand. But when he offered to sell factories and powder to the United States government at nominal prices (so long as he got the orders immediately, without waiting for a declaration of war), he was rebuffed. Instead, Congress passed a measure imposing a profits tax of 12.5 percent on sales of "gunpowder and other explosives" and made it retroactive to the beginning of 1916. Then, because Chilean nitrogen for smokeless powder was threatened by German submarine warfare and shipping shortages, he offered to utilize a Du Pont patent for extracting nitrogen from the air—so long as the company was allowed to develop a water site at Muscle Shoals, on the Tennessee River. Congress called it a "grab" and passed a law, instead, allowing the government to use and exploit nitrogen-from-air patents on its own.*

By the time of the 1916 presidential election, P.S. had become so aggrieved with the powers-that-be he was rumored to have issued an order forbidding employees to wear "Wilson for President" buttons. He denied this but commented in a public statement:

> There is a growing realization that many acts of the present administration have been inimical to the interests of the company and therefore inimical to the individuals who, as employees or stockholders, depend on it for their daily bread. Men of both national parties, who have studied these acts in an impartial, nonpartisan light have reached the conclusion that they and their families will benefit by a change at Washington. They have expressed their views openly both within the plants and without; and neither they nor those who think otherwise have been interfered with in the slightest degree.

Here again he was being disingenuous. He was quite well aware that there was a movement in Delaware Republican circles to put up his cousin Coleman as a possible presidential contender in the coming election—and, in fact, had contributed heavily to it. Cousin Coleman had bounced back again, not only out of his hospital bed but out of the bed of his latest *amour,* the dark-eyed movie star Pauline Frederick, who had been told to get back to the film studios while her lover did some politicking.

Coleman was by now very popular indeed in Delaware, with both voters and politicians. He had forged ahead with his road project despite all kinds of opposition, and the most modern highway in the United States was now pushing its way from Wilmington through lower Delaware to Dover. As soon as it was nine-tenths complete, Coleman announced he would hand it over to the state free of charge, a ninety-seven-mile gift of smoothly navigable pavement worth four million dollars.** He had also taken an interest in education and went around the state kissing babies and

---

* Du Pont had stolen them from Germany, anyway.
** In fact, this did not happen until 1924.

congratulating their parents; and he constantly talked about the need to keep the United States out of the war. No longer connected with Du Pont, he could honestly claim he had no pecuniary interest in involving his country.

The idea was to bring Colonel Henry Algernon du Pont from Washington, where he was just about to retire from the Senate, and have the Republicans elect him as a delegate to the convention in Chicago, where he would drum up support for Cousin Coleman.

But it did not quite work out that way. If Alfred I. was on bad terms with his cousin P.S., he had even more reason to dislike, even hate, his Cousin Coleman. Coleman had messed up both his private and professional life. He had done everything he could to make life difficult for Alfred I. and Alicia, and had turned the family against them. And then he had cheated him over the sale of the shares.

There was nothing Alfred I. could do about Coleman in business, since he had simply pocketed his thirteen million dollars and got out of Du Pont. But he could torpedo his political ambitions. By this time Alfred I. had drawn his money out of the family bank, the Wilmington Trust Company (of which P.S. was the principal shareholder), and between them, he and Willie du Pont bought a bank of their own, the Delaware Trust Company. Alfred I. was touched to hear that hundreds of the Brandywine powder men transferred their savings to the new bank as soon as they heard the news.

Through the Delaware Trust he now began buying up downstate Delaware newspapers, six in all: the Harrington *Journal,* the Dover *Sentinel,* the Seaford *News,* the Laurel *Leader,* the Middleton *Chronicle,* and the Newark *Ledger.* He already had the controlling interest in the Wilmington *Morning News.* Through these papers he began to attack both Senator Henry Algernon du Pont and Coleman, ridiculing the praise lavished on the two men in the Colonel's own paper, the *Evening Journal.*

Alfred I. had two tame men in the Dover legislature. One was Senator J. Frank Allee and the other, Representative Edward Bradford, Jr., Alicia's brother. Allee was influential among the Republican delegates, and Alfred I. paid heavily for his support, handing over to his son the proprietorship of the Dover *Sentinel* and backing Allee's own investments in oil to the tune of eleven thousand dollars. Eddie Bradford acted as his paymaster among the Republican representatives and ward heelers, cashing Alfred I.'s checks and paying them in untraceable cash.

They worked smoothly and quietly, so that when the party members

[263]

came to meet in Dover to elect their delegate to the Republican convention, the Colonel was so sure of his victory he decided he did not even have to bother coming down from Washington. But Alfred I. was there. Because he knew what was going to happen.

After an uproarious session the members of the party committee voted not for the Colonel, who got only fifteen votes, but for Alfred I., who got twenty votes.

"BANG! T. C. DU PONT'S PRESIDENTIAL BOOM BLOWS UP," said Alfred I.'s Wilmington paper the following morning.

Alfred I., who had written the headline himself, surveyed it with satisfaction. It was only the first step.

Next he attacked not just Coleman but all the du Ponts in the state. He issued a statement calling for legislation to rewrite Delaware's state tax laws, which were archaic in that they heavily taxed farmland, real estate, and livestock but completely exempted dividends and other "wealth of an interest-bearing character."

"Delaware is actually living under the most obsolete laws of any state," he declared.

> The most marked of these iniquitous statutes are those relative
> to revenue and taxation. In the main they are a century and a half
> old—fair and equitable enough in the day of their creation, but in
> view of the changed forms of wealth that exist in the present day,
> wholly inadequate.

He asked the legislature to pass two measures, one providing for a graduated inheritance tax for state purposes, and the other equalizing tax so that all real and personal property would be taxed alike, without regard to the form in which it existed.

It was a move likely to cost the du Ponts millions, and they piled into Coleman, telling him to get out there and fight the threat to their fortunes.

It was quite a campaign, and much money changed hands in the corridors of the legislature at Dover, with lobbyists scurrying this way and that as they tried to satisfy the demands of Coleman's whips on the one hand and the paid hacks of Alfred I. and Eddie Bradford on the other. The result was a tie. Alfred I. got an inheritance tax through but failed to get the legislature to accept a satisfactory tax on interest-bearing investments.

He had, nevertheless, given the du Ponts the fright of their lives and made Coleman afraid for his political future. Coleman knew by now that

Alfred I. was not finished with him and was out to make him regret that he had ever humiliated Alicia and cheated him out of those shares.

Early in 1917 P.S. decided to take Alice away on a belated honeymoon that would relieve some of the tension that seemed to be growing between them. It had been a trying summer and fall, and Alice's diary signposts its difficulties.

She wrote on June 6, 1916:

> Uncertain weather. Fussed over patience all day. Lost temper a little. Very hectic supper but show went o.k. All went at 11.

> [Next day] Terrible weather. Very sulky household. Wrote & felt rotten. Cried all day. Went in & met P.S. Nap.

> July 2, 1916. Sunday. P.S. worked all day—I helped him. Callers in p.m. & scene.

> July 3, Monday. Home all day. Very apologetic to P.S.

> July 4. O.L.

It might be unfair to draw conclusions about Alice's feelings from these curt entries were it not for the fact that her later letters, which flow much more freely, confirm the significance of the indications in her diaries. There cannot be much doubt that by the beginning of 1917 the autumnal marriage of P.S. and his cousin was beginning to show signs of blight. Perhaps a change of scene would help.

The "honeymooners" did not go alone but took a small party along with them: P.S.'s sister Lou and her husband, Charles Copeland, Alice's sister, Mary, and her husband Nathaniel Robertson, and two married friends. They climbed aboard a private coach, Commonwealth, which was attached to a transcontinental train, and set off for a twenty-eight-day trip to San Francisco, Del Monte, Santa Barbara, Pasadena, and then on to the Grand Canyon in Arizona. But there were too many things going on in Washington and Wilmington to allow the tourists a peaceful and harmonious time together. The other couples decided to go back when they got word of America's imminent involvement in war, but Alice and P.S. persisted. Still, by February 3, 1917, when President Wilson announced he had broken relations with the imperial German government, both husband

and wife must have realized it was useless. Alice was only too well aware that P.S.'s mind and emotions were further away from her than ever.

"When Pierre and Alice left the train at Santa Cruz for a side trip to view the big trees," P.S.'s official biographers report,

> he could think of little else except the responsibilities that he felt war would thrust upon his company. Early the following day, Pierre telegraphed Irénée from the Hotel Del Monte that he would come to Wilmington immediately if his services were needed. Irénée's return telegram encouraged Pierre to continue his trip.

But it was no use. They arrived back in Philadelphia on February 20, 1917, and P.S.'s chauffeur, Charlie Mason, was there to drive them back to Longwood. During the journey Charlie announced that if and when the United States entered the war, he would volunteer. He added that his boss need not worry about a replacement as Charlie's brother, young Lewes, had been taking lessons and was now an expert driver. With P.S.'s permission, Lewes would take over.

Both Alice and P.S. agreed that that would be fine. Charlie Mason was assured that his wages would be paid "for the duration" and his job kept open for him.

CHAPTER 19

Double-dyed Villains?

D u Pont reports take pains to show that the company made compara-
tively little out of supplying explosives to the United States government during World War I. The company's extraordinary gains came almost wholly
from the British, French, and (at the beginning) Russians. Du Pont shipped
so much gunpowder to the Allies in the period 1914–18—and made so
much money out of it—that large profits from the United States would only
have added to the embarrassment the family was later made to feel.

By 1917 the business genius of P. S. du Pont had changed the nature
of the company from that of a prosperous but tightly knit family business,
concentrated mainly on the Brandywine, into a vast corporation which,
though still family-owned, now had its centers of production spread throughout the nation. The company itself, as an industry, was also in a process of
transformation, changing slowly, imperceptibly to the eyes of the outside
world, from a company of explosives manufacturers into something much
more diverse: a chemistry combine.

Long before the war, P.S. and his brothers had become interested in the by-products that they knew could be spun off the manufacture of explosives. One of the main attractions P.S. had found in the proposition put to him back in 1906, when Du Pont had been asked to tie up with the French branch of Nobel, was that its wily Austrian president, Dr. Siegfried Singer, held patents for certain chemical formulae which included a form of cellophane and artificial silk. Singer had even gone so far as to prophesy he would soon make his company independent of dynamite products. It was only Singer's aggressive forays into Du Pont's Mexican market that made P.S. reject Nobel's offer.

P.S.'s younger brother Lammot, the brightest chemist in the family, was now beginning to visualize Du Pont as a mainly chemical rather than a mainly explosives corporation, and he had persuaded his fellow directors to make him head of a new Miscellaneous Manufacturing Department. Through this operation he had pioneered developments in Fabrikoid material (based on a British patent), paints, celluloids, and preservatives. His most promising expansion had been in the field of dyestuffs.

The war with Germany might have been expected to put German patents for dyestuffs—in which that nation was the acknowledged expert—on the open market in America, since those patents now belonged to the enemy. But the Germans had always been extremely cagey with their dye-stuff formulae, using German chemists to oversee their manufacture even in America, and when war began, Du Pont found it could not make the dyes on its own. Instead, they made do with processes purchased from England. Both Lammot and P.S. realized that once the war was over, the dyestuff market would revert to the Germans, but Du Pont's labs were working hard to duplicate or improve German methods, and meanwhile the company was selling all the inferior product it could produce.

From a strictly business point of view, it did not matter whether Du Pont sold explosives to the United States government or not, even after America had entered the war. Du Pont could still sell every pound of explosives it made to the British and French at a large profit. The company also had more than capacity orders for all its chemical products. P.S. made a plausible case, later on, when he argued that only patriotism finally persuaded him to cooperate with the United States government and make powder for them too.

It was not until America's participation in the war was six months old—in October 1917—that the government made up its mind what kind of role it was going to play. Reluctantly, the men in Washington came to the conclusion that a mass American army would have to be shipped to Europe; and once they cleared that hurdle, it became obvious that the army would need powder to put in its guns. Unprepared for war as usual, officials then began a mad scramble to organize supplies. The Ordnance Department eventually produced a contract with Du Pont whereby the company would build a new explosives plant for the manufacture of powder for the army. The plant would be built at cost. The powder-making process would be operated on a basis of 9.5-percent commission for Du Pont. At the end of eighteen months the plant would revert to the government.

It was not a particularly profitable contract, but when Secretary of War Newton D. Baker looked it over, he hit the roof, declaring neither he nor Congress would stand for it. His objections were leaked to the newspapers, and by the time they reached the press they were somehow twisted to indicate that for an initial outlay of $90 million (which would be reimbursed by the government) Du Pont was about to make a profit amounting to something between $20 million and $30 million. This exaggeration of the facts hardly did Du Pont any good with anti-big-business interests, most of whom took to calling the company merchants of death.

It was not until 1918, when the war was nearly over, that Du Pont was allowed to build the Old Hickory Powder Works in Tennessee. The cost of the plant was $83,820,000, and from it Du Pont produced powder for the armed forces worth $24,320,000 before the armistice finally arrived. Their total gross profit on the operation, for building the plant and making the powder, came to $2,670,000, which is rather less than they were making *a day* on their trade with the Allies. Nevertheless, in later years, when Alger Hiss appeared as counsel for a government committee investigating Du Pont's wartime activities, he accused the company of having made a profit of 39,321 percent out of their dealings with the United States government between 1917 and 1918. He based this figure on the fact that after being reimbursed for building costs, Du Pont had expended only $5,000 on creating the company that ran the Old Hickory plant, and had come up with over $2 million in profit. P.S. replied that the Du Pont brains and expertise that had gone into the operation were worth much more than that.

His experiences with the government during the war, and particularly with the mud-slinging congressmen who now began attacking the company, embittered him. From this time on he began questioning the way the government of the United States was run and the processes by which it was elected. The du Ponts had always tried to be a law unto themselves and cherished a strong suspicion of outside authorities that tried to regulate their lives. P.S. himself was in many ways a kind and forward-looking man, but he had always been one who "knew better" than his so-called representatives in Washington. Now, increasingly, he began to resent the ways in which the elected governors of the country interfered with the way he and other businessmen ran their organizations. What did it matter how much profit Du Pont made so long as he paid his taxes, adequately remunerated his employees, paid them in sickness and health, pensioned them off with liberal stipends? What right had the government to question his own rewards and those of his family so long as they had been earned by their sweat or their brains?

One of his more remarkable relatives was Cousin Zara du Pont. Zara had been a convinced socialist since she was a girl in her teens, and had been fighting for justice and equality all her life. As early as 1891 she was writing to P.S. to plead with him for a contribution toward a scheme she was organizing to get hospital and nursing training for black girls:

> My heart goes out to the negroes, they struggle under such a handicap, intense poverty, low pay, injustice and an enforced inferiority complex, in spite of which they are such a kindly race.

She was always on the side of the workers and would be found in the picket lines outside the Du Pont plants in the years to come. But during the war she had been out in Ohio, fighting not just for peoples' jobs but also for women's suffrage. Once more she wrote to her cousin for financial help:

> We are having a very short & strenuous campaign in Ohio, little or no work having been done throughout the state to educate men or women to see that with only half of the people represented we have not a true democracy. . . . It has made our expenses very heavy & unfortunately our opponents the anti-suffrage party, as always, is composed of the rich. . . . If you are with us, please help us promptly. . . . Love to all

P.S. was fond of his crusading cousin and never failed to give her a welcome whenever their paths crossed, which was rarely, for he did not frequent the back yards of factories or the mean streets where she was usually to be found supporting a cause. But though he forgave her for what she did within the family—opposing his purchase of Coleman's shares, for instance—he neither understood nor was prepared to swallow her "silly ideas" about equality. Nor did he ever send her any money. His reply to her pleas was usually a lecture, and he sent her one in this case—and it

pretty well summed up his criticisms of the United States system as he feared
it was developing:

Dear Zadie,

I do believe in equal suffrage for men and women as a princi-
ple, but I do not believe in extending the suffrage at present until
we are in a position to limit the suffrage of both men and women.
I believe it is a fact that a majority of our men are unfitted to vote
on the great questions of the day. They are misled by demagogues
and writers who make their money through talking and writing
without much regard for the principles which they promote. A
cure for this is education. . . . There is plenty of work and opportunity for all men and women who are willing to exert themselves and live reasonable lives and there is boundless room at the
top for those who can qualify for success. Our present day politician makes his living by causing the unworthy to believe they
are entitled to everything without effort. They cannot succeed in
their teaching, for reward without effort is impossible.

Candidly, Zadie, I believe that you are entirely on the wrong
track in your present effort.

In 1918 the du Ponts were worrying about the election of a new
senator from Delaware, for they badly needed a friendly representative to
take the place of the Colonel, whose sun had set after his humiliation by
Alfred I. in 1916. Once more Coleman was on the scene, this time seeking
the Republican nomination for senator. Would Alfred I. step in and again
sabotage the chances of his least favorite cousin?

He did more than that. He decided he would choose the state's next
senator himself, and such was the control he now exerted over the Delaware Republicans that many of his cohorts pleaded with him to choose
himself as the nominee. He refused to be drafted. But he made it plain that
Coleman would not get the nomination either. When friends of both men
came together and proposed a reconciliation between the cousins in the
name of party unity, he angrily rejected it. Instead he issued a statement:

Any good Republican properly qualified to represent Delaware in the United States Senate will meet with my approval, but
it must be clearly understood that he must not be dominated by
any political machine or by any group of individuals. . . . The
people of Delaware will in future do the bossing. . . . Nomi-

nees must receive their nominations honorably. . . . This is a matter for the immediate consideration of the State Committee.

He agreed to meet for a "harmony conference" in the state capital, Dover, but insisted that neither Coleman nor any representative of what he called company interests would be acceptable to him. Confronted with this statement, P.S. called a meeting of his directors in the Du Pont Building and, recognizing that Cousin Coleman now had no chance of nomination, charged John J. Raskob to find another candidate suitable to the company who could be slipped in without acknowledging his Du Pont backing.

Raskob, who was beginning to have king-making ambitions in politics as well as big business, organized Service Citizens of Delaware, a committee that called for social reforms in the state "on a scale never attempted before," and promised to come up with a man of the people to carry them through. It was not mentioned, of course, that Du Pont money was behind the committee.

But Alfred I. knew too much about the way Cousin P.S. and Raskob worked to be fooled for long. Within a week his Wilmington *Morning News* was exposing the Du Pont backing behind the Service Citizens of Delaware.

Then he produced his own candidate, a country doctor named Lewis Heisler Hall, and forced his nomination through the party caucus. The incumbent senator, Willard Saulsbury, was the Democratic candidate for reelection and Saulsbury, who had suffered at du Pont hands himself,* had always stood by Alfred I. in family matters. But neither friendship nor past services prevented Alfred I. from ordering an expensive and unscrupulous campaign against him. When the voting was over, Alfred I.'s nominee was home and dry, defeating the incumbent Saulsbury by 1,589 votes.

The result would have made P.S. more bitter than ever over the state of American politics had he given himself time to think about it. But he was preoccupied with something much more important. Lewes Mason was dying.

In a way, Alice Belin du Pont enjoyed the war. It gave her an excuse to get away from Longwood, where she was apt to brood about the state of her

_____
* He had, it will be remembered, been "banished" by the Colonel after marrying Willie's ex-wife, May du Pont.

marriage, and contribute to the war effort. She was, of course, elected to all the committees and made a sponsor of all the bond drives; that she was the wife of the richest and most powerful man in the state of Delaware meant that her name was one to wave in the face of reluctant givers and use as a persuader.

What she liked best was working for the Red Cross in downtown Wilmington chatting with the other women as she rolled bandages or packed parcels for the doughboys "over there," and when she and P.S. drove back to Longwood in the evening, with young Lewes Mason at the wheel, she was often bubbling with anecdotes and gossip to which her husband listened with his usual tolerant good humor. There are traces of this exuberance in her diaries, for she was wont to copy into the back of them verses she had heard or her own limericks, which she had been inventing since she was a schoolgirl. She wrote one about the daughter of one of the matrons who worked with her at the Red Cross:

> There was a young lady named Maisie
>   Who in cheek was a regular Daisy,
> She took her Ma's clothes
>   And her poor sister's beaux
> And was quite inexpressibly lazy.

She recited to P.S. one of the verses current at the time, depicting the way in which "we poor civilians" were suffering as a result of wartime restrictions:

> My Tuesdays are meatless
>   My Wednesdays are wheatless
>   I'm getting more eatless each day!
>
> My home it is heatless
>   My bed it is sheetless
>   They're all at the YMCA!
>
> My clubrooms are treatless
>   My coffee's now sweetless
>   Each day I grow poorer and wiser!
>
> My stockings are feetless
>   My trousers are seatless
>   My gosh, but I do hate the Kaiser!

Like many of the Belins and the du Ponts, Alice, since childhood, had suffered from hereditary deafness. In a way, it was lucky that the affliction had struck so early, for even while she was still at school she learned to lip-read, and the ability to see what people were saying even when she could not hear them had proved invaluable to her during lectures at Bryn Mawr.

It was of course no secret to P.S. that his wife was deaf. However, he does not seem to have realized that she could read lips, and that was the reason, perhaps, why he rarely bothered to halt the flow of his conversations with young Lewes Mason when she came upon them in P.S.'s great study at Longwood, or walking together in the gardens. It seems never to have occurred to Alice (at least not before his death) that there was anything unnatural about her husband's closeness to Lewes Mason, and any spiteful remarks she did make about it came more from snobbishness than from sexual jealousy. In May 1918 she met P.S. at the opera in Philadelphia. He had come up from Wilmington, driven by Lewes, and appears to have asked her if she minded having the young man in their box with them, since he was fond of music.

That night she wrote:

> 1918. May 1. Wednesday . . . P.S. came up and we went to Galli-Curci concert. Surrounded by chauffeurs.

But what she resented about her husband's relationship with his servant was that it was so much more intimately easy and relaxed than her own association with him. It caused as many differences between them as did their lack of physical contact, and the problem seems to have reached a peak in June 1917, shortly after Charlie Mason went off to the war. Her entry for June 5, 1917, reads:

> O.L. Went to Phila and spent day with Mother & Father. Home late and had a long & very terrible talk w. P.S. No sleep.

Thereafter, what some experts on the du Pont papers call "Alice's hints" are increasingly frequent. Entries like "Silent evening," "Long talk with P.S. but got nowhere," or "Asked P.S. why" pepper the pages, evidences of the unhappiness she confessed only to her father and mother. Harry Belin was a patient and understanding man, but to judge from his letters, all he could do was counsel his daughter to cultivate patience and forbearance. In the circumstances, there was little else he or anyone could do.

The great influenza epidemic of 1918 was the moment of revelation for Alice. The virus was mowing down hundreds of Du Pont powder men. In normal circumstances P.S., always deeply concerned about the welfare of his workers, would have been out visiting families, comforting the widows or the bereaved, as he did when there was an explosion in the mills. He had important preoccupations at the office; the decision on Alfred I.'s appeal in the Coleman shares case was about to be given. And many of his du Pont relatives and in-laws had been badly stricken by the flu, two so badly that they subsequently died.

But he neglected them all to sit by the side of his young chauffeur. And when Lewes Mason died on October 19, 1918, P.S. was inconsolable. He did not even go to the funeral of his close Du Pont colleague, Ham Barksdale, or that of Cousin Ethel du Pont's brother, but he arranged all the details of Lewes's funeral, looked after Charlie Mason's family, shepherded Lewes's grieving fiancée away from the graveside, and negotiated with the McLaury Marble and Tile Company of New York for the best Italian marble for the young man's tombstone. (He had already paid for the perpetual care of the grave in Union Hill Cemetery.)

The "hard realization of my place" about which Alice du Pont wrote in her diary immediately after Lewes Mason's death became even harder to bear as the days, the weeks, and the months passed. P.S. could not seem to accept the loss of his beloved young man, and his pain seemed to increase as time passed. He began visiting the cemetery regularly each week, and although Alice often went with him, she must have felt like a being apart, for he took no notice of her as he stared down at the grave.

"Pierre very miserable," Alice confided to her diary.

As if he could not bear to be without the young man's presence, P.S. spent hours looking after his affairs, administering his will,* approving the tombstone design. He commissioned Clawson S. Hammit of Wilmington—an artist who specialized in portraits, painted from photographs—to do one of Lewes, and he even traveled to the home of Lewes's mother in lower Delaware to pick out a suit from the boy's clothes so that the painter could use it to secure better verisimilitude.

By December he had devoted so much time to Lewes's affairs that Alice told him he needed some relaxation, and persuaded him to accompany her to the opera for a performance of *Pagliacci.*

"P.S. very uncomfortable," she noted of the outing.

---

* Lewes left forty-six thousand dollars, entirely from the investments P.S. had made on his behalf.

Next day he was down with a boil, and the doctor was called in to apply poultices.

Dec. 11. Fri. Awful day. P.S. home all day. Poultice every hour. Doctor decided to have surgery. . . .

Dec. 12. Sat. Horrible day. P.S. went to cemetery. Mother and I to town. Waited for doctor after lunch. They came at 4 p.m. Operation. P.S. pretty light headed.

Dec. 13. Sun. P.S. in bed all day but good appetite.

On Christmas Day, 1918, she noted:

Alone in evening.

If Alice had ever imagined the death of Lewes Mason would improve her relationship with her husband and bring them to a closer understanding, she must have begun to realize by the beginning of the new year that it was, in fact, making P.S. more remote from her than ever.

Much of his spare time in the early weeks of 1919 was spent conferring with Clawson Hammit over the painting of Lewes's portrait. He was not satisfied that the artist had "caught" the young man's "special look" and he kept urging him to try again and again. Finally, not entirely happy with the two portraits Hammit had made, he paid him off with a check for a thousand dollars.

His grief failed to diminish as the months went by. He saw no reason to conceal it any longer and sought a way of letting the community at large know what Lewes Mason had meant to him. He told Alice he was proposing to make a gift to a Pennsylvania hospital where Lewes had once been treated for a hip injury, and that he wanted to do it in Lewes's name. This caused Alice some distress, and she urged him to wait awhile.

"Awful morning writing & thinking," she wrote on June 18, 1919, but added three days later:

Golf with P.S. Long talk on golf course and I hope better understanding.

He had apparently agreed to postpone his gift, but he did not forget it. On Saturday, September 19, 1925, he laid the cornerstone of a new hospital at West Chester, Pennsylvania, which he had financed at a cost of $1.2 million on condition that it be named the Lewes A. Mason Memorial Hospital.

"Lewes A. Mason prompted me to make this gift," he declared,

and it seems only right that the hospital should bear his name. Had he not been in West Chester Hospital I would never have known how badly a new one was needed. Had he not died, I would not have been moved to do what I have done. He did good work, and he was great in inspiring others.

Shortly afterward he wrote to a young painter in New York, Miss Eleanor Crownfield, and asked her whether she would be willing to paint a picture of a young man he had known, one Lewes Mason, for a fee of three hundred dollars. In fact, she painted two portraits, for which he paid her thirteen hundred dollars. One was hung in the hall of the Lewes A. Mason Memorial Hospital, and the other he kept for himself. But P.S. was not satisfied with either of them. He wrote to Miss Crownfield:

> It is a great deal to expect you to obtain a good likeness without your having known the original and with no very satis- factory photographs to copy from. Perhaps I am too exacting in asking for a reproduction of my mental impression which may not be that of the photographer or of any other individual.

As if realizing that his days at the powder mills were over, Alfred I., even before the court of appeal threw out his suit against the new regime at Du Pont, had begun diversifying his activities. With some of the monies he had made from the company's sales to the Allies, he bought the Grand Central Palace on Lexington Avenue in New York, at a cost of one million dollars, and set up what he called the Merchants and Manufacturers Ex- change. This was a consortium of European and South American manufac- turers who would import goods duty free and then use the Grand Central Palace as a showcase for displaying and drumming up orders for those goods, which they would then bring in from abroad. It might have worked had Alfred I. given it his full attention, but he left the running of the show to others, and soon they began cheating him. By the time he had poured in another one million dollars, he found that he was being asked for more, which prompted him to take a closer look. He decided to liquidate the operation.

In the meantime there were rumors from Washington that the Internal Revenue Service was getting ready to investigate his income taxes, having decided under pressure from Congress to "get after those war profiteering du Ponts." Alfred I. had been chosen because he was so much more in the public eye than his quiet, retiring cousin P.S., who had, in fact, made at least ten times as much out of the war.

Altogether, Alfred I. was at a loss now that he had left Du Pont, and more aware than ever before that he was really ignorant of the world of big business, a babe in the woods outside the Brandywine and beyond the smell of gunpowder. His sense of isolation might have been easier to live with had his personal affairs been in good order, but things were going wrong there too. Alicia was now a semi-invalid, able to walk only with difficulty, and when her husband started his New York project, she began complaining bitterly about his absences from Wilmington. To appease her, he bought a superb stretch of two hundred and fifty acres along the north shore of Long Island, at Sands Point, for $236,000, and there built a magnificent Georgian mansion, which he handed over as a present to his wife. He called it White Eagle, and Alicia moved in as soon as it was ready, taking with her Alfred I.'s stepdaughter, Alicia ("Pechette"), and a French war orphan whom the couple had adopted and renamed Adelaide Camille Denise du Pont.

Alfred I. was now fifty-five years old. Though blind in one eye and almost totally deaf, he still felt life pulsing through his veins and was determined not to be like his wife, that is, bitter and totally withdrawn from life. If Alicia had thought she would see more of him by living on Long Island, she was wrong. He was rarely with her. Though he could not hear a note, he still went to concerts, following the music with a score. He patronized the Shakespearean plays in which his actor friend, Jimmy Hackett, was playing, again with a copy of the script before him; or would go night after night to see the melodrama in which his old chum and boxing partner, John L. Sullivan, was then appearing. The great John L., now a mere shadow of his old bareknuckle-champion self, was getting on in years, but physically he was a good deal better than he might have been had he not decided to go on the wagon. He would stop the action in midscene every time Alfred I. appeared in his theater, and in stentorian tones calculated to penetrate even the thick walls of his friend's deafness, he would declare:

"My greetings to Mr. Alfred I. du Pont!"

Alfred I. had never been a celibate or a one-woman man, and even if he had been, Alicia's persistent maladies made it certain there was no longer any comfort for him in that quarter. The only woman he really loved was the lovely Jessie Ball, but she was now living and teaching in California, three thousand miles away. He could only dream about her and sublimate his feelings with less idealistic attachments. But each one was messier and more expensive and left him unhappy, guilty, and dissatisfied.

After a miserable Christmas at Nemours in 1919—Alicia had reluctantly made the journey back from Long Island and never stopped complaining about it—he decided he could bear his loneliness no longer. He told Alicia he was badly in need of a change of scene and just had to get away. His yacht was laid up, and he did not wish to go to Florida where he might run into "enemy" du Ponts. He would be going to California. As if guessing why he was going there (and if she still went through his letters, she would not have needed to guess), Alicia insisted he take little Alicia with him. She too could do with a change of scene.

He was too glad to get away to complain about that, and he immediately sent a telegram to Jessie Ball in San Diego announcing his imminent arrival. She was at the station to greet him when he and Pechette stepped down from the train on the morning of January 7, 1920, and though, for the child's sake, they did not embrace as passionately as they might have done in other circumstances, they felt as if a new era had begun for both of them. Jessie Ball, though sixteen years had passed since their first meeting, and though she was now an attractive woman of thirty-two, had never married and made it plain there would never be anyone in her life but Mr. Alfred I. du Pont. She accompanied father and stepdaughter to the Coronado Hotel, gaily reestablishing contacts on the way, and then hurried off to her afternoon classes, but not before promising to join Alfred I. for lunch the following day.

It was a date never kept. When Alfred I. got up to his room, there was a telegram waiting for him.

"RETURN AT ONCE," it said. "ALICIA DEAD."

Alicia had been stricken while traveling to Charleston, South Carolina, in the company of a du Pont cousin with whom she was to attend a coming-out party for one of her southern relatives. She was found gasping and moaning in her berth just before the train arrived at the Charleston station, and was rushed to Charleston Hospital, where she expired a few hours later. The family firmly denied the rumors circulating in Wilmington that she had died from an overdose of painkilling medicine; and the Du Pont newspaper, the Wilmington *News,* in reporting her death, pointedly mentioned that only a few days previously, she had accompanied her husband to the railroad station and bidden him good-bye "with a loving kiss" when he had left on his trip to the West.

Alfred I. telephoned Jessie Ball to tell her that Alicia was dead and he was leaving at once to arrange for her funeral. A week later he was the chief mourner when she was buried on the grounds of Nemours, beside the bodies of her baby son and daughter. To the surprise of those du Ponts who attended the funeral—P.S., Coleman, and Alicia's father, Judge Bradford, were not among them—the ceremony turned out to be a solemn religious one. Alfred I. had always proclaimed himself an atheist, but it was he who had arranged for the interment service to be conducted by Dean Robbins of the Cathedral of Saint John the Divine of New York, and fourteen cathedral choir boys sang as Alicia was lowered into her grave. What the rest of the du Ponts had not realized until now was that Alfred I. had embraced religion after the death of his day-old son and henceforth never retired to bed without first falling to his knees in prayer. He was on his knees now, loudly praying for his sins to be forgiven.

CHAPTER 20

Internal Combustion

CURIOUSLY enough, it was the swashbuckling and ruthless cousin Coleman du Pont who made the first peace overtures to Alfred I., and the gentle, civilized, mild-mannered P.S. who remained determinedly unforgiving.

P.S. had always been proud of the fact that the rest of the du Ponts looked up to him as the incorruptible member of the family whom they could always trust. When Alfred I. charged him with underhanded motives over the share transfer, he felt his honor had been impugned, and this cut him to the quick. It also exacerbated his resentment against his cousin for the way he had treated his ex-wife and his children. But what finally decided him that Alfred I. was a scoundrel who could never be forgiven was his behavior over bonuses for the executives and department heads of the Du Pont company.

P.S. believed strongly in the old-fashioned virtue of hard work and felt it should be rewarded. Early in his career as treasurer of Du Pont he had persuaded his two cousins that regular bonuses to the hard workers and good producers in the yards and offices would result in an eager work force always striving to do better. One of the moves they had agreed upon before the quarrel began was to allocate blocks of five hundred shares each to ten senior members of the staff. Alfred I.'s subsequent suit succeeded in having this bonus gift abrogated, and P.S. was furious about it. He sent a memorandum to the executives concerned:

It is doubtful if the benefits of cooperation have ever been more forcibly exemplified than . . . in the crisis of the world's history today. Had it not been for the prompt cooperation of the Allies, France would now be overrun and Britain threatened if not overpowered by German savagery. The cooperative forces . . . have won victory where defeat awaited separate effort. In the Du Pont company the result of the efforts to master a task that has never before been accomplished has been due to the perfect cooperation of the departments, whose leaders by unselfish devotion to the cause have set an example of loyalty for all to follow.

It is impossible to estimate completely the far reaching effects of your efforts. In Britain and France it is acknowledged that the Du Pont company, which means you, has saved the day for the Allies. . . . It is not improbable that civilization itself owes its continued existence to you and your associates. . . .

At such a time it is pitiful that a Court of Justice takes from you the well earned fruits of your endeavors and *that a handful of evil doers who have bourne* [sic] *no part of the burden but who have shared liberally in the rewards* [italics mine] should seek to deprive you of the payments which their own agreements gave you under the bonus plan. It is their intention to leave you as your whole compensation for two years of unremitting effort, a salary no greater than some of them were willing to draw from year to year for trifling time and efforts on behalf of the company. Though flaunting the name of du Pont, they have brought it to shame and dishonor.

He would not let them get away with it, P.S.'s memo continued. Rather than have the executives lose their bonus, he was immediately setting aside shares from his own common stock in Du Pont, "which shares [would] accrue to [their] benefit in the event of a final adverse decision of the Du Pont Securities Company case."

The transfer of stock would cost him $600,000, in addition to the $2.5 million in stock that he had already promised his executives as a result of the Coleman transfer. It was true that he could afford it. As he remarked in his memo:

> Though the total of [this gift] will be large I assure you that its loss will cause no personal inconvenience to me nor to those in any way dependent upon me. There will remain with me a quite sufficient amount of stock of E. I. du Pont de Nemours and Company whose value your united efforts have so greatly increased.

But it was the meanness of the gesture, against men who had been his colleagues, that made P.S. so angry and unforgiving of his cousin. He had no wish whatsoever to make up with him.

Coleman, on the other hand, thought it was about time the cousinly quarrels were forgotten. When he heard that Alicia was dead, he immediately wrote Alfred I. a note of sympathy in which he made it obvious he regretted some of the things he had said about her in the past. Then news began to spread of Alfred I.'s financial difficulties. The government had started a suit against him for $1,576,015.86 additional tax on his 1915 income. His losses on the Nemours Trading Corporation were still coming in, despite its liquidation. He was so strapped for ready cash that when he was asked to make a contribution to an M.I.T. building fund, he wrote to that institution's president, Dr. Richard MacLaurin:

> I cannot begin to tell you how sorry I am not to have been able to participate in this wonderful work. . . . I am busy trying to arrange to keep out of jail.

Altogether he owed $10,030,000, and the problems of finding the money to pay it off were driving Alfred I. to the edge of a nervous breakdown. It was at this point that Coleman attempted to come to his rescue by offering him a loan to tide him over the crisis. The offer was ill received. Alfred I. let it be known that he saw ulterior motives behind it, and claimed that Coleman was trying to get him on his side in the struggle for control of the Delaware Republican party. This may have been true, but if so, Coleman was prepared to pay millions for it. Bruised at the rebuff, he retired to Colorado Springs, suffering from a sudden bout of lung trouble, and it was there that Alfred I.'s shrewish sister, Marguerite du Pont Lee, wrote him. She had always maintained that Coleman had been overcompensated in their grandmother's will, and that her cousin owed his ill health to overindulgence.

"Dear Coly," she wrote on May 28, 1921,

> Extremely sorry to hear of your lung trouble. I fancy the enclosed news [that shares in which he was an investor were rising] will effect a speedy cure. I diagnose your malady as one affecting your stomach, rather than your lungs, and doubtless was produced by the too rich diet of "Goodstay" [Coleman's home in Wilmington] upon the top of so many of Granny's securities. Leaving you to digest this, in addition to all the rest, I remain as ever Your cousin.

Coleman was so shocked by the savage tone of the letter that he sent a copy to P.S. who wrote back to him:

> I was interested in noting the cheerful letter written to you by Marguerite. It was quite unnecessary for her to sign the document, one would have guessed it as coming from her pen. She seems to have "broken loose" lately, for I received a similar letter apropos of the final liquidation of the Johnson Company, in which she suggested, sarcastically, that my signature on the stock certificates should be worth more than 36¢, and invited me to pay her something additional for her shares. I replied that I could make all the signatures I wished for less than 36¢, therefore was not in the market to acquire more.

Alfred I.'s money troubles inevitably weakened his hold on the Delaware Republican machine, and if Coleman had been trying to "buy" his cousin's political support it was soon unnecessary. Though no longer concerned with the management of the Du Pont company, Alfred I. still had stock in it worth $24 million, of which he pledged $12 million against a loan from J. P. Morgan and Company to pay off his debts, at the same time liquidating some of his other assets. One of these was the only morning newspaper in the state, the Wilmington *Morning News,* which he sold off for $190,000. The buyer was a Delaware corporation, which turned out to be owned by P. S. du Pont, and the newspaper immediately changed sides and began proclaiming the virtues of Coleman du Pont as the next United States senator from Delaware. Alfred I. also gave away his five remaining downstate newspapers, all of which had been losing money, and soon they too began discovering good qualities in Cousin Coleman.

Not that Alfred I. seemed to worry very much about Delaware any longer. The woeful countenance he had worn at Alicia's funeral in January was transformed two months later, in March, when he went to the depot in New York to meet the train from Chicago. Jessie Ball had decided she needed to return to the East for a time, and had secured a six-month vacation from her school in San Diego. She was to stay with her sister in New Jersey, but in the weeks that followed she was often at Nemours, or spending weekends on Cherry Island with Alfred I., Maurice and Margery, Mr. and Mrs. Francis I. du Pont, and Eddie Bradford.

In June 1920 Alfred I. gave what he called a Ball's Neck Reunion at Nemours, and all members of the Ball and Harding families who were in the East were there. It was just like old times, with the old musicians from Ball's Island performing on their fiddles and banjoes, old and young feasting and celebrating, and Alfred I. leading a radiant Jessie Ball around the dance hall to music that he could not hear.

Little Pechette sang songs for them in a voice that was much more than a childish soprano, so much so that Jessie praised her talents highly to Alfred I. and, egged on by Pechette, urged him to have her professionally coached. (He told Jessie later that he was sending the child to France, accompanied by a chaperone, to study under Jean de Reszke.)

That autumn, after seeing his stepdaughter off to Europe, he followed Jessie back to California. When he and his valet, Thomas Horncastle, arrived in Los Angeles on January 20, 1921, Jessie was once more waiting for him on the platform. With her was the brother, Edward Ball, whom Alfred I. had not seen since he was a bright little lad dancing ahead of the hunting parties in the Ball's Island woods seventeen years earlier.

Alfred I. du Pont and Jessie Dew Ball were married by an Episcopal clergyman in Los Angeles on January 22, 1921, with Edward Ball as best man. As Alfred I. came out into the California sunshine with his new bride on his arm, Edward grasped his sister's other arm, and they posed as a trio for a photograph.

The newspapers proclaimed it the wedding of a backwoods Cinderella to a fabulous merchant prince and captioned their pictures of Jessie Ball:

"This girl has married into millions."

In fact, Alfred I. had never come nearer to bankruptcy. He had paid off many of his debts, but he still owed the United States government $1.5 million in back taxes, and new liabilities of $7 million were threatening to engulf him. To make matters worse, the market had gone down, and his Du Pont shares that had been worth $24 million a year ago were now valued at $9 million. He warned his new bride that far from having married a multimillionaire, she might have entrusted her life to a pauper.

He was exaggerating, of course. He was hard hit, but such was his happiness that he no longer seemed to care. As he told Jessie:

> After all I've said about wealth being a mere trust in the hands of those who possess it, I'd be a poor sport of a man not to be able to part from mine a little in advance of normal expecta- tions, and begin over again without recriminations against others or bitterness of heart.

Jessie did not seem to care either.

"I don't think Mr. du Pont was ever happier than I saw him that day," Ed Ball said later. "He was fifty-seven years old, but he looked as if he had the whole of his life before him."

Ever since the development of the internal-combustion engine, the du Ponts had been fascinated with motor cars and their possibilities. At a time when people were still arguing that nothing would ever replace the horse and buggy, the three cousins were vying with each other to buy (or design) the fastest and most reliable automobiles ever to be seen on the Delaware high- ways. The motor car was, in fact, one of the reasons why they became so interested in roads. P.S. wanted a smooth route from Longwood to Wil- mington, so he paid for construction of a turnpike out of his own pocket, charging a small toll to other users.* Coleman pictured himself being driven the ninety-seven miles from Wilmington to Dover in style, as well as in triumph, when he became one of the state's United States senators, and it was worth four million dollars to make it a possibility. Alfred I. contributed to the construction of a road from Wilmington to Philadelphia so he could drive to concerts and operas in his homemade automobile, straight from the powder yards.

It was John J. Raskob who finally persuaded P.S. to invest and involve himself in the automobile industry. Now one of the busiest bees in the American business world, in addition to being a good and watchful treasurer for Du Pont, a fond (if not exactly faithful) husband, a proud father of an

---

*He handed the road over to the Delaware and Pennsylvania authorities in 1919.

ever-growing family, a good Catholic, a faithful supporter of orphanages and other worthy charities, Raskob also spent a great deal of his time in New York meeting bankers and big-business men and generally making contacts. Among the enterpreneurs he met, one from the automobile industry particularly struck him as a man to know and watch. He was William C. Durant and he ran an operation called the General Motors Company. From the way Durant talked, Raskob became convinced that though his company was not doing well at the moment, once he got its problems straightened out, General Motors would develop into the most promising company in the automobile industry.

In February 1914 Raskob bought five hundred shares in General Motors and persuaded P. S. du Pont to buy two thousand. The price was seventy dollars for a hundred-dollar share, and he explained, "only the fact that they were not paying dividends" accounted for the low price. But they would, he assured P.S., they would.

He was quite right. The outbreak of World War I gave America's motor-car industry just the boost it needed, and General Motors was in the forefront of those producing trucks, troop carriers, and staff cars for the western front. By the summer of 1915 its stock had risen to $200, and by December it was selling at $558, advancing the value of P.S.'s two thousand shares by over a million dollars. This sudden rise, however, started an internal fight for control of General Motors, and when the subsequent strife threatened to wreck the company's plans, P. S. du Pont was called in as peacemaker.

The upshot of all the conciliation meetings was a deadlock solved only when P.S. was elected chairman of the board of General Motors. He was pleased. He needed the distraction. He brought three members of his entourage to join him on the board: John Raskob, J. Amory Haskell (once president of Laflin and Rand, who had moved over when Du Pont bought the company), and his brother-in-law Lammot Belin, in whose New York apartment he and Alice had been married.

P.S. and Raskob set out for Detroit to learn something about the automobile business. It was a moment when the two men had come close to each other again, in a way that had not happened since Raskob's marriage. Raskob was once more P.S.'s adoring slave and admirer, and his boss returned his adulation in the only way he knew how, by making gifts to him. Just before the Detroit trip he had given Raskob yet another block of Du Pont shares and in return received this letter from him:

Dear Daddy,—

It is hard for me to express myself in words under ordinary circumstances and it seems impossible to properly do so when my heart, always so full of love and affection for you, is filled to overflowing with the thought that you too really care so much for me who at times, I fear, has been very unruly and sorely tried your patience.

Nothing counts quite so much in life as love in its full sense and meaning embracing as it does complete confidence in honesty and integrity. There is no one thing which has helped me quite as much as your complete confidence in me. One could hardly fail under the circumstances and you must appreciate, Daddy, that I am very proud to have had the privilege of association with you and to have had that association ripen into such a strong bond of love and friendship. . . . [T]he magnificent credit you always give me is really a reflection of you and your work in a mirror which you have succeeded in polishing after a very great deal of hard work. Remember, Daddy, it is always possible to ruin mirrors through breaking them, and aren't you very afraid of spoiling me through your continued praise?

To me the splendid opportunity given me in the Du Pont Securities Company through your generosity and thoughtfulness will ever stand as a monument in my memory of you. It has made so many things possible especially for Helena and the children that it is ever pleasant to think about as it associates you so closely and intimately to me in my home life.

Now I am going to build another monument by keeping your gift as a fund separately invested to grow and be used in the future in some way that will ever make me think of you in my endeavors to handle it in a way that I think will make my Daddy love me more if that is possible.

or a car enthusiast of P.S.'s caliber Detroit was as exciting as a modern
ıild's visit to the John F. Kennedy Manned Space Flight Center. With
askob in tow, he met characters like Louis Chevrolet, Walter Chrysler,
dward Fisher, and Henry Ford. He also got to know more about Will
'urant, a genius of the internal-combustion engine, who, practically single-

handed, had organized car divisions called Buick, Cadillac, Oaklands, Olds, and the General Motors Truck Company, in addition to having imported the brilliant Frenchman Louis Chevrolet to build the car that bore his name.

Unfortunately, what he learned of Durant confirmed the man's strength as an automobile engineer but revealed his alarming weakness as a company president. As someone confided to him in Detroit:

> Durant is a genius, and therefore not to be dealt with on the same basis as ordinary business men. In many respects he is a child in emotions, in temperament, and in mental balance, yet possessed of wonderful energy and ability along with certain well-defined lines. He is sensitive and proud; and successful leadership, I think, really counts more with him than financial success.

He also wanted to run the whole show and soon made it plain to P.S. he was welcome as chairman of the General Motors board only so long as he did exactly what Durant wanted. It was not how P.S. had envisioned his new role. He was in the motor business now, and he wanted to participate in every way—in the design of models (he particularly liked the new five-hundred-dollar Buick), in sales promotion, in financing, and, of course, in profits.

He did not interfere at first while he learned the rudiments of the industry; but then, after a three-year boom the United States entered the war, and private car manufacture for a time dropped practically to zero. Steel was short, which put a damper on production, and General Motors stock dropped disastrously on the market.

Will Durant panicked as he saw the value of his shares going down to $100, $98, then $84, from near $600. He began buying up shares from his own resources, in the hope of mopping up the surplus and stopping the rot. It was at this point that John Raskob came to tell him that he would like to help him in his campaign to purchase the plummeting shares. Although he was no longer a pauper, Raskob was certainly not in the du Pont's financial class, and one can only wonder where he got the money to go into the market and begin spending so wildly (almost $2 million) on falling General Motors shares.

Then Durant ran out of cash. He was so strapped for money that Raskob asked P.S. to persuade the General Motors board to raise the president's salary to half a million dollars a year and pay him two years in advance. The chairman's evident sympathy with Durant's plight and his eloquence on his behalf persuaded the others to go along, and Durant got his one million dollars. But it did not last long. It merely paid off part of his collateral, and he was quickly in trouble again.

Once more Raskob approached P.S. on behalf of his collaborator. Had this been part of the plan all along? That Raskob would partner Durant in a wild, but obviously hopeless, buying spree so that eventually only P.S. would be able to help him—on P.S.'s terms? Certainly P.S. was now the only one around with enough cash on hand to bail out Durant.

P.S. offered to inject $12.5 million of his own money into General Motors. But on one condition: A new company must be formed, controlling both Chevrolet and General Motors, and P.S. would be given joint control over it with Will Durant.

Never. Durant was adamant. Never would he share his babies with anyone, not even P. S. du Pont.

Raskob then retired to Longwood to discuss the situation anew with his boss. If Will Durant's obduracy had disappointed him, he gave no indication of it. Raskob bounced back to Detroit with a new idea calculated to cut through the impasse. He pointed out to Durant that, as treasurer of Du Pont, he was aware that the company was up to its ears in surplus cash made during the war and was looking for a safe channel into which to sluice it. He proposed that Du Pont invest in General Motors twenty-five million dollars of this surplus, thus enabling Durant to remain head of his company without having an individual majority stockholder breathing over his shoulder.

Durant liked the sound of it and asked Raskob to take it up with P. S. du Pont. If P.S. liked the plan, perhaps he would push it with the Du Pont company. Since Raskob had already talked it over with P.S., that was no problem. P.S. replied that he was in favor of the plan and would take it before the next meeting of the Du Pont board.

Curiously enough, P.S. did not have so easy a time convincing his fellow du Ponts as he had expected. There were many hesitations about going into the automobile business, and a feeling among some that they ought to stick to explosives and chemicals. But both his brothers, Irénée and Lammot, came to his support, and his own persuasive powers and those of John Raskob finally won the day. What probably decided them on the idea was one stipulation P.S. had made: If Du Pont went into General Motors, the new company would be run along Du Pont lines. Although Durant would still be president, there would be an executive committee with powers to vote on policy, and a finance committee with powers to decide on expenditure.

Furthermore, he added, he would see to it that John Raskob was elected chairman of the finance committee. Raskob would relinquish his duties as treasurer in Wilmington in order to look after money matters in Detroit. Du Pont's own executive and finance committees then voted to go along, and twenty-five million dollars of the company's money was released for the purchase of General Motors shares.

Thereafter, though he may not have realized it, Durant became a cipher, and Raskob never made a move without first consulting P.S. By 1922 the Du Pont company had invested a total of $79,537,095 in what came to be known as the General Motors Corporation, and Will Durant had been replaced by a new president, none other than P. S. du Pont himself. Not so long afterwards, a jubilant Raskob was writing P.S. to boast that General Motors's income before taxes was no less then $426,900,000 and its net worth more than two billion dollars.

It was something of a financial triumph considering the initial investment had been only twenty-five million, and it brought the Du Pont company vast new markets and financial returns in ways other than dividends from the sale of cars. P.S. once more showed his gratitude to Raskob by lending him money to get in on the bonanza, and on October 4, 1919, his friend wrote back (in a letter marked "Confidential"):

Dear Daddy:

In paying my note may I yet again record my appreciation of the many wonderful opportunities you have and are continually giving me. The opportunity to purchase two thousand shares of Chevrolet Motor Co. stock through your loan nets me a profit at today's market of over four hundred twenty five thousand dollars. The results in this case can be stated in dollars, a definite foot-rule, but the opportunities extended to me in other directions have produced results for me which cannot be measured. Notable among such is the opportunity to take the Chairmanship of the Finance Committee of the General Motors Corporation. Really, when I think of the magnitude of the position and its responsibilities, I wonder if I am properly meeting them. One is such a poor judge for oneself. Opportunity of practically continuous consultation with you is, I am sure, the only thing that keeps me from being really scared at times. As it is, somehow I never seem to have the least fear. Oftentimes I wonder whether anyone has ever had my opportunities and how much better others might have handled them. It has been my good fortune to win your confidence and love which, after all, is the greatest reward anyone could ask. Financial success is a mere incident compared with that.

Its [sic] just splendid to know you, Daddy, as I do and you know much better than I can tell you exactly what my feelings are.

At least the maneuvers connected with the affairs of General Motors served to wrench P.S.'s mind away from the death of Lewes Mason, but for Alice there was no similar anodyne. For a time, it seems she could not bear to watch her husband suffering, and she began to go away for longer and longer periods, to Atlantic City, to her parental home at Scranton, on cruises to Europe. Under the pressure of her life with P.S. her health had begun to decline. First it was haemorrhoids ("I can't say I like a doctor examining my tail," she wrote to P.S. in 1919) and then what she called nerves.

The custodians of the du Pont Papers have refused the author permission to quote from two letters that Alice sent P.S. about this time, on the grounds that they were written when she was probably suffering from "menopausal depression (temper tantrums, sleeplessness, baseless fears, irregular periods, indecision, ardent behavior to spouse, etc.)," and therefore do not reflect her normal self. This is a pity, because the letters do indeed have their "ardent" passages and illustrate vividly Alice's deeply felt love for her husband, her longing for his embrace, and her painful sense of deprivation.

There is, however, another letter she wrote in this period that may be quoted from. In the fall of 1922 Alice was away from Longwood on a cruise to Europe with some of her younger du Pont relatives. Just before sailing, she had gone with P.S. to Newark, Delaware, for a ceremony at the young university that the du Ponts had helped to fund and get started, and on that occasion he had been presented with a degree. She wrote from the steamhip *Cretic:*

> . . . Just at this time a week ago today we were starting off to Newark for your latest honor. I say latest but perhaps there has been another since I left. Every one you get rejoices my soul,

for no one knows better than I do how much each one is deserved. Sometimes I think you would prize these honors more highly if you had someone to whom to hand down the visible signs. But again I realize more and more that you do not need actual children & grandchildren to treasure your memory & the traditions connected with it, for you are going to be looked back on as almost a saint or hero in the history that is read in future years. I wish I could feel sure that I would have the place of a proper helpmate in this same history, but if I don't do better in the future than in the past I won't deserve it. Already I think my nerves are in better shape however for I can realize what a fool I was about lots of things before I left home. Let us hope some serenity will stick to me on my return. . . .

Oct. 4. . . . I do feel very far away from the one I love best and many times a day I wonder where you are and what you are doing. . . . You have been so good about writing me and your letters have been so amusing and have also said such nice things about missing me that I have been very happy over them.

Coping with John Raskob was so much easier than handling a wife, P.S. must often have thought. There were never any attacks of nerves, or implied rebukes. He was so easy to please. He never made demands or hinted at them. Make him a gift, send him a commiserating letter about a cold or an absence, and his response was uncomplicated and unstinting.

Part Five

ALL IN THE FAMILY

CHAPTER 21

Spreading the Load

By the 1920s the du Ponts were fast becoming the richest family in the United States and probably the world. The Rockefellers, the Mellons, and the Guggenheims might have possessed larger individual fortunes, but the aggregate amount of money possessed by the du Pont clan far surpassed that of any other family. They kept quiet about it.

The sixty du Ponts who, unlike the rebellious five, had supported P.S. in the suit over Coleman's shares were, of course, by far the most affluent. P.S.'s brothers and sisters were the richest of all, because they now controlled over sixty-four percent of the stock. To make sure that it could be handled as a block, P.S. had hidden it safely away (together with their shares in General Motors) in a holding company called Christiana Securities. With the exception of certain offspring of the Old Guard, all pro-P.S., and his family, other stockholders were barred from Christiana. So the third stage of the development of the Du Pont empire had been reached: Begun as a joint effort of the clan, it had then passed on to the three cousins and was now controlled by one single family. P.S.'s plan had come to pass, and he and his two brothers, Irénée and Lammot, with fifty-two percent of the shares among them, had taken over. So long as they held on to Christiana, they would control Du Pont and be impervious to takeover bids whether from enemies in the family or without.

Alfred I. was still the most powerful of the potential enemies, for he had held on to his share of the stock, amounting to 19.627 percent of the total. He tried to raise some money during the worst of his financial crises by offering to sell it to his cousins, but (fortunately for him) he had asked too much and was turned down. He found other means of raising money and thus kept his Du Pont holding, which multiplied twentyfold in the years to come.

Of the Old Guard shareholders, the richest was Colonel Henry Algernon du Pont, with 5.03 percent of the stock. He had put his Du Pont holdings in a blind trust while he was in the United States Senate but had now reclaimed them. The Colonel was eighty-three years old in 1921 and racked with the aches and pains of age. The dank mists of the Brandywine had given him rheumatism, and the rich foods from Winterthur's kitchens plus the good clarets, burgundies, and ports from its cellars had left him with a painful legacy of gout. Agonized in practically every joint, he had given up the research into family history to which he had devoted himself since leaving the Senate, because his eyes were failing him too.

He sometimes complained he had lived too long, and he was weary enough to wish he could die. Unfortunately, that was not possible. At the time of his quarrel with his only brother, William, the Colonel had vowed that when Willie died, he would not be buried in the family cemetery at Sand Hole Woods, and had secured a pledge from the rest of the family that they would carry out his wishes. But as the years passed, Willie had begun insinuating himself back into everybody's affections. Even P.S. had forgiven him, as he had not forgiven Alfred I.

The Colonel feared that if he died before Willie, the family would get soft-hearted and allow Willie a plot in the cemetery. So he was hanging on, to see it did not happen. Sand Hole Woods must *never be sullied* by Willie's foul body.

The only trouble was that Willie du Pont was eighteen years younger than his brother, and no matter how hard the Colonel willed it, Willie refused to die first.

It was a race against time, which soon all the other du Ponts were watching with morbid fascination, and it went on until 1926, when, at eighty-eight, the Colonel could no longer keep his grip on life. He died with Willie's name—like an imprecation—on his lips to the last. As if he too had been holding on, Willie du Pont then proceeded to waste away, and he died two years later. Both were buried in Sand Hole Woods.

With the exception of Alfred I., all the other du Pont rebels were forgiven, one by one. It was difficult to do otherwise, since a number of them had relatives who had sided with P.S. and these loyalists now pleaded for the recalcitrants to be welcomed back to the fold. Philip du Pont, for example, was the son of Alfred I.'s mortal enemy, Elizabeth Bradford du Pont. She told P.S. she had made Philip see the error of his ways. Another member of the opposition, Paul du Pont, had brothers who rallied to P.S. and were now ready to use their fraternal influence; but most influential of all was the fact of his relationship to P.S.'s brother, Irénée du Pont—they were brothers-in-law. In the end none of the offending five was deprived of his or her first million dollars by the break, even if they never quite amassed the sums achieved by the virtuous sixty.

Not a single one of them, however, was invited back to work for Du Pont, and this created bitterness in some. One who had shared P.S.'s passion for automobiles, and who would have relished working for General Motors, was Paul du Pont, Irénée's brother-in-law; he not only liked motor cars but had a genuine talent for building them.

As a gesture of defiance toward his smug and successful cousins, he announced he was going into the automobile business on his own, and that, moreover, the vehicle that he and his colleagues had designed and built would soon go on the market and be called—what else?—the DuPont car. He wrote to tell P.S. about it. P.S. turned the letter over to his brother Irénée, now president of Du Pont, to deal with. It goes without saying that both brothers were appalled at the prospect, and Irénée hastened to convey his disapproval to Paul, to whom he wrote on July 9, 1919:

> I am certain that you are not intentionally trying to reap a benefit at the expense of the Du Pont Company in naming your new company du Pont and think your desire to couple your own name with your venture is otherwise a commendable one and a move that shows your faith in the undertaking. You probably are

not as familiar as I am with the tremendous advertising and prestige that the du Pont name has in the motor field. It has been published broadcast over the country and abroad that du Pont has gone into the motor industry in a very large way. It has, and to a considerable extent the reputation of the Du Pont Co.'s success has reflected on General Motors, so that the stock has increased tremendously in value and part of the rise is doubtless due to the Du Pont's interest.

The du Pont car would likely be considered by the buyer as a specially good product, put out by General Motors, possibly through a subsidiary. . . . Mr. Durant recognized this and sometime ago had up the question of producing a du Pont car which would be the last word in car construction. Should this materialize there will be considerable confusion to the detriment of the Du Pont Company interests and probably to your financial benefit.

I do not think you would care to put yourself in a position where others will think you had an ulterior motive in choosing the name and embarking in the business at this juncture. . . .

If he thought this would scare off Paul du Pont, he was mistaken. The reply that came back was positively defiant.

"Dear Irénée," Paul wrote,

Regarding you letter of the 9th, I will say that I am unable to see the matter as your letter would seem to wish me to see it.

You imply that my motives in using my name in connection with the business is open to question. I cannot agree with you.

Your argument, carried on to its conclusion, becomes untenable. It would prohibit my use of my own name in any business whatsoever in which the powder company might at any time choose to invest a part of its surplus capital, and in which it might later wish to use the name of du Pont—unless I first gained the Company's permission.

In effect, coming from you, who are President of E. I. Du Pont de Nemours & Company, this amounts to an assertion of the Company's authority to deny me my birthright. I cannot consent to that. Nor do I believe that you, after reasonable reflection, will seriously seek to maintain so preposterous a position.

You need have no fear but the "duPont Car" will be entirely

worthy of the name. I am going to sell you one of the first lot, and I am certain that you will concede that it is as good as can be made.

But the DuPont car never came on to the market in any serious way. Irénée and P.S. saw to that. Irénée lent Paul some fifty thousand dollars to get going. But while outwardly pretending to support his brother-in-law's venture, Irénée made certain it was starved of capital just when it was needed. To Coleman, who offered to invest twenty-five thousand dollars "for family reasons," Irénée wrote: "If you are willing to put in $25,000 I think it will tend to help, especially if you write Paul telling him frankly that you are not making it as an investment but purely as an aid to give one of the young fellows of the family an opportunity to make good if he has got it in him. If we can get Paul into the attitude of mind that he must make good, it will do more towards straightening him out of the troubles of the past than any amount of coaxing or threatening."

Paul du Pont was convinced he simply needed additional capital to exploit his product—generally accepted to be a good one—and he went back to his brother-in-law to solicit more money for further production and advertising. But to his consternation, Irénée, who must by that time have been worth at least seventy million dollars, wrote:

Dear Paul:

I have been very negligent in replying to your letter of Septemper 7th [1920]. It is very hard to write when you don't know what to say. Frankly, I have no funds for investment, having spent or committed myself to the spending of all my income, and more, this year, and my forecast for next year is all taken up as far as income is concerned. Therefore, in order to subscribe further to your project, it would necessitate selling some other investment to obtain funds.

The vast bulk of my investments were made at low figures and if I should sell them I will be subjected to an income tax of about half of the total proceeds. . . . Therefore, from a business point of view, I would surely decline a subscription. On the other hand, if I felt sure that a reasonable size subscription would be of material benefit to you, I would be willing to make it on your account.

Felix tells me he has put in an additional $50,000. If I do

likewise, how much will you put in and will the aggregate be enough to see the proposition through for a reasonable time, say, six months?

As Paul du Pont said later, he needed at least a year and a million dollars to make his car a viable commodity. But there were no more infusions of money from Irénée, Felix, or Coleman. The Du Pont car went out of existence shortly afterward, without having offered any competition to the automobiles produced by Du Pont's own company, General Motors. But at least no one in the family could accuse Irénée, his brothers, and his cousins of not having tried to be a help to Cousin Paul.*

While P.S. was organizing General Motors in Detroit, and Irénée was easing himself into the Du Pont presidency in Wilmington, their third brother, Lammot, was showing his muscle inside the company by developing and improving the nonexplosive side of its products. Lammot had always been the most modest of the brotherly trio, and there were some who would have said that he had much to be modest about. A favorite family story tells how one day he forgot whom he was supposed to meet and wired Cousin Coleman for information. Coleman wired back:

NAME YOUR DATE DWIGHT MORROW. YOUR NAME LAMMOT DU PONT.

Lammot was a shy man who, more even than the rest of the clan, eschewed outward show and favored the simple life. He was one of the du Ponts who remained pretty well unfascinated with the automobile, and preferred riding his bicycle to work. His favorite occupation was stripping to the waist and chopping trees in his back yard; it helped him to think, he said. He was not, however, exactly backward where it came to women, and had married early. His wife gave him eight children before rebelling. She decided to become an invalid instead and eventually died of cancer. Lammot soon afterward married his housekeeper, a charming and worldly-wise woman who gave him no children at all. She once remarked to one of her in-laws:

* Paul fooled them in the end by making a success of one of his ventures. Later in the 1920s he designed and put on the market a powerful motorbike, which he named the Indian. As president of the Indian Motorcycle Company, he made a prosperous business out of catering to the motorbike craze of the 1930s and, in the style of his in-laws, bought himself an ocean-going yacht on the proceeds.

"What a difference there is between Lammot and his brother, Irénée. They both like women, but Lammot just has to make it legal. I'm sure of one thing—when I die, Lammot will marry again."

He did, twice. Irénée, on the other hand, stayed married for life to his cousin Irene, by whom he had ten children, of whom eight daughters and one son survived. He was like Cousin Coleman in his appetite for female adventure and was known to some members of the family as the Fanny Patter. And like Coleman but unlike Lammot he paid off his women and never thought of marrying them.

Lammot shone in the chemistry division of Du Pont, where he and Ruly Carpenter, his brother-in-law, had worked well to develop products to take the place of explosives. One of the reasons why Lammot had been pleased by the company's acquisition of General Motors was that its automobiles would provide an automatic market for many of the Du Pont products he had had a hand in developing: paint, leather substitutes, rubber-coating, battery solution, and preservatives. He said he hoped P.S. would have no silly ideas about being "impartial" and looking outside Du Pont for such materials, and was assured that General Motors would indeed use Du Pont products exclusively. Irénée let it be known among company employees that if and when they bought a car, it would be looked on with favor if they made it a Chevrolet, Buick, or other General Motors product.

The company also developed thriving markets in acetates, airplane dopes, naphthalene, transparent sheeting, fabric, cleanable collars and cuffs, leads, wax, and charcoal. But what Lammot considered his most valuable achievement was securing the formula for dyestuffs that would enable Du Pont to compete with the quality aniline dyes that were once more available from Germany. His efforts had been successful, thanks to the expenditure of a large amount of money, and a commando operation that required the aid of the United States government.

The dyes that Du Pont had been making during the war were based on a patent the company had bought in 1916 from a company in Manchester, England, and though not nearly so good as the German dyes, they had been good enough so long as the war lasted. But just before the armistice Du Pont heard through the British that two of the most important men in the German chemical industry had escaped into Switzerland. One was Dr. Carl Duisberg, head of the German aniline-dye industry, and the other, Dr. Fritz Haber, who had crossed the frontier wearing a false beard and carrying with him, it was believed, the formula for a startling new process he had invented during the war. Haber had found a way of making synthetic nitrates, and in 1918 his factory at Oppau had produced ninety thousand tons, equal to one fifth of the output of Chilean natural saltpeter.

The chief chemist in Du Pont's labs, Dr. Charles Lee Reese, had been trained in Germany and knew both Duisberg and Haber. He was asked to get hold of them and bring them back to Wilmington. But before he could do so, the Allied armies poured into the Rhineland, took over the chemical factories, and demanded that the Swiss return the two fugitive German scientists. They came back of their own accord but, when they saw what the Allies were doing to their factories, refused any cooperation whatsoever. Du Pont and Nobel Industries of Britain had hastily renewed their global agreement the moment the war was over, and they hoped, when things were less passionate, to bring Germany back into the cartel. As a result, they prevailed upon the British and American armies of occupation to go easy on the chemical factories and staffs. The commanders thereupon told the German chemists that although they were determined to have their formulae for explosives and poison gases, they would not ask for dyestuff or nitrate patents and would refrain from prying "into secrets of commercial value in times of peace."

Not so the French—who simply occupied the factories, rounded up the chemists, and demanded they demonstrate how their formulae worked, on pain of dire consequences. The Germans refused and were upheld by the British and Americans. Then came Versailles. The French, already disgusted with the "softness" of the Anglo-Americans, advocated the complete destruction of all German armament plants, including the dyestuff and nitrate factories in the I. G. Farben conglomerate, which, insisted Field Marshal Foch, the French commander in chief, was a nonnegotiable condition of the peace talks. In the face of this seeming catastrophe, Dr. Carl Bosch, chief chemist to the German delegation at Versailles, made a secret offer to the French: If they would reprieve I. G.'s factory at Oppau in Germany, and allow it to continue to make synthetic nitrates, I. G. would go into partnership with them, in France, for the manufacture of dyestuffs. He offered more than that. He rightly pointed out that no one in the world, no matter how hard they tried, had been able to make the German dyestuffs formulae work, not even the experts at Du Pont. The key to the secret was locked away inside the heads of not more than five or six Germans, and they would never be forced to reveal it. On the other hand, Bosch would *hand over* the secret to the French—in return for that reprieve.

It was too tempting an offer for the French to resist. They agreed to the deal. The great Oppau factory was saved, and almost immediately its work force of nearly five thousand returned to the production of nitrates.

When Lammot du Pont heard the news, which had leaked out in Paris, he went to see his brother Irénée, who called an emergency meeting of the executive committee. Something would have to be done, for Du Pont just could not face the prospect of having to compete with the French *and* the Germans in the world market for dyestuffs, especially in view of the fact that their two competitors would be marketing a superior product. Bosch's action was particularly resented by Lammot and Ruly Carpenter, because they had tried to do a similar deal with Bosch themselves and failed. They had sent Dr. Reese, their chief chemist, to Versailles, and he had offered the Germans a joint Du Pont–I. G. Farben partnership in the dyestuffs business in return for the formulae. What they could not see was that Bosch was in the same position as the maiden who decides to sacrifice her virginity to save the family home. The villain who held the mortgage was France, not America. What good would it do to surrender to the villain's more amiable and less brutally determined brother? Rather curtly, Bosch had turned Du Pont down.

Lammot remained despondent over the dismal prospect for several months until Dr. Reese appeared to have some interesting news. The company had a representative in the occupied zone of Germany, an able, astute, and hardheaded German-American, Dr. E. C. Kunze. Dr. Kunze had unearthed four chemists in Germany who were known to understand German dyestuffs, and two of them had the formula. What inducements could he offer them in return for securing their "cooperation"? The executive committee met again and decided to instruct Kunze to offer the four men and their families free passage to the United States, plus five-year contracts with Du Pont at twenty-five thousand dollars a year—a magnificent sum in those days, especially to Germans making do on starvation rations in the midst of insane inflation.

Kunze told the four men to pack, then smuggled them aboard a train for Holland. They left their families behind (Kunze promised to look after them and send them on later) but brought with them a trunk containing a treasure of plans, diagrams, formulae, and other vital information about the operations of their company, Bayer, which had agreements with I. G. Farben. All went well until the trunk, which was filled with clothes to conceal the papers in its false sides and bottom, fell off a cart after passing customs at the Dutch frontier and some papers spilled out. After looking through them, the Dutch police allowed the four Germans to proceed but seized the trunk, "for inquiries."

Someone alerted the Bayer company in Cologne, and they in turn informed the police. The official prosecutor in Cologne demanded the immediate arrest of the four men for industrial espionage, and their return to Germany with the papers. Kunze, his plan rapidly falling to pieces, managed to spirit two of the men aboard a ship in Rotterdam before any action could be taken, and they made it to the United States. Unfortunately, these two, though likely to be invaluable employees, were the two members of the quartet of Germans who did not know the dyestuffs formula.

The two who did, Dr. Max Engelmann and Dr. Heinrich Jordan, had meanwhile been shipped back to Germany, and a great scandal had begun. The German press launched itself into a vehement attack against the United States, using such headlines as "DOLLARS BUY FOUR TRAITORS" and "AN AMERICAN PLOT AGAINST GERMAN DYESTUFFS INDUSTRY." The American chemical warfare expert, Charles Meade, wrote to Irénée:

> The Bayer Company has pretty effectively succeeded in getting the German government to do its will, in view of the fact that it has held Dr. Jordan in Holland and I presume by this time, under the Extradition Treaty, has had him returned to Cologne. [Dr. Engelmann] cannot secure a passport to this country under what we believe is a general order issued by the German government forbidding the issuance of passports to any German scientists.

Through one of their Belin cousins, the three du Pont brothers knew a young member of the Dulles family who had been part of the American delegation at Versailles, and when they consulted with Allen Welsh Dulles,* they were advised to contact his uncle, Robert Lansing. Lansing had also been at Versailles as President Wilson's secretary of state, and though his influence at the White House had faded, the State Department and the armed forces still jumped to when he asked for something—as he did now. Lansing, who had retired from the government to become a member of a well-known Washington law firm, requested the authorities to look after "one of [his] young men" when he reached Germany in the

* Later head of the Central Intelligence Agency.

spring of 1921. The young man, a former member of the American army of occupation, was one Clement Lincoln Bouvé, and when he turned up in Coblenz, he had half a million dollars of Du Pont's money to spread around.

The commanding general of the United States forces in Germany, Major General Henry T. Allen, assigned a commando team to Bouvé with no less than the chief of the United States Military Secret Police, Captain H. E. Osann, in charge of the detail. They were to act under Bouvé's instructions, and what Bouvé wanted, as he explained to Osann, was the rescue of Dr. Englemann and Dr. Jordan from the hands of the German civil authorities. It was not as easy as it sounded. Engelmann and Jordan were being held in Cologne, which was in the British zone of occupation, and Bouvé was aware that the British would be unwilling to let them get away with the two chemists; in fact, he could not understand why the British had not already shipped them off to England for the aid and comfort of Nobel Industries. So it had to be a clandestine operation.

As it turned out, kidnapping and violence were unnecessary, for it was a time when inflation was running wild, and the rate for British, French, or American currency in Germany was soaring up into the millions of marks. A dollar was far more effective than a bullet. One of them could buy a girl. A thousand could buy a man's soul. To make sure that no one made the slightest fuss, Bouvé dispensed dollars to every important official between Cologne and the North Sea and bribed thousands of minor fry as well. The commando brought Engelmann and Jordan (accompanied by Mrs. Jordan and a small son) to the United States Army transport *Somme,* waiting in Bremen harbor, and they landed at Hoboken on July 5, 1921. Dr. Reese was waiting to greet them and take them back to Wilmington, where houses had been furnished and made ready for them.

This time Du Pont had the right couple in its hands, with the dyestuff and nitrate formulae stored away in their heads, and a debt of gratitude to the company which they were eager and anxious to repay. Within a month of their arrival Du Pont was ready to enter the dyestuff and synthetic-nitrate markets on equal terms with the Germans and French.

More than equal, in fact, for in September 1921, two months after Du Pont captured Dr. Bosch's secrets, the great German synthetic-nitrate factory at Oppau, which Bosch had saved by his deal with the French, was blown out of existence. In one of the worst explosions ever recorded, the complex was completely destroyed, six hundred workers were killed, and another two thousand injured. No one ever solved the mystery of how it happened. The New York *Times* commented on October 31, 1921:

Nearly three years after the armistice, the Oppau plant of odious memory is blown to pieces by some mysterious explosive and 3,000 persons are killed, injured or missing, and the scientists, including Professor Haber, do not know how it happened, can't understand it at all. It may never be explained to the satisfaction of honest scientific men; but when the fact is well known that there is an unrepentant and revengeful military party in Germany that looks to another war to restore her baleful power, and when the world believes that these dangerous reactionaries would welcome the discovery by their chemists of annihilating gases of enormous power, it is not inconceivable that the disaster at Oppau may have been due to covert experimenting by those chemists.

Maybe. On the other hand, it could also have been the work of a rival eliminating the competition. Du Pont could count itself fortunate that it had got hold of those vital formulae just in time.

CHAPTER 22

Dirty Deals

P.s. du pont had never been as fond of music as was his cousin Alfred I., and as Alice reported in her diaries, he sometimes dozed off or fidgeted badly when she took him to the opera or the symphony in Philadelphia. (She could not hear much of the music herself, being deaf, but she never gave a sign that she was not passionately absorbed.) Her husband's interest had, however, seemed to quicken while Lewes Mason was alive. She had sometimes come across them listening together to records on the Victrola, and there had been one occasion when she found them in the ballroom, P.S. playing on the grand piano and Lewes singing the words of a song he was reading over P.S.'s shoulder.

The loss of Lewes seemed to heighten P.S.'s interest in music. In 1919 he told Alice that he was having an organ fitted into the house, and soon workmen and experts from New York were swarming all over the ballroom. Aside from the huge instrument Wanamaker had installed in its big store in Philadelphia, the organ at Longwood was the largest in the country, with 10,010 pipes and a vast electrical apparatus to keep it in working order. Thenceforward, P.S. began to give concerts for other members of his family, inviting organists from New York, Paris, and London to play on the mighty instrument, the great Marcel Dupré among them.

There was a phrase used at Longwood whenever P.S. wanted to be alone. He would have it announced that he had "gone to Africa," and during the time he was supposed to be away he cut himself off from everyone, including Alice, who would actually go on a trip. P.S. would then wander through the vast conservatories, contemplating the exotic blooms in the orchid house, poking around among the rare shrubs and flowers, though leaving them alone on strict orders from the head gardener. An organist would be summoned to play not for a weekend concert but for P.S. alone as he sat in the empty ballroom, his eyes closed, his face expressionless, listening to Bach and Buxtehude for hours on end.

His reputation as a gentle, kindly, and caring man was firmly fixed both among the du Ponts and in the state of Delaware, and it was not entirely a false myth that had been created about him. His old leanings toward paternalism were still evident, and no member of the family (except Alfred I.) ever appealed to him for help in vain. He settled family squabbles and marital tiffs. He bailed out relatives who had got into debt. His files are full of documents revealing how he subsidized widows of old colleagues for years and kept on a private (and secret) pension roll dozens of former partners or workmen whom he had not seen since the turn of the century and who had fallen on hard times.

It was as a result of his efforts that the pension and sick-benefits schemes at Du Pont were constantly improved, and from 1919 onward he began remedying another need in Delaware that the legislators in Dover refused to tackle. He became interested in education—an involvement that was initially prompted by his distaste for Alfred I. When Alfred I. set out to beat the Colonel and Coleman and gain control of the state Republican machine, he had won widespread public support by citing Delaware's lack of schools and promising to provide them. He kept his word by financing them out of his own pocket. But when he ran on hard times, P.S. took over and made the building of public schools his hobby. He built the best one near the Wilmington suburb of Greenville, around which most du Ponts now lived, so that the family's offspring would have good educational facilities; he had no compunction about seeing that the du Ponts always had the best. But 17,300 Delaware children also were given classrooms, and 86 schools were constructed solely for blacks, who had never before had any school facilities in the state.

"One of these days," he paternally told a local black leader, "I may even give your people a high school—when your children have demonstrated that they need one."*

It was du Pont feudalism at its most patronizing, but at least it got some of the state's deprived black youth into classrooms for the first time in their lives. Altogether he spent five million dollars of his own money on education in Delaware. But then, he could afford it, and he and his relatives were paying hardly any state taxes anyway.

So P. S. du Pont was an admired man in Delaware in the 1920s, and few people made any overt criticism of his extraordinary wealth. He kept quiet about it, in any case, and the Du Pont–owned newspapers were forbidden to discuss it, except on those occasions when he gave large sums of money away.

He was still convinced that politically the country was going to the liberal dogs. He was wary of every move to increase taxation on business profits, every move to extend the rights of unions, every attempt by officialdom to interfere in the operation of his or other companies, characterizing them as "blatant socialism." He had a deep suspicion of any politician who called himself "the people's friend," less because he was usually a fraud than because he might be genuine; but neither P.S. nor the rest of his family had any hesitation in aiding, with all the money needed, any candidate who promised to become "the businessman's friend."

Just as Alfred I. used Eddie Bradford, Jr. to run his political errands in the state capital, so did P.S. use John J. Raskob to perform similar services; and in the early 1920s, when Cousin Alfred I.'s hold on the Delaware Republicans had loosened after his series of financial disasters, Raskob moved in on P.S.'s instruction. His job was to maneuver Coleman du Pont into the United States Senate, where the company was badly in need of friends. There was no election coming up, and in any case, Coleman did not seem to have voter allure, but that did not deter Raskob, who could manipulate politicians as smoothly as he could bankers and motor magnates. Soon word reached Alfred I. that there was mischief afoot.

"I understand there is a scheme on foot to put Coleman in the Senate by governor appointment," he wrote to his sister, Marguerite, on May 6, 1921.

* He built the first Negro high school in Wilmington in 1927 at a cost of $860,000.

The plan is to get the present Democratic Senator, Wolcott, to resign by offering him the Chancellorship of the State, which appointment is made by the Governor next month, and then to have the Governor appoint Coleman Senator in his stead. . . . Coleman has recognized for some time that he has no chance of being elected to the Senate by people so long as I was alive and kicking.

The rumor was true, and in his present parlous financial state, there was little Alfred I. could do about it. The deal was made in May 1921, and Coleman was sworn into the United States Senate a few weeks later. Alfred I. made his opposition known and described the whole maneuver to Philadelphia and New York newspapers as "Delaware's Dirty Deal."

His other two cousins did not take kindly to his scorn and contempt. But they got their own back. Alfred I., desperately needing money to pay the extra tax the government had levied on his income, was finally forced to approach Du Pont and ask his relatives whether they cared to buy some of his shares, at their price. He made his approach at the same moment that P.S. decided to have Du Pont shares quoted on the stock exchange, which would undoubtedly mean a sudden rise in the price of the stock. But nobody told Alfred I.

Irénée wrote to P.S., who was in New York:

> Alfred was in my office last week and brought up the proposition of selling 25,000 shares of Du Pont Common. He said he was not in need of money but thought it would be a prudent thing to do and it would eliminate some rather high interest charges. He also said he thought "you boys" ought to have first chance at the stock and he would not consider selling it elsewhere until we had given him some reply. This did not ring altogether true so that I did not press very far the "olive branch" but did go so far as to say that it seemed foolish for us to deal through intermediaries when we might sit across the table and discuss the question frankly.

In fact, frankness was totally absent from the discussion. Without revealing anything of Du Pont's intentions with regard to going public, Irénée and his accountants drove a hard bargain. In the end Alfred I. sold twenty thousand of his shares for two million dollars. Six days after the deal was made, Du Pont's shares were being quoted for the first time on the New York Stock Exchange and went up immediately by fifty percent—which would have meant an extra one million dollars for Alfred I.

He needed the money because the Internal Revenue Service was pressing him for $1,961,597 in extra taxes and interest. These were the days of the Warren G. Harding presidency, and his administration did not suffer an excess of honesty. Alfred I. was told that he needed a friendly senator who could "persuade" Secretary of the Treasury Andrew W. Mellon to forgive large debts owed to the government. He had already done it several times for other large debtors. But Alfred I. did not have a friendly senator, he only had his cousin Senator Coleman du Pont, who made sure he was dunned for every cent he owed.

In later years Jessie Ball du Pont used to ride around Wilmington in the back of an olive-green Rolls-Royce with wickerwork body, driven by a liveried chauffeur, and in her funny hats, she reminded many who saw her of Queen Mary of England. But there was nothing of the *grande dame* about her when she was first married to Alfred I. Spiteful members of the du Pont clan sniffed that she had only married their cousin for his position and his money, which was a bit much coming from characters who had been doing that very thing for generations. In any case, if Jessie had done any such thing, she quickly discovered that money troubles were crowding in on her new husband from every side, and it did not seem to worry her a bit. With the possible exception of Margery, Maurice du Pont's wife, she was quite the most carefree and happy-go-lucky character ever to allow herself to be grafted onto the du Pont family tree. Despite their differences in age, moreover, she gave every sign of adoring her husband, and there were telltale clues to the depth of her affection whenever they were together: She was always gently tweaking his ear, stroking a wisp of his hair, or entwining her fingers in his. On his part, the expression of wonderment and pleasure on his face as he contemplated Jessie was something to see, and he did not try to conceal the joy he felt at having her. He began to call her by many pet names, but his favorite was the Brid (presumably for "Bride"). As he wrote later:

> I made a mistake in my first two marriages. I did not realize what a wife could mean until I married the Brid.

He had written on their first anniversary:

> As I am somewhat maudlin today, I will simply say that after one year with the Brid I must confess that she is a million

times more wonderful than I had hoped. Think of spending one whole year with a girl and never a cross word or having the slightest misunderstanding or receiving anything but constant loving, thoughtful devotion! However, such is the case and at times I have to scratch my cocoamat, alias my luxuriant locks, in order to realize that I am in the world, or, as the Prohibitionists say, am living still.

Jessie squeezed the bitterness out of him and injected part of her own adrenaline. She brought back the boyish exuberance and zest for life that had been missing for the last thirty years. She also set about the task of mending the fences he had trampled down on the Brandywine in his anger over the slights and insults he had received from his family and his clan.

She was wise enough to realize that despite the umbilical tug that Alfred I. still felt for the Du Pont company, there would be no future and no happiness for him in resuming his association there. In any case, what sentimental feelings could he possibly have for the organization as it had developed since he had severed his working contract with it? At the end of the war the Brandywine yards had been closed down at last, their mixing mills and grinding sheds made obsolete by new processes and manufacturing methods. When the shutdown was first announced, Alfred I. had made a handsome offer to buy the yards and Eleutherian Mills, the house that the founder of the family company had first set up in 1802. In one of their meaner-minded moments his cousins turned him down in favor of a much lower bid from a lesser cousin. Only Jessie knew how much the rejection had hurt him; and in truth, P.S. and his brothers should have been ashamed of themselves, for no living du Pont had earned a better right than Cousin Alfred I. to inherit the yards where he had been weaned on the company's black powder. It took Jessie's best efforts as an easer of pain to reconcile her husband to the rebuff, and the anguish he felt convinced her it was all the more urgent to find him some occupation that had nothing to do with the Brandywine and Du Pont.

Meanwhile she pursued her self-appointed task of bringing about a reconciliation between Alfred I. and his family. It was not easy. In the summer of 1923 she heard that his daughter Bep was on a visit to her mother, Bessie. She got a message to Bep and persuaded her to come round to Nemours with her two children. Alfred I., who had not even realized that Bep was married, did his best. He fussed over his two grandchildren and was obviously delighted with them. But the strain between father and daughter was too great to be eased by one visit, which, as it turned out, was not a wholehearted success.

Jessie had better luck with Alfred I.'s estranged sister, Marguerite du Pont Lee. Marguerite, as is evidenced by the nasty letter she wrote Coleman when he was ill, was not the nicest of characters, and she had uttered some choice adjectives about Alicia when she was still alive, thus angering her brother. Jessie brought them together for Christmas, 1923, and the reunion this time went well.

Word of Alfred I.'s new affability and of Jessie's good nature spread through the Brandywine and, though it did not heal all wounds, had a surprisingly anodyne effect in some quarters. Alfred I. was astonished to receive a letter from, of all people, the man who had been his mortal enemy during his love affair with Alicia and their subsequent marriage—Judge Edward Green Bradford himself. The judge asked Alfred I. to forgive him for his past conduct and begged a favor of him. Although he was not a du Pont, his wife, Eleuthera, had been, and she was buried in the family burial grounds, Sand Hole Woods. The judge feared that "others" might not feel he was qualified for a place in the cemetery when he died, so would Alfred I. see to it that he was buried beside his wife? He went on to say that "owing to past differences" he was not in contact with his only son, Eddie Bradford, Jr.—and he did not wish to alter this fact, so would Alfred I. please not inform Eddie that his father had written. But if Alfred I. himself was still alive when Eddie died, would he see to it that he too was buried in the grave at Sand Hole Woods, beside his father and mother?

Alfred I.'s instinct was to write back and tell the old man to rot in hell. But Jessie persuaded him to be gentle. He eventually responded:

My dear Judge Bradford:—

This is in acknowledgment of your communication of September 19th.

You may rest assured that so far as it lies in my power your instructions will be carried out.*

Truly, Jessie had changed Alfred I. for the better.

But she had her heart set on a much more serious exercise in reconciliation, and that concerned her husband's only son, Alfred Victor du Pont. One of the things that had shocked her during the semiabortive reunion with Bep had been a remark Alfred I. made in the course of the conversa-

---

* Judge Bradford died in 1928 and was buried in Sand Hole Woods.

tion, about his shame that neither he nor any of the du Ponts had served in the armed forces during the war.

"Alfred Victor did," Bep said proudly. "My brother volunteered and served in the Marines."

"I didn't know that," Alfred I. said.

Jessie was determined that from now on he should learn all there was to know about his son.

In fact, Alfred Victor du Pont's career in the marines had not been particularly distinguished. He had never seen active duty. He was too young and he had joined too late. When he came back from the war, he resumed living with his mother, Bessie du Pont, and his sister Victorine in the house P.S. had given them. P.S. was still as loyal as ever to Alfred I.'s ex-wife and had appointed himself Bessie's patron and her children's surrogate father. He made Bessie a generous allowance to bolster the payments she received from Alfred I. (which still continued to be extremely modest); he provided her with a house and a car, and he found her an occupation: the writing of a family history, for which he promised her all the financial support (including payment for trips to France) she might need in her research. This launched Bessie du Pont on a career as family historian, which kept her busy until the day of her death.*

It is not every son whose father humiliates him by trying to persuade a state legislature to change his name, and Alfred Victor continued to show signs of the traumatic experience through which Alfred I. had put him. He was bright, intelligent, but nervous and uncertain, quick to look for insults and take offense, and overeager to show the world (or, rather, his father) that he did not need anyone's help to make good.

During one of his vacations from Yale he signed up for a job with the Pennsylvania Railroad at a time when it was hit by a strike of several hundred of its staff, and someone tipped off the newspapers. A rash of stories broke out about the young du Pont strikebreaker, and all the old family scandals were raked up. P.S. took it upon himself to go to his nephew's defense, and even wrote to the newspapers deprecating the way in which the story of Alfred Victor's job had been handled.

He decided that if Alfred Victor was to be saved from himself, it was

* Volume I of the several books she subsequently wrote was the first in the United States to be bound in the Du Pont synthetic material Fabrikoid. P.S. was not satisfied with its quality and had subsequent volumes done in more conventional material.

time to get him away from Wilmington, away from the influence of his mother, away from the omnipresence of his father. After the young man graduated from Yale, P.S. found him a job as a chemist at a Du Pont plant in Louviers, Colorado, and promised him that if he worked hard and "went through the mill," he would see to it that he rose through the ranks to an important position in the company.

It did not work out well. Alfred Victor was too touchy and apt to flaunt his du Pont name before his foremen when they criticized his work. He even complained to P.S. when one of his bosses "bullied" him, and got a letter back gently chiding him for not pulling his weight. (With typical meticulousness, P.S. had first written to the factory superintendent for a private report on his nephew's work record.)

In August 1924 Alfred Victor telegraphed P.S.:

> MARCELLA MILLAR OF DENVER AND I WERE MARRIED QUIETLY LAST FRIDAY. SO SORRY YOU AND MOTHER WERE NOT HERE BUT WANTED YOU TO KNOW BEFORE AN-NOUNCEMENTS ARE OUT. PLEASE WIRE US WESTERN UNION YOUR LOVE AND BLESSINGS AT LOUVIERS COL. LOVE FROM US BOTH. ALFRED.

The good wishes were duly sent back, but P.S. confided to Alfred Victor's mother that he thought the boy had been hasty, and feared the marriage would not last.

By the autumn of 1925 Alfred I. had begun to get his finances back in order and was in the multimillionaire class again. His return to affluence might not have been so speedy had he not had the help and advice of his brother-in-law, Edward Ball. Even at thirteen—his age when Alfred I. had first encountered him in the Virginia woods—Ed Ball had been smart and quick, and he had developed considerably since then.

Alfred I., still as enthusiastic as ever over gadgets and new inventions, had been shown a new machine that not only boiled, washed, and peeled tomatoes but then went on to can them.

He bought the rights and opened a tomato-canning factory at Laurel, Maryland, which he called the Clean Foods Products Company. The process worked well, but the sales went badly. At Jessie's suggestion Alfred I. put in a call to her brother, Ed Ball, in California and asked him to come east and take over management of the factory at a salary of five thousand dollars a year. Ed was making eighteen thousand at the time as a traveling salesman for a furniture company, but he came. As he said:

"I loved my sister and liked Mr. du Pont and knew he would get into one of his messes if I didn't help him out."

He quickly discovered, however, that no matter how expertly he managed Clean Foods, there was no way of saving it from eventual bankruptcy.

"I could operate successfully, but the patient would still die," Ed Ball said later. "With thirty of those handy machines Mr. du Pont had bought, I could have canned all the tomatoes in the country—*if* I could have gotten them to the factory before they spoiled. But there was no way of doing that. And there was no way of making Clean Foods pay off. It was too far away from the growing tomatoes."

He advised Alfred I. to give up before he lost his shirt, and helped him to sell out at a good price. But then, instead of going back to California and the furniture company, he heeded the appeals of both his brother-in-law and Jessie and agreed to stay on as Alfred I.'s financial aide and adviser. Almost at once he found himself involved in Alfred I.'s troubles with the United States government. Despite a succession of appeals through the courts, the Internal Revenue Service was slowly and inexorably moving in on Alfred I. for extra tax on his 1915 earnings, roughly totaling a whopping two million dollars, to which he had also to add the legal costs now looming up on him.

His case finally reached the United States Supreme Court, where it was decided that he should pay the assessment demanded by the government, but would then have the right to sue the Internal Revenue Service for its return. Rather than face such a suit, and the large amounts it would add to his legal bills, Alfred I. agreed to a compromise with the tax authorities. They knocked $200,000 from his assessment, and he anted up $1,694,207.

It was then that Ed Ball pointed out that Alfred I. had received an equally formidable assessment (which he had not paid yet) for his 1918 tax. Why did he not take that one to court too? The lawyers said it would never work, but Ed persisted and eventually persuaded his brother-in-law to file suit. It took three years, but finally the collector of internal revenue admitted defeat. On January 22, 1926, he sent Alfred I. a refund of $1,461,-979 for overpaid taxes, plus $499,618 interest.

By that time Ed Ball had become his brother-in-law's closest business collaborator. And he was proving he could be smart in other ways too. If Alfred I. needed any friendly senators to help him in the future, Ed Ball would find them for him. But there was more to the association than business collaboration. The two men got on famously. Furthermore, Ed Ball, a confirmed bachelor who cold-bloodedly regarded women as useful only for recreational and therapeutic purposes, was always around after office hours to work or share amusements with Alfred I.

They often took trips together and proved congenial companions.

"Had a little stag boating party down the Bay yesterday," Alfred I. wrote to Ed's older brother, Thomas, after one such outing.

> Most of the men were in the elderly class, like myself, but Ed and I were the only ones who did justice to the rum bottle, deviled crabs, chicken salad, ice cream, etc. After we had each devoured four deviled crabs and then proceeded to superimpose upon the same several plates of ice cream, there was a unanimous vote taken that we could not possibly survive the night. This morning we both made an affidavit to the effect that we never had a finer night's sleep.

He added:

> Ed is surely a nice boy, the most lovable human being, next to the Brid, that I know. Being a Ball he is naturally a gentleman, and excuse me from living with anybody less. He is a little pig-headed—another Ball feature (also a du Pont feature, I being the exception)—so it is necessary to bat him over the head with a club once in a while; but he has a well-balanced cabeza and is a fine, loyal, hard worker, as tenacious as a bull dog on a tramp's pants—all qualities appealing most strongly to me.

Moreover, Ed went on rescuing him from his financial follies. In the aftermath of the collapse of the Nemours Trading Corporation, the White Shoe Company of Boston sued Alfred I. for a debt of 1.5 million. The legal advisers of White Shoe insisted they would never accept less than payment in full. Then Ed Ball took over. He argued with the lawyers for forty-eight hours, at the end of which time they said they would accept $750,000. He departed with the air of a deflated and disappointed man and did not reappear again for a month. This time the White Shoe lawyers offered to take $630,000, or Alfred I. would have to face the consequences. Ed Ball said his client had no other option but to do so, and departed once more. Less than a month later he was invited back to Boston to see the lawyers, who said they would accept $490,000.

"It's a deal," he said, and advised his brother-in-law to pay.

Alfred I. wrote a check and at the same time raised Ed Ball's salary to twenty-five thousand dollars.

Ed Ball regarded the increase as an incentive to start earning money for his brother-in-law instead of simply helping him cut his losses. He began looking out for prospects.

Jessie was always trying to find places where she and Alfred I. might run into one of his children, and in 1926 she took him to the Wilmington Horse Show. A small group of young women swept by them as they were making their way to the paddock, and Jessie caught her husband looking at the prettiest one among them.

"That's your daughter, Victorine," Jessie said.

He seemed utterly nonplussed for a moment, staring after the girl whom he had last seen when she was four years old. Finally he said:

"I don't like the way she's dressed."

Some months later he rolled over in bed and woke up his wife. It was three o'clock in the morning, she later recalled, and he said he had a plan. He had already talked over with Jessie what was to happen to his money when he died. She would have a life interest in Nemours and enough to live on there, but after her death he wanted the place to become a home for crippled children. He did not believe in large inheritances, maintaining they sapped initiative; therefore, he wanted the bulk of his fortune to go to charities. But he also wanted his children to enjoy some of his money now— he wanted Bep, for instance, to spend some on her children, and Victorine to spend some on clothes.

"I didn't like the way she was dressed," he said again.

As for Alfred Victor, well, the lad was trying hard to get on in the world, perhaps he ought to be given a little help.

Jessie told her husband it was a fulfillment of all she had hoped for; she was convinced it would bring about the reconciliation between Alfred I. and his children that she had been working toward since her marriage. Accordingly, on July 15, 1926, his father sent the following letter to Alfred Victor, who was by this time working for Du Pont in Wisconsin:

My dear Alfred:—

I am writing for the purpose of ascertaining your views in connection with a plan which I have in mind for making additional provision for your comfort, instead of deferring such action until the probate of my Will. My health is excellent and, so far as

I know, my prospect of life is good, and I, therefore, am willing to make the following arrangement:

I will turn over to you the sum of $200,000.00 in cash, to be your own absolute estate and to be disposed of as you desire.

My object in making the offer in your interest is that you may now enjoy the use of the above sum, which I desire you to have.

I am making a similar offer to your sisters, Bessie and Victorine, and there is but one condition that I attach to the above, namely, that you all three agree not to enter into or encourage any litigation having for its purpose the setting aside, modifying or changing any provision of my Will.

This is not to be construed by you that I have concluded not to make any further provision for you in my Will but as to that I will exercise my own discretion and judgment.

If you are not familiar with the Trust Agreement entered into by me with your mother in September, 1905, I beg to advise you that, under the terms of this agreement, you will ultimately, that is, upon the death of your mother, be provided with an income from securities, which, at the present rate, would net you $8000.00 per annum.

Your consideration of the above is requested and a definite reply within a month.

What should he do? Alfred Victor's immediate instinct was to get the advice of his uncle P.S. before making any reply to his father's offer. He sent an urgent letter to Longwood asking "Dear Cousin Pierre" to tell him what to do. P.S. wrote back at once to say that he had given his nephew's news careful thought, and then proceeded to weigh all the pros and cons:

To refuse would be construed to mean that you intended to dispute your father's will, a position you can not assume without knowing the terms of the will. Moreover, I feel certain that you and your sisters have no desire to stir up ill feeling. Your father states clearly the object of the letter, it is proper to take him at his word and accept the gift in the spirit in which it is offerred [sic]. To do otherwise would seem to me ungrateful and expressive of a disbelief in his motives.

He added:

[321]

There is only one point on which I feel uncertain, that is one of fairness to your Mother. Your father treated her with unfairness and unnecessary harshness, I might well add with cruelty. She has replied with a dignity of position and calmness of spirit that has met with general admiration. If you feel it unfair to her that you should accept from him, your feelings would be respected and admired if they by chance became known but I believe there would be more opportunity for misunderstanding than for correct reading of your motives.

He went on:

Looking at things from another angle:— Your father has given you little assistance and, as far as I know, made no effort heretofore. What he now seeks to make over to you is not a very large sum, in fact might be considered less than your due. You can not be considered ungrateful if you should, in the future, fail to support him, an embarrassment that might be caused were the sum very large. . . .

On the whole, Alfred, I must advise you to accept. By doing so you give up any thought of breaking your father's will to your own enrichment, but this is a manly act that you will not regret in fact I doubt if, when the time comes, you would be willing to undertake a course that would cause much publicity of an unwelcome kind.

I hope that this offer of your father means a softening of heart towards his children for whom he has so far done unnaturally little.

My best wishes and love to you all in this perplexing situation, whatever you do I am confident, will be in earnest desire to act for the best of all without selfishness.

It was lucky P.S. had advised in favor of accepting, because by the time his letter arrived Alfred Victor had already done so. His sisters Bep and Victorine had telephoned him to say they had decided to take their father's offer and give him the pledges he asked for. Alfred Victor, afraid that his own reply would therefore seem tardy and diminish him once more in his father's eyes, had already scribbled a hasty note to Alfred I. thanking him for his offer and promising not to contest his will. All he could now do regarding his previous approach to P.S. was to write his uncle expressing the hope that he did not think it unwise of him to have accepted.

"When this money is paid," he added, "will you help me to invest it properly?"

Jessie was pleased at the way things had worked out. What she wanted to do now was bring her husband and his children back together again, not just through money but through friendly contact, and this she managed to achieve later that year. His youngest daughter, Victorine, announced that she had become engaged to a young man named Elbert Dent, and wrote to ask if she could come and show him off to Jessie. Jessie was shrewd enough to realize that it was not for her sake that her stepdaughter wished to introduce her young man. She knew that Vicky had always adored her father from a distance and longed to be reunited with him but had been inhibited by loyalty to her mother and Alfred I.'s obvious lack of interest in the welfare of his children.

Before she could talk to her husband about Vicky's approach, she heard that Alfred I.'s son, Alfred Victor, and his wife, Marcella, were due in Wilmington shortly. They were coming east to attend a big party Irénée du Pont was giving for one of his daughters at the Hotel du Pont. Why not invite both Vicky *and* Alfred Victor around for a reunion and make a date for the evening of Irénée's party? Alfred I. and his children might find the meeting hard going, and if so, Irénée's party would give the young people a good excuse for leaving early.

After some hesitation Alfred I. agreed to the invitation, remarking, rather grumpily, that he hoped his children would not stay much longer than fifteen minutes.

Just before nine o'clock on the night of April 22, 1927, the four young people arrived at Nemours and rang the bell of the great house. The door was opened by the butler/valet, Thomas Horncastle, who took their coats and then led them, his face expressionless, across the vast hall into the Louis XVI drawing room, indicating that they should wait while he announced them to his master and mistress. Elbert Dent and Marcella du Pont gingerly perched themselves on the edge of a gilded chaise longue, but Vicky and her brother remained standing. Instinctively, she reached over and grasped Alfred Victor's hand.

"Isn't this just like a scene in a melodrama?" she finally said in a strained voice, and all four of them broke into giggles.

Then Alfred I. and Jessie appeared. Her father walked directly across to Vicky and put his huge arms around her in a warm hug. Then he reached out and pulled Alfred Victor toward him, including him in the embrace. Presently Alfred I. broke loose to kiss Marcella and shake hands with Dent.

No one had said a word so far, and as Marcella recorded in her diary later, "it was pretty strained at first." But then Jessie got to work. Moving easily among them, filling up the awkward silences with warm and affectionate chatter, she gradually thawed her husband and the four nervous young people. Soon Alfred I. was teasing Marcella about the responsibilities of marriage and, in mock-heavy fatherly style, questioning young Dent about his suitability as a husband for his daughter.

Instead of fifteen minutes the meeting lasted until well after eleven o'clock, and the young people left only because Jessie gently remarked that their uncle Irénée might well be offended if they left it very much later. When they went to the door to depart, it was Alfred I. who opened it for them, warmly embracing both Vicky and his son as he bade them goodnight. To Alfred Victor he said:

"I want to see a lot more of you. Come again, soon."

Marcella later recorded that in the car, on their way to the Hotel du Pont, both her husband and Vicky wept.

"They were very happy," she said.

For Alfred Victor, who had been so deeply humiliated by his father, it must have been hard to believe that the reunion had actually happened.

"Now I know how the prodigal son must have felt," he said later.

Even before the reconciliation with his father, but after he had received the gift of money from him, Alfred Victor had sworn that he had no plans for altering his life or giving up his career with Du Pont. His mother believed him, but P.S. was more skeptical. Shortly after Alfred I. had paid two hundred thousand dollars into his son's account, P.S. received a letter from the young man, in which he expressed great dissatisfaction with his work, his workmates, and his prospects and said he was thinking of giving up his job. P.S. wrote in reply:

> I have given your letter of November 28th much thought and have consulted with Lammot on the subject. He agrees that you should not feel discouraged even though the situation is not at present to your liking. As far as I can find, your progress, knowledge and experience is [sic] recognized, and I think will eventually find its reward if you stay with the company. . . .

During my younger years I suffered many pangs of disappointment concerning possibility of advance. I am happy that I stuck to the job, even though after nine years I broke away for a short period. I recommend that you stick to it for awhile longer at least. I hope you will write to me again on the subject when you feel like doing so.

But Alfred Victor was not to be persuaded. Suddenly his life had changed and working at Du Pont now seemed unnecessary drudgery. His father's money had given him a feeling of independence. His father's changed attitude had restored his self-confidence and sense of belonging somewhere.

Toward the end of 1927 he finally resigned from the company and appeared at Nemours to ask his father—and not P.S.—what he should do next. Alfred I. was delighted to be consulted, and asked his son what he particularly wanted to do. Alfred Victor took a deep breath and then paused, as if hesitating before putting his father to the test. Then he said:

"I'd like to be an architect."

"In that case," said Alfred I., "we had better start making some arrangements."

Jessie recalled later that it was one of the happier moments of her life. She suggested that they all have a drink, and mixed herself an extra large Scotch.

It was through Alfred Victor's mother, Bessie, that P.S. heard the news. Alfred Victor did not have the courage to tell him.

CHAPTER 23

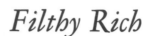

Filthy Rich

P. S. DU PONT was fifty-eight years old in 1928, and from then on, when asked to give his occupation in the forms he filed for tax purposes, he described himself either as "retired" or as a "conservationst and horticulturist." Officially he had stepped down from many of his functions at Du Pont, and he left to his brothers, Irénée and Lammot, the day-to-day decisions about finance and production. But he remained chairman of the board and kept a sharp eye on the management of the family money.

The 1920s were boom years for Du Pont, and dividends on the no-par-value common stock rose from $15.50 a share in 1926 to $19 in 1928, with earnings of $276.5 million in that year, the largest ever to be recorded by a single industrial corporation to that date.* Many other businessmen cast greedy eyes on such a phenomenally successful company, but P.S. had no fears of any threat to the family's control so long as he had the bulk of their shares tied up in the Christiana Securities. No one was allowed to own shares in Christiana except his immediate family and his trusted aides (like John

* That figure was not exceeded until after World War II.

Raskob). Raskob informed him that the British end of the global cartel, Nobel Industries (now known as Imperial Chemical Industries), which had come to P.S.'s aid in the early days of his takeover of General Motors by buying shares to bolster him, wanted to transfer those shares to Du Pont to benefit from the boom it was enjoying. P.S. agreed. He particularly wished to reward his good friend Sir Harry McGowan (later Lord McGowan), who was Imperial's chief and who often came to stay at Longwood. But when Raskob further suggested Imperial should be given shares in Christiana, P.S. emphatically refused.

He would not even allow Christiana's money to be invested outside Du Pont, and when Irénée and Lammot came to him with a proposition to purchase a large block of United States Rubber Company stock, he concurred, so long, he said, as the purchase was made "from our own pockets" and not from Christiana. In the meantime he tied up his global contacts even tighter by going into partnership schemes with his British and German associates. So far as Du Pont was concerned, the Germans had been welcomed back into the fold by the mid-1920s, when the company began granting patents to them for Du Pont products like shatterproof windshields and the new fadeproof Duco paint for automobiles. The next step was a three-way partnership, linking Du Pont, Imperial Chemicals, and BASF* of Germany, to market tetraethyl, the new booster for gasoline invented jointly by General Motors and the Standard Oil Company of New Jersey, which formed a company, the Ethyl Gasoline Corporation, to exploit it. Du Pont organized the global sales of this new firm.

Du Pont was also interested in discovering the process by which Germany was manufacturing its new synthetics in the factories rebuilt after the war. Because it was no longer possible to gain possession of such know-how by kidnapping chemists, the alternative was to "buy in." Luckily, the Germans were still desperate for foreign currency. For an expenditure of four million dollars Du Pont obtained a fourteen-percent slice of two of the biggest synthetic-making units in the I. G. Farben complex and thus had access to German advances in celluloid, cellulose, artificial silk, vulcanized fibers, and various viscose products. The labs in Wilmington promptly began using them as a base for experimentations of their own.

It was true that P.S. was devoting much of his time to what could be called extracurricular activities. He spent many hours in his conservatories and gardens at Longwood; his latest scheme was to electrify the fountains he had installed in the formal gardens, to regulate their flow by day and

* Badische Anilin und Soda-Fabrik, a subsidiary of I. G. Farben Industries.

illuminate them by night. In Longwood he now had one of the most spectacularly lovely estates in the nation, and he was gradually opening the house and grounds to the public for outdoor concerts (Gilbert and Sullivan) and garden parties in the summer, and recitals on the great organ in the winter. Many of the du Pont girls had their coming-out parties there, too, although Irénée, who preferred the Hotel du Pont for his daughters' coming-out parties, once complained, "The girls don't like it because the flowers are always so much more beautiful than they are."

Longwood was obviously P.S.'s home, but for tax purposes he was never prepared to admit it (Longwood was in Pennsylvania, where taxes and death duties are high), so he now kept a permanent suite at the Hotel du Pont for himself and Alice and registered them both as Delaware residents. As a result, he was appointed tax commissioner for the state and asked to revise Delaware's archaic tax laws. He evened up the tax burden somewhat by transferring part of it from the shoulders of the farmers and ordinary working people to those of the richer citizens, mostly du Ponts, many of whom promptly went to live elsewhere. But he did not tamper with the Delaware laws on corporate taxes or on death and estate duties, which, he remarked, "would be like cutting off my nose to spite my legatees." His other state preoccupations continued to be the pursuit of a better educational system for Delaware's children and the chairmanship of the state campaign against Prohibition, to which he was vehemently opposed, believing that it both encouraged rather than discouraged drinking and subsidized organized crime.

In addition to all this, he was at Du Pont headquarters in Wilmington at least four times a week when he was in Delaware, and went once a week to New York to consult John Raskob and Alfred P. Sloan, to whom he had handed over the presidency, about the affairs of General Motors. It was a busy life.

Alice saw less of her husband now, but she did not complain. The "nerves" from which she had suffered a few years earlier were under control. In the words of a young relative recalling her attitude, she was "steady, in charge, compassionate, and totally normal." And philosophical, no doubt.

As a result of his support for the forces fighting Prohibition, P.S. got involved with John J. Raskob in the presidential election of 1928. Aside from fulfilling his duties as chairman of the finance committee of General Motors and as a director of Du Pont, and having his financial finger in half a dozen other profitable pies, Raskob had also broadened his political interests. Now a well-known figure in the higher echelons of the Democratic party, he was well acquainted with Governor Al Smith of New York, and they had much in common, since both were dealers and manipulators, Roman Catholics, and enthusiastic wets. When Smith was nominated as Democratic candidate for the presidency against Herbert Hoover, he asked Raskob to mastermind his campaign, and Raskob eagerly accepted the challenge.

The night he agreed to manage Al Smith, Raskob returned to the Carlton House—where he and P.S. kept an apartment for their New York visits—with a bottle of champagne and a large chocolate cake for a "celebration." He knew P.S. doted on desserts, the gooier the better, and was equally partial to champagne. Presently he confided the good news to his friend, who congratulated him and then advised him to let Alfred P. Sloan of General Motors know as soon as possible, since this was a political job he had taken and a leave of absence from business might be considered necessary. Raskob said he would go to the General Motors headquarters at Fifty-seventh Street the following morning to tell Sloan all about it.

But next morning Raskob learned by telephone that his favorite son, William, had been killed while driving down to Wilmington from Yale. Raskob left for Wilmington at once, in deep distress, and forgot everything else for the next twenty-four hours. When he returned to New York on July 11, 1928, news of his appointment was in all the newspapers. That was how Sloan and General Motors first heard about it, and an angry Sloan demanded that Raskob resign at once from his chairmanship of the company's finance committee. Raskob maintained that he should only be expected to take a leave of absence, but Sloan vehemently disagreed, insisting that General Motors and partisan politics should not be mixed. He said he was issuing an immediate announcement that Raskob's resignation had been accepted.

When P.S. was informed of this, he handed in his resignation too. Sloan tried to persuade him to withdraw it, and when he refused, Sloan simply announced that he would not accept the resignation. But about Raskob he was adamant. Sloan made the following statement:

> General Motors is not in politics. It will not permit its prestige, its organization or its property to be used for political purposes.

P.S. deeply regretted the raw deal he felt Raskob had been given, and he almost immediately lost interest in General Motors affairs. After all, had it not been for Raskob, he would never have been involved to begin with. Quietly, he eased himself out of his job as chairman of the board, and though he remained a director, and Du Pont continued to be General Motors' main financial backer and beneficiary for several years to come, he never took part in its affairs again.

As for the presidential campaign, he gave all aid he could to Raskob and Al Smith. But neither his heart nor his mind was in it. After all, he was a lifelong Republican and had nothing in common with the honky-tonk razzmatazz of the New York Democratic machine. In addition, he was a quintessential WASP, and though he was prepared to pay lip service to the idea of a Roman Catholic president, he could not really stomach the prospect. He never said so, but he was almost certainly pleased when Hoover won and straightforward, honest-to-God Republican principles prevailed.

The Right Reverend Philip Cook had taken over as bishop of Delaware in 1920, and by the end of the decade he and his family were popular with everyone, including the du Ponts. Six feet three inches tall and a war hero, the bishop was young and good-looking (qualities he shared with his wife) into the bargain. Moreover, their three young daughters were delightfully pretty blondes, their four sons were well-mannered, and since Mrs. Cook had once been a roommate of Irene du Pont (Irénée's wife) at college, they were socially acceptable too. Every door was open to them. Bishop Cook earned an extra dividend because his birthday was on July 4, the day Irénée traditionally gave his great Fourth of July fireworks party, and henceforward the bishop was named guest of honor. The party was held on the grounds of Granogue, the great, ugly house Irénée had built for himself and his family on a hill just over the Pennsylvania border, and the host spent a considerable fortune on food, drink, and, of course, elaborate fireworks (for which, however, he demanded a rebate from the manufacturer, since, as he said, "we are both in the trade"). It had begun as a family gathering for about one hundred and fifty du Ponts and friends and gradually swelled to around five thousand, not counting those who gathered outside the walls.

By this time most of the du Ponts were filthy rich, even those members of the family who did not work for the family firm but only drew dividends from its profits. They used their money on various personal extravagances, some ostentatious and some tasteful. One spent ten thousand dollars installing a plumbing system for her kennel of pet dogs; another liked to boast she had never worn a raincoat, toted an umbrella, or put her foot down on "bare sidewalk" in her life, because she was always transported from carpeted doorway to carpeted doorway wherever she went. Some used their money wisely, others spent it wildly, and still others wielded it simply as an instrument of power. Inevitably, the extravagant spenders wound up in scandalous dilemmas. But they could count on either Bishop Cook or P.S. to be on hand when family matters needed straightening out, discreetly.

In P.S.'s generation it had usually been the du Pont males (such as William, Alfred I., and Coleman) who had kicked over the traces, defied family convention, or been guilty of some dreadful moral turpitude, but in the succeeding generation it seemed to be the du Pont girls who wished to thumb their noses at the rest of the family. One of the last of the du Pont males who should have been shocked at this was Philip du Pont, who had been quite a playboy in his time. But like many a reformed sinner, he had become puritanical in his later years and unforgiving of the transgressions of others. Philip was one of those former supporters of Alfred I. who had broken with P.S. and the syndicate during the 1915 controversy, but he had certainly not suffered for it—principally because he had inherited some ten million dollars from his mother, Eleuthera Bradford du Pont, who had sided with P.S. Philip proceeded to gamble his inheritance on the stock exchange, in between writing bad verse (he called himself poet on his tax returns), and by the twenties was worth fifty-four million dollars.

But the more money he made, the less he approved of "depravity and moral laxity," as he termed it, and when he discovered that one of his daughters was "morally weak," he was quite irate. Philip had two daughters by his meek and long-suffering wife. The youngest, Mary Jane du Pont, has been described by one of her contemporaries as having "not very much chin, very limp hair, a love for horses, a direct hook-up with the Lord, and an omnipresent sense of right and wrong. Her father adored her."

On the other hand, the elder daughter, Frances, was "a dancing darling, who climbed up on tables like Joan Crawford, and by age sixteen had developed a taste for bootleg gin, and boys and girls."

At a Wilmington party Frances fell for a handsome young man. His name was Richard D. Morgan, and he worked for the local telephone company. Shortly after her seventeenth birthday Frances came to her father to announce that she and Richard, then twenty-one, wanted to get married. She did not have time to mention that she was already pregnant, because Philip du Pont roared:

"Over my dead body. You're not going to marry anyone, especially a telephone lineman. You're a disgrace to the family."

At this, Frances swept out of the house, climbed into the driving seat of the family Pierce-Arrow, and took off for Rehoboth, the Delaware seaside resort, with Morgan in the back seat. Once arrived, she sent a message to her father via the bishop of Delaware:

> If you want me to have an illegitimate baby of which you'll be the grandfather, here I am. If and when you give your permission, we'll get married.

Bishop Cook took the message to Philip and asked him to face facts: This lovely girl, his daughter, was in love with this young man, and was, moreover, a tiny bit pregnant. Did he not think it was time to ask her to bring her young man home, and allow them to get married?

Philip reluctantly agreed, and Frances and Richard Morgan were married. But the father never forgave his daughter, and when he died in 1928, he left the bulk of his fortune (amounting to some fifty-eight million dollars) to his daughter Mary Jane and his alma mater, the University of Virginia. As for Frances, he cut her off with a mere two million dollars. That would teach her to shock the family!

It did not teach her at all, of course. After giving birth to two daughters in quick succession, Frances shucked off Richard Morgan and married a man from the theater, one Gordon Rust.

"They called Frances the 'Black Banana' in du Pont circles," said one of her friends, "and I leave it to you to work out the reason for the nickname. She used to go around upsetting everybody else's marriage. She would have bets with her husband, Gordon. She had this marvelous necklace of uncut diamonds, opals, and rubies, which she'd inherited from someone in the family, and Gordon would say at a party: 'I'll bet you this stone or that stone you won't get him into bed with you,' and he would pick out someone he knew was happily married. Then she would go up and make a dead set at the man, and she was quite a dish. What Gordon did with the stones he won I never found out—something pretty dreadful, I'm sure. Not that the Black Banana cared. She'd go to bed with anyone for a bet, male or female. I remember there was a big one with Lord Caernarvon, both here and in England. And then she started playing two of her friends, Joan Fontaine and Olivia deHavilland, against each other. She said it was marvelous fun."

By that time, of course, the bishop of Delaware had given up intervening. It would have usurped too much of his time.

Ironically enough, it was P. S. du Pont who was called upon to mediate in the case of Alicia Maddox Glendening—the child born to Alicia du Pont while she was married to George Maddox and having a violent affair with Alfred I.—and it was her husband who was complaining, not her father.

It will be remembered that shortly before his marriage to Jessie Ball, Alfred I. had sent Alicia (whom he still called Pechette), then sixteen years old, to Paris, accompanied by a chaperone, to study singing under Jean de Reszke. But the girl took after her mother and was soon adept at dodging her chaperone and going off on adventures of her own. In 1921 she met and fell in love with a young man named Harold Sanford Glendening. The son of a Connecticut mailcarrier, Glendening had won scholarship after scholarship to school and college and had finally gone to Oxford University as a Rhodes Scholar. Alicia wrote to Alfred I. and Jessie to tell them she wanted to abandon her musical career in order to get married, and since her mother was dead and Alfred I. was her guardian, would he give her his consent? The news worried Alfred I. He had settled a considerable fortune on Alicia himself and knew she had inherited a large sum from her mother, and he wondered whether young Glendening, who, after all, was from a poor background, was simply after her money.

He and Jessie therefore turned their honeymoon trip into a voyage to Paris, where it soon became apparent that Alicia was already having an affair with the young man. They talked to the couple and counseled them to wait a year or two, but Alicia was impatient. Since both he and Jessie liked Glendening and considered him trustworthy, Alfred I. finally gave his consent, and the young people were married. Alfred I. handed Alicia a check for fifty thousand dollars, and a gold locket from Cartier's marked "P" (for Pechette) as a wedding present, and all signs pointed to a happy marriage.

Then, in 1924, the couple returned to the United States, bringing with them their young son Alan. And almost at once the marriage seemed to go to pieces. When they first arrived, they were invited to stay at Nemours with Alfred I. and Jessie, and it was a disaster. Alicia seemed to have developed many of her mother's characteristics, and the realization must have given Alfred I. a sharp and unpleasant shock of recognition. She was willful, bored, unhappy, and viper-tongued. She not only nagged her good-natured husband but, when he refused to rise to the bait, turned upon her guardian's beloved wife. Alfred I. would brook no criticism of Jessie whatsoever, and the day he heard Alicia calling her "a peasant" and "an old man's darling" and worse, he angrily ordered the Glendenings from the house and announced that he would have nothing to do with them again. Jessie was unable to dissuade him, and so they were banished from his life.

When the marriage disintegrated and Alicia was reported to have gone to Reno, it was not to her guardian or to Jessie that her husband appealed but to P.S., who knew nothing at all about the situation until he received a melodramatic telegram from someone named Glendening, giving an address in New York City and the message:

WILL YOU PLEASE HELP ME SAVE MY SON FROM ALICIA. IF SO WRITE ME.

P.S. wrote back to say there must be some mistake; Glendening should perhaps be addressing his plea to Mr. Alfred I. du Pont at Nemours, Delaware. He was extremely embarrassed by the whole business and, in a note to his sister Lou, complained about being mixed up in "the questionable behavior of the questionable daughter of a questionable mother."

I think Alfred ought to be drawn in to it. After all, Alicia's his step-daughter—or is that the right term for her?

He refused to intervene, and eventually Alicia obtained a divorce in Reno. She subsequently married a Welshman named Victor Llewellyn and went to live in England. Neither her guardian nor her ex-husband ever forgave her.

Coleman du Pont relinquished his Senate seat in 1928, when it was obvious that his health would no longer stand the wear and tear, and it could hardly be said that his fellow members missed him. Nor did the nation. The citizens of Delaware would remember that he gave them a splendid road, the first real motoring road in the United States, but outside his native state few people realized he was responsible for U.S. Highway 13. He had fought a lifelong battle with various forms of cancer but had never once let them interfere with what he called his "unquenchable lust after good food, good drink and bad women."

Had he not been such a perennial optimist, Coleman would have been forced to recognize that of the three cousins who had so courageously joined forces back in 1902 to rescue Du Pont from failure, he was the one who had ended up with the least reward from the great adventure. It was his skill and braggadocio that had brought off the deal and launched the family company on its brave new era. Without his business flair—and his con man's sleight of hand—the venture would surely have foundered in those first few years. And what had he got out of it? Precious little compared with the vast fortunes his cousins had subsequently made. Even Alfred I., for all his stupid follies and reckless behavior, had restored his crumbling resources and become rich again. As for Cousin P.S., he now controlled two of the biggest organizations in the world, and such was the scale of his success that even his brothers, his in-laws, and his secretary were all worth more money than Coleman.

Not that Coleman was at a loss for the odd million when he totted up his resources. Of late he had not been too sensible in his investments, had lost a good deal of money in the Florida land boom, and had been forced to put his hotel holding company (Boomer du Pont Properties) into liquidation. But he could still rustle up ten to twelve million dollars in a pinch. The trouble was that in the eyes of other du Ponts, particularly his only surviving son, Frank, it was a trifle compared with what P.S. and Alfred I. had.

"Father," Frank had said to him one day, "why on earth did you sell out your Du Pont holdings? How could you have been so stupid?"

The only member of his family who did not look upon him with contempt or resentment was his youngest daughter, Renée, who loved him for himself.

His wife, Elsie, had never forgiven him for being absent on some amorous adventure in Florida, and untraceable, when their son Eleuthère had been taken ill at school and died at the age of eighteen. She now seemed no longer to care whether Coleman lived or died, and she stayed in New York or Wilmington while he lay suffering at Horn's Point, the farm in Maryland that he had bought for his retirement. A famous New York surgeon operated on him for cancer of the throat in 1928 and assured everybody who asked that Coleman, who was the world's most loquacious man, would soon be talking again. But by 1930 the hole in his throat had failed to heal, and he was suffering from tuberculosis as well.

This was the man who had been the jolliest du Pont of them all, full of tricks and high spirits, proud of his pretty girls, his Pierce-Arrow, from the back of which he distributed twenty-dollar gold pieces at Christmas, his New York police card, his senatorial office, his road. Now he lay in bed in a darkened room and tried to communicate with his visitors with his lips, or scribbled cheerful-sounding notes to his friends. None of his children, except Renée, came to see him, but his near neighbor John Raskob tried to keep him amused with a series of chatty letters. It was ironic, in the circumstances, that Raskob wrote him on August 26, 1930:

> I often think of you and want to run down and see you and have been on the verge several times but you have such a large family that it seems a shame to burden you with more calls. If, however, it is all right to come for a few minutes some day, I would like to do so. I am always down at Pioneer Point [the Maryland estate Raskob had bought for himself] on the Chesapeake weekends, and it is but a short run to Horn's Point Farm from there.

By the time that letter reached him, Coleman was really in no position to see anyone. His condition worsened in September, and he was in considerable pain. The only person allowed to visit him was Renée, and he made an effort when she arrived. Renée had taught herself to lip-read so she could understand what her father was trying to say, and they managed to exchange some merry if (on his part) silent remarks, until a comment from Renée would make Coleman choke with laughter and the nurse had to be called.

As Renée was leaving one day she said, "I wish there was something I could do for you, Dad."

Coleman looked up at her, trying to form words with his lips. Then failing to do so, he took up his pad and wrote on it:

"You can. Get a gun and shoot me."

He died in November 1930, leaving twelve million dollars to be divided among his family. His son, Frank, complained bitterly that it was a pittance compared with what he might have left had he held on to his Du Pont stock. The first thing Frank did after he went through his father's things was to take all his papers, letters, billets-doux, and make a bonfire of them in the yard. By destroying the evidence, he hoped to conceal the fact that his father had been a roué as well as a "poor" financial provider.

CHAPTER 24

---◆---

Floridian

ALFRED I. was snobbish only about his lineage. He liked to trace his ancestry back to the kings of France. When he and Jessie were in Delaware, they dressed formally each evening and dined in the great hall of Nemours, where a giant portrait of Louis XV hung on the wall, and Alfred I. often took pleasure in pointing out the likeness between himself and the supercilious monarch gazing down upon them.

In fact, his closest resemblance was to his forebear, Samuel du Pont, who five generations back had been a watchmaker in France. Curiously enough, Alfred I. had inherited his ancestor's fascination with clocks, and there were one hundred and twenty-nine of them in his Delaware mansion. One of his favorite rituals was going round them each weekend, "attending to the horlogerie," as he called it, winding, adjusting, listening to each clock until it ticked away to his satisfaction.

By the time Coleman du Pont died, Alfred I. had every right to feel superior. His cousin had left "only" twelve million dollars, whereas he estimated his own fortune as at least three times that sum, and probably nearer to forty million. And despite the depression, it was rising. That was mainly because he had the wisdom to follow the advice of his brother-in-law, Ed Ball, to invest in Florida.

The Florida he had chosen to put his money on was not, however, that stretch of the southeast coast along the Miami Beach strip where so many fortunes were made and lost in the 1920s. Jessie du Pont, in fact, had made a quick profit there by buying for $33,000 two small strips of land that she sold a few months later for $165,000. But that was before the crash came and land values slumped lower than the mud in the swamps the investors had been buying. Coleman confessed just before his death that he had lost millions in several misadventures in south Florida.

Ed Ball and Alfred I. favored the prospects further north, around Jacksonville and the Florida Panhandle, where the prospects seemed limitless and the land had been left untouched by the boom.

Alfred I. decided to become a Florida citizen shortly after his cousin P. S. du Pont became tax commissioner of Delaware. One of the first results of P.S.'s regime was the arrival at Alfred I.'s office in Wilmington of an assessor, who proceeded to go through his papers with ferretlike determination. Alfred I. was "all riled up at Pierre poking his nose into [his] affairs," as he put it, and he thought he knew why his cousin was harassing him. Alfred I. had recently aroused resentment among Du Pont's political interests in the state by lobbying to get a pension plan for old people through the Delaware legislature, and this had alarmed P.S. considerably, because of the potential expense to taxpayers in the family.

When he suggested, in a letter to his cousin, that a pension plan needed careful construction if it were not to prove too heavy a financial burden, Alfred I. scornfully replied that he himself was taking care of pensions for twelve hundred of the eight thousand aged and incapacitated people eligible for a pension in Delaware, and it was costing him three hundred thousand dollars a year. Indeed, he felt it shameful that a private citizen had to take over the rightful responsibilities of the state.

> [T]he state, in my opinion, should make provision for them and not transgress every principle of decency and every rule prescribed by the Christian religion by refusing them bread and clothing.

Then had come the visit from the tax commissioner's investigator, and it was too much for Alfred I. He announced he was changing his residency. He registered, under the laws of Florida, all his holdings (with the exception of Nemours) in two Florida companies, the Saint Johns River Development Company and the Brandywine Hundred Realty Company. Later he formed the Almours Securities and backed it with desposits amounting to thirty-four million dollars. From then on he was free from not only the prying eyes of his cousin and the Delaware tax collectors but also those of any tax collectors at all, for in those days Florida tax laws were liberal to the point of invisibility.

While Alfred I. stayed close to the telephone in Jacksonville and looked after the construction of a new home he was building for himself and Jessie on the outskirts of the city, Ed Ball took his Chevrolet and set out to traverse the neck of Florida and the Panhandle beyond, in search of likely land investments. It was wild country in those days. The paved road ended in Suwannee County and did not start again until Pensacola, more than three hundred miles away. In between was dirt road—rutted, tricky, bone-shaking when dry; a quagmire when wet.

Once this land had been a fertile zone of prosperity, with a great trade in lumber from the slash-pine forests and a thriving cotton crop grown in the clearings between. But the boll weevil had destroyed the cotton, wasteful lumbering methods and old-fashioned mills had slowed down timber production, and the roads had crumbled. It was the land of the poor Florida cracker and his humble farm, and all around were towns and villages gone to rot.

Alfred I. had told Ed Ball to buy up any likely land at up to fifteen dollars an acre. Ed soon sized up the situation. He saw that the timber forests were as rich as ever and knew there was a thriving market for them back in Wilmington. Du Pont had now become a busy producer of two new products, rayon and cellophane, and wood pulp was an essential ingredient of both. If they could only get the roads through, here was a practically endless source of supply.

With Alfred I.'s go-ahead, Ed started buying. Never once did he pay anything like $15 an acre. His first purchases, in Franklin, Bay, and Walton counties, plus the village of Carrabelle, on the Gulf coast, cost him something around $12 an acre, but after that he got tougher. By the 1930s he had bought up a large slice of northeast Florida amounting to some 466,747 acres, for which he paid an average price of $3.80. This territory stretched across the Panhandle as far as Apalachicola. Soon a railroad, the Apalachicola Northern, and a telephone and telegraph company were added, and development plans were begun for the restoration of one of the dying cities along the Gulf, Port Saint Joe.

It was a veritable kingdom, and what Alfred I. needed to make it viable was a banking system to finance its developments. He bought the Florida National Bank and appointed Ed Ball his lord chamberlain.

Mellow was now the word for Alfred I. No one watching him—whether aboard his new yacht, the *Nemenoosha,* cruising the Saint Johns River, a band of orphan children in tow, or in the ornamental gardens of his new Florida home, Epping Forest, walking hand in hand with Jessie—would ever have guessed that he had once been a wild man who stamped and roared with rage and frustration, inveighing against the world in general and against his du Pont relatives in particular. Marriage to Jessie had changed everything for him.

"My first marriage, as you know," he wrote to one of his daughters, "was a boy's marriage, with the outcome you also know."

> My second marriage was made very largely for the purpose of protecting a sick woman, who was persecuted by every human being who had every right to do the opposite. I failed in my first marriage and I failed in my second marriage. But thanks to Jessie, in my third marriage I succeeded.

He was still as romantically in love with her as ever. He even wrote her verses, scribbling in trains during their travels and passing his writings over to her, and watching her as she read them, blushing.

In 1928, when she was suddenly struck down in Baltimore and had to be rushed to the hospital for an operation, he sat in the waiting room and "faced up to the blackest moment of [his] lifetime," as he put it later, the prospect that Jessie was going to die. There was no chance of that. Jessie was carved out of long-living material, and no virus or ulcer was going to cut her down in her prime. Later, when she had recovered, he showed her the verse he had written in despair while waiting for news of her:

> Oh Beauty, thou flower of
> Unsurpassed fragrance,
> How brief is thy lifetime
> How fleeting thy breath,
> Today in the sunshine,
> Tomorrow the shadows
> Are casting their mantle
> In silence of death.

Jessie read it and laughed.

"You can't get rid of me like a sweet pea," she said. "I'm a perennial."

In 1929 he took Jessie on a convalescent trip to Europe, and they stopped off at Carlsbad, in Czechoslovakia, to take the cure. He made side trips to Munich to see his daughter Madie and her three children and invited his son, Alfred Victor, to come up from Italy where he was studying architecture. He gave daughter and son a Buick car each as a present and invited them all to join him back in Wilmington and Florida for a great reunion.

Before leaving America, he had begun to suspect that one day the booming stock market was going to bust, and in anticipation of any crisis he had given Ed Ball full power of attorney, as well as the right, at any time, to draw on his main investment corporation, Almours Securities, which now owned stock valued at $150 million.

On July 12, 1929, a run on Florida banks forced the closing of the Citizens Bank in Tampa, and fifteen others went with it. Soon banks all over the state were under pressure. Florida National, Alfred I.'s bank, had one of the biggest runs of all. Ed Ball showed his mettle by serving coffee and cakes to the long lines of waiting customers, figuring that the aggregate time it took for the clients to drink and munch would give him extra time to speed loads of money from branch to branch, as and when it was needed.

But the crunch came on July 22, when not even caviare on toast would have slowed down the clients in their demands for money. Ed Ball wired the banks in New York to send him fifteen million dollars against twenty million in Du Pont common stock held by Almours Securities. At the same time he wired Alfred I. in Europe to telegraph back his approval.

Alfred I. cabled back:

YOU'RE ON GROUND   USE OWN JUDGMENT BUT PULL OUR BANK THROUGH.

With this cable in his hand, Ed Ball drew up an announcement to the press, stating that Florida National had Alfred I.'s fifteen million dollars behind it and could withstand any run on funds that came along.

The word spread. By lunchtime the run was over, and Florida National depositors began to return. The $15,000,000 guarantee did not have to be touched, and by the time Alfred I. and Jessie arrived back from Europe, the $20,000,000 worth of Du Pont common was back in the strongbox of Almours Securities. At the worst moment of the crisis Florida National had lost nearly $5,000,000. By March 31, 1930, deposits were higher than ever before, at $20,238,180.19.

Time magazine gave credit to Alfred I. for saving the state from financial disaster. Alfred I. read the piece aloud to Jessie and her brother, then said:

"But we know better, don't we? They should have given the credit to a clever little man named Edward Ball."

Even P. S. du Pont and his brothers did not realize the major role Ed Ball had played in saving their cousin from disaster. At a meeting of the executive committee in Wilmington in 1932, Lammot du Pont proposed Alfred I. be asked back as a director of the company. It was unanimously decided to send him an invitation. When Alfred I. heard about it, he slapped his thighs with delight and said jovially to Jessie:

"What is it they find most attractive about me suddenly—my good looks or my money?"

He was tempted to accept, because ties with the old firm still tugged. But to Jessie's relief, he finally decided to turn down the offer. He wrote back to Lammot and proposed that one of his nominees should be elected to the board, in his stead, to look after his interests. He suggested Ed Ball. This proposal was coolly rejected by the company. Privately, Lammot was reported to have commented:

"We can't possibly have a type like Ed Ball on the Du Pont board. He's simply Alfred's brother-in-law and head ass-licker, a common little drummer."

When Alfred I. heard about the remark (for some kind friend on the Brandywine repeated it to him), it ended for all time any inclination he might have had to arrange a reconciliation with his cousins. He resolved never to mix with them again, and to confine all his correspondence with them strictly to the affairs of the Du Pont company.

By 1932 Alfred I. was indeed the strong man of Florida, and Ed Ball was his fixer behind the scenes. From a sixteen-room mansion on the outskirts of Tallahassee, known locally as the Highwayman's Hideout, Ed ran a lobbying organization that was solely devoted to the task of making the Florida legislature do exactly as Alfred I. wanted. What he wanted most at the moment was roads—roads that would link Jacksonville on the east coast to Pensacola on the other side of the Florida Panhandle, taking in all the isolated counties and Gulf coast ports in between. That was where Alfred I.

now owned land, and he wanted to develop it, for trade and for tourism, and especially for shipping timber from the great slash-pine forests that were now included in his fief.

Alfred I. had always been a curious mixture of ruthless robber baron and idealistic protector of the poor. In Delaware he had been a sincere and dedicated fighter for good government, universal education and scholastic opportunity, workers' insurance, and old-age pensions. But he had never let his ideals stand in the way of his drive for money and power. He had nothing but contempt for P. S. du Pont's "bloodless" attitude toward his workers, but when it came to a business recession, and the struggle began between Them and Us, he automatically moved to the same side as his cousin, whose moneymaking philosophy he shared.

During the great economic crisis of 1932 he had no doubt whatsoever how the situation could be remedied, and his was a simplistic solution, nothing like the all-in-it-together measures that President Franklin D. Roosevelt subsequently took under the New Deal.

"Were I dictator of the United States today," he wrote at this time,

the first thing I would do would be to cancel or repeal every bonus and every pension that might be termed as unearned, giving only to such as have suffered by injury or old age in the service. The next thing, I would visit every safe deposit box in the country and confiscate 50 percent of all the money I found in them; notify those who got the other 50 percent that, should the next visit disclose any, it would all be confiscated; and any discovered hoard outside the safe deposit box would result in a little shooting Bee. I would put every dollar to work in the country and in addition to that I would put every son of a gun, or daughter of a gun, back of that dollar and make them work.

I would have an island in the center of the Pacific Ocean, called Bum Island for people like some of our [du Pont] cousins who either refused to work or who were unable to work. I would have another island just out of reach, called Bummess Island, where all the ladies who were too fat to work or refused to work would be sent. Each would have a site where she could plant cabbages, turnips, beets and other necessities of life and keep alive if she wanted to, otherwise be thrown to the sharks.

Anyone who smoked more than five cigarettes a day would be sent to Dope Island, where they would join other inebriates, partakers of cocaine, opium, heroin, etc. They would be given plenty of poppy seed to plant. Trained sharks would be waiting nearby.

All Congressmen would be sent back home to go to work!

He added:

I would tax all sales about 2 percent, probably less, and I would get 2 billion dollars annually from taxing rum and another billion from cigarettes. If people want to have fun, or rather too much fun, they would have to pay for it. I am not yet certain whether I would tax babies or not, for the reason that I have not yet decided whether they are the direct result of fun!

And he concluded:

I certainly would have one dandy country to live in inside of five years.

Alfred I. was sixty-eight going on seventy in those years of the early thirties, a good-humored, benevolent-looking man, always bending down to pat the heads of children and give them money for a lollipop, gallant with the ladies, young and old alike, and never impatient when someone approached him with a hard-luck story. He could be genuinely kind and generous, and he could rightly boast that he had never turned a man or woman in need from his door. To hundreds of humble folk in distress he had always been a friend in need.

But in the world of Florida politics Ed Ball was his alter ego. It was Ed who cut the political corners, manipulated the smart deals, knew just which representatives to cultivate in order to stop a particular threatening piece of legislation in its tracks or drive a more favorable one through.

What Alfred I. wanted was roads—roads across the swamps and bayous between Suwannee County and the state capital, three hundred miles away. At the Highwayman's Hideout—with a white-gloved black servant dispensing bourbon and canapés, nubile college cheerleaders decorating the high-ceilinged, elegant rooms, and Ed Ball talking persuasively at the center of the throng—a powerful pressure group was organized. Called the Gulf Coast Highway Association, it proclaimed as its objective the building of roads across the sparsely-populated north portion of the state, and south from Tallahassee to Tampa and the Tamiami Trail. Everyone called it a Utopian scheme, especially so in a time of depression, and gave it no chance of ever being adopted. Because who would pay for this plan to open up the North? Why, the taxpayers of the heavily populated South, who would derive no real benefit from it.

They underestimated the strength of Ed Ball's formidable highway-man's lobby. His skillful maneuvering, Alfred I.'s money, politicians, and greed drove the scheme through the state legislature.* The result was that three main trunk highways were subsequently built: U.S. 90 from Pensacola to Tallahassee by the inland route through the bayous, swamps, and pine forests; U.S. 98 between the same points along the Gulf Coast; and U.S. 19 connecting Tallahassee with Tampa in central Florida. At the same time state funds were released to local cities in the area to begin construction of secondary connecting roads to provide a network of communications throughout the region.

There were grumbles from Southern legislators that most of the roads ran through Alfred I. du Pont's territory and would make all the difference to his lumber business. Now he could transport all the timber he could cut. The Northern pols were not worrying about that. They were getting their share. In fact, they were so grateful that they named one of the main bridges on the new Route 98 Alfred I. du Pont Bridge at the point where it spanned Saint Andrew's Bay at Panama City. Ed Ball had, of course, bought up Panama City for his boss, as well.

When it was all rammed through the legislature, Ed came to see Alfred I. and asked him what they should do next.

"Let's kill that proposal for a state income tax," said his boss. "It will keep moneyed people out of Florida, and it's money Florida needs."

The northern politicians duly killed the income-tax bill. After it was voted down, there was a celebration at the Highwayman's Hideout, and the representatives drank a toast of congratulation to "Mr. Ed." Alfred I. and Jessie were there, and a newspaper reporter asked them what they were going to do with the money they would save from the defeat of the bill.

"Every cent of it will go to our charity for orphans," said Jessie du Pont.

"And so will the rest of my money," said Alfred I.

Except for his deafness and the hunting accident that had lost him his eye, Alfred I. had never suffered from an illness in his life. If he called Jessie

---

* Which, under the voting system of the day, was controlled by the bloc of representatives from the North.

the Brid, she, when speaking to her sisters, referred to him as "my great big bull" and confidently predicted he would still be young and active when she had become "a respectable old lady."

But in the autumn of 1933 he suddenly collapsed at the wedding reception of his trusted aide. Ed Ball, after forty-six years of bachelorhood (though not exactly celibacy), had announced he was going to get married, and then presented his bride-to-be, an attractive young woman named Ruth Latham Price who had done some secretarial work for Alfred I.

"Yes, Ruth is a lovely girl," Alfred I. wrote to his sister, "but then you must not be surprised as I picked her for Ed."

Alfred I. and Jessie were the two chief guests at Ed's wedding, and at the reception afterward the groom drew his boss aside and confided to him that before going through with the wedding he had prevailed upon his bride to sign a marriage contract. It contained a number of clauses specifying what duties and obligations she would be expected to perform as Mrs. Ed Ball. He showed Alfred I. the document, which included clauses in which Ruth agreed not only to secure his approval of her dresses but to submit all her dress bills to her husband before paying them; to be "clean and tidy" in the presence of her husband, whether on public or private occasions, and never to be seen with her hair in curlers or her face "over-caked with makeup"; to refrain from forming close relationships with members of the opposite sex, and to limit her female friends to members of her own social stratum; and to refrain from "nagging, undue harassing or otherwise disturbing the smooth course of marital existence."

Alfred I. looked it through and then said:

"You don't mean to say she *signed* this screed?"

"I wouldn't have married her if she hadn't," Ed replied.

Alfred I. started to roar with laughter, then suddenly clutched himself and staggered. He had to be helped into another room, and a doctor was called. He was diagnosed as having suffered a mild seizure as a result of trying to laugh and swallow a mouthful of whiskey at the same time.

But he was really never the same again, and from then on it began to look as if Jessie's great big bull had been spavined.

CHAPTER 25

Harvesting

P. S. must sometimes have sorely envied the gregariousness of his brothers, Irénée and Lammot. They seemed to get so much more fun out of life than he did. As one of the richest and most powerful men in the nation, he should have been the last one to lack a close friend, but in truth there was not a single person in whom he could confide. John Raskob had gone off to play politics and build skyscrapers in New York and, in any case, had always been too deferential to his beloved Dad to be receptive to personal confessions; these would simply have revealed that his idol had feet of clay, and Raskob would have been embarrassed. Alice was not the answer because the gap between them had now widened to a chasm, bridged only by a span of surface politeness and concern, which swayed alarmingly every time it was buffeted by a difference of opinion or one of Alice's attacks of "nerves."

P.S.'s trouble was that he just could not unbend like his brothers, and none of his relatives would have dared to make the effort to help him. He had grown up as the father of the family, a role he could not shake off. Dad he would always be to the rest of them—and dads could not confess weakness and doubt.

Longwood Gardens was now one of the showplaces of the nation, and visitors came from all over the globe to see its orchids, its annual show of ornamental flowers in the great conservatory hall, its *son et lumière* on the grounds where the great fountains played. Distinguished guests were always coming to stay: Lord and Lady Melchett, Lord McKenna, and Lord and Lady McGowan from England; Herbert Hoover, Joseph P. Kennedy, the Mellons, John Foster and Janet Dulles, Charles and Anne Morrow Lindbergh, the Dwight Morrows, and scores of other political and financial leaders. P.S. and Alice moved easily among them, looking happy and serene. But the moment they were alone, they went their separate ways, and often P.S. repaired to his study to play checkers with one of his gardeners or his chauffeur.

As if to underline the way in which everyone was apt to put him on a pedestal, some anonymous donors, P.S. learned, had decided to finance the erection of a statue of him in downtown Wilmington, and he was deeply embarrassed. There was a statue in Wilmington of President Garfield with his hands behind his back, clutching a scroll; that statue had always aroused the derision of the du Pont cousins, P.S. included, in their childhood. The family joke was that the president had just emerged from the lavatory and was absentmindedly still clutching the toilet roll. P.S.'s shrewish cousin, Marguerite (Alfred I.'s sister), remembered this when she read the news of P.S.'s statue in the newspapers, and she promptly sat down to write him a letter:

> *My dear Pierre,*
> Visions of a Garfield in a long frock coat, done in bronze, standing in front of Granny's church on Delaware Avenue, arose from the misty past when I read in the [New York] Times— neatly framed—that you too are to be immortalized in the streets of our native borough! My dear Pierre, do beseech the sculptor to spare you and me, that roll of toilet paper you will recall our late lamented President grasped gracefully in one hand at the middle of his back! In the meanwhile accept my sympathy in this hour of your greatness.

[348]

P.S. wrote back:

Dear Marguerite:

A determined stand has, I believe, prevented the calamity foreseen by you in the possibility of my elevation to a pedestal in Wilmington. I have used every threat save that of application of dynamite to stop the project, which, I think, is successfully buried for all time. . . . Your sympathy is nonetheless appreciated because of the change in affairs.

The fact that Irénée and Lammot du Pont had now reached the eminence of president and chairman of the board of the Du Pont company (P.S. had taken over the chairmanship of the finance committee and still controlled Christiana) did not inhibit them in their enjoyment of the spoils of riches and power.

Irénée had never suffered any of P.S.'s reticence with pretty girls, and his pleasure in the enjoyment of them increased with the years. As early as the 1920s he had discovered a taste for caviare and delightedly reported to John J. Raskob, "It makes wonderful bait to attract the 'chickens.'" But as time went on, he offered bigger bait, and prettier and prettier fish swam into his net. In the twenties and thirties, most of his parties were held at Granogue, the family mansion, and that meant his flirtations inevitably came under the pained, long-suffering eye of his wife, Irene, and one or the other of his daughters who were just coming out or beginning to be married.

"Irene was a saint," said one of the regular guests at Granogue. "I mean saint in the Protestant sense of the word. She was devoted to her church, she was devoted to her children, and she was bewildered by her husband's interest in other females. He was a marvelously gay character and he had girls all down the block and she knew it. She was hurt by it, and no modern wife would have stood it. But in those days, at least in our circle, wives were brought up differently. If your husband went off and did those crazy things with other women, well, you waited until he decided to come back to you—which in Irénée's case, he always did."

One by one, eight daughters were given coming-out parties at the Hotel du Pont, with a Meyer Davis orchestra playing and limitless food and drink until dawn. One by one the girls were married at Christ's Church.

"That's all Irénée's daughters did," said their friend. "They just got married. Irénée gave each of his sons-in-law exactly the same wedding present—a million dollars and a job with the company. The only one who turned down the million was Crawford Greenewalt, who married Margaretta, and he was already working for the company, and not in any drag job, either."*

But as his daughters departed from the family estate, there were fewer excuses for parties, and so Irénée decided to broaden his horizons. In the late 1920s he bought four hundred and fifty acres of forest and bayou in Varadero Province, ninety miles southeast of Havana, Cuba. There, at a cost of three million dollars, he had James H. Guthrie construct a great house on a bluff overlooking one of the loveliest beaches in the Caribbean, which could be reached by elevator from the cliff. One of the features of the house was a great organ (Irénée also had an organ at Granogue), for which he had piano rolls of music especially adapted so that it could play automatically for dancing. The ballroom, with a floor of Carrara marble, was in a rooftop mirador with a sensational view across the Bay of Gardenas, and the organ dance music was piped through from below. There were also a nine-hole golf course carved out of the thick forest, a small cluster of houses for the Cuban staff (numbering two hundred), a pipeline for fresh water from across the bay, brought in at a cost of six hundred thousand dollars,** and, on the lawns, a dozen tame iguanas imported from Panama for the amusement of the guests.

He called his Cuban retreat Xanadu, and it was, in truth, a "stately pleasure dome." Irene was allowed to come over to stay for one short period every year, and on these visits she brought a few friends with her. But otherwise it was for "men only," which did not, of course, mean that it was without feminine company. There are more than a few once-famous American beauties who were regular visitors to Xanadu and who have prospered from the trust funds Irénée subsequently made over to them.

"He wasn't exactly harmless, but a girl didn't have to take anything she didn't want from Uncle Buss," said the daughter of one of his contemporaries. "He liked to get a nice seventeen-year-old girl and ask her down to the basement to look at the pipes in the organ, but all she had to do was yell when he made a pass at her and it was over. There were always lots of fathers around Wilmington who said they wouldn't let their daughters go to Granogue because Uncle Buss was such a roué, but I can't believe any girl

* "Drag job" was the family description for a du Pont who had been given a job for which he had no qualifications.
** Irénée tried to quell local resentment of his extravagance by arranging fresh-water outlets across the bay for the use of fishermen.

was naive enough to accept an invitation to Xanadu without knowing what she was getting into. I admit that when you're young and are wearing short shorts with brown legs, you don't think what effect it can have on a susceptible mature man. But if he walked into your bedroom with no clothes on and you told him to get, he *got.* Even at Xanadu. But I don't know any of the girls who later regretted it—not financially anyway—when they didn't say get. Of course, nobody ever brought up what went on at Xanadu with Irene. She would have maintained she didn't know what you were talking about. Her philosophy was, if you keep on ignoring something, it'll go away. And I guess in the end it did. But not till Irénée got to be a very old man."

On the other hand, he could be extraordinarily understanding when the sons and daughters of his friends had problems of the kind they could not take back to their parents and would never have dared to broach to P.S.

"He might not give you the advice you wanted to hear," said one of his young friends, "and he was apt to scoff at problems, any of which, he seemed to infer if you were a girl, could be solved if you acted feminine and got married. But the valuable thing was that he listened, and he was sympathetic. And he could be extraordinarily generous even if you were one of those girls who never let him get beyond patting your fanny. One Christmas he gave me and my sister two hundred shares each in United States Rubber. When he handed me mine, he said, 'I think this should give you enough dividends each year to buy yourself your own Christmas present, a nice vacation, maybe.' When the first year the shares didn't pay a dividend at all, I got a letter from Uncle Buss saying he was embarrassed that United States Rubber had let him down; it should have paid a dollar a share, and therefore he was sending a check for two hundred dollars." She added: "Do you know what? They subsequently split those shares, and I gave each of my sons two hundred shares, and it paid for their education through school, and they sold it for their college tuition and other things. We got one thousand shares out of it in all. Can you imagine what he must have given his real girl friends?"

In between his sessions at his Cuban pleasure dome, Irénée du Pont did well by the company. He guided Du Pont through some tricky financial crises and kept it afloat and paying a profit even during the depths of the depression, when, for the first time in decades, the shares plunged down to par.

P.S. had supported the election of Franklin D. Roosevelt mainly because he had pledged to bring Prohibition to an end, and as a reward the president made him first a member of the advisory board and then of the National Labor Board of the National Recovery Administration. But P.S. did not really care for Roosevelt's financial policies, particularly his failure to balance the national budget, and gradually he began distancing himself from both the president and the Democrats and seeking out his old Republican acquaintances again. His complete break with the Democrats came when a Senate committee, headed by Gerald Prentice Nye, began an inquiry into the big armaments companies and chose Du Pont as its principal scapegoat. P.S. complained bitterly that the evidence had been completely loaded against Du Pont's wartime policies, and asked how Roosevelt could have allowed a friendly firm to be so unfairly pilloried.

Irénée, who from the start had never concealed his dislike of the Democrats, especially Roosevelt, shrugged his shoulders. But when the fall-out from the Nye committee's hearings spread across the nation, and Du Pont began getting nasty letters from the public, it was Irénée who appointed himself the company's chief apologist. To one college debating society, which wrote him that it proposed to discuss the banning or restricting of Du Pont activities, he answered:

> First, let me say that the Du Pont Company were munition makers during the World War; the largest munition makers in the world during that period. They made approximately one-half of all the smokeless powder used by the Allies, including Russia, Italy, France, England and the United States. We thought we did a swell job, especially as notwithstanding the fact that every raw material at least doubled in price, we were able to reduce the cost of powder until we were selling it at 20% below pre-war prices. . . .
>
> The company did make a very large sum from the foreign governments from the sale of munitions. When the United States went into the War, the profits were reduced to substantially a nominal amount, with the entire accord of the management of the company. Incidentally, the taxes paid by the company to the United States Government in 1917 were greater than the profits on their U.S. business.

Irénée could not help adding a fact that had particularly embittered P.S. during the Nye committee's inquisition of Du Pont: that the company was no longer engaged in making munitions, anyway. In his words:

Since the War, the munitions business of Du Pont Company is almost negligible. Immediately after the War we demolished 98% of our smokeless powder manufacturing capacity and would have destroyed the other 2% excepting that with the advice of the United States government officials we preserved it and concurred in their thought that it was desirable to maintain a nucleus so that in case of war the art would not be forgotten.

Lammot du Pont was the only one among his brothers and sisters to marry more than once. Caroline Hynson Stollenwerk, wife number three, was a divorcée from a fashionable East Coast family. She made it clear from the start that she thought she was doing the du Ponts a favor by marrying into them. She was fond of quoting Cornelius Vanderbilt's contemptuous remark:

"The trouble with the du Ponts is they're so pathetically provincial."

Caroline du Pont decided she was going to change all that and, in particular, change Lammot, who, poor lamb, was just too unsophisticated for words.

In a way she was right. A humble and unassuming man, Lammot was a fine chemist, though he deprecated his abilities and many times remarked:

"If there weren't a lot of men in the Du Pont company who know more than I know, the company wouldn't last long."

Unlike P.S., he did not have a passion to make the countryside bloom. Unlike Irénée, he was not devoted to fireworks. He did not collect cars or hummingbirds or shells or racing stables, as some of his relatives did. True, he had a sailing yacht, but it was a modest one. Modest was the word for the way he lived, riding his bike, chopping his wood, watching over Du Pont developments with a dedicated devotion. Until Caroline Hynson Stollenwerk came along, that is.

"And then Lammot absolutely lost his mind," said one of his relatives. "Caroline blinded him. She was soon wearing enough diamonds to blind everybody, in fact. She decided she ought to introduce Lammot to the social swim, and she started throwing parties for him, for everybody who was anybody on the East Coast. She arranged parties for him in New York of the kind that make your head spin, and soon she had him so jazzed up he started acting like a playboy—Lammot, a sober, middle-aged businessman who symbolized America's dedication to the work ethic! She got him off his bicycle and into flashy limousines. There even came a time when he started giving his female guests presents at their dinner parties—souvenirs like flawed emeralds, that sort of thing. Can you imagine? Lammot, who kept mothballs in his wallet to stop his money from being eaten away!"

Of course, it did not last long.

"The whole thing was a good blast for a year," said his relative. "It should have been a weekend. With Irénée, it would have been."

Caroline Hynson Stollenwerk du Pont departed via the divorce court. Lammot dug his bike out of the shed and vowed he would never get married again.

"But bachelors have never really been safe in the du Pont family," his relative said. "There are too many cousins, and cousins of cousins, around who have them all staked out."

It was a cousin of a cousin who became Lammot's fourth wife.

Shortly after the advent of Adolf Hitler and National Socialism in Germany, Alfred I.'s daughter Madie arrived in America from her home in Munich with her third husband, Hermann Ruoff. Her father and Jessie entertained the couple both at Nemours and at their Jacksonville home, Epping Forest, and brought the other members of the family together with them for a series of happy reunions.

Alfred I. was worried about Europe. He had seen something of the Nazis during his last trip to Germany, and he heartily disliked the philosophy Adolf Hitler was preaching. He had some quiet talks with Madie's new husband and urged him to move himself and his family to America, where the future looked more secure. Ruoff, a reasonable and intelligent young man, had his own fears about the Nazis and was inclined to agree that such a move would be wise. But when Madie heard about it, she was furious. Under no circumstances would she consider leaving Germany, especially now that the Germans had a leader who could rid the nation of its "rotten elements." She proudly showed her brother and sisters snapshots of her sons back in the Reich, one dressed in Brownshirt uniform and the other in SS uniform. They had dedicated their lives to the Führer, she said, and she would never leave them. The Ruoffs sailed back to Europe in 1934, and Alfred I. accepted the fact that he had lost them to Germany for good.

Although he seemed to have no inkling that his life was nearing its end, he spent his seventieth year concentrating on personal affairs and left most of his business dealings to Ed Ball. He made many journeys back to Delaware from Florida and spent much time overseeing the completion of the great ornamental gardens he had ordered for the grounds of Nemours. Behind the nine-foot wall of the estate its three hundred acres had been transformed; water from a tributary of the Brandywine had been piped in to form a series of lakes, and the vista of water and shrubbery that now spread out from the terraces of the great house reminded visitors irresistibly of Versailles. That was hardly surprising, since one of the architects of the garden was Alfred I.'s son, Alfred Victor, who had done his studying in Paris and Rome and had now gone into partnership with Gabriel Massena, an architect who had also studied in those cities.* Alfred I. waited until they had designed and built a so-called Temple of Love against the boundary walls, then he erected two great iron gates to complete the approach to the house. One pair, known as "Kate's gates," had been made for Catherine II of Russia by the French ironworker Tijon. The other pair came from Wimbledon Manor, England, and had at one time been given by King Henry VIII to his sixth wife, Catherine Parr.

The lavishly furnished house and the elaborately planted gardens were a prop to Alfred I.'s pride, and he was convinced that everything about the great estate was superior to the trappings of Cousin P.S.'s Longwood. Since he was never invited to visit Longwood, he was never disillusioned on that score.

But if Nemours salved his pride, it did not give him the same satisfaction as a walk down the hill to the entrance of the old Hagley Yard and its powder mills. For the Du Pont centenary of 1902 Alfred I. had built the great gates that led into the yards, but now, though they stood open, he did not pass beyond them into the yards themselves. Having been thwarted in his attempt to buy the old mills and the big house when they were closed down after World War I, he now obeyed the notice at the entrance forbidding "trespassers" to enter. But he liked to stand at the gates and gaze through at the few old wheel mills that were still intact; facing toward the rushing creek, they were shrubbed and moss-grown. And in his deadened ears he must have heard the sounds of decades past—of men shouting and great millstones grinding as he and his fellow powder men turned out the famed Du Pont black powder.

Back in Florida there were no such disturbing memories, and Jessie made sure that life at Epping Forest, on the banks of the Saint Johns River, was always serene. Each morning she walked with him down to the water's

---

* They also designed a home for the elderly at Smyrna, in lower Delaware, at a cost of $500,000 (paid for by Alfred I.), and a public school near Nemours for which Alfred I. also provided $150,000.

edge, and while a servant raised the American flag Alfred I. put a touch to the nearby cannon and boomed out to Jacksonville the news that another day had begun.

In January 1935 he called in his lawyers and began making alterations to the will he had written a couple of years earlier. He calculated that his fortune by that time amounted to some $67 million, of which $30 million would go in state and federal inheritance taxes when he died. He had always made it clear to Jessie and his children that he wished most of what remained to be put into a perpetual trust, which was to be called the Nemours Foundation for the benefit of the orphaned, the crippled, the old, and the poor.

"The Nemours Foundation," his will stated,

> shall be created and maintained as a memorial to my great, great grandfather, Pierre Samuel du Pont de Nemours, and to my father, Eleuthère Irénée du Pont de Nemours . . . for the purpose of maintaining . . . a charitable institution for the care and treatment of crippled children, but not incurables, or the care of old men or old women, and particularly old couples, first consideration, in each instance, being given to beneficiaries who are residents of Delaware.

He directed that a hospital for this purpose be erected on the grounds of Nemours, and that the house itself be used as an administrative building, with the grounds as a recreational facility. It would all be run on earnings from the money turned over to the foundation.

As to the rest of his fortune, he directed that the following should benefit from it:

First, his wife Jessie. She would receive the house, Epping Forest, in fee simple, plus all the furnishings and paintings at Nemours and all other personal possessions, together with an annuity of two hundred thousand dollars for life—this to constitute the first claim on the earnings of the estate. After all other bequests and annuities had been discharged, Jessie would also receive the balance of the estate's earnings during her lifetime.

Alfred I.'s four children by his first marriage would each receive five thousand shares of Almours Securities common stock, which would mean around seven hundred and fifty thousand dollars apiece.

He made no provision for his stepdaughter, Alicia (Pechette), who had once been his favorite child, because, he coldly stated, "Mrs. Victor Llewellyn is amply provided for under the Will of her mother." He left another one million dollars for the provision of annuities for his brother Maurice and various nephews; and he did not forget Ed Ball, who was also to be given seven hundred and fifty thousand dollars.

There. It was done. Sixty-seven million dollars (less taxes) disposed of on four sheets of notepaper.

On Saturday, April 27, 1935, Alfred I. got up at dawn as usual and walked slowly down to the banks of the Saint Johns River to touch off the morning cannon. But on Sunday no sound reverberated over Jacksonville. Alfred I. had suffered a heart attack that morning, and in the evening an oxygen tent was moved into his bedroom. Jessie went to sit with him, wearing a pretty green dinner dress she knew he liked. He opened his eyes around eleven o'clock but did not see her. Instead, though there was no one else in the room, he said:

"Thank you, doctors. Thank you, nurses. I'll be all right in a few days."

At twenty-two minutes past midnight, on Monday, April 29, 1935, he died.

Alfred I. du Pont was buried on the grounds of Nemours on May 3, 1935, at a service conducted by the bishop of Delaware, the Right Reverend Philip Cook, and all the du Ponts were there with two exceptions. Bessie du Pont did not attend. Nor did P.S. He gave as his reason the fact that one of the mourners was Secretary of War George Dern, a member of the Roosevelt administration, which he loathed. But that was really a poor excuse.

His relatives were surprised. P.S. had always been so thoughtful, kind, and gentle, they had not realized that so far as Cousin Alfred I. was concerned, he was an adamantly unforgiving man. But why? After all, had he not been the winner, all down the line?

Part Six

THE END OF
AN EPOCH

CHAPTER 26

Purity Hall

S OME time in 1927, when Lammot du Pont was still running the Miscellaneous Manufacturing Department of the company, concentrating on artificial leather and silk, cellophane, paints, preservatives, and other cellulose products, Dr. Stein, assistant head of the Du Pont laboratories, came in to see him. Under the regime of the company's chief chemist, Dr. Charles Lee Reese, Du Pont was no longer a pioneer in the development of new processes and products. The policy was to buy up the patents of the company's global partners, Nobel and I. G. Farben, and others and pay a royalty on their use while perfecting and improving them, and it was in the pursuit of this essentially secondhand activity that most of the staff at the labs were engaged. Even a big discovery like the ethyl additive for gasoline, which General Motors/Du Pont and Standard Oil had begun marketing, was near enough to an I. G. Farben additive to make the Germans believe for a time that the Americans had stolen it from them.

Dr. Stein worried about this. He told Lammot he thought it shameful a great organization like Du Pont was relying so heavily on the foreign members of the cartel, and that it was about time they employed chemists to do more than just fiddle around with other men's inventions. Why didn't Du Pont revive tradition and follow the example of Lammot's own father, Lammot du Pont, Sr., whose work in the company's labs had repeatedly resulted in discoveries that had changed the nature and the fortunes of the firm? What Lammot senior had done could be done again. There was a whole new synthetics field waiting to be discovered.

Lammot was impressed. He retired to his back yard to chop wood and think it over. At the next meeting of the executive committee, he persuaded his two brothers that there was a need to adapt their research policy. They finally agreed to finance a new wing, which would be added to the company's General Research Station. Here chemists would concentrate not on finished or half-finished products, not on improving the company's lines, but on fundamental research. Their quest would be for new processes rather than new materials. Their budget would be large, but no specific targets nor time limits would tie them down.

The new wing, once it was erected across from the Du Pont experimental station in Wilmington, became known as Purity Hall—because of its dedication to pure research—and its chemists were inevitably called the Virgins by the old pros working at their test tubes across the way.

To Purity Hall in 1929 came a young man who, in the next decade, was to fulfill Dr. Stein's wish by changing the nature and the fortunes of the Du Pont company all over again. He was an owl-eyed, haunted-looking fellow named Wallace Hume Carothers, and what he did at Purity Hall was discover nylon.

By the 1930s there were a number of synthetic materials around, and probably the best-selling among them were artifical silk, cellophane, and rayon, all of which Du Pont manufactured. Thanks to the work of the General Research Station, the company had vastly improved the quality of these products. The Du Pont chemists had, for instance, taken cellophane and done with it something that its French discoverers had failed to do— make it waterproof.

But all these artificial products, as well as the cushion materials Du Pont made for cars, its paints, glassware, preservatives, were either viscose or cellulose products, which meant that their basic ingredients were derived from plants or natural raw materials processed and developed in various patented ways. No one had so far produced a totally *synthetic* material, conjured up, so to speak, out of the air. But chemists believed it was possible, and many dreamed of one day bringing it about.

Among them was Wallace Carothers. Born in Burlington, Iowa, on April 27, 1896, Carothers came from a family of Scotch immigrants, and perhaps because there were crofters (tenant farmers) in his background— of the kind who weave Fair Isle sweaters and Hebridean tweed—in his teens he became fascinated with fibers and pondered the possibilities of imitating them in the chemistry lab. The eldest of four children whose parents had no money to spare for fancy education, Carothers peddled fruit, swept snow, and had a paper route to pay his way through Tarkio College, Missouri, during World War I. In 1920 he won a scholarship to the University of Illinois, where he specialized in organic chemistry, and from then on he knew exactly where he was going.

He was teaching at Harvard in 1926 and, although only thirty years old, was already regarded as a chemist and innovator with a brilliant future (though everybody admitted he was a "lousy teacher"); he was beginning to attract attention because of his investigations into the nature of polymers and long-chain molecules.

In 1928, with Purity Hall established and a liberal budget provided for its operation, one of its most brilliant chemists, Dr. Julian W. Hill, began looking around for a man to head the department of organic chemistry. The head of the chemistry department at Harvard, James B. Conant,* spoke so highly of Wallace Carothers that Hill sought him out. The young man did not seem to be interested in the large salary Hill offered him, but his attitude changed when it was pointed out that at Purity Hall he would be working on a practically unlimited budget, and that pure research was the object of the exercise.

Carothers found the prospect of having his own laboratory and complete financial and professional freedom too much to resist. He signed on with Du Pont. And right from the start, as his bosses had hoped, he set himself a goal, a target.

What Carothers was setting out to do, in layman's language, was experiment in the test tube with the so-called giant molecule and persuade it to imitate the process by which a spider spins his web or a silkworm produces silk.

"If a silkworm can do it," he once said, "why can't I?"

Working in close collaboration with Julian Hill, he took only two

* Later president of Harvard.

years to get the results he was seeking. Or some of them, anyway. Around 1930 the two chemists produced synthetic fibers that actually stretched. With tweezers, Julian Hill pulled out of a test tube a blob of the thick, viscous liquid with which they had been experimenting and absentmindedly held on to it while he was called across the room. After he had taken a few steps, he turned to find Carothers staring at him: The thread, like a strand of molasses, had not broken. It hung in the air like a filament from a spider's web, shimmering in the reflection of light. They touched it, and it stayed whole; they pulled it, and it stretched and was flexible. Had they made the breakthrough and come up with a rival to nature, a genuine synthetic? Not quite.

On September 1, 1931, there was a meeting of the American Chemical Society at the Statler Hotel, in Buffalo, New York, and two of the main speakers were Dr. Wallace Hume Carothers and Dr. Julian W. Hill, who discussed their work at Du Pont's experimental station in Wilmington. In the course of their remarks to a group of organic chemists, they mentioned that as a result of their experiments they had produced "a clump of filaments rolled into a small ball and compressed [which] showed a remarkable springiness resembling wool. In their elastic qualities these fibers [were] very much superior to any known artificial silk."

The next day the New York *Times* announced, "CHEMISTS PRODUCE SYNTHETIC 'SILK.'" On September 14, 1931, *Time* magazine published a story under the head "CASTOR OIL SILK," saying:

> By heating castor oil and an alkali and mixing the result with the motor antifreeze compound called ethylene glycol, Wallace Hume Carothers and Julian W. Hill, Du Pont chemists, produced an artificial silk fiber. Theirs is an entirely synthetic fiber. Rayon is natural cellulose processed by machine in imitation of the silk worm's processing cellulose for its cocoon. The Carothers-Hill fiber is as lustrous as real silk, stronger and more elastic than rayon fibers, as strong and elastic as real silk. [But] it is expensive to manufacture commercially and it is mainly a demonstration of chemical knowledge and skill.

But the fiber was not quite as good as *Time* magazine seemed to imply. Carothers soon found that after about six week the material began to disintegrate. Hot water melted the fibers, and so did ironing. More experimentation was in order before it could be called a viable discovery. Wallace Carothers was completely uninterested in whether these synthetic fibers could be turned into a product. That they might one day be marketable was of no concern to him. But he was still passionately determined to show he could do what a silkworm could do, and do it as well. It was for that reason that he went back to the test tube. He discarded these first polyesters and started all over again.*

Wallace Carothers was a workaholic who thought nothing of putting in a straight thirty-six hours at the Du Pont labs, forgetting about food, drink, sleep, in his obsession with what was going on in his test tubes. When he emerged into the daylight he was apt to be moody, remote, or abrupt, and around the experimental station it was said that he had a bad case of nerves. A fellow chemist confided that one day he had run across Carothers in the toilets, where he was staring at a small phial in the palm of his hand. When asked what it was, he said:

"It's cyanide. I carry it around with me all the time. One day I'll use it."

He confined his social life to the circle of chemists with whom he worked, his favorite hosts being Julian Hill and his wife. Polly Hill was a gardener, and Carothers sometimes toured the flower beds with her to look at her blooms and discuss cross-pollination. He did not seem to go in for girl friends. His interest in the opposite sex was confined to his sister, Isobel, who was famous in those days as a member of the singing trio Clara Lu and Em, which performed on the radio. Isobel was Lu, and Wallace, whose musical tastes were otherwise strictly classical, never missed one of her programs if he could help it. He once remarked that all other girls paled in comparison to Lu and added:

"If she wasn't my sister, I'd have married her."

Most of the Du Pont chemists with whom Carothers worked not only were distinguished in their profession but also came from the kind of milieu a Middle Westerner of his background could never have encountered back home. They taught him the joys of symphony concerts and theater, good food and fine wine, and he was so appreciative that soon their wives were vying with each other to feed him exotic dishes, introducing him to his first pâté de fois gras, his first caviare, shrimp cocktails, avocados, and crepes suzette. From then on, when he remembered to eat, he ate only the best. Julian and Polly Hill would sometimes come back from a journey to find

---

* Two English chemists began working on them and some fifteen years later developed what became known as Orlon and Dacron.

the door of their house open and Wallace Carothers inside, sprawled on a couch with a jar of caviare and toast, a glass in his hand, an empty and a half-full bottle of Niersteiner beside him, and Mozart playing on the phonograph. Locked doors never deterred him.

With the Hills, at least, he demonstrated he was not always introverted, brooding, and lacking in a sense of fun. Once when Polly was away, Carothers telephoned Julian, who had invited him over for dinner, to say that he would be bringing the hors d'oeuvres. One of the other guests remembers how Carothers entered the room, his eyes gleaming, clutching a box that, he said, contained "rare Pacific molluscs," which few people had ever tasted before.

"Wallace said they were absolutely delicious, so long as they were cooked properly," she said, "but if a mistake was made they could be ruined. He then took us all into the kitchen and instructed Julian to take a pan of water in which he would add a cupful of soy sauce. The secret, Wallace said, was to bring it to the boil but *not to a raging boil*. That was important. So Julian did as he was bid, got the pan of water and soy simmering nicely, at which point Wallace opened his package and took out what looked like scallops and told Julian to drop them in the pan. 'But for God's sake don't let them boil madly,' he beseeched. 'Gently, gently, gently.' So we all watched with bated breath while the scalloplike fish floated around for a bit in the pan, looking most peculiar, I must say. Then Wallace signified that they were done and we must sit down at once and sample them. So we put a heapful on each plate, adjourned to the living room, and between sips of our martinis sampled these exotic and rare fishes from the Pacific. Ugh!"

What Wallace had done, in fact, was produce the first synthetic sponges for Du Pont and brought them straight from the Wilmington lab, having first cut them up into scallop shapes. His face was a picture of delight as he watched his host and the other guests chewing, nodding politely, then chewing again, until they desperately spat them out.

"It was Wallace's way of getting nicely back at us," said one of the guests, "for having lifted our patrician eastern eyebrows the first time he had eaten caviare with us and pronounced it 'fishy.' "

In 1935 Carothers achieved his breakthrough—he came up with a new material. Made from acetylene polymers and their derivatives, it had qualities uncannily like those of rubber. It would stretch and revert to its original condition. It was hard wearing. Du Pont was delighted. Carothers had laid the foundation of a new substance that was to revolutionize the motor industry and save the United States from disaster during World War II, when supplies of raw rubber were cut off by the Japanese conquests in Asia. The new substance, named neoprene, was so akin to rubber that it was hard to tell the difference. P.S., Irénée, and Lammot, who had bought large stocks in United States Rubber, made an additional fortune for themselves as a result of neoprene.

Nor did Carothers stop there. He and Julian Hill refined their processes and came up with sensational results—an altogether more refined kind of fiber. It had all the toughness of cotton, all the delicate fineness of silk, and, when woven, all the qualities of the best silken cloth. As the discovery became known, there was jubilation at Du Pont and admiration throughout the academic world. Though still under forty, Carothers was elected in 1936 to be the youngest member the National Academy of Sciences, and its first organic chemist. Invitations flowed in from colleges all over the world, offering him distinguished academic positions with their own scientific departments attached. He said no to all of them.

Meanwhile Du Pont geared up to manufacture this amazing new fiber. A hard-wearing cloth had been produced from it, and also a pair of remarkably gossamerlike synthetic silk stockings. Lammot boasted to his brothers that the possibilities were limitless.

"But what are we going to call it?" he asked.

It was a question to which Wallace Hume Carothers never heard the answer. Early in 1936 word reached Wilmington that Wallace's beloved sister, Lu, had died of a heart attack. A childhood bout of rheumatic fever had left her vulnerable. The shock to her brother was staggering, and he seemed neither to reconcile himself to it nor recover from it. For days he wandered around Wilmington like a lost soul, walking through the streets with tears streaming down his face; he often got drunk and neither bathed nor shaved.

After three weeks Carothers turned up again at the labs and resumed work. And then a strange thing happened. Four weeks after his sister's death he told Julian Hill that he had got married. He produced his bride, a Wilmington girl named Helen Everett Sweetman who worked in the experimental laboratories.

For the next twelve months there were all sorts of rumors about Carothers and his wife. He was said to have begun an affair with another woman with whom he was madly in love, but was meanwhile still living at home. In the spring of 1937 Mrs. Carothers announced that she was pregnant.* When her husband learned about it, he seems to have suffered almost as profound a shock as that he had experienced when his sister died. It was compounded when the woman with whom he was having an affair told him she did not propose to leave her family and marry him.

He still came to the laboratory and still pored over his polymers. "But really, he wasn't doing anyone any good," a fellow chemist said. "He was just like a zombie. I have never seen a man so depressed."

In May he announced he was going away for a couple of days, but did not say where. He did not travel far, in fact: At a hotel in Philadelphia he rang for room service and ordered a glass of lemon juice. Into it he poured his phial of cyanide, and he was found dead the following morning.

What Wallace Carothers might have gone on to discover had his personal problems not overtaken him is anyone's guess. As it was, he had already made his mark in organic chemistry, and Du Pont proceeded to reap the benefit of it.

But they still did not have a name for the new miracle fiber. When the executive committee met, they were asked for ideas. P.S. suggested "Duparooh" and "Duproh" accompanied by the slogan "Du Pont brought a rabbit out of a hat." His brother Irénée offered "Duperon" with the catchword "Du Pont pulls rabbits out of nitrogen." Lammot came up with "Delawear" and "Neosheen." Ruly Carpenter suggested "Duponese," "Pontella," and "Lustrol."

Since none of these quite rolled off the tongue, the problem was passed on to the employees, who were asked to send in names. One that they rather liked was "Exton," but it turned out to be an already registered trademark. Others were "Wacara" (for Wallace Carothers), "Nuyarn," "Norun," and "Nulon." Another one was "Nilon," which was passed over until someone doodled with it, changing the *i* to a *y*. Nylon it was.

The appearance of nylon on the American market had almost as much impact on the nation as Henry Ford's Model Ts and Model As. With the first cheap motor cars, the American people were able to leave their homes and broaden their horizons; and when their sons and daughters discovered

* A daughter was born in November.

the delightful hurly-burly as well as the delicious privacy of the rumble seat, national morals were liberated too.

The effect of nylon was equally salutary. The first product Du Pont put on the market utilizing the new process was, it is true, not very revolutionary. It was a nylon toothbrush, which made hardly a ripple except in the trade where the makers of horse bristles saw the writing on the wall. But by 1939 the first nylon-yarn factory went into production at Seaford, Delaware, and in the spring of that year a note was sent to all Du Pont female employees telling them they could buy two pairs each of the "new Nylon stockings," sizes 8½ to 10½, at $1.15 a pair. Their comments on quality and wearing would be appreciated.

The moment the girls smoothed the new stockings over their limbs and began strutting around the office and factory floors in them, they felt as if they had been made over.

"I felt different," one of the secretaries said. "My legs felt different. I felt like kicking them up in the air."

Right from the start they were conscious that the men's attitude had changed too. It was not that they all began staring at the girls' legs.

"Somehow, they made you feel you had gone to town on yourself, like spending fifty bucks on a hairdo, a facial, a bottle of perfume," the secretary said, "when all you'd done was put on a new pair of stockings."

They had further reasons for preening themselves in the weeks to come, because they were allowed to sample Du Pont's ventures in nylon underwear, and for girls who had never been able to afford real silk panties and slips, it was a revelation. Soon in downtown Wilmington it was possible to identify a Du Pont female employee simply by the elegance of her legs and the confidently easy way in which she walked.

"Even the misogynists have started watching our girls," a delighted Lammot reported.

As word of mouth spread, Du Pont was bombarded by public and manufacturers alike, asking when they too could start taking part in the nylon revolution.

The first public sales were confined to Wilmington itself. A local department store was sent the whole of the factory's first shipment—four thousand pairs of stockings. An ad in the Wilmington *Morning News* warned it would be first-come-first-served, and sales would be limited to three pairs per person. Forty-five-gauge pairs would be $1.15, forty-eight-gauge $1.25, and fifty-one gauge $1.35. A queue started to form in the early hours of the morning. The four thousand pairs were gone in a little over an hour.

One of P. S. du Pont's nieces, Louisa d'Andelot Carpenter, worked as a dress designer in the New York theater, and she wrote to her father, Ruly Carpenter, in an attempt to get in before the rush began:

> We go into rehearsal with the show, "The Little Dog Laughed," to be produced and directed by Eddie Dowling, on Wednesday, July 10th. In doing an investigation of our costumes I thought it a swell idea to dress all the girls, including the principals, of course, in Nylon stockings. Do they make them in opera length? Also I would like to make a good deal as we want as many as 200 pairs to start with, and undoubtedly another order, that is if the show is successful, which I hope. Of course, the Nylon stockings would receive advertisement in the theater programs etc.
>
> Let me know if you think this is a good idea, and what kind of deal we can make.

Louisa's father wrote back to tell her that there were as yet no opera-length nylon stockings available, nor any others, since Du Pont was so overwhelmed with orders he did not have a dozen pairs to spare.

By this time everybody wanted nylon stockings. The newspapers were full of stories about them. Women's magazines pictured slim models, their long limbs swathed in gossamer sheaths, wearing the latest in nylon panties and slips. Gossip columns named society beauties and Hollywood film stars who had jumped aboard the nylon bandwagon. *Motion Pictures* magazine reported:

> Myrna Loy used to sleep in the buff but now she wears a nylon nightie, and she says she feels even silkier. Wait till she gets nylon bedsheets!

Somehow a rumor started that the principal ingredient of nylon was coal, which was not true, but it did give writers a chance to have some fun. Margaret Fishback wrote a verse about it:

> Said Dad to his expensive daughter
>   These stockings made of coal and water,
> With just a little air thrown in,
>   Sound economical as skin.

With summer here I've coal to burn
Left in the bin, so kindly learn
To knit your own, since we have air
And also H_2O to spare.

In August 1940, at the New York World's Fair at Flushing Meadow, Du Pont's exhibition of nylon products—consisting of a model wearing a gorgeous nylon evening gown, and others in stockings, nylon-satin slippers, and underwear—was the hit of the show. It was said that Du Pont had even succeeded in making nylon lace. Almost immediately, Cannon Mills, one of the biggest American producers of silk and artificial-silk stockings, announced it was abandoning production of these in favor of nylons, and before the end of the year sixty-nine other companies had followed suit. By that time Du Pont had invested forty-nine million dollars in its nylon plant and development, plus four million for experimental purposes.

But the profits were rolling in. The first shipments of stockings to Philadelphia and New York, five million pairs in all, were snapped up in hours. Someone wryly commented that women were becoming prouder of their nylons than they were of their diamonds.

In a way, they were quite right. For suddenly in 1941, when the United States went to war, nylon stockings became almost as precious. With all imports of raw silk from the Far East halted, nylon replaced it in all fields. The production of nylon stockings was halted, and the nylon yarn was utilized for parachutes and other war materials instead. In the next eighteen months fifteen million pounds of Du Pont nylon yarn was produced, but only a fraction was set aside for stockings, and those that did get produced were largely reserved for the military post exchanges. GIs took stockings with them when they sailed in the convoys to Britain in 1942–44, and it was there and in France and, later, in Germany that girls learned what it was like to roll on a pair of nylons—though most of them paid different currency for the privilege of wearing them.

The ban on mass production held until September 1945, when the stocking machines were geared up again and the first consignments came back into the big stores. This time every woman in the country wanted a pair. To begin with, there was only one shade of brown obtainable, at $1.12 a pair, but the name of nylon was enough to start lines in every big city from Los Angeles to New York. Women bit and scratched each other for possession of the last few pairs. In Flatbush special police details had to be called in to control the vast crowds.

In Chicago a girl dancer was found murdered. "Robbery is not thought to have been the motive of the crime," a local newspaper reported.

The dead girl was still wearing her nylons, and there were five more pairs in her wardrobe.

One woman to whom the whole nylon craze meant nothing was Alice Belin du Pont. P.S.'s wife had long since passed the stage when personal vanities were important to her, and, in any case, as she told one of her nieces:

"Who would want to use substitutes for undergarments when silk is still available! And it is available—at a price."

As she had done in World War I, Alice went to work for the Red Cross in World War II, but this time she did not bother going into Wilmington. She and P.S. had part of Longwood turned into a military hospital for seventy-two patients, and she helped with the nursing chores on the spot. Her sister-in-law Irene du Pont came over to work with her. As one of their nieces reported:

"When you listen to them talking, it's mostly grumbles about husbands."

Irene had quite a bit to grumble about. Although Irénée was sixty-seven years old in 1942, he was still as fond of his amorous adventures as ever and had gone off for a party at Xanadu as if determined to ignore the war. P.S. commented:

> When he gets down there, it is very hard to induce him to reply to letters or give attention even to the most important affairs. To him Cuba seems to be a carefree resort where he can shake off the bothersome troubles of the United States. I do hope he will not be disillusioned later on.

P.S. was content with a short winter holiday on the island of Boca Grande, on Florida's Gulf coast, where his sister Bella and her husband, Rodney Sharp, had built themselves a house so ornate that it was known in the family as the Taj Mahal. P.S. was always unlucky with Florida weather, and in any case, since he was totally disinterested in swimming, fishing, tennis, or bird-watching, he was very soon bored. His brother-in-law tried to involve him in the local passion for shelling on the well-strewn beach and proudly showed him the collection of junonias, lion's paws, crown conches, and other treasures that he had dredged from the sands in front of the great house. But P.S. was not to be persuaded. For in the early hours of the morning he had already glimpsed from his bedroom window the figure of Rodney Sharp's butler on his way to the beach carrying a tray of rare shells, which he proceeded to place in strategic positions so that unwitting guests would stumble upon them in their shelling expeditions later in the day.

P.S. brought with him to Florida one of the latest of the company's developments in synthetics—false teeth. He had kept his own teeth until his seventieth year, but had now "had the darned things disposed of," and he was pleased with the result.

"The only fault in your make-up," he wrote to one old colleague,

> is the fact that you are still plodding along on nature-made teeth. You should follow my example and have a new set "made by Du Pont"—very satisfactory and to me a great improvement on nature's manufacture. If you will try a set you will never use others. Whenever I see pictures of grinning girls with a full set of teeth, I always feel like writing below: "teeth by Du Pont." In their perfection they always look to be of that kind.

On his seventy-second birthday, January 15, 1942, he signed an official form in which he described his occupation as "conservation and enhancement of [his] estate." He gave his income as "about $300,000 per annum" adding underneath, "nothing at all after the payment of taxes"). He noted that "cash in hand" was "in excess of $500,000" and "personal property" was worth "about $5,000,000."

Over the past five or six years he had been quietly divesting himself of his wealth in anticipation of inheritance taxes. John J. Raskob had fixed him up a pension fund at a cost of ten million dollars, and the two men had then executed a tax-dodging maneuver whereby Raskob bought the reversionary rights. The bulk of his personal wealth P.S. turned over to his two brothers, as well as his holdings in Christiana.

"Just see that Alice and I don't starve to death," he told them, and Irénée and Lammot had solemnly assured him that they would always be there to keep the wolf from his door. Altogether he calculated he had passed over $137 million to his brothers and other members of the family by 1944. He still, in fact, had about $20 million left.

Though P.S. would always remain Du Pont's *éminence grise,* he had resigned most of his official positions both with the company and with General Motors. When news of this reached Raskob, he wrote P.S.:

The only objection I have to your resignation is that you didn't finish your job before quitting. Perhaps, however, you can explain more or less satisfactorily why the great chemical concern with which you have been associated for some fifty years has developed no method of preventing old age creeping up on all of us and rendering us more and more impotent. Perhaps, too, the reason is that you feel something should be left for your successors to accomplish.

To which P.S. might well have replied:

"Ah, yes, but will my successors be du Ponts?"

For that was what was troubling him and his brothers now. Age had overtaken Irénée and Lammot as well. Already they were beginning to search for in-laws, having run out of cousins of the blood capable of keeping the organization thriving. When Lammot resigned as president during World War II (Irénée had already chosen pleasure domes over the Du Pont boardroom), the first of the remoter du Pont connections was made president. Walter S. Carpenter, brother of Ruly,* took over. It was supposed to be temporary while they groomed a genuine du Pont heir. But whom could they possibly choose? P.S. did not see a promising member of the family anywhere.

In the summer of 1944 as she walked back down the corridor after serving a shift in the hospital wing at Longwood, Alice collapsed. Doctors diagnosed a thrombosis, which paralyzed her right leg and affected her speech. At first everyone was optimistic about her chances for recovery, and P.S. wrote to one of her nieces, Aileen du Pont:

Alice seems better today and quite her cheerful self, which I attribute to rest augmented by [an] appropriate amount of whiskey. It is a curious thing that she continues this taste, which in moderation belongs to all the Belin tribe, while on the other hand she has developed a liking for beef, which is quite unusual for her but will help her get back her strength.

Three days later he mentioned she had drunk the greater part of a glass of milk—"about as near a miracle as I have experienced in our family," he said, and continued:

* Ruly Carpenter was married to P.S.'s sister Meta.

Being deaf makes the speech question much more difficult as one cannot be certain that she adjusts her accousticon properly (nobody else can do it for her) and therefore we do not know how much she hears. . . . When she does speak and makes mistakes she laughs it off. Like most deaf people she dreads mistakes due to failure to hear properly.

There were four nurses to look after her, and P.S. fretted that they did not have much to do: "Most of their time is expended in eating, sleeping, playing solitaire, and doing picture puzzles." But Alice, accommodating as always, did not keep them in idleness for long. She had one last glass of whiskey on the afternoon of June 23, 1944, and died later in the evening. She was seventy-two years old.

There was only one complication about Alice's death. The Pennsylvania doctor who signed the death certificate gave her place of residence as Longwood, near Kennett Square, Chester County, Pennsylvania. P.S. pointed out the error. Alice was a legal resident of Delaware and her official home was the Hotel du Pont, Wilmington. The death certificate would have to be changed, because considerable money was at stake: Alice had left several million dollars, and inheritance taxes in Pennsylvania were high. P.S. swore out an affidavit before the authorities in both states and succeeded in getting the death certificate altered. At the same time he put in a claim for $2,345,042.50 from his wife's estate on the grounds that she had been holding this sum in her account on his behalf, and this too was granted. Alice would have been distressed to learn that in dying where and when she did, she had nearly cost her husband $6,000,000.

But at least in this instance it worked out all right in the end.

CHAPTER 27

Class Action

Iɴ 1945, just before the end of World War II, P.S. wrote to ask John Raskob if he would like to buy the reversion in yet another of his annuities —a maneuver to avoid taxes on both sides. This one was, at least for a du Pont, a modest little pension. As P.S. wrote:

> If you are in any way interested, I have an annuity which returns $3,000 a month, or $36,000 a year, issued by the Equitable Life Assurance Society. Knowing my age to be 75½ years, you can probably figure on the value of this annuity as well as anyone. For the record, I find that my expectation of life, as shown by the American Experience Table, is 6.1 years; by the Commissioner's Standard Ordinary Table, 6.6 years; by the American Men's Experience Table 6.5 years; by the Fraternal Congress Table 5.75 years. You will see that there is no very great variation in the results derived from these tables. However, by the Standard Annuitants Table, I am rated at an expected 11.1 years. This I am

led to believe is the expectancy used in determining the cost of an annuity for a man of my age, and this cost may be written up in order to cover the lack of average data. If you are not interested in this, I shall be glad to know of any suggestions that you have as to a likely purchaser.

Whoever did finally buy the reversion rights (Raskob does not seem to have done so) cannot have made much of a profit out of it. Five years later P.S. was still alive at eighty and, except for a touch of arthritis, seemed to be as fit as ever, with quite a few years ahead of him.

Du Pont and General Motors (which the du Pont family continued to control) were now the biggest and richest corporations in the world. Both had done well out of the war. Du Pont had reverted to powder making for the duration as part of its wartime effort and produced nearly five billion pounds of explosives, which constituted seventy percent of the nation's output and three times as much as the company had made during World War I. Lammot du Pont was able to boast:

"In one day, every day, we are producing more explosives than we made in the whole of the four year period of the Civil War."

But that was only a portion of Du Pont's activities. As Gerald Colby Zilg has recorded:

> Du Pont nylon replaced Japanese silk in parachutes, and was used in everything from glider tow ropes to tropical mosquito screens. Du Pont paints coated the hulls of whole naval fleets, Du Pont dyes were used in uniforms, Du Pont antifreezes kept army trucks going in winter, and Du Pont cellophane wrapped rations, drugs, and supplies. A single Du Pont factory turned out eighty-six products that went into the Superfortress bomber alone. The war economy consumed 50,929 miles of Du Pont 35mm film, 38 million miles of nylon parachute yarn, 92.9 million pounds of cellophane, and 11 million pounds of [the insecticide] DDT. . . . Artificial rubber also enjoyed a boost: by May 1941 Du Pont was producing 6,000 tons of Neoprene a year.

From the moment America's involvement in the war seemed inevitable, Lammot persuaded his brothers and the Du Pont executive committee to let him pour unlimited funds into the company laboratories of the General Research Department, and the chemists in Purity Hall were urged to bend their principles and apply fundamental research to the war effort. The budget of the department was upped to eight million dollars in 1941 and went on rising.*

The result was a whole new line of products. There were insecticides for fighting Asian bugs, a sideline that would become one of Du Pont's most profitable operations; food preservatives; transparent plastic hoses for aircraft; camouflage paints impregnable to infrared rays; preservatives for wood, textiles, and metals, cold- and heat-resistant clothes; and a whole new line of plastics.

By 1942 Du Pont had its biggest sales turnover of all time, with $498 million worth of goods sold, giving the company a profit of $55 million. At the same time General Motors was grossing $14 billion in government contracts for cars, trucks, tanks, and, later, planes. From these activities Du Pont received an average of $45 million of General Motors' profits, for each of three years, which, when added to the wartime profit of Du Pont itself, a total of $741 million, meant that Du Pont earned $876 million in profit, three times as much as the company had made in World War I. Of this, Du Pont paid out $288 million in dividends to its stockholders, most of whom, of course, were members of the du Pont clan. Of this amount, nearly $200 million went into Christiana Securities, P.S.'s family trust.

From one wartime activity, however, the company made no profit at all. In 1942 General Leslie Groves asked Du Pont to build and operate a plant for the production of material for an unspecified weapon. The undertaking turned out to be the Manhattan Project, and the weapon the atom bomb. Irénée's son-in-law, Crawford Greenewalt, who supervised the factory operation, was present when Enrico Fermi removed the cadmium controls from the radioactive pile in the University of Chicago's Staff Field Stadium, and watched the chain reaction begin. He was also in New Mexico when the first test bomb was exploded. In between, he and a team of Du Pont scientists and engineers designed and built two factories, at Oak Ridge, Tennessee, and Hanford, Washington, for the induction and control of atomic fission.

The company received one dollar in payment for its efforts. But there were, of course, those other compensations.

Altogether, the du Ponts had no reason to grumble about what World War II did for them. As a family, they suffered only one casualty. Eight members of the family served in the navy, the air force, or the Office of Strategic Service, among them, Lammot's son (Lammot du Pont), Coleman's son (Reynolds du Pont), and Richard du Pont, son of Felix du Pont,

* It reached its peak after World War II when it amounted to $350 million a year.

Sr. Richard had for years pioneered developments in gliding and was the national champion and world long-distance champion in 1938. He became assistant to General Henry Arnold in World War II and was put in charge of preparations for the glider landing on Sicily in 1943. Trying out a new glider at March Field, California, in September 1943, he fell to his death when his parachute failed to open. He was buried in a place of honor at Sand Hole Woods.

Otherwise, Reynolds was the only one wounded (during navy combat). The rest came back unscathed, to find that the Du Pont boom had done wonders for their incomes in their absence.

On New Year's Day, 1950, P.S., Irénée, and Lammot were joint hosts of a party to celebrate the one-hundred-and-fiftieth anniversary of the arrival of Pierre Samuel du Pont and his family in America. Since they were all over six feet tall and still straight as ramrods, the three brothers made a brave sight standing in the large conservatory at Longwood, their "teeth by Du Pont" and their long noses gleaming under the bright lights as they welcomed fellow members of the clan to the celebration. Only P.S.'s bald head and white moustache betrayed him as the eldest brother—he was then eighty—for in some ways Lammot at seventy seemed years his senior. The youngest brother looked thin and careworn, his clothes hung loose about him, and he was reputed to be wilting under the iron regime imposed upon him by wife number four.

Like his ancestor and namesake, Pierre Samuel du Pont, P.S. was now patriarch of the clan, for there was no longer a single du Pont around who could equal him in years or in labor for the family. At the last celebration (the centenary in 1900) P.S. had had to defer to the whims and prejudices of old Colonel Henry Algernon du Pont, then father of the clan. But the tyrant was long since dead and his hatreds buried with him. His son, Henry Francis du Pont, spent his time filling the family home at Winterthur with choice pieces of American furniture and had no time for engaging in family feuds. In any case, P.S. would never have thought of consulting him about which du Ponts should come to the one-hundred-and-fiftieth birthday party, and a blanket invitation had gone out to all of them.

From all parts of America and the world the relatives arrived in Delaware. "Six hundred and thirty descendants of the original du Pont de Nemours attended the simple meal with appropriate improvements becoming to this age" (P.S. wrote afterwards) and all enjoyed the occasion very much, particularly the rule that there should be no speeches, which greatly comforted those who might be called upon and caused the audience a like satisfaction. We escaped with a few pictures, which in such a gathering could not be classed as good. To all of us it was a revelation to see so many strange faces but as [they] were all tagged with name-plates, we were able to greet each other by affectionate first names from the start.

On Sunday I shall celebrate my eightieth birthday. I am beginning to realize that the epithet "patriarch and venerable citizen" may apply to me although I cannot say that such terms apply to my personal feelings.

In fact, for P.S. there had been two shadows hanging over the birthday celebrations, and one of them had caused him much personal sorrow—more, perhaps, than he had felt over the death of his wife. Bessie du Pont, Alfred I.'s ex-wife and a du Pont herself, had been ill for some time and was doing her damnedest to hold on to life long enough to attend the celebration, but she died a few days too early. P.S., who had stood by her ever since Alfred I. had first walked out on her, was much distressed by her passing. He had never seen Bessie du Pont as clearly as had some of the other people who had been close to her, and had tended to idealize her as a gentle, feminine, undemanding, and courageous person. On the other hand, on receiving news of her death, Marcella du Pont, wife of Bessie's only son, Alfred Victor, wrote a letter to P.S. containing a description of her mother-in-law that was probably much more accurate, if less sentimental, than the one P.S. cherished:

I seldom thought of her as a Mother-in-law, but rather as a strong-minded, gifted woman of great taste and one who laid about her on all sides with unswerving ideas, which, on occasion, cut across one's own beliefs like a flail.

For P.S., Bessie had always symbolized the early days on the Brandywine, when she and Alfred I. had lived happily together at the Swamp, and the cousins were friends and collaborators. With her death an era was truly ended for him. He wrote to another of Bessie's old intimates:

Your letter . . . takes me back to the days when the "Swamp" was at its best, with its interesting and entertaining host and hostess and the many friends that we met there. The breaking up of this home was a tragedy that cannot be explained, though it was regretted by all, none more than the writer of this letter.

Bessie herself changed very little. She bore the burden of the tragedy with great calm and bravery and all admire her for the stand that she took. I never heard her make a complaint about her hard luck.

Except for his mother, she was the only woman in his life who had really meant anything to him, and he would miss her.

The second shadow hanging over the celebration concerned all three brothers particularly and the du Pont clan in general, and it seemed likely to cost them money. What most business and political leaders in the United States considered inevitable had come to pass: The United States government was prosecuting Du Pont, General Motors, and United States Rubber under the Sherman Antitrust Act. Not even P.S. was particularly surprised about that, and no one around Du Pont's legal department was prepared to deny that the government had a good case. For years Du Pont not only had been taking a large slice of the profits of General Motors and United States Rubber but also had been chief supplier of many of the products and accessories the other two firms used. General Motors cars and trucks used over a hundred Du Pont materials, and United States Rubber, while making tires with Du Pont's neoprene, went on to sell the tires to General Motors. It was a cartel all right, and the company was ready to defend itself on that score.

But the government did not confine its case to a suit against Du Pont. Asserting that it was resolved to break up what it termed "the largest single concentration of power in the United States," it involved other targets as disparate as all the family holding companies, the banks and, of course, Christiana Securities. And on top of this, it then filed a class action against no less than one hundred and eighty-six members of the du Pont family, all of them closely related by blood or marriage to P.S. and his brothers.

The government justified this move by pointing out in its brief:

Evidence in the record of this case shows it is the practice and policy of senior members of the class and their defendant representatives to distribute during their lifetimes a substantial portion of their stock holdings to minors in the family, usually by setting up trusts of stock.

P.S. was depressed by the government suit and indicated to the legal staff of Du Pont that he wanted as little participation in it as possible. He had experienced the exhaustion and frustration of an antitrust suit once before in his lifetime—when Du Pont had been sued the first time, in 1907—and he did not think he had the strength or tenacity to go through another four years of legal argument and political polemics. But when he realized that not just the company but the whole family was being involved, his paternal instincts (or were they now his patriarchal instincts?) were aroused, and he suddenly found in himself a burning desire to come to the defense of the younger members of his family. He signified to Du Pont's legal staff that he would be a willing witness in the forthcoming suit, and would meanwhile go through his papers for relevant facts.

From that moment on he had time for little else and spent much of his days writing long memoranda about the early days of the company and the takeover of General Motors. To an old colleague he wrote on June 16, 1952:

> The government seems to have outstripped its own method in the suit which is now being brought against the Du Pont Company. This suit includes all members of the du Pont family descended from Pierre S. du Pont who died in 1817 and the wives and husbands of such descendants. Few of these people know anything whatever about the business of the Du Pont Company and the majority are minors. The judge has ruled that each one of these people named by the government must be dealt with in a separate suit.

He added:

> I have spent a great deal of my time during the past two or three years digging out facts concerning happenings about which I am the only living person qualified to testify. I am fortunate in being able to remember much of this business without trouble but the documentary evidence must be presented in addition to my testimony. The government does not have to prove any of its claims and, of course, we are not faced by our accusers, who are

really unknown persons. Those who signed the papers are only clerks or lawyers hired to work up the case.

All three brothers had been called as witnesses when the trust suit opened in Chicago, but one of them never made it. In 1952 Lammot du Pont was felled by a heart attack at his summer home on Long Island and died alone on July 24. Ironically enough, the rest of his family were on the Brandywine, celebrating the one-hundred-and-fiftieth anniversary of the Du Pont company in the Hagley Mills powder yards where the enterprise had first begun. The rest of the clan were all there too, and eighty thousand Du Pont employees in sixty-eight plants around the country had been given a holiday to celebrate the great day.

P.S. and Irénée joined Lammot's fourth wife and his ten children at the burial service in Sand Hole Woods and then went back to Chicago.

Irénée was the first of them to be called as a witness, and his easy aplomb both impressed and irritated the court. He blew smoke rings from his large Havana cigar as he discussed the case with reporters. In Chicago's stifling summer heat he did not neglect a boost for Du Pont products in pointing out that he was wearing one of the company's new nylon shirts ("It dries on you when it gets sweaty") as well as a light-weight nylon suit ("It never needs pressing"); and he raised a laugh when he had the lawyers continually repeat their questions because his hearing aid was malfunctioning.

"These things are very badly made," he remarked. "The Du Pont Company ought to go into the business."

But it was P.S. whose manner and testimony influenced the proceedings the most. Unlike Irénée, he did not indicate he found the proceedings contemptible, nor did he betray his sense of indignation at the attack on the lesser members of the family clan. With flawless memory, he recounted the history of the Du Pont enterprise from the takeover by the cousins in 1902, through the struggle with Alfred I. in 1915, to the involvement with General Motors. He spoke calmly but convincingly of Du Pont's patriotism in two world wars and could not be shaken from his assertion that national interest rather than monetary gain had motivated his family in their company policy.

P.S.'s testimony took several days to deliver, but he showed no sign of fatigue or annoyance when the government prosecutors harried him. His legal staff was delighted with his performance, and Ethel Scott, wife of Philip C. Scott, one of the two principal Du Pont lawyers, wrote to him:

I'm not sure you have the reports of the trial—one you may not have, as it was told me privately by my little friend, the newspaper man. He told me not to tell but he said: "There won't be any more witnesses in this trial to compare with Pierre and Irénée du Pont. They were the top for us."

Life magazine did a large piece on the trial and made it plain P.S. had come out the hero of the proceedings. But no one liked the photograph the magazine used of him, and at the request of John Harlan, the chief Du Pont counsel, he sent another for distribution to the press. P.S. noted:

[It] has been signed in order to be sure that you recognize the countenance of the original in the photographic reproduction. If this should cause you embarrassment it may be kept under cover or in a dark room.

He also sent a copy to Ethel Scott, with his autograph on it, and the words "Unfortunately, it is said to look like me."

By the time his birthday came around again in 1954, the case was under advisement and there would be a long wait before the judgment was announced. P.S. wrote to a colleague on January 27:

My eighty-fourth birthday passed over without congratulations from Washington or from any United States court, which is something to be thankful for. Silence is the best gift from that source.

We finally closed the hearings of the Du Pont–General Motors–U.S. Rubber case at Chicago and await the decision of the judge. I know and I believe the judge knows, without further thought, what the verdict should be. Only matters political can alter the decision and at present I see no reason why that interference should be injected at this time but I should like to see the case ended by a favorable decision in order to end the matter.

But time was against him in that. He had already cheated most of the statisticians and gone well beyond the "expectation of life" forecasts that four major insurance actuaries had made about him in 1945. He was now shooting for the 11.1 years calculated by the Standard Annuitants Table, which would take him up to 1956.

He passed most of his time at Longwood now, making notes for his autobiography—the one, he said, "I intend to write in my old age"—and recollecting his associations with John J. Raskob for a biography A. Rae duBell was writing about Raskob (who had died in 1950). Otherwise he liked to wander through the conservatories and gardens and, when the weather was good, enjoyed playing on the console that controlled the great fountains he had established in the forecourt of Longwood House. The jets had been designed to lift the streams of water to eighty feet in the air, but P.S., with a series of manipulations which he preferred to keep to himself, could get them to shoot up to one hundred feet, a spectacle that never failed to delight him. He still kept up a voluminous correspondence with his nephews, nieces, and their progeny, to whom he was still Dad or Uncle Dad. He was not too well in the spring of 1954, but who could expect to be at eighty-four?

"I have been visited for about a month," he wrote to one of Raskob's daughters,

> with one of those indeterminate ailments which come with no apparent cause &, fortunately, leave without ill effects. Next week may find me back at the office, meantime I go out for a brief walk each day & return completely satisfied. Such is life at 84, plus a residue of ill health, soon to be forgotten, I hope.

He was slightly cast down and kept reminding himself of it, because he had not entirely completed the ritual New Year's Day round of visits to the du Pont ladies on the Brandywine at the beginning of 1954. In fact, he had done better than most of the earlier du Pont patriarchs. There were fewer du Pont females then, and they gathered in groups at only six or seven houses; whereas P.S. had got around to twelve of the thirteen Brandywine houses and personally presented boxes of candy to the one hundred and sixty-eight du Pont ladies who had gathered to receive him. But he had become so fatigued toward the end that he had missed the house of his nephew E. Paul du Pont, and this irked him because it was well known that he was not overfond of Cousin Paul. He sent round fifteen boxes of candy and fifty letters of apology to Mrs. Paul du Pont and the other ladies who had waited in vain to receive him, but his failure kept nagging at him. He felt he had let down the family tradition. On New Year's Day the head of the du Ponts was obligated to bring good wishes to every one of their ladies, and old age and physical disability were no excuse for failure to do so.

On February 11, 1954, he made a special effort and gave what was to be his last big party at Longwood. He invited the whole of the Du Pont roster of lawyers and their wives to a banquet in celebration of the end of the government suit. There were no speeches, but the dinner was one to remember, both for its splendidly luxurious dishes and for its impeccable wines, the best in P.S.'s cellar. He had been tempted to choose the dessert course himself, since sweet dishes were his passion, and he had taken out the book of recipes he had kept over the years, with lovingly remembered dishes like spiced peaches, baked Alaska, and johnnycake. There was also a section headed "Other good desserts I have met," which included boiled apple pudding and boiled Indian pudding, after which he had written, "likely to die after eating but worth while." He reluctantly decided he did not want dead lawyers on his hands, and served them crepes suzette instead.

One of his major preoccupations was keeping up with the pensions he paid privately to old colleagues, their widows and children, who had been with him at Du Pont over the years, and some even went back to Lorain, Ohio (he was paying the college fees of a grandson of one of his former clerks there). He had provided a generous pension for the mother of his old protégé, Lewes Mason, until her death a few years back and had then taken it upon himself to subsidize and educate the children of Charlie Mason, Lewes's brother. Charlie too was now dead, but during his service in France in World War I he had made friends with a French peasant named Henri Petit, and they had corresponded.

In the spring of 1954 a neighbor of Petit's who understood English wrote on his behalf to P.S. asking for news of Charlie. How was he? What was he doing now? Why had he not written?

The letter seemed to rekindle in P.S. all the old memories of the Mason family and particularly of its most cherished member, Lewes. As if to reestablish a link with a precious period in his past, he sat down to pen a long letter to the neighbor, asking him to bring Henri Petit up to date with all that had happened to the Masons, including the deaths of Lewes and Charlie. Then he added:

> And please tell me in confidence how is Monsieur Petit himself? I understand from your first letter that he is sixty-nine years old and having a hard time on his small farm. Will you please tell me how much Monsieur Petit would need to supplement his pension and make life pleasanter for him? It would give me great pleasure to be able to help him.

It was one of the last letters P.S. wrote. On the night of April 3, 1954, he complained of a pain after a bout of coughing, and when the doctor examined him he was found to have ruptured a blood vessel. He was rushed to Wilmington Hospital, where he was given blood transfusions; but he failed to revive and died in his sleep two days later.

Henri Petit never did get his pension, because the reply from France to P.S.'s offer did not arrive until the morning of April 6, and by that time he was already dead.

Judge Walter la Buy delivered his judgment in the case of *United States* v. *du Pont* in December 1954, some nine months after P.S.'s death. The rest of the family were sad about that, for the verdict would undoubtedly have given him great satisfaction. The company came out of the ordeal practically unscathed. First, all the du Pont relatives, with the exception of seven principal members of the family, were dismissed from the suit. Then the judge ruled that P.S. and the executive committee of the company had not *intended* to create a monopoly when they had bought into General Motors, and he therefore exonerated all concerned of any ulterior or criminal motives.

The news caused a boomlet on the New York Stock Exchange, which put up the price of Du Pont shares by 4.5 points. The president and two ex-presidents of the company (Crawford Greenewalt, Irénée's son-in-law; Walter Carpenter, Jr., P.S.'s brother-in-law; and Irénée himself) were pictured happily congratulating each other in the Du Pont offices in Wilmington.

"We were confident this would be the result," said Greenewalt.

"We owe it all to my brother and to a brilliant legal staff," said Irénée.

The trio then drove to Sand Hole Woods to lay some flowers on P.S.'s grave and say thank you to him personally.

In death as in life, he had been most circumspect. All his vast wealth (calculated as amounting to some $450 million) had been given to his brothers, nephews, and nieces long enough ago to cause no trouble with the tax authorities. His estate was valued at $80 million, and this he left in a charitable trust charged with the care of Longwood Gardens, which, he specified in his will, would be open to the public and serve as the center of the Longwood Foundation.

So, though the state would receive nothing in taxes, the public got one of the showplaces of the nation. The du Ponts were holding on to more money than ever, but at least the people were benefitting from the death of some of them. Henry Francis du Pont had already made Winterthur into a foundation and stocked it with antiques for visitors to see and admire. Nemours had been made into a home for crippled children—though there would be trouble about that in the future. And now Longwood, with its flowers, its shrubs, its orchids, its gardens, and its fountains, would go on show.

Had P.S. lived, he would undoubtedly have urged the executive committee of the company to keep a low profile from then on. Unfortunately, his successors had inherited none of his modesty, circumspection, or discretion.

A year after the verdict was given, the jubilant members of the executive committee of the Du Pont company met to discuss ways of conveying their feelings of justification to the government in Washington and the public at large. There was no one present with enough common sense to urge them to keep their mouths shut and their triumphant feelings reined in. And so, when the meeting came to an end, an announcement was issued: The Du Pont company had voted to invest a further seventy-five million dollars in General Motors.

The reaction on the stock exchange should have warned them that the decision was stupidly provocative. Both Du Pont and General Motors shares dropped.

But the most serious effect was in Washington, where the Justice Department was incensed by this open display of du Pont arrogance. The department's lawyers decided to press with all due speed an appeal against the Chicago verdict, and application was made to the Supreme Court for a review. Even then, the new generation at Du Pont did not seem to realize the danger they were in. As one of them pointed out to Irénée when he wondered out loud what P.S. would have done, there was no need to worry. The company had friends on the Supreme Court now. John Harlan, who had so brilliantly led the Du Pont legal team at Chicago, had been rewarded by appointment to the Court. Another associate justice was Tom Clark, who had previously worked as a lobbyist for the Ethyl Gasoline Corporation, a Du Pont subsidiary. With friends like that, they could not lose.

But they did. Harlan and Clark cited conflict of interest and excused themselves. The remainder of the Court reversed the Chicago verdict by a vote of 4 to 2. The Court decided that commercial and financial domination by the du Pont family had been proved, and it was something the Court was not willing to tolerate. They sent the case back to Chicago for Judge la Buy to set forth a plan for divestiture without delay. They made it plain that they wanted to see not simply a divorce between Du Pont and its subsidiaries but an end to the family's monopolistic control of a large segment of business in the United States.

P.S. must have turned in his grave.

Or would he have cared—conscious as he had been toward the end of his life that no matter what the Court ruled, his family's grip on Du Pont had become loose and limp after one hundred and fifty years, and soon it would be a business like any other?

CHAPTER 28

Chain Reaction

IN 1963, nine years after P.S. died, Irénée followed him at eighty-seven. Like many an old roué, Irénée had passed the last years of his life in peaceful harmony with his wife, Irene, on his estate at Granogue. He had long since given up the pursuit of blond Lolitas, and in any case, his pleasure dome in Cuba, Xanadu, had been seized by Fidel Castro after the revolution in 1959.* He still gave his Fourth of July fireworks parties— though the guest of honor, Bishop Philip Cook of Delaware, had died in 1939—until Irene fell ill, and the sound of the bursting rockets and the flicker of baleful bright lights on the windows of her bedroom proved bad for her nerves. Then the great ceremonial was abondoned, and Irénée did not revive it after his wife died in 1961. He sorrowed greatly over her death. After a lifetime of neglecting her, he missed her in the evening of his life and had no wish to stay around without her.

* It is now a restaurant.

He left one son to inherit his fortune and, maybe, his control over the family company. But Irénée du Pont, Jr., had neither the will nor the capacity to lead the powerful chemical combine that Du Pont had become, and he had to reconcile himself to the realization that in spite of his background and his share of the Du Pont stock, he would never be of more than vice-presidential caliber.

Other du Ponts hoped for a time, to do better. There was Henry (Hank) Belin du Pont, the son of P.S.'s brother Belin, who had died of tuberculosis back in 1902. The sickly child of a cousinly marriage, Hank du Pont had become one of P.S.'s many wards and had grown up strong in body and promising in managerial capacity. But his main interest was aviation. The collapse of a disastrous first marriage seemed to sap any latent business ambition he might have had to succeed at Du Pont. When he married a second time, it was to a du Pont cousin, Emily, whose chief passions in life were foxhunting and sailing. Being a strong-willed woman, she soon persuaded her husband that with the exception of flying, nothing else in life was much worth bothering about. In any case, why did he need to work at a job he loathed? He was one of the richest members of the family and could do what he liked.

From that time on, Hank lost interest in his Du Pont activities, taking up aviation and sailing instead. He had a long-standing rivalry with his cousin, Pierre Samuel du Pont III, Lammot's son, and they competed against each other in races to Bermuda and across the Atlantic, sparing neither themselves nor their crews in their effort to be first over the line.

On one of these trips a member of the volunteer crew, a Mr. Blaff of New York, had a heart attack and died before they could reach shore. When Hank finally made it to Bermuda, a friend was waiting to commiserate with him.

"What a terrible time you must have had," he said.

"What do you mean?" asked Hank in astonishment. "It's the best trip I've ever had. We had twenty-knot winds all the way across—no gale force winds at any time. It was absolutely wonderful. And we won!"

"But," said his friend, "wasn't it awful what happened to poor Mr. Blaff?"

"Well, yes, that was unfortunate," admitted Hank. Then he brightened. "But even he must have known it was the best sail we ever had."

As his friend remarked later:

"Hank du Pont has become a very one-track guy."

But not the kind Du Pont was looking for.

The remaining direct descendant in whom the family had great hopes was Reynolds du Pont. The youngest son of Lammot by his first marriage, Reynolds was acknowledged to be the nicest and most personable member of his generation of du Ponts, despite a mixed-up childhood. Someone asked him why he went to so many boarding schools (four) when he was young, and he replied:

"Because I kept running out of mothers."

His real mother died while he was a child, as did his first stepmother. The third departed after a divorce, and the fourth stayed on to push him around.

"She was an absolute pain in the ass," he once said about number four, but his tone was mild and he gave little sign that she ever succeeded in upsetting him unduly.

Reynolds went to work in true du Pont tradition at the bottom and labored hard and long in branches of the company all over the nation.

"He was in the front line of the plastics revolution," said another member of the family. "He didn't have anything to do with inventing or developing them. All that was done at Purity Hall by the experimental chemists. But Reynolds was working on the machines that turned them out, and after about three years he had rayon, dacron, orlon, polystyrene, and all that plastic junk coming out of his ears."

After three years of working on the night shift, he thought it about time he was given a break, and he went to Irénée du Pont, who was still alive at the time, and asked him to use his influence. Irénée sent for his record and then said:

"Rennie, my brother P.S. always had a rule about members of the family he liked who went to work for the company. If he thought they were never going to make it to the top, he called them in and told them not to stick around—it would only make them bitter and frustrated."

He looked his nephew straight in the eye, and then went on:

"Why don't you go in for politics? That's where personality pays off."

Reynolds took the hint. He could afford to. The money Lammot had left him in 1952 (about forty-three million dollars) had been held in trust for him, and the members of the family who had looked after his inheritance had more than tripled it in the meantime. Even if the influence of the du Pont family was no longer as strong in Delaware politics as it had been in the heyday of the Colonel, Alfred I., and Coleman, a heap of money could still make an impact, especially if it was backed by the public support of the family newspapers in Wilmington. Reynolds became first a state representative and then a senator, and set about his political duties with enthusiasm. But he had come too late into the field. Although Delaware politics was just as venal and malleable as ever, it was no longer the du Ponts or even the Republicans who manipulated the votes, but hardheaded Democrats from Wilmington. This was not the launching platform Reynolds had expected it to be, and he gradually realized that his political career was not likely to go far beyond Dover. He gave up in frustration.

"And there he was," said a member of the family. "Poor Rennie, one of the family's brightest. Pushed out of Du Pont, embittered over politics, left high and dry in middle age, with nothing to comfort him but his one hundred and fifty million dollars."

Then the du Pont in-laws at last came into their own. They had been allowed to marry into the family for that very purpose, but only now were they given the chance to make good. Some of them did. Perhaps the most successful was Crawford Greenewalt; married to Irénée's sister, Margaretta, he saw the company safely through the General Motors breakup and the plastics revolution. Perhaps the least successful was not an in-law but the son of one. Lammot du Pont Copeland was the son of Charles Copeland and Lou du Pont, P.S.'s favorite sister. He did well by the company and the family's interests so long as he served under Greenewalt, and it was during this period that he spread Du Pont's interests overseas and opened thirty-five plants in thirteen different countries. But when he took over from Greenewalt in the 1960s, he made the first of his big mistakes.

One of his family heroes had been Lammot du Pont, without whose influence and enthusiasm, he believed, nylon would never have been discovered. Copeland encouraged Purity Hall, by generous funding, to discover yet another synthetic that might have the revolutionary effect upon people's habits that nylon had achieved, and in the early part of his reign he believed the formula had been found. Du Pont's chemists came to him with a new synthetic material that seemed to have all the qualities of genuine leather.

Copeland was excited. He charged the publicity department with finding a name for the new synthetic, and they finally came up with Corfam. In the meantime he pushed through the executive committee an extra sixty million dollars for Corfam's development and then announced that Du Pont itself proposed to market the new product.*

* The company's usual practice was to sell yarns and synthetics to other factories for preparation and marketing.

A great publicity campaign was organized to launch Corfam in the shops as the miracle substitute for real leather in footwear. Slogans began to appear in Du Pont's newspaper ads: "Get swept off your feet" and "Du Pont invites you to step into the future." But there was a snag. Corfam was very expensive to make. The development budget had gone to the labs in an effort to help the chemists find a cheaper production process, but they failed. When Du Pont began marketing Corfam shoes, the public found it would have to pay as much for them as for high-class leather. And not only that. Unlike ordinary leather, Corfam never seemed to become really supple, and a pair of Corfam shoes never felt "worn in." True, they never wore out either, but they were never actually comfortable.

Lammot would have seen the danger at once. He had exploited nylon not only because it had marvelous qualities for a synthetic but because it was cheap to produce. When Corfam proved so expensive, he would have cut his loses and withdrawn it—or P.S. and Irénée would have forced him to do so. But Copeland was one of those bosses unwilling to admit a mistake. He could not bear to see his chance for fame fading and falling. He went on pushing the new product, pouring money into a futile campaign long after the public had stopped buying. By the time he finally gave up, Du Pont had lost $150 million in its attempt to replace real leather.

It could not have happened at a worse time, for by 1966 the economy was slowing up, and there were now scores of rivals in the synthetics field, most of them using patent processes that Du Pont had originally invented but had been forced to give up, for fear of new antitrust prosecutions. By 1967 profits were down twenty-four percent and Du Pont stock had fallen by fifty percent.

Even so, Copeland might have survived had not the family made a dreadful discovery. His son, Lammot du Pont Copeland, Jr., had gone into the newspaper business in California and run into trouble. His father helped him out to the tune of seven million dollars, but it was not enough. It was a moment when even the most powerful du Ponts did not have much ready cash around, for the company's shares had plummeted still further. But Copeland did manage to get a loan of five million dollars from a Swiss bank and passed it over to his son hoping it would be enough for him to pay off his creditors and bail out.

Unfortunately, Copeland's $12 million in loans was nothing like enough. In 1970 his son filed for bankruptcy, admitting debts amounting to some $50 million. And it was then the family found out that among the loans still outstanding, were two large ones from, of all people, labor unions. He had borrowed $2.7 million from the International Brotherhood of Electrical Workers and $4.5 million from the International Union of Barbers. And not only that: As collateral for the loans, he had pledged the family's most closely guarded treasure—nothing less than stock in the du Pont family trust, Christiana Securities.

What shocked the du Ponts even more was the discovery that Copeland had known all about it and had failed to prevent his son from pledging what one of them called "our blood bank." It was as bad as pledging flesh to a Shylock, and the family found it just as painful as losing a limb when the bankruptcy court awarded Christiana Securities stock to the unions in lieu of their money.

Copeland was never forgiven. He not only gave up the presidency of Du Pont but also any part in the direction of the company's affairs. The family abruptly lost its taste for the activities of in-laws and sons of in-laws and sighed for those happier days when their full-blooded cousins had run the company for them, and Christiana Securities meant what it said.

Back in 1927 F. Scott and Zelda Fitzgerald had come to live in Wilmington for a time, but such was the pervasive power of the family throughout the community that it was the du Ponts who made a lasting impression on the Fitzgeralds rather than vice versa. Scott wrote to his editor, Maxwell Perkins:

> There's a kind of feudalism [here]. The du Ponts, an immense family, mostly female, dominate the town. They marry whom they will. A strong, practical race of vast wealth. We went to a du Pont wedding and saw most of them, and found them almost the whole show. They have an eccentricity and independence—not arrogance, for they are simple and natural—that comes from their position, and offer a most interesting subject for conversation.

But that was forty years earlier. Their position had changed as they lost control of the great combine to which the family had given its name. It was not that there were fewer du Ponts in Delaware. It was not that they had less money. It was just that the separation between family and enterprise, which increased inexorably from year to year, seemed to diminish them in influence, power, and importance. They no longer even found it easy to get jobs with the company.

[395]

"Indeed," says an official history,

> as the members of the clan eligible for posts in the Du Pont Company grew, those who reached the upper echelons of management progressively decreased.

The last great hope of the du Ponts finally called it quits in 1968. Pierre (Pete) du Pont IV, Lammot's grandson, had signed on with Du Pont after leaving law school with high hopes of becoming the first lawyer, and the first nonchemist, to be president of the company. He felt he had the brains and energy for the job, and even if his father, Pierre III, had turned out to be a spendthrift and a playboy, his hard-driving mother, Janis (known to all the other du Ponts as Janis-Planis), put a poker up his spine and pushed hard for his promotion. The trouble was, no one else thought as much of Pete as his mother did. He just did not seem to have the dynamic, or the flair, for running the giant organization that Du Pont had become. There were too many outsiders who had vastly superior capabilities.

So in 1968 Uncle Rennie (Reynolds du Pont) gave up his senatorial seat in Dover, Delaware, in favor of his nephew, and Pete embarked on a political career instead. The family was proud of the fact that he did better than Reynolds, launching himself out of local politics and into the United States Congress. Like a true son of Janis-Planis,* he drew up a blueprint for his future. He would do a good job in Congress and then return to Delaware to polish his local image by becoming governor of the state. Then, after two years in office, he would resign, run against the incumbent United States senator, and go back to Washington in a blaze of glory. Who knows what would happen after that? Any job in politics could be open to him. Having failed to become president of Du Pont, he might well end up by becoming president of the United States.

Unfortunately, he did not draw his blueprint carefully enough—which is possibly why Du Pont had let him go in the first place. He got himself elected governor of Delaware all right. But in doing so, he failed to protect his political flanks, and when the elections were over, he found that as a Republican governor he had been saddled with a Democrat as his lieutenant governor. That meant he could not resign without a Democrat taking over, and the Republicans would never forgive him for that. Meanwhile, as the Republican governor of a Democratically controlled

---

* Who kept a "Think" book of her projects for a year ahead.

state house, he was rarely allowed to get away with anything that would give him political charisma.

What must have added to Pete du Pont's chagrin was an action taken by Du Pont in 1974. The company broke precedent and at last appointed a lawyer to be chairman of the board and chief executive. But it was not Pete who was sent for. The man chosen could hardly have been more of a stranger to the family's traditions. His name was Irving S. Shapiro, and as *Fortune* magazine remarked at the time:

> In several respects, Shapiro seems a wildly improbable choice to head Du Pont. It is one of the most science-minded of companies and spends $250 million a year on research, but Shapiro is a lawyer who is baffled by any technology more complex than a screwdriver. What is most astonishing of all is that the son of a poor Jewish shopkeeper should move to the top of the most family-dominated of the nation's major corporations. In all its century and three-quarters of existence, Shapiro is only the second chairman who is not related to the du Pont family.*

But Shapiro had been brought in because he had just those qualities that Pete du Pont, for all his charm, and the rest of the du Ponts, for all their money and tradition, lacked. He knew how to lead. He was a squat, solid man with a big nose, a dark complexion, and a slight hunch, as if his shoulders bent from his constant shoving of something or someone. He was the son of a Lithuanian immigrant who had settled in Minnesota where he opened a pants-pressing shop and made enough money to help his son get to the University of Minnesota. From there he had gone to Washington as part of the legal staff of the Office of Price Administration and had stayed on until the end of World War II, when he joined Du Pont's legal staff in Wilmington.

The only goal he had at that time, for all his ambitions, was to become general counsel of the company. He knew it would never occur to P.S. or any of his brothers to think of a legal man for anything except the company's legal business.

---

* The first was Charles B. McCoy, whom Shapiro succeeded. And even McCoy had family connections: His brother-in-law was a du Pont.

"Historically, lawyers had never moved beyond the legal department of Du Pont," Shapiro said later. "In the early days of Pierre's administration, the head of the legal department was always closely involved with him. Pierre always treated him very generously in terms of financial consideration, but he never moved him out of the legal department, and so there had been this tradition that one simply didn't find lawyers in the central part of the administration. Indeed, as I remember, when Mr. [Crawford] Greenewalt first became president he made some comment about lawyers being inappropriate to run a business. Much too conservative."

What changed everything was the antitrust suit. When the Supreme Court overturned Du Pont's victory at Chicago, and ordered the company to divest itself not only of General Motors but of its monopolistic holdings all down the line, Irving Shapiro was the lawyer who drew up the plan the Court eventually accepted. It was said to have been so carefully and brilliantly constructed that it saved the du Pont family nearly a billion dollars in stock it might otherwise have had to sell. Shapiro denied that.

"It was not nearly as good a settlement for the du Ponts as you might suppose, and as rumor has it," Shapiro said later. "We got a substantial amount of relief for the ordinary stockholders, du Ponts among them. But a substantial part of the burden was picked up by the stockholders of Christiana. It was the price of getting relief. In a very real sense, the members of the du Pont family took a substantial tax load in order to take care of other shareholders of the company. Everything considered, it was a favorable result, but I think history has tended to neglect the fact that the du Pont family could have done better than it did. They willingly gave up tax benefits in order to protect ordinary stockholders."

He did not suggest they had been pauperized in the process, and in any case, it is highly unlikely that his legal efforts would have been so substantially rewarded had he not done well by them in the final settlement. Anyone going back over the commentaries made by financial and political specialists in the early 1960s, when the antitrust settlement was finally resolved, cannot help noting that the experts thought Du Pont had "got away with it," and the family business had emerged from its ordeal intact.

It was not true. The efforts of Irving Shapiro saved the du Pont family fortunes, but in a way, he lost them something much more important: the power to control the family company. Thereafter strangers, outsiders, moved in. Alfred I. and Coleman du Pont would have been outraged at the idea that non–du Ponts were at last taking over the company for whose destiny they had fought successfully in 1902. P.S. would have been deeply saddened. There were still members of the family prejudiced enough to suspect a deep, dark Jewish plot when Irving Shapiro came back from Chicago and began to rise in the organization, over the heads of the du Ponts who still worked there. Pete du Pont, a member of the legal staff at the time, can hardly have shouted for joy when Shapiro leapfrogged him and was promoted to assistant general counsel of Du Pont in 1965.

But what could he do about it? What could any of them do about it? No du Pont had the necessary expertise to maintain control, even if it could be wrested from the hands of strangers. The point about Shapiro was that by the time he settled the antitrust case, he knew more about Du Pont than any of the family. He could hardly help absorbing the details.

"In the role of being counsel," he said later, "I became involved in [the company's] thinking, in the problems the management was solving, in the solutions they were proposing. In a very real sense, I wandered into it in my role as a lawyer."

But from the moment Shapiro ceased to be simply a legal adviser, and became head of Du Pont's corporate planning department, which is what happened in the sixties, it was the beginning of the end of Du Pont as a family company. Pete du Pont resigned to go into politics. The other family members on the staff eased themselves out and looked around for more promising occupations. By the mid-1970s, with Irving Shapiro as chairman of the board, there were two thousand du Ponts living in and around Wilmington, but not a single one was on the board of directors or a member of the planning committees. They who had once been the owners of Du Pont were now its *rentier* class, living on the dividends earned for them by other men.

Only the artifacts remained behind to remind visitors of how the du Ponts had once lived and worked. Longwood Gardens with its orchids and Winterthur with its antique Americana were on public show. A hospital for crippled children was rising on the grounds of Nemours, and a tower with a carillon had been erected over the spot where Alfred I., Alicia, their two doomed babies, and his third wife, Jessie, were buried.

Down below in the woods the Brandywine still flowed over the dams beside the old powder mills in Hagley Yard. Eleutherian Mills, the house that the founder of the company had built for himself back in 1803, had been restored, like the mills themselves, to pristine condition by one of the du Pont foundations. Sometimes, in the summer, with members of the Hagley Associates dressed up as powder men and their wives, the mill wheels were allowed to turn, and an attempt was made to simulate what this place had been like in the heyday of the Du Pont family firm, when this was the center of the world of black powder.

The efforts were laudable; the spectacle was entertaining. But inevitably authenticity was lacking. The essential ingredients were missing. There was no noise. There was no acrid stench of powder. There was no prickling sense of danger. And there were no cousins.

Source Notes

PROLOGUE: DEATH OF A LOVED RETAINER

In describing the circumstances surrounding the death of Lewes Mason during the influenza epidemic of 1918, I have relied both on documentary sources and the recollection of individuals. Alice Belin du Pont's diaries in the Historical Library of the Eleutherian Mills–Hagley Foundation chart the progress of Mason's illness and the steadily increasing distress of her husband, P. S. du Pont, as his favorite servant's condition worsened. I have also had access to letters from Lewes Mason's mother and sister dealing with his life at Longwood. For what was happening at the Du Pont company while the drama was being played out, I have used company records and reports. Several old Wilmington residents recalled details of the great epidemic as it affected them and their neighbors. The incident at Wilmington railroad depot, where the platform was strewn with coffins, was recounted by Mrs. Adeline Cook Strange, who passed through with her mother and two sisters in October 1918 on the way from Baltimore to New York. Mrs. Cook was only a baby at the time, but her mother often recalled the incident.

CHAPTER 1: AIDE-MÉMOIRE

In the Historical Library there is much documentary evidence about the arrival of the du Pont family in America. The patriarch of the family, Pierre Samuel du Pont, and his son, Eleuthère Irénée, both wrote many letters about it, as did the women of the family. There are also many books dealing with the period, including a three-volume history written by the late Bessie Gardner du Pont with the encouragement and financial help of her friend and sponsor, P. S. du Pont.

CHAPTER 2: THE REIGN OF HENRY THE RED

The description of the explosion at the mills in March 1818 is taken from documents in the Historical Library. The quotations from Eleuthère Irénée about his financial difficulties are to be found in the P. S. du Pont Papers (hereafter PSdP), also in the library, as are the details of how he and his cousin Victor died. The estimation of the qualities of du Pont women, particularly Evalina and Margaretta (Meta) du Pont, is derived from a close study of the letters they wrote and the comments of other members of the family in their correspondence with each other. Bessie Gardner du Pont's history of the family also proved useful in tracing the development of the company after Irénée's death, particularly with reference to the period when Antoine Bidermann and Irénée's eldest son, Alfred Victor, temporarily took over.

To find out what sort of a man was Henry (the Red) du Pont, I consulted not only PSdP and the Winterthur Papers in the Historical Library but army and other records in the Library of Congress and the National Archives. Letters to his former fellow students both at West Point and in the army give some interesting sidelights on the ruthless nature of his personality.

CHAPTER 3: THE BROTHERS

The task of building up a picture of Lammot and Mary Belin du Pont was made much easier for me by Lammot du Pont Copeland's recent gift to the Historical Library of about five thousand letters and other documents written by or concerning his maternal grandparents. The description of Lammot's journey to the Crimea is based on several different documents in this collection and PSdP, including Lammot's own letters and those of a former business associate, Theodore Grasselli. There seems to be no evidence that Lammot ever confronted Henry du Pont over the "misunderstanding" about payment for the explosives that the younger man had run through the Anglo-French blockade.

The description of the explosion in which Alexis du Pont was killed comes from a manuscript in the Historical Library, entitled "History of Explosions at Brandywine Mills Compiled from Records by Francis Gurney du Pont and Also from His Own Experiences." The account contains reports of all major disasters from 1815 to 1902.

The story of the courtship and marriage of Charlotte Henderson and Irénée du Pont II comes from family correspondence in PSdP, the Winterthur Papers, and the A. I. du Pont Papers (hereafter AIdP) in the library.

CHAPTER 4: THE WAR BETWEEN THE DU PONTS (AND THE STATES)

For the Civil War background as it concerned the family and the Du Pont company I have relied on the family letters, accounts of the period written by Colonel Henry A. du Pont in the Winterthur Papers, and a long piece entitled "My Father," by P. S. du Pont (in his papers at the library). Charlotte Henderson du Pont's tragic story is recounted in various letters exchanged between her in-laws, and in her correspondence with Sophie du Pont.

The letter from Ellen du Pont to her brother Henry Algernon about the election of President Lincoln is in the Winterthur Papers.

There are three accounts of Lammot du Pont's trip to England during the Civil War in PSdP, including some of Lammot's own letters about it. But many of the details of his stay in London (particularly of a meeting at Morley's Hotel with Lord Palmerston) cannot be confirmed from British sources, and I have not used them.

CHAPTER 5: NEW BLOOD

For the background to the marriage and career of Lammot du Pont I have relied on several sources, particularly P. S. du Pont's "My Father," the letters of Lammot's mother, Meta du Pont, and other family correspondence (PSdP). The letters of Mary Belin to Lammot, and, subsequently, to her family and other du Ponts, also provide a very full account of her thoughts and feelings. General Henry's gesture in visiting Mary on New Year's Day is described in "My Father."

For background to the activities of the Powder Trust I have gone to *History of the Explosive Industry in America* by Arthur P. Van Gelder and Hugo Schlatter (New York: Columbia University Press, 1927).

The account of the life, marriage and illness of Charlotte and Irénée du Pont is based on their letters to Sophie du Pont, and on correspondence between Sophie and other members of the family, in PSdP.

CHAPTER 6: "FROM SUDDEN DEATH, GOOD LORD, DELIVER US!"

Lammot du Pont's successes in tying up the Powder Trust and buying control of California Powder is described in P. S. du Pont's "My Father," and Henry's machinations in arranging the success are revealed by a study of the letters in the Winterthur Papers.

The description of Lammot's experiments in treating nitroglycerine were described by Theodore Grasselli in a letter to Lammot du Pont II. The account of Lammot's death in the explosion at Repauno comes from an annex to Francis Gurney du Pont's "History of Explosions at Brandywine Mills . . ." together with reports from survivors and F. G. du Pont's own letters to his brother Alexis in PSdP. Sophie du Pont's description of the funeral is taken from her diary in PSdP.

CHAPTER 7: THE CHILDREN OF THE SWAMP

The story of the orphans' defiance of a family decision to remove them from Swamp Hall is a favorite du Pont legend, and Alfred I. wrote about it later at some length in letters to be found in his papers. He also told the story many times to both his third wife, Jessie, and his brother-in-law, Edward Ball.

The story of Alfred I.'s younger days is built up from the recollections of it, which he gave Edward Ball, and references in family correspondence, particularly letters from P. S. du Pont (the cousins were still close at this time). I have also relied on Marquis James's *Alfred I. du Pont, the Family Rebel* (Indianapolis and New York: The Bobbs-Merrill Company, Inc., 1941) for much information on his early life. James was able to talk to many contemporaries who were then still alive.

For the background to the work of Thomas Alva Edison, and for his association with Alfred I. du Pont, I have relied on correspondence between James Dashiell and S. F. Mathewson in PSdP, and on James. Background to the marriage of Alfred I. and Bessie Gardner is provided by family correspondence, particularly from Marguerite du Pont Lee, in AIdP. Accounts of Alfred's journey to Paris appear in PSdP.

CHAPTER 8: LEAVE IT TO "DAD"

Background for the activities of Coleman du Pont in his early days in Kentucky come from a privately printed reminiscence written by his son-in-law, John W. Donaldson (*Caveat Venditor: A Profile of Coleman du Pont;* privately printed, Wilmington, 1964), a copy of which was lent me by a member of the family. Alfred I.'s clashes with his uncles after Henry du Pont's death are described in his own accounts of the period in his correspondence in PSdP. P. S. du Pont's progress I have followed in his and his mother's letters in the same collection.

CHAPTER 9: BROTHERLY HATE

Though the du Ponts were unfailingly deferential to Colonel Henry Algernon du Pont to his face, they could be exceedingly irreverent in their references to him in their letters, and it is from this correspondence that I have built his portrait. In particular, the letters of Mary Belin du Pont, Louisa d'Andelot du Pont, and her brother P.S. are illuminating when they purvey family gossip. It is from this correspondence and references in the Colonel's own letters in the Winterthur Papers that I have taken much information for the reconstruction of the feud between him and his brother, William du Pont.

For the story of the breakup of Alfred I. du Pont's first marriage the correspondence of Mary Belin, Lou, and P. S. du Pont in PSdP has also been of value. I have, in addition, consulted the depositions of Alfred I. and Bessie Gardner du Pont made before the Seventh District Court of South Dakota (at Sioux Falls), together with those of their daughter Mrs. Marguerite du Pont Lee and T. W. Huidekoper, R. V. Abbott, and I. M. Williamson, all of them testifying to the difficulties of the marriage. I have also heard the comments of Alfred I.'s brother-in-law, Edward Ball, on the subject, though his memories of the divorce came at second hand, via Alfred I. and his sister, Jessie.

The scandal over Maurice du Pont's marriage to an Irish girl is dealt with at length in family correspondence, and I have quoted from Lou du Pont's letter to her brother, which is in PSdP. I have also studied newspaper accounts of the young couple's homecoming.

Alfred I.'s appearance, musical activities, and work in the mills are referred to in many family letters, and there is also a sharp picture of Brandywine life in articles in *Du Pont Magazine,* particularly "Old Black Powder Days" in the issues of August-September 1927 and January 1928. For the details of the death of Louis du Pont I have consulted Wilmington, Philadelphia, and New York newspaper articles about the tragedy, and Alfred I.'s own references to it in his letters to his sister Marguerite.

P. S. du Pont described his debut as a du Pont employee in a long article he wrote in 1945, entitled "My Induction to Explosives Manufacture." Details of the change in shareholdings in the Repauno Mineral Company are also referred to in this document, which has been deposited with his papers in the Historical Library. The quotation regarding P.S.'s attitude toward the Du Pont company administration in these early days is taken from *Pierre S. du Pont: The Making of a Modern Corporation* by Alfred D. Chandler, Jr., and Stephen Salsbury (New York: Harper & Row, Publishers, 1971). P.S.'s description of how he invented smokeless powder for shotguns is also taken from "My Induction. . . ." His willingness to share credit with his uncle Francis Gurney with only modest compensation in royalties did not meet with approval in his family, and his brother Belin was particularly incensed by his modesty. In return for handing over the patent he said, "it would not be at all too high to ask say a half share in the firm with the privilege of subscribing for another half at the end of a year."

The scandal over William du Pont's marriage to Annie Zinn and his brother's subsequent maneuvers is taken from PSdP and the Winterthur Papers.

CHAPTER 10: COUP DE GRACE FOR UNCLE FRED

The story of Montchanin's affair and the subsequent marriage is to be found in PSdP. The reconstruction of the circumstances in which Alfred (Uncle Fred) du

Pont died in a bordello in Louisville has been made from contemporary newspaper accounts (the Cincinnati *Enquirer* had a field day over the scandal) and from certain documents in the family papers in the Historical Library that are still sealed but have been read by officials of the library. Their gist was conveyed to the author. The terms of Uncle Fred's will were registered in Louisville. The quotation regarding it comes from Chandler and Saulsbury. Correspondence between P.S., Belin, and Louisa du Pont is to be found in PSdP. So is Frank Gurney du Pont's letter of October 1, 1894.

CHAPTER 11: SPLIT

The correspondence concerned with P.S.'s departure from the company and his transfer to Lorain, Ohio, comes from PSdP. Alfred I.'s work in the mills during the Spanish-American War is described in Du Pont company records, and there is also a good account in James, from which the quotation is taken. Cousin Eugene's letter is in the Du Pont company records.

The du Pont family correspondence is well salted with descriptions of their involvement with automobiles, particularly in the early days of the internal-combustion engine, and it is from many of these letters that Alfred I.'s motoring adventures were reconstructed.

Much of the correspondence and other documents concerning Alfred I.'s liaison with Alicia Bradford is still restricted, but the account of their affair and subsequent marriage has been based on information provided by those who have read and studied the correspondence. Louisa du Pont's letters to her brother about Alicia are in PSdP. The same papers have helped me to build up a picture of the early association of P.S. and John J. Raskob. The centenary celebrations on the Brandywine are fully described in the letters of Louisa du Pont.

CHAPTER 12: TROIKA

There are many documents in PSdP about the takeover of the Du Pont company by the three cousins. All of them wrote copiously about it, and P.S. subsequently did a paper entitled "Reorganization of 1902," which he dictated in 1948. There are many letters from Alfred I. and Coleman concerning the transfer, and also a typewritten sketch of P.S. by John J. Raskob that deals with it, all to be found in PSdP. Some of Colonel Henry A. du Pont's views on the transfer are to be found in the Winterthur Papers.

CHAPTER 13: GUNPOWDER PLOT

Details of the maneuvers Alfred I. and Alicia Bradford indulged in during their clandestine affair come from those who have been able to read the restricted letters and correspondence in AIdP. The story of Alfred I.'s association with Thomas

Alva Edison and Dr. Miller Reese Hutchinson is based on accounts in James and in *Edison, the Man and His Work* by George B. Bryan (1926). Alfred I.'s growing regard for Jessie Ball has been reconstructed from letters in PSdP and James, and from conversations with Jessie's brother, Edward Ball, as has the account of the shooting accident.

The subsequent behavior of Bessie Gardner du Pont while her husband was hospitalized was described by Marguerite du Pont in a deposition before the divorce court in South Dakota. Louisa du Pont's letters to her brother about the situation come from PSdP.

CHAPTER 14: COLEMAN'S NEW ROLE

The study of Coleman du Pont's political activities in Delaware is based on contemporary newspaper accounts. John J. Raskob's account of his honeymoon comes from the Raskob Papers in the Historical Library. Alfred I.'s continuing affair with Alicia Bradford, his divorce, and other matters pertaining to his break with Bessie are reconstructed from a study of the records in South Dakota, letters in PSdP, and accounts given by those who have read the restricted letters in AIdP. The legal exchanges between the two trustees of the children are in PSdP, as are accounts of the death of William du Pont.

CHAPTER 15: UNTRUSTWORTHY

The account of the antitrust suit is based on the evidence given in Circuit Court of the United States, Delaware, No. 280 in Equity, United States of America, Petitioner V. E. I. du Pont de Nemours and Company et al. Defendants, Petitioners' Brief, Defendants' Brief, Petitioners' Testimony, Defendants' Testimony, vols. 1–5. P. S. du Pont's comment on the case in a letter to Coleman is in PSdP, and further references are taken from "My Induction. . . ."

The exchange of correspondence between G. Q. Horwitz and P. S. du Pont over the care and maintenance of Alfred I. and Bessie du Pont's children is taken from PSdP, as is Alfred I.'s letter concerning the education of his son, Alfred Victor. The story of the quarrel over the Wilmington Symphony Orchestra is based on these same documents and contemporary press reports in Philadelphia and New York newspapers. Alfred I.'s farewell to the powder men is taken from E. I. du Pont de Nemours' records, and his remarks to Edward Ball are those remembered by Mr. Ball.

CHAPTER 16: COUSINLY COOLNESS, BROTHERLY LOVE

Alfred I.'s comments on the new Hotel du Pont are to be found in PSdP. His remark about the wall at Nemours is repeated in many family documents, reminiscences, and letters. The description of Longwood comes from Chandler and

Saulsbury. The story of Coleman du Pont's road and his adventures in New York is told in Donaldson.

The account of Alfred I.'s bill to have his son's name changed is based on records in the Delaware State House of Representatives for 1913, his statements to the press, and contemporary newspaper reports. Coleman's letter to P.S. is in PSdP. Irénée du Pont's proposal to divide up the world markets is taken from the Irénée du Pont Papers (hereafter IdP) in the Historical Library, as is Judge Laffley's letter. P.S.'s letters to Coleman about Du Pont's wartime boom and the Kraftmeier visit are in PSdP.

CHAPTER 17: PATIENCE REWARDED

The story of Alice Belin's wedding is based on a study of her diary extracts, entries in her notebooks, and letters in PSdP.

For the story of the takeover of the Du Pont company by P.S. and his brothers I have used several sources, including evidence subsequently given in the suit *Philip F. du Pont et al.* v *Pierre S. du Pont et al.,* in the Circuit Court of the United States for the Third Circuit; the studies of it by P. S. du Pont in "Coleman Sells Out," which he wrote in 1941; and Alfred I.'s version of the affair as recounted in James.

The account of Alicia's sojourn in Europe and the death of her baby is told in family letters in PSdP.

CHAPTER 18: FEUD

Once more I have used evidence given before the Circuit Court of the United States for the Third District in the suit *Philip F. du Pont et al.* v. *Pierre S. du Pont et al.* for background to my account of what happened after P.S. bought out Coleman. The family letters quoted come from PSdP. Alfred I.'s comment on the verdict comes from AIdP.

P.S.'s comments on the Wilson administration are taken from Chandler and Saulsbury.

Alfred I.'s political activities in Dover against Coleman du Pont are described in contemporary newspaper accounts and in family correspondence in the Historical Library. The "second honeymoon" trip taken by P.S. and Alice is described in his letters to his sister Louisa. His decision not to cut it short is mentioned in Chandler and Saulsbury.

CHAPTER 19: DOUBLE-DYED VILLAINS?

Du Pont's chemical activities and its explosives production during World War I are fully dealt with in Chandler and Saulsbury, and I have based portions of this account on that work. The description of P.S.'s gradual disenchantment with the government in Washington was developed from his writings, culminating with his correspondence with Zara du Pont, which is in PSdP.

The activities of the du Ponts in Delaware politics are described in both PSdP and the Raskob Papers, and it is on these as well as contemporary newspaper accounts that I have based my description.

Alice Belin du Pont's wartime activities are traced in her diaries and notebooks, in which the verses quoted are contained. The death of Lewes Mason is also described in these diaries, P.S.'s subsequent efforts to procure an adequate portrait of him are described in his letters in PSdP. The speech he made on September 19, 1925, is to be found in contemporary newspapers.

The account of the death of Alicia Bradford du Pont and her funeral is based on contemporary newspaper accounts and James.

CHAPTER 20: INTERNAL COMBUSTION

P. S. du Pont's memorandum to his executives is to be found in PSdP. Marguerite du Pont Lee's letter to Coleman is also there, as is his subsequent account of it to P.S. The reunion of Alfred I. and Jessie Ball, and his marriage to her, are based on contemporary newspaper accounts, comments in family letters, James, and conversations with Edward Ball.

For my account of Du Pont's association with General Motors I have relied on the Raskob Papers, which give a full account, and Chandler and Saulsbury, and *Strategy and Structure* (M.I.T. Press, 1965) by Alfred D. Chandler, Jr.

Alice's letters to her husband are in PSdP.

CHAPTER 21: SPREADING THE LOAD

The account of Paul du Pont's venture into automobile manufacture is based on a study of family correspondence, particularly letters between him and his brother-in-law in IdP.

Lammot du Pont's marital adventures were described by a member of the family who knew him well. The account of Du Pont's efforts to secure German chemists after World War I is based on documents in company records and on a report on the activities of German chemical firms in Joseph Borkin's *The Crime and Punishment of I. G. Farben* (New York: The Free Press, 1978).

CHAPTER 22: DIRTY DEALS

For the activities of P. S. du Pont in building and establishing gardens and greenhouses at Longwood, I have relied on the documents in the Longwood section of PSdP. P.S.'s efforts to improve Delaware education are also well documented in his papers. Marguerite du Pont Lee's letter to P.S. is in PSdP, and Irénée's letter about Alfred I. comes from IdP.

The account of Alfred I.'s jousts with the United States tax authorities is based on his available papers in the Historical Library, newspaper accounts, James, and conversations with Edward Ball. His letters concerning Jessie are in AIdP. P.S.'s letter concerning Alfred Victor and his treatment in the press is in PSdP, as is Alfred Victor's telegram announcing his marriage. Jessie du Pont's efforts to bring about a family reconciliation are told in AIdP, where her husband's letters to his son are to be found. P.S.'s comments on the situation are in PSdP. The description of the family reunion at Nemours is based on a later account written by Marcella du Pont, and on James. The story of how Alfred Victor decided to leave his Du Pont job is told in letters exchanged between him and P. S. in PSdP.

CHAPTER 23: FILTHY RICH

The account of the formation of Christiana Securities and P.S.'s tight hold on it is told in company records and in Chandler and Saulsbury. Details of activities at Longwood come from the Longwood documents in PSdP. John J. Raskob's account of his fall from General Motors is in the Raskob Papers, and P.S.'s decision to resign is recounted in his own description of his General Motors association, in PSdP.

Mrs. Adeline Cook Strange told me some absorbing stories about her father, Bishop Philip Cook, and his (and her family's) association with the du Ponts. But the account of his involvement in the trouble with Philip du Pont's daughter comes from a source within the family.

Harold Glendening's letter to P.S. about Pechette is taken from PSdP.

The death of Coleman du Pont is described in Donaldson. Raskob's letters to Coleman are to be found in the Raskob Papers.

CHAPTED 24: FLORIDIAN

For the details of Alfred I.'s and Edward Ball's activities in Florida I have relied upon the available papers, accounts by Edward Ball in conversations with the author, and contemporary newspaper accounts. The account of Ed Ball's marriage is based on stories told by members of the family.

CHAPTER 25: HARVESTING

The letter from Raskob is in his papers, and that from Marguerite du Pont Lee is in PSdP. Irénée du Pont's character and activities have been reconstructed from accounts given by his relatives and those who were close to him in his lifetime, and it is upon them that I have relied for my description of Xanadu. The letter from Irénée to the college debating society is in IdP. These sources have also given a thorough description of Lammot du Pont's character and background.

The account of the building of Nemours and of Alfred Victor's architectural activities comes from his papers at the Historical Library. Descriptions of Alfred I.'s death and his will were repeated from accounts given by Edward Ball, members of the family, and James, as well as contemporary newspaper accounts.

CHAPTER 26: PURITY HALL

For my account of the invention of nylon and the background of its creators, Wallace Carothers and Julian Hill, I have studied the Du Pont records, Dr. Hill's own privately printed booklet about his collaborator (*Wallace Hume Carothers,* reprinted from Proceedings of The Robert A. Welch Foundation Conferences on Chemical Research, Houston, Texas, Nov. 8–10, 1976), many books about the development of polymers, and conversations with those who were associated with the research, notably Nathaniel Wyeth. The correspondence between Carothers and his old mentor at Cornell is taken from the Du Pont Papers in the Historical Library, as are accounts of how the name *nylon* was chosen and the story of nylon's progress to the marketplace. The death of Wallace Carothers was described in contemporary newspaper accounts, and my own account was reinforced by information from those who had known and worked with him.

The description of Alice's death, and P.S.'s letters about her during her final illness, are in PSdP, as are details of how her death certificate was changed.

CHAPTER 27: CLASS ACTION

For the account of Du Pont's activities in World War II, I have relied on company records and Gerald Colby Zilg's well-researched *Du Pont: Behind the Nylon Curtain* (Englewood Cliffs: Prentice-Hall, 1974). I have also used Du Pont records as published in *Moody's Industrial Manuals* for the period 1945–46 to show the rate of the company's postwar development. Descriptions of the one-hundred-and-fiftieth birthday celebrations are to be found in PSdP, and letters of condolence to P.S. after Bessie's death are also to be found there.

The antitrust suit that eventually led to Du Pont's divestment of General Motors was a long and complicated case, and for background to it I have studied petitions and statements in the suit *United States Government* v. *Du Pont, General Motors, and United States Rubber Company.* Letters referring to the suit are in PSdP.

P.S.'s letter regarding a present for Henri Petit is also in PSdP.

CHAPTER 28: CHAIN REACTION

For my account of P.S.'s successors I have relied upon Du Pont company records and stories told by members of the family or those close to them. The account of the failure of Corfam is in the company records, and the bankruptcy of

Charles du Pont Copeland's son is well documented in Zilg and contemporary newspaper accounts.

Irving Shapiro spent some time talking to me about Du Pont developments and his own assumption of power, and it is on those conversations that I have relied for my quotations. The description of Pierre du Pont IV's political career as congressman and governor of Delaware comes from newspaper accounts and conversations with his political friends (and enemies) in Wilmington and Dover.

INDEX

Acetates, 303
Acetylene polymers, 366
Addicks, John Edward O'Sullivan, 195, 196
Air-conditioning, 185
Airplane dopes, 303
Akouphone, 185, 186
Alexandra, Queen of England, 185
Alfred I. du Pont: The Family Rebel
 (James), 92*n*, 95*n*, 146*n*
Alfred I. du Pont Bridge, 345
Alicia (yacht), 203
Allee, J. Frank, 263
Allen, Major General Henry T., 307
Almours Securities, 339, 341, 356
Al's Band. *See* Tankopanicum Orchestra
American Chemical Society, 364
American Eagle (ship), 21
American Powder Company, 69
American Tobacco Company, 210, 211
Angell, Louise B., 224
Aniline dyes, 303
Antifreeze, 377

Antitrust legislation. *See* Sherman
 Antitrust Act
Apalachicola Northern railroad, 339
Arnold, General Henry, 379
Atlantic City, N.J., 148, 149
Atlas dynamite, 77
Atlas Powder Company, 211
Atomic bomb, 378
Aufschlager, Dr. G., 234
Austin Powder Company, 69
Automobile industry, 287–292, 299–302,
 377, 378
Automobiles, 147, 286, 368

Badische Anilin und Sodafabrik (BASF),
 327
Baker, Newton D., 269
Ball, Edward, 186, 219, 285, 286
 financial adviser to Alfred I., 317–320,
 338–345
 marriage of, 346
 and politics, 342, 344, 345

Ball, Jessie Dew. *See* du Pont, Jessie Dew Ball
Ball, Ruth Latham Price, 346
Ball, Thomas, 319
Ball family, 186–187, 285
Ballistite, 233
Ball's Island, Va., 186, 188, 218, 285
Bancroft, John, 205, 212, 213
Barbary Coast pirates, 26
Barksdale, Hamilton M., 167, 218
    death of, 275
Barre, Mrs., 14
BASF (Badische Anilin und Sodafabrik), 327
Bates, Mrs. Lindon, 261
Battery solution, 303
Battles, Dr., 154
Bauduy, Ferdinand, 28, 33
Bauduy, Jean-Pierre, 28
Bauduy, Victorine. *See* du Pont, Victorine (d. 1861)
Bayer company, Cologne, 305, 306
Belgium, 99
Belin, Greta, 241
Belin, Henry (Harry), 57, 82, 123, 151, 239, 274
    and Du Pont, 40, 53, 65, 179
Belin, Henry Jr., 240–241
Belin, Lammot, 287
Belin, Mary. *See* du Pont, Mary Belin
Bell, John, 54
Bellevue-Stratford Hotel, Phila., 12
Bergen Point, N.J., 22, 23
Bidermann, Evaline. *See* du Pont, Evalina
Bidermann, Jacques, 21, 23, 27
Bidermann, Jacques (James) Antoine, 27–28, 34
    death of, 63
    and Du Pont, 30, 33, 35, 36, 37
Bijou Theater, Boston, 90
Black powder, 3, 59, 181, 211–212, 218
Blacks, and education, 311
Blaff, Mr., 391
Blaine, James G., 100
Blasting powder, 75
    prices, 68, 69
    soda, 91–92
Boca Grande (island), 372
Bois des Fosses (estate), 20
Bonaparte, Napoleon, 29, 30
Boomer du Pont Properties, 335
Bosch, Dr. Carl, 304, 305, 307
Bosphorus Strait, 45
Bouvé, Clement Lincoln, 307
Bradford, Alicia. *See* du Pont, Alicia Bradford Maddox

Bradford, Edward Green, 148, 315 and *n*
    relationship with daughter Alicia, 148, 158, 160, 161, 166, 188, 202, 280
    U.S. Circuit Court Judge, 148, 257–258
Bradford, Edward Jr., 203, 241, 285, 315
    in politics, 263
Bradford, Eleuthera (Eloo). *See* du Pont Eleuthera Bradford
Bradford, Eleuthera Paulina du Pont, 149, 158, 161, 315
Bradford, Elizabeth. *See* du Pont Elizabeth Bradford
Bradford, Joanna du Pont, 217
Brandywine Creek, 23, 24, 40
Brandywine Hundred Realty Company, 339
Brandywine River, 4, 23, 24
Breckenridge, John C., 53, 54
Brereton, Ruth, 257
British India, 60
Broom, Jacob, 24, 25
Brown, Harry F., 248
Brown prismatic powder, 145
Bryn Mawr College, 238
Buchanan, Mr. and Mrs. Albert, 95*n*
Buckeye Powder Company, 208
Buckner, Col., 236
Buffington, Joseph, 260
Buick, 289
Bush, Mary, 217

Cadillac (auto), 289
Caernarvon, Lord, 332
California Investment Company, 211
California Powder Company, 74, 75, 76, 170
Cannon Mills, 371
Cannons, 59
Carlton House, N.Y., 329
Carney's Point factory, 122–125, 132–135, 140–143
Carothers, Helen Sweetman, 367–368
Carothers, Isobel (Lu), 365, 367
Carothers, Wallace Hume, 362, 363–367
    death of, 368
    marriage of, 367
Carpenter, Louisa d'Andelot, 370
Carpenter, Ruly, 206, 245, 246, 303, 370
Carpenter, Walter S., 374
Carpenter, Walter Jr., 387
Cars. *See* Automobiles
Castro, Fidel, 390
Cathedral of Saint John the Divine, N.Y., 280
Catherine II, Empress of Russia, 355
Cedar Creek, Battle of, 59
Cellophane, 268, 339, 361, 362, 377
Celluloid, 268, 327

Cellulose, 327, 361, 362
Central America, powder market, 183
Central Coal and Iron Company, 102, 103, 130
Central Park (mansion), 130
Century Club, Wilmington, 217
Cervera Y Topete, Pascual, 144, 146
Chalfont, Catherine, 12, 14
Charcoal, 91, 303
Cherry Island, 186, 285
Chevrolet, Louis, 288, 289
Chevrolet Motor Company, 291
Chicago Opera, 6
Chicago *Tribune,* 210
Christiana Securities, 247*n*, 297, 298, 326, 327, 349, 373, 378, 381, 395, 398
Christina River, 24
Christ's Church, Wilmington, 49, 87, 94, 115, 160, 161, 349
Chrysler, Walter, 288
Cincinnati *Enquirer,* 130
Cinecameras, 185
Citizens Bank, Tampa, 341
Civil War, 3, 4, 50, 51, 52–61, 62, 63
Clara Lu and Em (singing group), 365
Clark, Ethel, 109
Clark, Tom, 388
Clean Foods Products Company, 317–318
Clothing, 303
    cold-and-heat resistant, 378
    nylon, 369–371
Coal mining, 102–103
Cocoa powder, 99, 105
Coleman, Ellen. *See* du Pont, Ellen Coleman
Coleman, Bishop Leighton, 155, 158, 202 and *n,* 203
Conant, James B., 363 and *n*
Connable, Mr., 201
Constitutional Union Party, 54
Cook, Jim and Araminta, 119
Cook, Bishop Philip, 330, 331, 332, 357
    death of, 390
Cook, Mrs. Philip, 330
Coopals and Company (Belgium), 100, 105, 106
Copeland, Charles, 134
    and Du Pont, 194, 254
    and Lou du Pont:
        marriage, 154, 206, 265
        son of, 393–395
Copeland, Lammot du Pont, 393–395
Copeland, Lammot du Pont, Jr., 394–395
Copeland, Louisa (Lou) d'Andelot. *See* du Pont, Louisa d'Andelot
Copper mining, 76

Corfam, 393–394
Correspondence between Thomas Jefferson and Pierre Samuel du Pont de Nemours 1798–1815, 30*n*
Cowan, William, 39
Coyne, William, 248
Cretic (steamship), 292
Crimean War, 43–45
Crownfield, Eleanor, 277
Cuba, 3, 146, 390

Dacron, 365*n,* 392
Dallas Streetcar Company, 153
Dalmas, Charles, 25
Dashiell, Jimmy, 184, 216, 217
Daw, John, 238
DDT (insecticide), 377
Dearborn, Henry, 27
DeHavilland, Olivia, 332
Delaware:
    Brandywine County, 54
    Christian Hundred County, 54
    and Civil War, 50, 52, 53, 54, 57
    climate, 25, 27
    Kent County, 52, 54, 57
    newspapers, 263, 284–285, 311
    public schools, 310–311
    Republican Party, 283, 284, 311
    Sussex County, 52, 54, 57
    tax laws, 264, 328
Delaware (battleship), 216
Delaware Investment Company, 180, 211
Delaware River, 24
Delaware Security Company, 180, 211
Delaware Trust Company, 263
Delmarva Peninsula, 52
Dent, Elbert, 323, 324
Depression, 343, 351
Dern, George, 357
Derna, Libya, 26
Dewey, Admiral George, 4, 144
Divorce, 125, 126, 127, 202
Douglas, Stephen, 54*n*
Dover *Sentinel,* 263
Drown, Dr. D., 108–109
DuBell, A. Rae, 385
Duco paint, 327
Duisberg, Dr. Carl, 303, 304
Dulles, Allen Welsh, 306 and *n*
Dulles, Janet, 348
Dunham, L. L., 243
Du Pont, Adelaide Camille Denise, 278
Du Pont, Aileen, 374
Du Pont, Alexis I. (1816–1857), 35–38, 40, 47, 76
    death of, 48–49

Du Pont, Alexis I. (1843–1904), 80, 176
  death of, 166*n*
  and Du Pont, 106, 166
Du Pont, Alexis I. (Lex) (1869–1921),
    109–110, 114, 135*n*
  and Du Pont, 194, 246
Du Pont, Alfred I.:
  and Alicia Bradford:
    friendship of, 148–150, 158–161,
      174, 184, 186, 187–188, 198, 199,
      200
    marriage of, 201–202, 203, 216–217,
      278–280
  and Bessie Gardner:
    children of, 203–205, 212–215, 230–
      231, 320–325
    friendship of, 96–98
    marriage of, 98, 107, 108, 116–121,
      145, 146, 149–150, 158, 161–162,
      186, 191, 192, 199, 200
  business ventures, 277–278, 317–319
  childhood of, 71, 81, 82, 86–88
  deafness, 146–147
  death of, 357
  and Du Pont, 91–94, 104, 115, 116
    Hagley Mills, 140–141, 143
    lawsuits against, 225–260, 282, 283
    1902 purchase of (with T. Coleman,
      P.S.), 165–172
    smokeless powder, 99–100, 105, 106
    vice-president and general manager,
      173, 178, 180, 194, 203, 211, 212,
      213, 214, 218, 219, 228
  education (M.I.T.), 89–90
  finances, 224, 283–286
    income taxes paid, 283, 285, 312, 313,
      318
    stock in Du Pont, 236*n,* 242–243,
      284, 286, 298, 312–313
  inventions of, 95, 119 and *n,* 184, 185
  investment in Florida, 338–345
  and Jessie Ball:
    friendship of, 186–189, 219, 229,
      278–279
    marriage of, 285, 313–316, 323, 324,
      333–334, 340–341, 345–346, 355–
      357
  loss of eye, 189–191, 199
  and music, 119, 120, 146–147, 184, 185
  and politics, 263–264, 271–272
  relationship with cousin P.S., 198–202,
    228–231
  will of, 320–322, 356–357
Du Pont (Alfred I.) Bridge, 345
Du Pont, Alfred Victor (1798–1856),
    35–39

Du Pont, Alfred Victor (1833–1893)
    (Uncle Fred), 40
  death of, 129–131
  business ventures, 102, 130
  estate of, 130–131
  as guardian of Irénée's children, 71, 73,
    86, 87, 89, 91
  as guardian of Lammot's children, 81,
    82, 107, 123
  in Kentucky, 46, 47, 53, 65, 101–102
Du Pont, Alfred Victor (1900–1970), 316
  and architecture, 325, 341, 355
  birth of, 150, 161
  and Du Pont, 317, 324–325
  marriage of, 317
  relationship with parents, 188, 192,
    203–204, 214–215, 230–231, 320–
    324
Du Pont, Alice (Elsie), 103, 151, 188,
    213–214, 227, 335
Du Pont, Alice Belin:
  death of, 375
  and Pierre Samuel du Pont:
    friendship of, 151–152, 179, 226,
      238–241
    marriage of, 10–15, 249–251, 265–
      266, 274–276, 292–293, 347
  Red Cross work, 273, 372, 374
Du Pont, Alicia Bradford Maddox, 138, 257
  and Alfred I. du Pont:
    children of, 213, 242
    friendship of, 148–150, 158–161,
      174, 184, 186, 187–188, 198, 199,
      200
    marriage of, 201–202, 203, 216–217,
      278–280
  death of, 279–280
  health of, 225, 229
  marriage to George Maddox, 159–162,
    174, 184, 200, 201
Du Pont, Amelia, 27, 29, 110, 119, 134
Du Pont, Anna (1860–1899), 71, 73, 86–
    88, 91, 96, 97, 126
  marriage of, 98
Du Pont, Annie Rogers Zinn, 125–127,
    155, 156
Du Pont, Bella (Bella du Pont Sharp),
    206, 372
Du Pont, Bessie (Bep 1889–1973), 145,
    188, 192
  birth of, 116
  relationship with father, 314–315, 316,
    320, 321, 322
Du Pont, Bessie Gardner, 96, 97, 100, 104,
    107, 216

Du Pont, Bessie Gardner (*continued*)
and Alfred I. du Pont:
children of, 203–205, 212–215, 230–
231, 320–325
friendship of, 96–98
marriage of, 98, 107–108, 116–121,
145, 146, 149–150, 158, 161–162,
186, 191, 192, 199, 200
death of, 380
in Europe, 188–192
as family historian, 316 and *n*
friendship with P. S. du Pont, 203–205,
212, 214, 316, 317
Du Pont, Bidermann, 40, 81–82, 130–131
coal mines of, 102–103
in Kentucky, 46, 47, 53, 65
marriage of, 65
Du Pont, Caroline Hynson Stollenwerk,
353–354
Du Pont, Charles, 53, 55, 67, 139, 176
death of, 166
and Du Pont, 115–116, 121, 167
Du Pont, Charlotte Henderson, 49–61, 70–
73
death of, 73
Du Pont, E. Frances (the Black Banana),
331, 332
Du Pont, E. Paul, 385
Du Pont, Edward, 138, 139
Du Pont, Eleuthera (Eleuthera du Pont
Smith), 35 and *n*
Du Pont, Eleuthera (sister of Henry the
General), 63
Du Pont, Eleuthera Bradford (Eloo), 138–
139, 148, 331
Du Pont, Eleuthera Pauline (1848–1906).
See Bradford, Eleuthera Paulina du
Pont
Du Pont, Eleuthera Paulina (1912–1912),
213
Du Pont, Eleuthère (son of T. Coleman),
335
Du Pont, Eleuthère Irénée (1772–1834),
20–25, 32, 33, 171*n*
death of, 34
Du Pont, Eleuthère Irénée (1829–1877):
death of, 73
and Du Pont, 36–40, 46, 49, 50, 54–61,
65, 76
marriage of, 49–51, 70–73
Du Pont, Elise (Lisa) Simons, 109
Du Pont, Elizabeth Bradford, 166, 216,
217, 255, 299
Du Pont, Ellen Coleman, 65
Du Pont, Emily Bradford, 202, 391
Du Pont, Ethel Hallock, 154, 206

Du Pont, Eugene (1840–1902), 48, 134
death of, 165
and Du Pont, 76, 80, 104, 105, 106, 109,
112, 114, 116, 122, 141, 145
estate of, 172
Du Pont, Eugene (1863–1916), 254
Du Pont, Evalina (Evalina du Pont Bidermann), 34–36, 53, 55, 56
death of, 61, 63
home of, 64
marriage of, 28
Du Pont, Felix (Lex), 135 and *n*, 136,
137, 201, 302, 378
Du Pont, Francis Gurney, 176
and Du Pont, 76, 80, 81
Hagley Yard, 91, 92, 95
senior partner, 104–125 *passim*, 131–
133, 145, 166–168
relationship with P. S. du Pont, 132, 133,
135–137, 140–143
Du Pont, Francis I. (1873–1942), 133,
135, 176, 285
Du Pont, Frank, 335, 336
Du Pont, Henry (the General) (1812–
1889), 35, 37–38, 66, 67, 85, 86,
87, 98, 99
death of, 100, 101
and Du Pont, 37–64 *passim*, 75, 76, 77,
80, 81, 122
and Gunpowder Trade Association, 68–
70
Du Pont, Henry Algernon (the Colonel)
(1838–1926), 72, 81, 155, 176,
255
death of, 299
and Du Pont, 76–77, 104, 112, 166, 168,
298
military career, 49, 58–59, 64, 113
in politics, 195, 209, 227, 255, 263, 298
relationship with brother William, 113,
125–127, 298–299
Du Pont, Henry Belin (Bese) (1873–
1902), 141, 142, 147
death of, 177
and Du Pont, 133, 137
health of, 134, 138, 139, 154
and Louviers, 174–175, 257
marriage of, 138
Du Pont, Henry Belin II (1898–1970),
139, 391
Du Pont, Henry Francis (1880–1893),
379, 387
Du Pont, Irene, 142–143, 157, 206, 303,
330, 349, 350, 351
death of, 390
Red Cross work, 372

Du Pont, Irénée (Buss) (1876–1963), 157
  death of, 390
  and Du Pont:
    antitrust suit against, 383, 387
    executive committee, 6, 206, 229
    president of, 299–300, 301, 302, 312,
      349, 351
    vice-president of, 232–234, 236, 245,
      246, 248
  and Irene du Pont:
    children of, 303, 328, 349–350
    marriage of, 142–143, 159, 303
  and Xanadu (home), 350, 351, 372, 390
Du Pont, Irénée, Jr., 391
Du Pont, Isabella d'Andelot, 70
Du Pont, Janis, 396 and *n*
Du Pont, Jessie Dew Ball, 338
  and Alfred I. du Pont:
    friendship of, 186–187, 188–189, 219,
      229, 278–279
    marriage of, 285, 313–316, 323, 324,
      333–334, 340–341, 345–346, 355–
      357
Du Pont, Joanna Smith, 63
Du Pont, Lammot (1831–1884):
  death of, 80–82
  and Du Pont, 39–54 *passim*, 59, 60, 63
  estate of, 107
  and Gunpowder Trade Association, 68,
    69, 70
  and Mary Belin:
    children of, 70, 106, 107
    marriage of, 65, 68
  and Repauno Mineral Company, 77–80,
    107
Du Pont, Lammot (1880–1952):
  death of, 383
  and Du Pont, 218, 229, 245
    chairman of the board, 349
    Miscellaneous Manufacturing Depart-
      ment, 268, 361
    products developed, 303
    president of, 374
    stock in, 245– 248
  marriages, 302, 353–354
  at M.I.T., 123, 154
Du Pont, Louis Cazenove, 70, 86, 87, 96,
  97, 117, 119
  death of, 120–121
Du Pont, Louisa d'Andelot (Lou), 114,
  118, 126, 138–139, 191, 206
  birth of, 70
  correspondence with brother P.S., 114,
    118, 126, 132, 134, 136, 146, 150,
    152, 154, 160, 165, 192, 200, 202,
    230

Du Pont, Louisa d'Andelot (Lou) (*con-
    tinued*)
  and Du Pont family centennial celebra-
    tion, 155, 156, 157 and *n*
  marriage of, 154, 191, 206, 265, 393
Du Pont, Louisa Gerhard, 38, 109, 110
Du Pont, Margaretta (Margaretta du Pont
    Bancroft Hiebler Ruoff), 100, 188,
    190–191, 192
  birth, 99
  marriages of, 204, 205, 212, 213, 214,
    354
Du Pont, Marcella Millar, 317, 323, 324,
    380
Du Pont, Margaretta (Margaretta du Pont
    Greenwalt), 350
Du Pont, Margaretta (Peg), 107, 206
Du Pont, Margaretta LaMotte (Meta), 35–
    39, 46, 47, 50–61, 66, 71, 73, 131,
    150
Du Pont, Margery Fitzgerald, 101, 148,
    149, 157, 158, 285, 313
  marriage of, 117–119
Du Pont, Marguerite (Marguerite du Pont
    Lee), 71, 86, 87, 157, 189, 190,
    284, 315, 348–349
  marriage of, 96, 97, 157
Du Pont, Mary Belin (1893–1913), 54,
    126, 134, 175
  death of, 226, 239
  and Lammot du Pont, 79–82, 106, 107
    children of, 70, 108
    marriage of, 65–68
Du Pont, Mary d'Andelot, 206
Du Pont, Mary Jane, 331
Du Pont, Maurice, 86, 87, 101, 148, 149,
    157, 158, 203, 285
  marriage of, 117–119
Du Pont, May, 125, 155, 156, 158, 202,
    255
Du Pont, Nathalie, 206
Du Pont, Paul, 299–302
Du Pont, Paulina, 30, 131
Du Pont, Pauline, 76, 112
Du Pont, Philip, 254–257, 299, 331, 332
Du Pont, Pierre Samuel (Pierre Samuel du
    Pont de Nemours, 1739–1817),
    20–23, 28, 29–31
  birth of, 20
  death of, 31
  debts of, 33, 35
Du Pont, Pierre Samuel (1870–1954):
  and Alice Belin:
    friendship of, 151–152, 179, 226,
      238–241
    marriage of, 10–15, 249–251, 265–
      266, 274–276, 292–293, 347

Du Pont, Pierre Samuel (*continued*)
  birth of, 70
  correspondence with sister Lou, 114, 118,
    126, 132, 134, 136, 137, 146, 150,
    152, 154, 160, 165, 192, 200, 202,
    230
  death of, 387
  and death of father, 81–82
  and death of Lewes Mason, 5–15, 275–
    277, 292, 309
  and Du Pont, 110, 111, 121
    antitrust suits against, 381–384, 387
    Carney's Point factory, 122–125, 132,
      133, 135, 140–143
    finance committee, 349
    president of, 9, 254
    purchase of (with Alfred I., T. Cole-
      man), 167–172
    purchase of T. Coleman's stock in,
      243–249
    treasurer of, 173, 178, 180, 181, 183,
      194, 202, 203, 212, 214, 218, 228–
      237
  finances of, 224, 236*n*, 287, 373, 376
  and General Motors:
    chairman of the board, 287, 289, 329–
      330
    president of, 291, 292, 302
    shares in, 287
  as guardian of brothers and sisters, 11,
    132, 134, 153, 154, 228, 297
  home of. *See* Longwood Gardens
  and Johnson Steel Company, 141–143,
    150–153, 169
  at M.I.T., 104, 107–110, 121
  nicknamed "Dad" by family, 123 and *n*,
    197 and *n*, 385
  old-age, 384–386
  pensions paid by, 386
  public schools built, 310–311
  relationship with Alfred I., 198–202,
    228–231, 281–283, 357
  relationship with Frank Gurney, 132,
    133, 135–137, 140–143
  retired, 326, 373, 374
  as trustee and patron of Bessie G. and her
    children, 203–205, 212, 214, 316,
    317
  turnpike built by, 286 and *n*
Du Pont, Pierre Samuel III, 391, 396
Du Pont, Pierre IV (Pete), 396–397, 399
Du Pont, Renée, 335, 336
Du Pont, Reynolds, 378, 379, 392, 393
Du Pont, Richard, 378–379
Du Pont, Samuel (French watchmaker),
  20, 337
Du Pont, Samuel (1914–1914), 242

Du Pont, Samuel Francis (the Admiral),
  27, 35, 53, 56, 58
  death of, 63
Du Pont, Sophie Dalmas, 23, 25, 27, 33
  death of, 34
Du Pont, Sophie Madeleine (1810–1888),
  27, 35, 46–47, 49, 50, 51, 53, 55,
  56, 58, 81
  death of, 113
  income of, 63
Du Pont, Sophie M. (1871–1894), 123,
  134–136
  death of, 136
Du Pont, Thomas Coleman:
  and Central Coal and Iron Company,
    102–103
  childhood, 65, 81, 82
  death of, 336
  and Du Pont, 224
    president of, 173, 178, 180–183, 193,
      194, 196, 202, 203, 209, 212–214,
      218, 228, 231, 235–237, 247
    purchase of (with Alfred I., P.S.),
      168–172
  health of, 227, 334–336
  and Johnson Steel Company, 131, 141
  at M.I.T., 89–90
  in politics, 195–196, 209, 262–264, 271,
    272, 284, 285, 311, 312
  U.S. Highway 13 built by, 227–228, 262,
    334
Du Pont, Victor (1767–1827), 20, 21, 22,
  27, 29
  death of, 33–34
Du Pont, Victor (brother of Charles), 194
Du Pont, Victorine (d. 1861), 34, 35
  death of, 63
  marriage of, 28
Du Pont, Victorine (1903–1965), 188,
  192, 320–324
  birth of, 162
Du Pont, William (Willie, 1855–1928),
  255
  death of, 299
  divorce from May, 155, 202
  and Du Pont:
    partner in, 76, 77, 104, 114, 127
    president of Repauno Mineral Com-
      pany, 114, 127
    stock in, 236*n*, 242, 243
  marriage to Annie Rogers Zinn, 125–
    127, 155, 202
  relationship with brother Henry A., 113–
    116, 125–127, 156, 298–299
Du Pont, William K. (1874–1907), 154,
  170*n*
  death of, 10, 206–207

Du Pont, Zara, 255, 270–271
Du Pont Building, Wilmington, 3, 193, 223
Du Pont Car, 299–302
Du Pont Circle, Washington, D.C., 63
Du Pont (E. I.) Company, 182, 183
Du Pont (E. I.) de Nemours and Company:
  antitrust suits against:
    1907, 205, 208–211
    1950, 381–384, 387, 388–389, 398, 399
  assets of, 170, 172, 184
  Carney's Point factory, 122–125, 132–135, 140–143
  centenary celebration of founding of, 175–176
  Civil War powder production, 4, 58, 59, 60, 62
  domestic markets, 182, 183, 194
  explosions and fires at, 29, 30–33, 39 and *n*, 47–48
  founded, 35–36
  French business ended, 35
  General Research Station, 362, 377
  global partners, 183, 194, 210, 232, 233, 327, 361, 362
  government contracts, 26, 28, 58, 60, 124, 145, 268, 269, 378
  government investigation of wartime activities, 269
  houses owned by, 85, 138, 174
  investment in General Motors, 290, 299, 300, 388
  laboratories, 121–122, 361
  Miscellaneous Manufacturing Department, 268, 361
  nylon plant, 369, 371
  plants and mills, 110, 170, 174, 188–189, 218, 393
  products (non-munitions), 268, 303, 327, 361–363, 367–368, 377, 378, 393–394
  profits, 70, 211
    Civil War, 62
    1913, 228
    World War I, 378
    World War II, 251, 260–261, 267, 269, 378
  Purity Hall, 362, 363, 377, 392, 393
  renamed E. I. du Pont de Nemours and Company (1902), 172
  renamed E. I. du Pont de Nemours Powder Company (1903), 181, 183
  reorganized, 211
  rival companies, 68, 69, 74, 179

Du Pont (E. I.) de Nemours and Company (*continued*)
  sold to Alfred I., P.S., and T. Coleman (1902), 8, 167–172
  Spanish-American War production, 145–146
  workers' pensions and benefits, 29 and *n*, 174, 282, 310
  World War I powder production, 4, 7, 235, 245, 251–252
  World War II powder production, 377
Du Pont de Nemours Père Fils et Cie, 21, 22, 23, 35
  bankruptcy, 28
Du Pont family:
  control of Delaware, 257
  diminished in power and wealth, 395–399
  and divorce, 125–127, 202
  intermarriage of, 27, 38, 66, 117–118
  lawsuits against, 381, 382–384, 387, 398
  New Year's Day visiting custom, 21, 67–68, 87–88, 385
  one-hundred-and-fiftieth anniversary of arrival in America celebration, 379–381, 383
  one-hundredth anniversary of arrival in America celebration, 154
  photo album of, 155–157 and *n*
  wealth of, 297, 330–331
  women of, 34
Du Pont Papers, 292
Du Pont Securities Company, 247 and *n*, 253, 254, 255–260
Dupré, Marcel, 310
Duquesnoy, Louis, 23
Durant, William C., 287, 288–289, 290, 291, 300
Dyestuff industry, 268, 303–307
Dynamite, 75–77, 181

Eastern Dynamite Company, 211
Edison, Thomas Alva, 90, 94, 95, 119, 147, 184, 185
Edison Laboratory, Menlo Park, N.J., 90, 94, 184, 185
Edward VII, King of England, 185
Electricity, 90, 115, 119
Eleutherian Mills (home), 27, 28, 31, 33, 34, 82, 105, 314, 399–400
Eleutherian Mills Historical Library, x, 229
Engelmann, Dr. Max, 306, 307
England. *See* Great Britain
Epping Forest (home), 340, 354, 355, 356
Equitable Life Assurance Society, N.Y., 228, 376

Essones, France, powder works at, 22, 23, 26
Ethyl Gasoline Corporation, 327, 388
Explosives industry (global), 183, 210, 232–234, 304, 327, 361, 362

Fabric, 303
Fabrikoid, 268, 316n
Farben (I. G.), 193, 304, 327, 361
  Oppau factory, 304, 305, 307–308
Fermi, Enrico, 378
Film, 35mm, 377
Fishback, Margaret, 370
Fisher, Edward, 288
Fitzgerald, F. Scott, 395–396
Fitzgerald, Margery. *See* du Pont, Margery Fitzgerald
Fitzgerald, Zelda, 295
Florida, 338–345
  roads, 342, 344, 345
  tax laws, 333
Florida National Bank, 340–342
Flu epidemic. *See* Influenza epidemic
Foch, Field Marshal Ferdinand, 304
Fontaine, Joan, 332
Food preservatives, 268, 303, 361, 362, 378
Ford, Henry, 288, 368
Ford family, 7
Fort Sumter, 57
Fortune magazine, 397
Foster, John, 348
France, 24, 147
  assistance to Eleuthère Irénée (1772–1834), 23
  and Crimean War, 43, 44, 45
  Directorate of Powders and Saltpeters, 100
  dyestuff industry, 304, 305, 307
  explosives industry, 232, 233, 234
  and rayon, 362
  and smokeless powder, 99–100
Frederick, Pauline, 262
Freedom trains, 52–53
French Ministry of War, 99–100
French Revolution, 20

Galt Hotel, Louisville, 86
Garden, Mary, 6
Gardner, Bessie. *See* du Pont, Bessie Gardner
Gardner, Coz, 191, 192
Gardner, Dorsey, 96
Garfield, James A., 348
General Motors Company, 287, 289
General Motors Corporation:
  antitrust suit against, 381–384, 387
  net worth (c. 1922), 291

General Motors Corporation (*continued*)
  and tetraethyl, 327
  World War II government contracts, 377, 378
General Motors Truck Company, 289
Gentieu, Pierre, 176
Gerhard, Louisa, 38
Germany:
  dyestuff industry, 268, 303–307
  explosives industry, 183, 232–234, 327
  National Socialism, 356
Gifford, U. Grant, 9, 13, 14
Gilbert and Sullivan, 328
Gish, Lillian, 102–103
Glassware, 362
Glendening, Alan, 333, 334
Glendening, Alicia Maddox. *See* Maddox, Alicia (Pechette)
Glendening, Harold Sanford, 333, 334
Gliding, 379
Gold mining, 70, 74, 76
Good Stay (home), 22, 23, 284
Gordon, Michael, 95
Graining mill, 93
Grand Central Palace, N.Y., 277
Granogue (home), 330, 349, 390
Graphite, 93
Grasselli, Theodore, 44–45 and n
Great Britain, 23, 29
  and American Civil War, 60
  and Crimean War, 43, 44, 45
  dyestuff industry, 307
  explosives industry, 183, 232–234
Green, Helen Springer. *See* Raskob, Helen Springer Green
Greenewalt, Crawford, 350, 378, 387, 393, 398
Greenewalt, Margaretta du Pont, 350
Greenleaf, Dr., 154
Groves, General Leslie, 378
Guggenheim family, 297
Gulf Coast Highway Association, 344
Guncotton, 124
Gunpowder. *See also* Explosives industry
  black, 3, 59, 181, 211–212, 218
  blasting, 68, 69, 75, 91–92
  brown prismatic, 145
  cocoa, 99, 105
  manufacturing process, 91–93, 99
  prices, 62, 68, 69
  rifle, 69
  smokeless, 99, 105, 106, 123, 124
  triton, 235
Gunpowder Trade Association (Powder Trust), 68–70, 78, 122, 144, 167, 179, 181, 209, 210
  collapse of, 182

Guns, 124
Guthrie, James H., 350

Haber, Fritz, 303, 304, 308
Hackett, Jimmy, 278
Hagley Associates, 400
Hagley Yard, 48, 59, 91, 92, 115, 141, 257, 355, 383
Hall, Lewis Heisler, 272
Hallock, Ethel. *See* du Pont, Ethel Hallock
Hallock School, 231
Hammit, Clawson S., 275, 276
Hamon, William, 24
Harding, Fanny, 186
Harding, Warren G., 313
Harding family (of Ball's Island), 186, 285
Harlan, John, 384
Harrington *Journal*, 263
Harvard University, 117, 120, 363
Haskell, Henry G., 248
Haskell, J. Amory, 167, 287
Haynes-Apperson (auto), 147 and *n*
Hazard Powder Company, 69, 170, 179, 211
Hearing aids, 147, 185
Hecla Powder Company, 69
Henderson, Charlotte. *See* du Pont, Charlotte Henderson
Henry VIII, King of England, 355
Hercules Powder Company, 211
Hercules Torpedo and Powder Company, 69
Hiebler, Max, 205, 213, 214
Highwayman's Hideout, 342, 344, 345
Hill, Dr. Julian W., 363–367
Hill, Polly, 365, 366
Hill, Walter N., 78, 79, 80
Hiss, Alger, 269
Hitler, Adolf, 354
Homberg, Moses, 65
Hoover, Herbert, 329, 330
Horncastle, 229, 285, 323
Horn's Point (farm), 335, 336
Horwitz, George Quintard, 201, 204, 205, 212
Hotel du Pont, Wilmington, 5–6 and *n*, 223–224 and *n*, 323, 328, 349
used as official residence for tax purposes, 9
Hughes, Charles Evans, 259
Huidekoper, Wallis, 190
Hutchinson, Dr. Miller Reese, 185

Imperial Chemical Industries, 327
India, 60
Indian Motorcycle Company, 302*n*
Influenza epidemic (1918), 5, 6, 12–13, 274–275

Insecticides, 377, 378
Internal combustion engine, 286
Internal Revenue Service (IRS), 277, 313, 318
International Brotherhood of Electrical Workers, 395
International Union of Barbers, 395
Irish immigrants, 53

James, Marquis, 92 and *n*, 146*n*, 182
Japan, 367
Jefferson, Thomas, 20–23, 26, 29, 30 and *n*, 31
Johns Hopkins University, 101
Johnson, Tom, 131, 132, 141, 142, 150, 151
Johnson Company, 131, 132, 141, 150–153, 169
Johnson Steel Company, 130
Jordan, Dr. Heinrich, 306, 307
J. P. Morgan and Company, 234, 235, 246, 247, 252, 261, 284

Kaufman, George S., 113
Kennedy, Joseph P., 348
Kraftmeier, Edward, 234, 235, 236, 245
Krupp (German company), 193
Kuhn, Loeb and Company, 236, 237, 245
Kunze, Dr. E. C., 305, 306

Labor unions, 311
La Buy, Walter, 387, 388–389
Laffley, John P., 234
Laflin and Rand Powder Company, 68, 69, 167, 179, 211
sold to Du Pont, 180–181, 183
La Follette, Robert M., 261
Laird, William Winder, 206, 254
Lake Superior Powder Company, 69
LaMotte, Ellen, 121
Lansing, Robert, 306
Laurel *Leader*, 263
Lavoisier, Antoine Laurent, 22, 26
Lead, 303
Leather, artificial, 303, 361, 393–394
Lee, Annie, 96
Lee, Cazenove G., 96
Lee, Marguerite du Pont. *See* du Pont, Marguerite
Lee, Robert E., 58
Lenning, Charles, 110
Life magazine, 384
Lincoln, Abraham, 53, 54, 57, 58, 60
Lindbergh, Charles A., 348
Little Choptank River, 119
Llewellyn, Alicia Maddox Glendening. *See* Maddox, Alicia (Pechette)

Llewellyn, Victor, 334
Locomobile, 147
Longwood Gardens (estate), 9, 13, 225–226, 240, 310, 327–328, 348, 355, 387, 399
World War II military hospital, 372, 374
Longwood Foundation, 387
Louis XVI, King of France, 20
Louisiana Purchase, 29–30
Louisville, Kentucky, 101, 102
Louisville *Commercial,* 130
Louisville *Courier-Journal,* 130
Louviers (home), 138, 174, 175, 188, 191, 257
Lower Yard, 91
Loy, Myrna, 370
Lyttle (coachman), 87

McAlpin, Hotel, N.Y., 228
McCoy, Charles B., 397*n*
McGowan, Sir Harry, 194, 327
McGowan, Lord and Lady, 348
McKenna, Lord, 348
McKinley, William, 215
Macklin, Bill, 88
MacLaurin, Dr. Richard, 283
McLaury Marble and Tile Company, 275
Maddox, Alicia Bradford. *See* du Pont, Alicia Bradford Maddox
Maddox, Alicia (Pechette), 162, 217, 278, 279, 285, 333–334, 356
Maddox, George, 159–161, 174, 175, 184, 191, 200
Madison, James, 127
Maine (battleship), 143
Mammoth Powder, 59
Manhattan Project, 378
Manila, 4
Marcellus Powder Company, 69
Maryland, 52, 57, 58
Mason, Anna, 14
Mason, Charlie, 11, 240, 266, 274, 275, 386
Mason, Mrs. Charlie, 14
Mason, Lewes A., 7, 9, 11–13, 240, 266, 272, 273, 274
death of, 14, 15, 275, 276, 277, 386
Mason (Lewes A.) Memorial Hospital, 276–277
Mason-Dixon line, 52, 57
Massachusetts Institute of Technology, (M.I.T.), 89, 90, 101, 104, 107
Massena, Gabriel, 355
Mathesius, Mr., 234
Mathewson, Frank, 189
Mathewson brothers, 94, 95, 98, 115
Mayo Clinic, Minnesota, 235, 244

Meade, Charles, 306
Melchett, Lord and Lady, 348
Mellon, Andrew W., 313
Mellon family, 7, 297, 348
Merchants and Manufacturers Exchange, 277
Merrimac (ship), 59
Mexico, 183, 194–195
Miami Powder Company, 69
Middleton *Chronicle,* 263
Millar, Marcella. *See* du Pont, Marcella Millar
Mining, 70, 74, 76, 102–103
Model A (auto), 368
Model T (auto), 368
Molecules, long-chain, 363
Monitor (ship), 59
Monroe, James, 31
Montchanin, Anne de, 128*n*
Montchanin, Pierre de, 128–129
Montpelier (estate), 127
Morgan, Frances du Pont (the Black Banana), 331, 332
Morgan, Richard D., 331, 332
Morrow, Anne, 348
Morrow, Charles, 348
Morrow, Dwight, 234, 246, 348
Motion Pictures magazine, 370
Motorbikes, 302*n*
Movement for National Preparedness, 261
Moxham, Arthur J., 152 and *n*, 153, 194

Naphthaline, 303
National Academy of Sciences, 367
National Bank of Louisville, 130
National Recovery Administration, 352
Nazism, 354
Necker, Louis, 23
Nemenoosha (yacht), 340
Nemours (home), 40, 50, 60, 66, 67, 218, 224–225, 241, 339, 354, 355, 357
Nemours Foundation, 356, 388, 399
Nemours Trading Corporation, 283*n*, 319
Neoprene, 367, 377
New Castle, Del., 125
New Deal, 343
New York *Herald,* 118
New York Stock Exchange, 312, 387
New York *Sun,* 230
New York *Times,* 230, 307, 364
New York *World,* 217
New York World's Fair, 371
Newark *Ledger,* 263
Nitrates, synthetics, 303–304, 307
Nitroglycerine, 75, 78, 79, 80
Nobel, Alfred, 75

Nobel-Dynamite Trust Company, 233, 234, 235
Nobel Explosives Company, 191, 193, 194
Nobel Industries, 304, 307, 327, 361
Nye, Gerald Prentice, 352, 353
Nylon, 367, 369–371, 394
    named, 368
    stockings, 369–371
    war materials made of, 371, 377

Oakland Motor Car Company, 289
Office of Price Administration, 397
Office of Strategic Services, 378
Old-age pensions, 338, 343
Old Hickory Powder Works, 269
Olds Motor Works, 289
Oppau, I. G. Farben factory at, 304, 305, 307–308
Oriental Powder Company, 69
Orlon, 365n, 392
Osann, Captain H. E., 307
Oxford University, 333

Paints, 268, 303, 327, 362, 378
Panama City, Fla., 345
Paper mills, 102
Parr, Catherine, 355
Payne, Maggie, 102, 129–130
Pearl Street Station, N.Y., 90
Pensions, old-age, 338, 343
Perkins, Maxwell, 395
Petit, Henri, 386–387
Philadelphia *North American,* 217
Philadelphia *Public Ledger,* 256
Phonographs, 185
Pierce's Park (home), 196, 202. *See also* Longwood Gardens
Pioneer Point (estate), 336
Plastics, 378, 392, 393
Polyesters, 365 and *n*
Polymers, 363, 366
Polystyrene, 392
Pontiana, 22
Porter, William H., 246
Potash, 92
Powder. *See* Gunpowder
Powder industry. *See* Explosives industry
Powder Trust. *See* Gunpowder Trade Association
Preservatives, 268, 303, 361, 362, 378
Presidential elections:
    1860, 53
    1928, 328–330
Presscakes, 93
Price, Ruth Latham, 346

Princeton University, 215, 216
Prohibition, 328, 352

Raskob, Helen Springer Green, 196–198, 288
Raskob, John J.:
    death of, 385
    and Du Pont, 287–288, 328
    and General Motors, 286–287, 290–291, 328
    marriage of, 196–198
    in politics, 272, 311, 328, 329–330
    and P. S. du Pont, 152, 153, 170, 182, 183, 244–246, 248, 347, 373
Raskob, William, 329
Rayon, 339, 362, 392
Recessions, 105
Red Cross, 12, 13, 273, 372
Reese, Dr. Charles Lee, 304, 305, 307, 361
Religion, 20
Repauno Mineral Company, 77–80, 104, 114, 122, 167
Repauno River, 77
Reszke, Jean de, 285, 333
Rheostat, 95
Rifle powder, 69
Rifles, 124
Roads, 286
Robbins, Dean, 280
Robertson, Mary, 265
Robertson, Nathaniel, 265
Robespierre, Maximilien Francois Marie Isidore de, 20
Rock Farms (estate), 200, 202, 203
Rockefeller family, 7, 297
Rodemann, August, 216
Rodman, Captain Thomas J., 59
Roosevelt, Franklin D., 343, 351–352
Roosevelt, Theodore, 4, 44, 210
Rough Riders, 144
Rowan, Andrew Summers, 144
Rubber, 366, 367
Rubbercoating, 303
Ruoff, Hermann, 354
Ruoff, Madeleine. *See* du Pont, Madeleine
Russia, 43, 44, 251
Rust, Gordon, 332

Saint Amour (home), 123, 133, 205
Saint James's Church, Philadelphia, 98
Saint Johns River, 355
Saint Johns River Development Company, 339
Saint Joseph's Roman Catholic Church, 94, 115
Saltpeter, 26, 60, 91, 133

Sand Hole Woods (du Pont family grave-
 yard), 31, 34, 47, 63, 81, 82, 165,
 208, 226, 298, 299, 315, 379, 383
Saulsbury, May du Pont, 125, 155, 156,
 158, 202, 255
Saulsbury, Willard, 155, 156
 in politics, 272 and *n*
Schweintz, Dr. G. E. de, 189, 190, 191
Scott, Bill, 224
Scott, Ethel, 383, 384
Scott, Philip C., 383
Scott, Father W. J., 190
Scott, William, 188–189
Seaford, Del., nylon factory at, 369, 371
Seaford *News,* 263
Sebastopol, 3, 45
Seitz, George, 209
Senate Appropriations Committee, 209
Service Citizens of Delaware, 272
Shapiro, Irving S., 397–399
Sharp, Bella, 206, 372
Sharp, Rodney, 14, 206, 254, 372, 373
Sherman Antitrust Act, 182, 205, 209, 381
Shotguns, 124
Silk, 371, 372
 artificial, 268, 327, 361, 362, 364
Silver mining, 70, 76
Singer, Dr. Siegfried, 194
Skimmerhorn, "Professor," 94
Slavery, 52, 53
Sloan, Alfred P., 328, 329
Smith, Al, 329, 330
Smith, Eleuthera du Pont, 35 and *n*
Smith, Thomas Mackie, 35 and *n*
Smokeless powder, 99, 105, 106, 123, 124
Smyth, James, 218, 224
Sobrero, Ascanio, 75
Société Nobel, 191, 193, 194
Soda powder, 91, 92
Somme (U.S. Army transport), 307
South Carolina, 54, 57
Spain, 141, 144
Spanish-American War, 4, 143–146
Sphinx (bordello), 151
Sponge, synthetic, 366
Staël, Mme de, 23
Standard Oil Company, 210, 211, 327
Stanley (auto), 147 and *n*
Statler Hotel, Buffalo, N.Y., 364
Steel companies, 150
Stein, Dr., 361, 362
Stock market crash of 1929, 338, 341
Stockings, nylon, 369–371
Stollenwerk, Caroline Hynson, 353–354
Stone, William J., 261
Streetcars, 102, 132, 150
Sulfur, 91

Sulfuric acid, 78, 79
Sullivan, John L., 89, 278
Superfortress, bomber, 377
Sutter's Mill, 74
Swamp Hall (home), 60, 61, 71–73, 85–
 88, 96, 117, 119, 120, 161, 174,
 188, 218, 380
 electricity installed, 94–95
Sweetman, Helen Everett, 367–368
Sycamore Mills, 69
Synthetics, 327, 362, 363, 364, 366, 394

Taft, William Howard, 210, 215
Talleyrand, 33
Tallman, F. G., 248
Tankopanicum Orchestra (Al's Band), 94,
 95, 98, 119, 146, 184, 216
Tarkio College, 363
Teeth, false, 21, 373
Telegraphy, 185
Telephone, 78
Tetraethyl, 327
Thompson, Henry B., 215
Thompson, Mrs. Henry B., 215, 216, 217
Thompson, J. Whitaker, 258, 259, 260
Tiffany's, N.Y., 157
Tijon (French ironworker), 355
Time magazine, 342, 364
Transparent sheeting, 303
Tripoli, 26
Triton powder, 235
Turkey, 43
Typhoid, 134, 206

Union, during Civil War, 54, 58, 59, 60
Union Hill Cemetry, 275
Union navy, 59
United States Hotel, Philadelphia, 34
United States Rubber Company, 327, 351,
 367
 antitrust suit against, 381–384, 387
United States Steel Corporation, 151
United States v. *du Pont,* 381–384, 387,
 388–389, 398
University of Chicago, 378
University of Illinois, 363
University of Pennsylvania, 39, 189
University of Virginia, 332
Upper Yard, 93, 110
U.S. Air Force, 378
U.S. Army, 26
 Corps of Engineers, 143
 Du Pont Powder supplied to, 4, 26, 28
 and smokeless powder, 106, 122
U.S. Congress, 113, 261–262, 396
U.S. Department of Justice, 210, 388

U.S. government:
  antitrust suits against Du Pont
    1907, 205–208–211, 232
    1950, 381–384, 387, 388–389, 398,
      399
  contracts with Du Pont, 26, 28, 58, 60,
    124, 145, 268, 269, 378
U.S. Highway 13, 227–228, 262, 334
U.S. Highway 19, 345
U.S. Highway 90, 345
U.S. Highway 98, 345
U.S. Navy, 26, 378, 379
  Du Pont powder supplied to, 26, 124,
    209
  experiments with guncotton, 124
  Torpedo Station, R.I., 124
U.S. Senate, 271, 311, 312, 352
U.S. Supreme Court, 318

Vanderbilt, Cornelius, 353
Versailles, Treaty of, 304, 306
Virginia, 52, 57
Viscose products, 327, 362
Vulcanized fibers, 327

Waddell, Robert J., 208–209, 210
Waldorf-Astoria Hotel, 228
Waller, Absalom, 96–98
Wanamaker's, Philadelphia, 309
Wapwallopen, Pa., mills at, 188–189
War of 1812, 28
Washington, George, 21, 186
Wax, 303
Weapons, 124
Weldy, 189
Welpen, Minn., powder plant at, 218

White Eagle (mansion), 278
White House, Washington, D.C., 60
White Shoe Company, 319
Wilmington Cathedral, 197
Wilmington Club, 120
Wilmington *Evening Journal,* 118, 120,
  255, 263
Wilmington *Evening Star,* 227
Wilmington Horse Show, 320
Wilmington *Morning News,* 263, 272, 284,
  369
Wilmington *News,* 255, 279
Wilmington Opera House, 94
Wilmington *Sunday Star,* 248
Wilmington Trust Company, 263
Wilson, Woodrow, 216, 262, 265
Windshields, shatterproof, 327
Winterthur (home), 55, 64, 76, 112, 114,
  115, 155, 379, 387–388, 399
Wolcott, Senator, 312
Women's suffrage, 270
World War I, 233–237, 242, 265, 266
  Du Pont gunpowder produced, 4, 7, 235,
    245, 251–252, 268, 269
World War II, 367, 377, 378
  materials for, made from nylon, 371, 377

Xanadu (home), 350, 351, 372, 390 and *n*

Yale University, 96, 97, 117, 316, 317

Zilg, Gerald Colby, 377
Zinc mining, 76
Zinn, Annie Rogers. *See* du Pont, Annie
  Rogers Zinn

Born in Manchester, England, and educated at the Wil-
liam Hulme School, the Sorbonne, and Berlin University,
Leonard Mosley has been a foreign correspondent most of
his working life. He joined Kemsley (now Thomson)
newspapers and worked for their Berlin Bureau in 1939,
and his experiences there—including interviews with
Hitler and most of the Nazi leaders—provided the basic
material for his book On Borrowed Time: How World
War Two Began, *which was a Book-of-the-Month Club*
selection in 1969.

When World War II began, he became chief war
correspondent for the London Sunday Times *and associ-*
ated newspapers, and reported the Battle of Britain, the
Middle East campaign, and the Allied landings in Greece
and Italy. He was part of the small expedition that went
through the Italian lines and restored Emperor Haile
Selassie to the throne of Ethiopia. While in the Middle
East, he took a course in parachuting and on D-Day
dropped into Normandy with the first wave of the Allied
invasion of Europe.

In the postwar years, he covered the Nuremberg
trials and traveled widely in Africa, the Middle East and
the Far East. From a long stay in Japan he produced
Hirohito: Emperor of Japan, *which was a Book-of-the-*
Month Club selection in 1966 and the first biography of
a Japanese ruler to be published in Japan, where it be-
came an instant best-seller. Power Play, *published in 1973,*
was the first book to warn the world of the strength of
OPEC and of the oil crisis to come. His two most recent
books, Lindbergh *and* Dulles, *were full selections of the*
Literary Guild and the Book-of-the-Month Club, respect-
ively.

In addition to writing nineteen books of history and
biography and five novels, Mr. Mosley has worked as a
theater and film critic in London and as a scriptwriter in

Hollywood. For his literary works and war correspondence, he was made an Officer of the Order of the British Empire, and for his writings about the Middle East, a Commander of the Order of Saint John of Jerusalem. He now lives on Sanibel Island, in Florida.